Deep Learning Tools for Predicting Stock Market Movements

Scrivener Publishing
100 Cummings Center, Suite 541J
Beverly, MA 01915-6106

Publishers at Scrivener
Martin Scrivener (martin@scrivenerpublishing.com)
Phillip Carmical (pcarmical@scrivenerpublishing.com)

Deep Learning Tools for Predicting Stock Market Movements

Edited by

Renuka Sharma

Chitkara Business School, Chitkara University, Punjab, India

and

Kiran Mehta

Chitkara Business School, Chitkara University, Punjab, India

Scrivener
Publishing

This edition first published 2024 by John Wiley & Sons, Inc., 111 River Street, Hoboken, NJ 07030, USA and Scrivener Publishing LLC, 100 Cummings Center, Suite 541J, Beverly, MA 01915, USA
© 2024 Scrivener Publishing LLC
For more information about Scrivener publications please visit www.scrivenerpublishing.com.

Wiley Global Headquarters
111 River Street, Hoboken, NJ 07030, USA

For details of our global editorial offices, customer services, and more information about Wiley products visit us at www.wiley.com.

Limit of Liability/Disclaimer of Warranty
While the publisher and authors have used their best efforts in preparing this work, they make no representations or warranties with respect to the accuracy or completeness of the contents of this work and specifically disclaim all warranties, including without limitation any implied warranties of merchantability or fitness for a particular purpose. No warranty may be created or extended by sales representatives, written sales materials, or promotional statements for this work. The fact that an organization, website, or product is referred to in this work as a citation and/or potential source of further information does not mean that the publisher and authors endorse the information or services the organization, website, or product may provide or recommendations it may make. This work is sold with the understanding that the publisher is not engaged in rendering professional services. The advice and strategies contained herein may not be suitable for your situation. You should consult with a specialist where appropriate. Neither the publisher nor authors shall be liable for any loss of profit or any other commercial damages, including but not limited to special, incidental, consequential, or other damages. Further, readers should be aware that websites listed in this work may have changed or disappeared between when this work was written and when it is read.

Library of Congress Cataloging-in-Publication Data

ISBN 978-1-394-21430-3

Cover image: Pixabay.Com
Cover design by Russell Richardson

Set in size of 11pt and Minion Pro by Manila Typesetting Company, Makati, Philippines

Printed in the USA

10 9 8 7 6 5 4 3 2 1

Dedicated to our Parents and God

Contents

Poorna Shankar, Kota Naga Rohith
and Muthukumarasamy Karthikeyan

Preface

Predicting the movement of stocks is a classic but difficult topic that has attracted the study of economists and computer scientists alike. Over the last couple of decades, several efforts have been made to investigate the use of linear and machine learning (ML) technologies with the objective of developing an accurate prediction model. New horizons, such as deep learning (DL) models, have just been brought to this field, and the pace of advancement is too quick to keep up with. Moreover, the stock market behavior and pattern have perplexed researchers and mathematicians for decades. Therefore, it is crucial to familiarize oneself with the many investment opportunities, styles, tools, and techniques to study the stock market volatility, and portfolio management solutions that exist in the case of a global financial catastrophe. Therefore, the objective of the current work is to give a thorough view of the evolution and development of DL tools and techniques in the field of stock market prediction in the developed and developing worlds.

Stock market interest has grown in recent years. Investors exchange millions of dollars in assets every day to profit. If an investor can predict market behavior, they may earn higher risk-adjusted returns. DL, ML, soft computing, and computational intelligence research have produced accurate stock market predictions. Financial research is tough but essential for stock market predictions. The efficient market hypothesis (EMH) may not be compatible with investors beating the market in risk-adjusted returns, but it does not imply that it is untrue. Its assumptions have been questioned. Momentum, reversal, and volatility contradict the EMH. Institutional investors can adjust for random over- and underreactions. This led to models that include how individuals think and behave, casting doubt on the premise that investors are always fully rational due to defects like loss aversion and overreaction. Fundamental and technical analyses are used to forecast stock prices. Previous research predicted stock prices and returns using statistical time series methods. Moving averages, Kalman filtering, and exponential smoothing are typical methods. Logistic regression and support vector machines have acquired appeal in stock market forecasting research with the introduction of AI and soft computing. These algorithms can handle more complex time series data to produce better predictions. These novel and helpful financial market forecasting tools intrigue academics. DL techniques and prediction models are evolving. Programming languages have evolved to make DL model creation and testing simpler. Online news or data adds to stock market forecasts. Knowledge graph-based graph neural networks are a new innovation. DL is used to recognize objects, classify images, and forecast time series. DL models outperform linear and Machine learning (ML) models for stock market prediction because they can handle vast volumes of data and grasp nonlinear associations. Asset management businesses (AMCs) and investment banks (IBs) are expanding their funding for AI research, which is currently represented by DL models. The objective of the current work is to give a thorough view of the evolution and development of DL tools and techniques in the field of stock market prediction.

We hope that the present work serves as a guiding beacon in your exploration of this captivating intersection. May the insights within these pages empower you to navigate the complexities of finance with newfound confidence and a deeper understanding of the transformative potential that lies at the nexus of DL and stock market predictions. In compiling this work, we have drawn from a myriad of sources, ranging from academic research and industry case studies to real-world applications. Our intent is to offer a balanced perspective—one that not only imparts technical knowledge but also fosters critical thinking and the cultivation of a discerning approach to market analysis.

Chapter 1 delves into the development of an ensemble model for stock market prediction, combining long short-term memory (LSTM), autoregressive integrated moving average (ARIMA), and sentiment analysis. The research captures long-term dependencies using LSTM, linear relationships through ARIMA, and public sentiment from tweets using sentiment analysis. Experimental results reveal the ensemble model's superior accuracy over individual models. The study underscores the significance of sentiment analysis, extracted from tweets, in enhancing stock market predictions. This innovative approach offers improved insights into stock price movements, benefitting investors and financial institutions.

Chapter 2 explained that the rapid expansion of quantum computing (QuCo) technologies, which will change software engineering, confronts the software market. The evaluation and prioritization of QuCo problems, however, are fragmented and immature. The preliminary nature of QuCo research and the growing demand for multidisciplinary studies to address these challenges were shown by a thorough literature analysis using data from several digital libraries. Insights from the study include the necessity for significant organizational efforts to properly take advantage of QuCo's benefits, documenting processes, needs, and fundamental norms for effective QuCo deployment, and addressing issues in scalability and resource performance evaluation. Researchers should look into how the assimilation of new technologies might lessen the organizational learning curve and encourage adoption. The study's implications include the need for substantial organizational efforts to fully harness QuCo's advantages, documenting processes, requirements, and inherent rules for effective QuCo adoption, and addressing challenges in scalability and resource performance evaluation. Scholars should investigate how the technology assimilation process can ease organizational learning load and promote the uptake of new technology.

Chapter 3 delves into the intricacies of open interest in the derivative market, emphasizing its importance in predicting market sentiments. By tracking variations in spot price, open interest, and delivery data, traders can gauge operator intentions. The chapter underscores the significance of analyzing open interest alongside technical charts, pointing out key indicators like put-call ratios to determine market positions. Through a comprehensive analysis of stock data and open interest trends, investors can make well-informed decisions. Yet, it is pivotal to remember that multiple factors should influence market strategies, and intraday Open interest (OI) data play crucial roles in understanding market dynamics.

Chapter 4 provides an overview of DL techniques for forecasting stock market trends, examining their effectiveness across different time frames and market conditions. It explores architectures like recurrent neural networks, convolutional neural networks, and transformer-based models, highlighting data preprocessing, feature engineering, and model complexity. Future research directions include hybrid models, exploring alternative data sources, and addressing ethical concerns. This guide is valuable for researchers and practitioners seeking to navigate the evolving landscape of stock market prediction through DL.

Chapter 5 has examined the repercussions of the 2008 financial crisis and the potential of another in 2023, emphasizing the advancements in artificial intelligence (AI) and QuCo for stock market predictions. Techniques like blind QuCo (BQC) and quantum neural networks (QNNs) have emerged, with models designed for precise stock predictions. The chapter's focus is to analyze and recommend the most accurate AI and QuCo-based algorithms. However, challenges persist, such as limited data, noisy market data, model interpretability, and the need for real-time predictions. Addressing these will pave the way for DL to revolutionize stock price predictions, ensuring enhanced forecasting and risk management.

Chapter 6 has explored the applications and implications of various models for causality, volatility, and co-integration in stock markets. By utilizing models such as the Granger causality, VAR, GARCH, and co-integration models, researchers can analyze and understand the intricate dynamics of financial systems. These models play a pivotal role in understanding causal relationships, predicting volatility, and identifying long-term economic equilibriums in stock markets. Practical applications extend to portfolio management, risk assessment, and guiding investment decisions. The chapter emphasizes the profound impact of these models in advancing the knowledge of finance, offering insights to investors and policymakers, and promoting a deeper comprehension of complex financial interrelationships.

Chapter 7 explains that the financial market is crucial for economic development, with the secondary market dealing with the share market. It offers long-term investment opportunities for investors and is used by small businesses and financial sectors. Stock dealing relies on predictability, which offers superior financial advice and forecasts the direction of the stock market. Techniques like Bayesian models, fuzzy classifiers, artificial neural networks, SVM classifiers, neural networks, and ML have been used to predict the stock market. Whereas AI-based prediction models can guide investors, they may not always account for unexpected occurrences.

Chapter 8 examines the increasing role of AI in stock market trading, highlighting free AI-driven programs that assist traders in making informed decisions. These AI systems enhance the efficiency of stock market operations by providing vast data-driven insights. The research focuses on the current and potential impact of AI in forecasting stock market trends. The study methodology, including data collection and analysis, is meticulously presented, with an exploration of future trajectories and implications of AI applications in stock market research.

Chapter 9 analyzes the relationship between monetary policy decisions and stock returns using an event study methodology. It finds that unexpected changes in policy decisions have the opposite effect on stock returns, emphasizing the importance of market conditions in assessing the relationship. The analysis also shows that the impact of monetary policy on stock returns is not uniform across sectors, emphasizing the need for a sector-specific approach. Financial constraints play a limited role in explaining differences in stock returns' responses to monetary policy surprises.

These findings contribute to the literature by offering diverse insights into the relationship between monetary policy decisions and stock returns in emerging markets.

Chapter 10 emphasizes the significance of AI in predicting stock market movements. Whereas stock market volatility can be daunting for investors, AI's ability to rapidly process vast datasets and detect patterns offers an edge over traditional prediction methods. The study presents a systematic literature review, highlighting that whereas AI models have shown promise, there is a consistent oversight in selecting and processing input data, which forms the foundation of any predictive model. The research emphasizes the importance of model validation, which is often neglected, and the need for accurate multistep forward predictions. The findings suggest that leveraging advanced AI models can benefit various stakeholders in the financial sector, potentially enhancing confidence and participation in stock trading. This could, in turn, stimulate economic growth, inviting more investment and fostering trust in predictive models among the larger population.

Chapter 11 emphasized that AI is a widely used technology in various sectors, utilizing computer sciences to make decisions and solve problems. It comprises DL and ML, which are often referred to simultaneously. The finance sector is also adopting new technologies to improve operational efficiency. DL and ML approaches share similar principles, but they differ from each other. This book chapter aims to compare and contrast ML and DL strategies to identify their main distinctions. Understanding the benefits, drawbacks, and applicability of each method is crucial before adopting it. The study will provide information on the use of both strategies and their unique advantages for users.

Chapter 12 has explained that the financial market is known for its volatility and unpredictable nature, making accurate stock price predictions challenging. ML techniques, such as Random Forest (RF), k-nearest Neighbours (KNN), SVM, and Naive Bayes, have been used to predict stock values and market trends. This study analyzed various algorithms, including sentiment analysis, time series analysis, and graph-based methods. The results showed that ML algorithms outperform human predictions and save time and resources. To improve stock price prediction, research should prioritize integrating stock trend analysis with historical stock data, generating more accurate and effective stock recommendations. Advanced learning-based techniques can also be used to extract relevant features, improving the accuracy of stock price predictions. Further research should explore the complexities and gradients of networks with numerous nodes, providing insights and potential directions for future research in this area.

Chapter 13 delves into the stock market's economic impact, investor participation for gain optimization, and risk reduction. Forecasting stock markets proves challenging due to economic uncertainties. The study explores predictive techniques like technical and fundamental analysis, alongside ML. It conducts a thorough systematic review and bibliometric analysis of 89 research works (2002–2023), focusing on fundamental analysis and stock market prediction. It highlights influential authors, institutions, countries, and sources while revealing intellectual structures using bibliographic coupling. ML algorithms, feature selection criteria, training/testing ratios, and accuracy metrics are discussed. Technical indicators and fundamental variables used in forecasting are examined. Overall, the study examines ML algorithms, feature selection, training/testing ratios, accuracy metrics, technical indicators, and variables for market forecasting.

Chapter 14 investigates the influence of emotional intelligence (EI) on investment decisions among Indian investors. Through a survey involving 239 seasoned investors from major metro cities, the research identifies four key factors linking EI with investment choices: attitude, emotions, perception, and risk aversion. The findings emphasize that those with higher EI tend to make wiser investment decisions. The study underscores the importance of fostering EI skills for investment stakeholders, suggesting that recognizing and nurturing these skills can optimize investment outcomes. Future research avenues in diverse cultural contexts are also recommended to expand on this understanding.

Chapter 15 discusses the challenges behavioral finance presents to traditional finance, which emphasizes rational decision-making processes in investments. Focusing on three cognitive biases, i.e., overconfidence, optimism, and the illusion of control, the research utilized a structured questionnaire completed by 362 participants to analyze their impact on financial decisions. The findings reveal a significant correlation between overconfidence and investment choices, whereas optimism and the illusion of control showed no notable influence. Although it offers critical insights into behavioral biases among investors in Delhi/NCR, the study's scope remains limited. The research underscores the importance of investor awareness of these biases for informed decision-making and has implications for financial advisors, brokerage firms, and stock market policymakers.

Chapter 16 examines the role of alternative data in investment management. This nontraditional, unstructured information offers unique insights but comes with challenges such as data quality, privacy, and lack of standardization. Effective governance, validation, and best practices can enhance the utility of alternative data. The future demands collaboration among stakeholders, advancements in data analysis technologies, evolving regulatory frameworks, and ongoing education for investment professionals. The study's findings offer guidance to investment firms, data providers, regulatory bodies, and the academic community on harnessing alternative data for better investment decisions and strategies.

Chapter 17 discusses that traditional finance theories rely on rational behavior in investors, focusing on optimizing returns through fundamental analysis, technical analysis, and personal judgment. However, recent research has identified inconsistencies in these theories when applied in practical scenarios. Retail investors in the equity market are prone to various influences, biases, and emotional factors that can impact their decision-making process. Behavioral finance, an interdisciplinary field, aims to understand irrational decision-making by integrating psychological principles and human behavior theories. It examines the influence of investors' emotions and psychology on their investment decisions, highlighting the importance of understanding how emotions contribute to irrational behavior. Warren Buffet emphasized the need for intellectual acumen and emotional restraint for rational conduct. The field of psychology remains relatively nascent, but it is crucial to examine the dynamics of group behavior within markets and individual investors' behavioral characteristics to achieve success in investment endeavors.

Chapter 18 examines the concept of volatility and its significance in interconnected financial markets, particularly focusing on its transmission between India's commodity and equity futures markets. By utilizing various statistical tests and models on data from 2007 to 2022, the study determines the extent of volatility spillover among different indices. Initial results highlight energy's index as the most volatile, with the Comdex index being the primary volatility transmitter. The findings provide valuable insights for portfolio managers, investors, and policymakers to strategize effectively in the face of volatile market conditions.

In closing, the journey into the realm of DL tools for predicting stock market movements is one of continuous discovery and innovation. As the financial landscape continues to evolve and the boundaries of technology are pushed further, the insights gleaned from this book are meant to be a stepping stone, not an endpoint. The path forward requires ongoing exploration, adaptation, and collaboration among researchers, practitioners, and visionaries. As you delve into the pages that follow, we encourage you to embrace the challenges, embrace the opportunities, and embrace the transformation that these tools can bring to the intricate world of stock market analysis.

Renuka Sharma
Chitkara Business School, Chitkara University, Punjab, India
Kiran Mehta
Chitkara Business School, Chitkara University, Punjab, India
January 2024

Acknowledgments

Writing a book is a journey that stretches far beyond the author's efforts. It is a collaborative endeavor fuelled by inspiration, support, and guidance from countless individuals whose contributions shape the final work. As I reflect on the completion of this book, I am profoundly grateful for the diverse and dedicated community that has enriched my path.

In awe and humility, we extend our thanks to the divine presence that has illuminated our path throughout this creative journey. Your guidance, whether through moments of clarity or challenges, has been our constant source of inspiration and strength.

Heartfelt gratitude goes to the exceptional authors and contributors whose collective insights, expertise, and dedication have brought this book to life. Your willingness to share your knowledge and perspectives has enriched every page, and we are humbled by the collaborative spirit that drove this endeavor.

We extend our appreciation to the dedicated team at *Scrivener Publishing LLC,* for believing in the potential of this book and for bringing it to fruition with unwavering commitment. Your dedication to quality and your belief in the power of ideas have made this venture a reality, and we are truly thankful for our partnership.

We express gratitude to the insightful critics whose thoughtful perspectives have pushed us to refine and polish this work. Your constructive feedback has been instrumental in shaping the final narrative, and we are thankful for the opportunity to grow and improve through your valuable insights.

With sincere gratitude, we acknowledge the reviewers whose time and expertise were invested in evaluating our book. Your thoughtful analysis and constructive critiques have played a pivotal role in refining the book, ensuring its precision, coherence, and resonance. Your dedication to the thorough review process is deeply valued, and we are thankful for the vital role you've played in elevating the quality of this publication.

Renuka Sharma
Kiran Mehta

Design and Development of an Ensemble Model for Stock Market Prediction Using LSTM, ARIMA, and Sentiment Analysis

**Poorna Shankar[1]*, Kota Naga Rohith[2]
and Muthukumarasamy Karthikeyan[3]**

[1]Department of MCA, Indira College of Engineering and Management, Pune, India
[2]Salesforce Consultant, Essen, Germany
[3]Chemical Engineering and Process Development, National Chemical Laboratory,
Pune, India

Abstract

The accurate prediction of stock market movements is a challenging task due to its complex and dynamic nature. In recent years, machine learning techniques have shown promise in addressing this challenge. This study focuses on the design and development of an ensemble model that combines long short-term memory (LSTM), autoregressive integrated moving average (ARIMA), and sentiment analysis to enhance stock market predictions. The ensemble model leverages the strengths of LSTM, which captures long-term dependencies in sequential data, and ARIMA, a statistical model known for its ability to capture linear and autoregressive relationships in time series data. Additionally, sentiment analysis is incorporated to analyze and quantify the impact of public sentiment expressed in textual data on stock market dynamics. The research methodology involves collecting historical stock market data, sentiment analysis data, and performing preprocessing steps to ensure data quality. The LSTM and ARIMA models are developed and trained using the collected data. Sentiment analysis techniques are applied to extract sentiment scores from the effect of public sentiment on stock market movements generated through Twitter application programming interface (API). The ensemble model is developed by fusing the predictions from LSTM, ARIMA, and sentiment analysis, with careful consideration of the weights assigned to each

---

*Corresponding author: poornashankar@indiraicem.ac.in

Renuka Sharma and Kiran Mehta (eds.) *Deep Learning Tools for Predicting Stock Market Movements*,
(1–38) © 2024 Scrivener Publishing LLC

model. The integration of sentiment analysis enriches the model by incorporating qualitative features derived from public sentiments. Experimental results using real-world historical stock market data demonstrate the effectiveness of the ensemble model. It outperforms the individual LSTM and ARIMA models in terms of accuracy and robustness. The inclusion of sentiment analysis further enhances the prediction performance by capturing the influence of public sentiment on stock market dynamics. The ensemble approach effectively leverages the strengths of each component to improve prediction accuracy and adaptability. The results of this study demonstrated that there is a high correlation between stock price rises and falls and public sentiment expressed in tweets. The findings offer valuable insights for investors, financial institutions, and policymakers, aiding in informed decision-making in the dynamic stock market environment.

Keywords: LSTM, ARIMA, NLP, sentiment analysis, RNN, stock market prediction

1.1 Introduction

Trading in the stock market and getting returns from it have become popular nowadays around the world. Predicting stock price has long been considered one of the most delicate yet critical undertakings. Understanding and predicting the behavior of stock prices have been the focus of extensive research and analysis for decades. The stock market is a dynamic and intricate system influenced by a multitude of factors, including economic indicators, company performance, geopolitical events, and investor sentiment. The stock market's prices are highly volatile. According to the efficient market hypothesis (EMH), financial market movements are influenced by news, tweets, and other factors, all of which have a substantial impact on a company's stock. Because the stock request is a nonlinear and dynamic system, sentiment values in tweets are one of the most important factors in the monetary request [1–4].

As a supplement to traditional stock market data, the development of news, blogs, social networking websites, and textual content on the Internet provides a valuable source to reflect attitudes and predict stock values. It is a difficult process to identify the collection of significant criteria for creating correct predictions; thus, regular stock market study is critical. Stock market values follow a random walk pattern and cannot be anticipated with more than 50% accuracy because of the sheer unpredictability of news and current events. Investment opportunities for individual investors or business opportunities in the stock market will increase if there is an efficient algorithm that can predict the short-term price of a stock of a certain company with the news/tweets around that company [5–7].

The main objective of this study is to give future stock price insights with deep learning algorithms and prevent future losses for investors and investment companies by providing accurate results using sentiment analysis.

1.2   Significance of the Study

Predicting stock market movements accurately is a challenging task due to the complex and volatile nature of financial markets. The relationship between stock price movements and public sentiment has long been a topic of interest in financial research. Traditionally, financial analysts relied on economic indicators, company performance, and market trends to forecast stock prices. In particular, the explosion of social media platforms, such as Twitter, has led to a vast amount of user-generated content being shared in real time. This content often reflects individuals' thoughts, opinions, and sentiments on various topics, including the stock market. As a result, researchers have increasingly explored the relationship between public sentiment expressed in tweets and stock price movements.

According to the EMH, financial market movements are influenced by news, tweets, and other factors, all of which have a substantial impact on a company's stock. Stock market values follow a random walk pattern and cannot be anticipated with more than 50% accuracy because of the sheer unpredictability of news and current events. Many studies have used Twitter as a primary source for public opinion research [8, 9].

In addition, this study will fill a gap in the scientific stock market literature by predicting stock market movements utilizing a variety of current news articles and tweets from various sources. In addition, a variety of machine and deep learning algorithms are employed to create models that can forecast stock market behavior. These models are tested using a variety of datasets, sentiment analysis methods, and whether or not a technical price indicator is used. As a result, the datasets and sentiment analysis methods are compared, and the accuracy of news article sentiment prediction is evaluated.

In recent years, machine learning techniques have gained significant attention as a promising approach to tackle this challenge. Among these techniques, long short-term memory (LSTM), autoregressive integrated moving average (ARIMA), and sentiment analysis have emerged as powerful tools for stock market prediction. This research focuses on the design and development of an ensemble model that combines these three approaches to improve the accuracy and robustness of stock market predictions [10].

LSTM, a type of recurrent neural network (RNN), is well suited for capturing temporal dependencies and patterns in sequential data. In the context of stock market prediction, LSTM can analyze historical stock market data, identify intricate patterns, and make predictions based on learned patterns. By leveraging the memory and hidden state of LSTM, the model can capture long-term dependencies and nonlinear relationships present in the stock market data [11].

ARIMA, on the other hand, is a classical statistical model widely used in time series analysis. It is particularly effective in capturing the linear and autoregressive nature of stock market data. By incorporating ARIMA as a component of the ensemble model, we can harness its strengths in modeling the time series aspects of stock prices and augment the predictive power of the overall model [12].

In addition to LSTM and ARIMA, sentiment analysis plays a crucial role in understanding the influence of public sentiment on stock market dynamics. The sentiment values of tweets will be tested to check whether it has an impact on stock request movements. Investors are veritably interested in the exploration area of stock price forecasts since the stock demand has gotten a lot of attention. Investors and investment businesses have become a popular choice for stock forecasts for secure investment results as a result of the stock request's irregularities.

Sentiment analysis involves the application of natural language processing (NLP) techniques to analyze textual data, such as news articles, social media posts, and financial reports, to determine the sentiment expressed within them. This study will fill the gap in the scientific stock market literature by predicting stock market movements utilizing a variety of current news articles and tweets from various sources. The task of assessing a text's viewpoint as good, negative, or neutral is known as sentiment categorization. The information gleaned from tweets is extremely important in generating predictions. By quantifying sentiment scores associated with the stock-related textual data, we can capture the effect of public sentiment on stock price movements [5].

The proposed ensemble model combines the strengths of LSTM, ARIMA, and sentiment analysis to improve stock market predictions. This study aims to contribute to the field of text analytics in forecasting using tweet sentiment and predicting stock market movements with statistical models such as ARIMA with artificial neural network (ANN) and LSTM.

The integration of these approaches aims to leverage the advantages of each technique, addressing their individual limitations and creating a more robust and accurate prediction framework. By combining the quantitative features captured by LSTM and ARIMA with the qualitative information derived from sentiment analysis, the ensemble model can potentially capture a broader range of factors that impact stock prices.

This research aims to design and develop an ensemble model for stock market prediction using LSTM, ARIMA, and sentiment analysis. Real-world historical stock market data will be used to evaluate the performance of the ensemble model against individual LSTM and ARIMA models. The study will also assess the impact of incorporating sentiment analysis on prediction accuracy and reliability. The predicted outcome of the study is to create a highly accurate algorithm that determines the correlation between sentimental analysis and the respective stock price.

The outcomes of this research have significant implications for investors, financial institutions, and policymakers. Accurate stock market predictions can assist investors in making informed decisions, financial institutions in managing risks, and policymakers in formulating effective economic policies. The ensemble model, combining LSTM, ARIMA, and sentiment analysis, represents a comprehensive and innovative approach to enhance stock market prediction capabilities and contribute to a deeper understanding of the intricate dynamics of financial markets.

1.3   Problem Statement

Accurately predicting stock market movements is a complex and challenging task, primarily due to the dynamic and unpredictable nature of financial markets. Traditional models and techniques often struggle to capture the intricate patterns, nonlinear relationships, and the influence of external factors on stock prices. Additionally, the emergence of social media platforms has introduced a new dimension to stock market analysis, with public sentiment expressed in platforms like Twitter showing a strong correlation with stock price rises and falls. Investment opportunities for individual investors or business opportunities in the stock market will increase if there is an efficient algorithm that can predict the short-term price of a stock of a certain company with the news or tweets around that company. However, effectively incorporating sentiment analysis into existing prediction models remains a significant challenge.

1.4   Research Objectives

The main objective of this study is to provide future stock price insights using ML algorithms and prevent future losses for investors and investment companies by providing accurate results using sentiment analysis by executing the following process.

- Develop an ensemble model combining LSTM, ARIMA, and sentiment analysis to improve stock market prediction accuracy.
- Investigate the impact of incorporating sentiment analysis on stock market predictions.
- Evaluate and compare the performance of the ensemble model against individual LSTM and ARIMA models using real-world data.
- Analyze the strengths and limitations of the ensemble model to identify areas for improvement.
- Provide valuable insights for investors, financial institutions, and policymakers to support informed decision-making in the stock market.

1.5   Expected Outcome

- The research will result in the design and development of an ensemble model that incorporates LSTM and ARIMA for time series analysis of stock market data and sentiment analysis techniques to analyze public sentiment expressed on Twitter.
- This model will effectively leverage the strengths of each component to improve stock market prediction accuracy and robustness.
- This analysis will provide insights into the factors contributing to the model's success and identify any potential limitations or challenges associated with incorporating social media data.
- The findings will enhance our understanding of the relationship between Twitter sentiment and stock market dynamics, providing practical implications for decision-making in the financial industry.

1.6   Chapter Summary

The research study is narrated in five chapters. The first chapter provides an overview of the research topic, highlighting the challenges of stock market prediction and the potential of machine learning techniques. It introduces the concept of ensemble modeling, which combines LSTM, ARIMA, and sentiment analysis to improve prediction accuracy. The significance of this research, problem statement, research objectives, and the importance of this research in enhancing stock market predictions are discussed.

The second chapter reviews relevant literature on stock market prediction, LSTM, ARIMA, and sentiment analysis. It explores previous studies that have examined the correlation between public sentiment expressed in tweets and stock price movements. The chapter also discusses the strengths and limitations of LSTM, ARIMA, and sentiment analysis, as well as existing research on ensemble modeling for stock market prediction.

The third chapter outlines the design and development of the ensembled model. It describes the data collection process, including the acquisition of historical stock market data, sentiment analysis data, and the preprocessing steps applied to ensure data quality. The chapter provides a detailed explanation of LSTM and ARIMA models, including their architectures and training procedures. It also describes the sentiment analysis techniques used to extract sentiment scores from textual data.

The fourth chapter presents the development of the ensemble model that integrates LSTM, ARIMA, and sentiment analysis. It outlines the fusion approach used to combine the predictions from the individual models, emphasizing how the weights are determined to optimize the ensemble's performance. The chapter also discusses the integration of sentiment analysis into the ensemble model and the methods employed to combine the sentiment features with the quantitative features derived from LSTM and ARIMA.

The fifth chapter discusses the experimental results obtained from applying the ensemble model to real-world historical stock market data that are presented and analyzed in this chapter. The performance of the ensemble model is compared against the individual LSTM and ARIMA models. Various evaluation metrics, such as accuracy, precision, recall, and F1 score, are used to assess the predictive capabilities of the ensemble model. The impact of incorporating sentiment analysis on prediction accuracy is also examined.

The findings of the research are discussed in detail in the sixth chapter. The strengths and limitations of the ensemble model are highlighted, along with the potential reasons for its performance. The implications of the research for stock market prediction and the insights gained from the integration of LSTM, ARIMA, and sentiment analysis are discussed. The chapter concludes with a summary of the research outcomes and suggestions for future work to enhance the ensemble model and further advance stock market prediction capabilities.

1.7   Theoretical Foundation

1.7.1   Sentiment Analysis

The practice of analyzing and interpreting the remarks, thoughts, and emotions made by people with emotional tendencies is known as sentiment analysis. For mining online reviews, sentiment analysis technology has been frequently deployed. The findings can aid firms in making changes to their future marketing strategy, such as examining the benefits and drawbacks of items from multiple perspectives in order to improve product quality and customized suggestions [2].

Due to their unpredictable nature and the large amount of noise and variables involved, financial markets are one of the most difficult systems to anticipate. For years, complex statistical approaches have been employed to forecast the stock market, allowing for the creation of robust prediction models with low error [4].

1.7.1.1   Subjectivity

Subjectivity refers to the degree to which a piece of text expresses subjective or opinionated content rather than objective facts. It represents the subjective perspective, beliefs, emotions, or personal opinions of the author. Text that contains subjective content often involves expressions of sentiments, emotions, evaluations, or judgments. The degree to which a person is personally connected with an object is referred to as subjectivity. Personal connections and individual experiences with that object are most important here, which may or may not differ from someone else's perspective. For example, the sentence "I am really delighted with my new smartphone because it offers the best performance on the market," has strong subjectivity. The user is actually talking about his experience and how he feels about an object, therefore the phrase is plainly subjective [3].

1.7.1.2 Polarity

Polarity, on the other hand, refers to the strength of the sentiment or emotional orientation expressed in the text. It indicates whether the sentiment conveyed is positive, negative, or neutral. Polarity classification assigns a sentiment label to a given text, indicating the overall sentiment polarity of the content. For example, a positive polarity indicates a positive sentiment such as trust, love, or admiration, whereas a negative polarity indicates a negative sentiment like "I don't think I will buy this item." Neutral polarity is assigned when no clear positive or negative sentiment is expressed [4].

Several studies have explored the potential of sentiment analysis of Twitter data to improve stock market prediction. The use of sentiment analysis, which involves extracting and analyzing emotions, opinions, and attitudes from text data, has shown promise in capturing market sentiment and predicting stock price movements.

The tweets were classified into three levels of polarity using sentiment analysis on each of the hashtag datasets: N, NEU, and P. Negative polarity (N) is formed for a negative view in the text, whereas positive polarity (P) is generated for a favorable opinion. For neutral opinion (NEU) or when

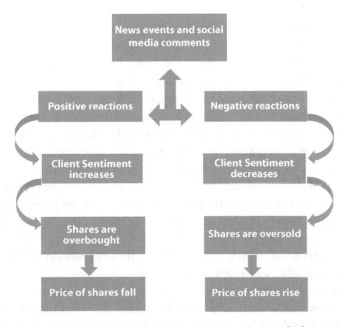

Figure 1.1 Representation of share value as per sentiments. Source: [39].

Table 1.1 Representation of
sentiments polarity and weight.

Polarity	N	NEU	P
Weight	−1	0	+1

the polarity cannot be estimated, NEU polarity is generated. The weights attributed to the standard polarities are shown in Table 1.1. Polarities in the NEU category tweets are given a 0 (zero) weight because they contain impartial opinions regarding the concept or thing. Negative opinion tweets (N) were given a "−1" weighting based on the magnitude of the negative sentiment. Positive opinion tweets (P) receive "+1," respectively. A sentiment dictionary is essential for recognizing sentiment tokens in any document during sentiment analysis [5].

This study's results can assist investors in anticipating and predicting whether their investment will be profitable or lose money, as well as preventing large margin losses and keeping their stock investments on track.

1.7.2   Stock Market

Stock price forecasting has recently gained more attention in the financial industry. The continued use of the Internet in the modern age has reached extraordinary levels, which suggests it may have something to do with stock price behavior. The aim is to detect association patterns and use them to predict how different stock prices will perform in the future [6]. Undoubtedly, even when individually boring, aggregated tweets can provide a satisfying representation of public attitudes. Today, a large volume of data, containing information on many topics, is transmitted online through various sources. A good example is Twitter, where more than 400 million tweets are sent daily. Whereas each tweet may not be meaningful as a unit, a large collection of them can provide valuable data on general opinions on a particular topic [7]. Assessing public sentiment by retrieving online information from Twitter can be helpful in developing trading strategies. Accurately predicting stock price movements depends on many factors, and certainly public sentiment is included [8].

The wealth of the inventory marketplace can sell the boom of purchaser demand. However, in different circumstances, the common fluctuations in inventory fees have led to the growth of macroeconomic uncertainty. Especially after experiencing unheard-of big fluctuations inside the A-proportion marketplace in 2015, the self-assurance of purchasers has been substantially undermined, which is not conducive to reaching the intention of increasing home demand. Therefore, many pupils have performed studies on inventory forecasting. Cheng *et al.* use historical stock market data and technical indicators to predict future stock price movements using an attention-based long-term memory model [9].

1.7.3   Sentiment Analysis of Twitter in Stock Market Prediction

Several studies have explored the potential of sentiment analysis of Twitter data to improve stock market prediction. The use of sentiment analysis, which involves extracting and analyzing emotions, opinions, and attitudes from text data, has shown promise in capturing market sentiment and predicting stock price movements. Bollen *et al.* conducted a pioneering study that demonstrated a correlation between Twitter sentiment and stock market performance. By analyzing the collective mood expressed in tweets, they found that changes in Twitter mood could predict changes in the Dow Jones Industrial Average. Their research highlighted the potential of sentiment analysis in capturing public sentiment and its relevance to stock market dynamics [10].

Building on this work, Sprenger *et al.* focused on sentiment analysis of individual stocks in the year 2016. They found that sentiment scores derived from tweets related to specific stocks exhibited a positive correlation with future stock returns. The study concluded that sentiment analysis of stock-specific tweets could provide valuable signals for predicting stock price movements [11].

Zhang *et al.* examined sentiment polarity in tweets and its impact on stock market prediction. Their research revealed that the volume of positive and negative tweets about particular stocks was significantly correlated with future stock returns. This finding indicated the predictive power of sentiment analysis in capturing investor sentiment and incorporating it into stock market predictions [13].

In a more recent study, Chen *et al.* combined sentiment analysis with machine learning techniques to improve stock market prediction accuracy. By integrating sentiment analysis features into their predictive model, they achieved superior forecasting performance compared to traditional models. The study highlighted the benefits of leveraging sentiment analysis to capture the influence of public sentiment on stock price movements [14].

Overall, the literature suggests that sentiment analysis of Twitter data can be a valuable tool in stock market prediction. By capturing and analyzing public sentiment expressed on Twitter, sentiment analysis provides insights into market sentiment, investor sentiment, and collective opinions, which can enhance the accuracy and robustness of stock market forecasts.

1.7.4 Machine Learning Algorithms in Stock Market Prediction

Machine learning has emerged as a powerful tool for stock market prediction due to its ability to analyze vast amounts of data, identify patterns, and make predictions based on historical trends. The application of deep learning, particularly convolutional neural networks (CNNs) and RNNs, has gained attention in stock prediction. Wang *et al.* applied CNN to analyze stock price data and showed its capability in capturing spatial and temporal patterns, leading to more accurate predictions [15].

LSTM and ARIMA models have been widely employed in stock market prediction due to their ability to capture complex temporal patterns and trends in financial time series data.

In the context of LSTM models, Fischer *et al.* in the year 2018 conducted a study on stock market prediction and demonstrated that LSTM-based models outperformed traditional approaches. They found that LSTMs effectively captured long-term dependencies and exhibited superior predictive accuracy in forecasting stock prices [11].

In terms of ARIMA models, Tsantekidis *et al.* investigated the application of ARIMA models in stock market prediction and found that they produced satisfactory results in short-term forecasting. Their study emphasized the usefulness of ARIMA models for capturing seasonality and trends in stock price data [16].

It is worth noting that the combination of LSTM and ARIMA models has also been explored in stock market prediction. Zhang *et al.* proposed an integrated LSTM-ARIMA model and demonstrated its superior performance in predicting stock prices compared to individual models. The integration of LSTM and ARIMA allowed for capturing both short-term dynamics and long-term trends, resulting in improved forecasting accuracy [10].

The statistical model unobserved component model is compared with the ML models LSTM and ARIMA for predicting the stock market in the study [12]. The experiment results revealed that LSTM demonstrated its superior performance in predicting stock prices compared to individual models.

In summary, both LSTM and ARIMA models have shown promise in stock market prediction. LSTMs excel in capturing complex dependencies and long-term patterns, whereas ARIMA models are effective in modeling linear trends and seasonality. The combination of these models can provide a comprehensive approach to stock market forecasting, taking advantage of their respective strengths in capturing different aspects of stock price data.

1.8   Research Methodology

1.8.1   Stock Sentiment Data Fetching Through API

Stock tweets were used to extract sentiment data (tweets) for Tata Motors. It is a social networking platform that offers large-scale text data as well as high-quality data for mining. In 2016, stock tweets had a global user base of over 40 million people. Filtering away nonfinancial tweets and spam communications is a priority. It also allows users to indicate whether a tweet is bullish or bearish [17]. It has two APIs, search API and stream API, for gathering various types of data. Through a query, the Twitter API returns the tweets of a certain user, company, or set of criteria. An authentication key is needed to get tweets from Twitter. The server will establish a connection between a Twitter server and the local machine and request the tweets to the user once the user has been authenticated [18].

1.8.1.1   Stock Market Data Fetching

Stock market data of Tata Motors company from "TATA Group" was obtained from Yahoo Finance for the years 2017 to 2023. The data were downloaded in an Excel sheet and attributes were noted.

1.8.1.2   Sentiment Data Preprocessing

As we all know, not all users follow the same pattern when it comes to tweets. In their messages, users can include numbers, emojis, punctuation marks, special symbols, and other elements. We preprocessed tweets to remove emojis, punctuation, URLs, stop words, and numbers, among others, to make reliable predictions from text data [19].

- **Text Processing:** The tweet text contains words that are not suitable for sentiment analysis such as tweets containing URLs, tags, and icons. To remove these words to improve accuracy, we used the R command for NLP [20].

- **Tokenization:** The classifier was trained from the tweets which were separated based on white space to create a list of words.
- **Removing Stop words:** Stop words have been excluded from the list through the Natural Language Toolkit (NLTK). It has a dictionary of stop words. Each word in the word list is compared with the words in the dictionary, each match, the corresponding word will be removed from the list [20].
- **Twitter Symbols:** Tweets mainly contain special characters like @ and #. Extra spaces and punctuations were used for different purposes. All symbols are removed as they are of no value to sentiment analysis except for $. Words starting with $ are matched with company names so that it could help filter them out because they can contain information useful for sentiment analysis. To clean up the symbols, we used the "Re" library in Python [21].

1.8.1.3   Stock Data Preprocessing

Stock market data extracted from Yahoo Finance is used to decide if a stock's price goes up or down on a particular day. To make this decision, today's closing price is subtracted from yesterday's closing price, if the result is more than 0, then it means that the security (shares of a company) is appreciated and the person's stocks can be sold for profit. Conversely, if the spread is less than zero, then the price of the security will decrease, and the investor can buy or keep the security if available [22]. The only problem that was faced was that the stock data were missing for the weekends but for the tweets, the data were available throughout the week. Last observation carried forward (LOCF) was used to calculate the missing values. It takes the stock close value of the previous day and will put it for the next day [23].

1.8.2   Project Plan

The workflow diagram of the project is illustrated in the Figure 1.2. The project focuses on analyzing the stock data of "Tata Motors," which is a company under the "Tata Group." The stock data were collected from Yahoo Finance, covering the period from 17 October 2017 to 3 February 2023. Additionally, tweets were collected using the Twitter API to analyze sentiment values [24].

The first step in the workflow involved gathering the stock data of "Tata Motors" from Yahoo Finance. This dataset contains valuable information

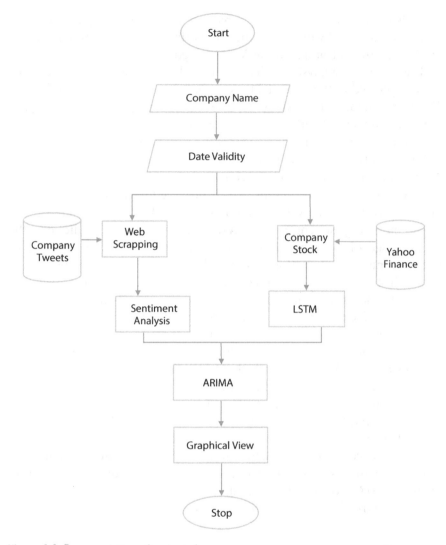

Figure 1.2 Representation of project plan.

such as stock prices, trading volume, and other relevant variables, which serve as the primary input for subsequent analysis.

Simultaneously, tweets related to the "Tata Motors" stock were collected using the Twitter API. The purpose of collecting these tweets was to perform sentiment analysis, aiming to understand the sentiment expressed by Twitter users regarding the stock.

After collecting the Yahoo Finance data and conducting sentiment analysis using Twitter data, the next step involves integrating the sentiment analysis results and LSTM predictions into the overall analysis. This integration is achieved by incorporating the sentiment analysis and LSTM outputs as additional features in the ARIMA algorithm.

The sentiment analysis results provide valuable insights into the sentiment expressed in the collected tweets related to the "Tata Motors" stock. These sentiment values, which capture the positive, negative, or neutral sentiment associated with each tweet, can be used as supplementary information to enhance the predictive capabilities of the ARIMA model.

Similarly, the LSTM algorithm generates predictions based on the historical stock data, taking into account the sequential dependencies and patterns. The LSTM predictions, which provide forecasts for future stock prices, serve as another valuable input to enrich the ARIMA analysis.

By combining the sentiment analysis results and LSTM predictions, the ARIMA algorithm can benefit from the additional information and incorporate it into the forecasting process. This integration allows for a more comprehensive analysis that takes into consideration both the historical stock data and the sentiment signals derived from the Twitter data.

The ARIMA algorithm leverages the combined information to refine its predictions and generate more accurate forecasts for the future price movements of the "Tata Motors" stock. By incorporating the sentiment analysis and LSTM outputs into the ARIMA model, the overall analysis becomes more robust, capturing both the quantitative patterns and qualitative sentiment signals in the stock data.

In summary, the sentiment analysis results and LSTM predictions are integrated into the ARIMA algorithm, enabling a more comprehensive analysis that combines the historical stock data, sentiment signals, and sequential patterns. This integration enhances the predictive capabilities of the ARIMA model and contributes to a more accurate forecast of the future price trends of the "Tata Motors" stock.

1.8.3   Use Case Diagram

The Figure 1.3 shows a representation of the use case of the diagram. Here, it shows two input points as shown: one is admin and the second is investor which follows the prediction process path before investment. The admin starts the initial step of the data collection process. After collecting the previous stock data, the preprocessing of the data is done to remove the unwanted columns from the data. After preprocessing the data stock trends are checked how it is going UP or DOWN, HIGH or LOW, or NEUTRAL also depending on the tweets that will affect its movements. It is also used

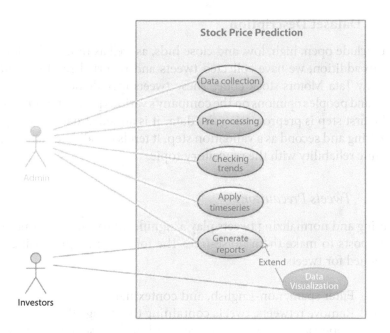

Figure 1.3 Representation of use case diagram.

to show its sentiments whether it is POSITIVE or NEGATIVE resulting in stock's ups and downs [25]. After checking the trends, the time series data method is used to check real-time values of stocks as in the stock market every second is important, delay also results in stock's ups and downs movements which can result in a company's profit- or loss-making results. After completing the process from the admin, the reports are generated in a graphical format to give clear insights to the investors. It is represented as a data visualization for the investors to clearly give them an idea about investment, whether to invest or not and how the company stock will be going ahead.

1.8.4 Data Collection

Data for stock prediction were collected from "Yahoo Finance," and to get sentiments, we collected tweets from "Twitter API" for the respective company. From Yahoo Finance, we have collected the previous data and from Twitter, we have conducted the sentimental analysis because we consider Twitter to be a major social media that will influence the stock market with a single tweet, it can move the stock upside or downside.

1.8.5   Dataset Description

Data include open, high, low, and close bids, as well as time and volume of bids. In addition, we have collected tweets and reported results about the company Tata Motors stock code. These tweets include both stock-related tweets and people's opinions on the company's various products and services.

The first step is preprocessing the data. It is aimed at data cleaning and formatting and second as a validation step. It tends to validate data for their semantic reliability with the repository topic.

1.8.5.1   Tweets Precautions

Cleaning and normalizing tweets play a significant role in analyzing social media posts to make them noise-free. The following preprocessing steps are applied for tweets.

a) Filter spam, non-English, and contextual.
b) Remove retweets, tweets containing the string "RT."
c) Uppercase letters are replaced with lowercase letters, thus preventing the repetition of the same words in the feature vector.
d) Remove punctuation, URLs, hashtags, and user IDs from tweets.

1.8.5.2   Consolidation of Sentiment and Stock Price Data

As we know, there can be more than one tweet per day about a company; the data we obtained from past sentiment projections are aggregated every day. This means that on a day, if there are more positive tweets than negative, then we say the stock market sentiment is positive that day and one can buy the stock. In this step, we have merged stock market data and sentiment-matching dates. At the end of the preprocessing stage, the file contains three attributes, i.e., date, stock price and sentiment for a given day [26].

1.8.6   Algorithm Description

1.8.6.1   ARIMA

The ARIMA method has been published for the first time with a box and Jenkins and the ARIMA model is often called the Box-Jenkins model. This model is also called as ARIMAX model if it has a series of time differently with input variables. The ARIMA analyze and predict a series of uniform distance changes. The conversion function affects data, it combines the values of the time series with previous values, past errors, and the linear combination of the present and past. The ARIMA process provides a complete set of tools. For unit timing chain modeling, estimates and parameter predictions, providing excellent flexibility for ARIMA or ARIMAX models, can be analyzed.

In the ARIMA model, the forecast value of a variable is the linear combination of previous values and previous errors, shifted as follows:

$$W_t = \mu + \frac{\theta(B)}{\phi(B)} a_t$$

Equation 1.1. ARIMA equation.
where
t   is index times
W_t is the response series Y_t or a difference of the response series
μ is the mean term
B   is the backshift operator; that is, $BX_t = X_{t-1}$
$\phi(B)$ is the autoregressive operator, represented as a polynomial in the backshift operator:

$$\phi(B) = 1 - \phi_1 B - \dots - \phi_p B^p$$

$\theta(B)$ is the autoregressive operator, represented as a polynomial in the backshift operator:

$$\theta(B) = 1 - \theta_1 B - \dots - \theta_p B^p$$

a_t is the independent disturbance, also called the random error.

In the identification phase, it specifies the response set and identifies candidate ARIMA models for it. In addition, it reads the time series to be used in the next statements, can distinguish them, and calculates autocorrelation, inverse autocorrelation, partial autocorrelation, and cross-correlation. Stability tests can be performed to determine if a difference is needed.

The estimate and diagnostic verification step specifies the ARIMA model to match the variable specified in the validation step and also estimates the model's parameters. It also generates diagnostic statistics to help you assess model fit. Checking for significance on parameter estimates indicates whether certain terms in the model may not be relevant. If the diagnostic tests show a problem with the model, you try another model and then repeat the diagnostic and estimating step.

In the prediction step, future values of the time series are predicted and confidence intervals for these predictions are generated from the ARIMA model generated by the previous estimation step.

1.8.6.2   LSTM

ANNs are very good at recognizing hidden patterns in data. The ANN will go through a training process where it records previous time series data points and adjusts them using the hidden layer and produces outputs. LSTM is a subset of cyclic neural network (RNN), where it is a subset of ANN. Long-term memory (LSTM) is an advanced regenerative neural network (RNN) and allows the analysis of data from a longer time series. When the RNN model is compared with LSTM, the LSTM model adds three more memory modules, input information at time t, select useful information with a certain probability, and finally extract useful information through the gate output as a state of the last hold layer, and then participate in the calculation of the next time.

The first step involved in the LSTM is deciding what information should go through the state of the cell. These will include a sigmoid class called "Forget Gate Layer." It looks at h_{t-1} and x_t and outputs between 0 and 1 for each number in the cellular state.

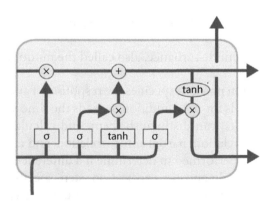

Figure 1.4 Long short-term memory network cell state. Source: [40].

$$f_t = \sigma(W_f.[h_{t-1}, x_t] + b_f$$

Equation 1.2 Forgot layer of LSTM.

The next step is to decide if the new information should be stored in the cell state. It has two phases. First of all, the sigmoid layer called the "gateway layer" decides which values have been updated. Then, a class tanh creates a new class that generates a new candidate value. Then, these two values will be updated to the state.

$$i_t = \sigma(W_i.[h_{t-1}, x_t] + b_i$$
$$\tilde{c}_t = tanh(W_C.[h_{t-1}, x_t] + b_C$$

Equation 1.3 Input layer gate of LSTM.

After this C_{t-1}, the old cell state will be updated to the new cell state C_t, multiplied by the value of the forgotten state, and then added to $\tilde{c}_t$. This will be the new candidate value.

$$C_t = f_t * C_{t-1} + i_t * \tilde{c}_t$$

Equation 1.4 New candidate equation of LSTM.

The final output will be the clean version of the cell state. First, we run with a sigmoid layer that decides the output we need based on the state of the cell, then we set the state of the cell through tanh and multiply by the output of the sigmoid gate, to decide the exit.

$$o_t = \sigma(W_o.[h_{t-1}, x_t] + b_o$$
$$h_t = o_t * tanh(C_t)$$

Equation 1.5 Output of sigmoid gate.

1.8.6.3   TextBlob

TextBlob is a Python library for NLP. TextBlob has actively used the NLTK to fulfill its mission. NLTK is a library that allows easy access to many lexical sources and allows users to work with classification and many other tasks. TextBlob is a simple library that supports analysis and complex operations on text data. For lexical-based approaches, a feeling is determined by its semantic orientation and the intensity of each word in the sentence and positive words. Typically, a text message will be presented with a series of words. After assigning individual scores to all words, the final sentiment is calculated using an aggregate operation, such as the average score of all sentiments. TextBlob returns the polarity and subjectivity of the words. In the sentence "The middle pole [1,1]," 0 identifies negative feelings and 1 identifies positive feelings. The negative word reverses polarity. TextBlob has semantic tags for detailed parsing [27], for example, emoji, exclamation marks, and emoticon. Subjectivity is in the range [0,1]. Subjectivity quantifies particular opinions and factual information contained in the textbook. Greater subjectivity means that the textbook contains particular opinions rather than factual information. TextBlob has a redundant parameter position. TextBlob calculates subjectivity by looking at "intensity." Intensity determines whether one word modifies the coming. In English, adverbs are used as modifiers ("veritably well") TextBlob uses a weighted average sentiment score for all words in each sample. This fluently makes the effect of centralizing rulings different between words in our case" useful" and "but" [28].

1.9   Analysis and Results

Upon analyzing the graph, we can observe that the majority of the tweets obtained exhibit a positive sentiment value.

The graph (Figure 1.5) provides a visual representation of the sentiment distribution within the collected tweets. By examining the data points or bars on the graph, we can discern the prevalence of different sentiment categories, such as positive, negative, or neutral.

In this specific case, the graph indicates that the neutral sentiment category encompasses the largest proportion of the tweets. This suggests that the sentiment expressed in most of the collected tweets is distinctly neutral and negative. Instead, the majority of the tweets tend to have a positive sentiment associated with them.

Analyzing the sentiment distribution in this manner helps us understand the overall sentiment landscape surrounding the subject of interest, in this case, Tata Motors. It provides insights into the sentiment tendencies or preferences expressed by Twitter users when discussing or referring to Tata Motors.

The prevalence of neutral sentiment in the collected tweets may imply that the sentiments expressed are relatively balanced, lacking strong positive or negative inclinations. It could indicate a neutral or objective tone

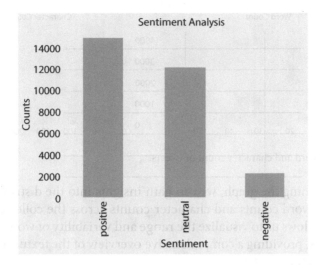

Figure 1.5 Count of tweets as per sentiment value.

in the discussions, where Twitter users are providing information, sharing factual details, or expressing opinions without a significant emotional leaning.

Understanding the sentiment distribution through the graph enhances our comprehension of the general sentiment atmosphere and can guide further analysis or decision-making. It enables us to identify any noteworthy patterns or trends in sentiment and helps in gaining insights into the public perception or sentiment toward Tata Motors based on the collected tweets.

In summary, the graph illustrating the sentiment distribution within the collected tweets highlights the prevalence of neutral sentiment values. This information provides valuable indications about the overall sentiment landscape surrounding Tata Motors on Twitter and assists in understanding the sentiment tendencies expressed by users in their discussions related to the subject.

The graph (Figure 1.6) presented visually illustrates the word counts and character counts derived from a collection of tweets gathered from Twitter specifically related to Tata Motors.

In this graph, the x-axis represents the different tweets within the dataset, whereas the y-axis represents the respective counts of words and characters. Each data point on the graph corresponds to a specific tweet and its associated counts.

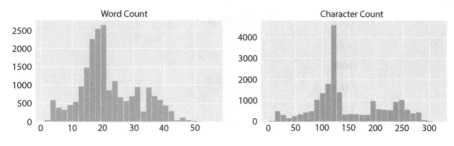

Figure 1.6 Word and character count of tweets.

By examining the graph, we can gain insights into the distribution and patterns of word counts and character counts across the collected tweets. The graph allows us to visualize the range and variability of word and character counts, providing a comprehensive overview of the textual characteristics within the dataset.

Analyzing the word counts helps us understand the length and complexity of the language used in the tweets. It allows us to identify common or frequently occurring words as well as the presence of longer or more elaborate expressions.

Similarly, observing the character counts enables us to gauge the overall length and brevity of the tweets. It allows us to assess the level of conciseness or verbosity in the text and identify any notable trends or outliers.

This graph serves as a valuable tool for exploring and summarizing the textual content of the tweets related to Tata Motors. It facilitates the identification of patterns, trends, and potential insights into the nature of the tweets, such as the use of specific keywords, the overall length of the messages, or the prevalence of shorter or longer posts.

Overall, the graph depicting word counts and character counts of the collected tweets offers a visual representation of the textual characteristics within the dataset. It aids in the analysis of the language patterns and content specific to Tata Motors on Twitter, providing valuable insights into the textual nature of the tweets.

The graph (Figure 1.7) represents the performance of a multinomial naive Bayes (NB) classifier in predicting labels for negative, neutral, and positive categories. Each cell in the graph corresponds to a combination of the true label and the predicted label. Darker colors indicate correct predictions, whereas lighter colors represent incorrect predictions. By looking at the colors, we can quickly assess the classifier's accuracy and identify any patterns or biases in its predictions. This graph provides a visual summary of how well the classifier performed in classifying the different label categories.

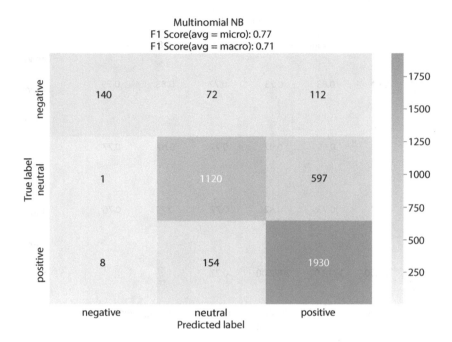

Figure 1.7 Multinomial naive Bayes classifier for true vs. predicted label.

The graph (Figure 1.8) represents the performance of a multinomial NB classifier in predicting labels for negative, neutral, and positive categories, along with additional metrics such as accuracy, weighted average, and macro average.

The confusion matrix in the graph displays the number of correct and incorrect predictions made by the classifier. Each cell in the matrix corresponds to a combination of the true label (rows) and the predicted label (columns).

In addition to the confusion matrix, the graph incorporates three important metrics:

1. Accuracy: Accuracy measures the overall correctness of the classifier's predictions. It represents the proportion of correct predictions to the total number of predictions. The accuracy score is typically displayed prominently and provides an overall assessment of the classifier's performance.
2. Weighted Average: Weighted average is a metric that takes into account class imbalance in the dataset. It calculates the average performance of the classifier across all classes, weighted by the number of samples in each class. This metric

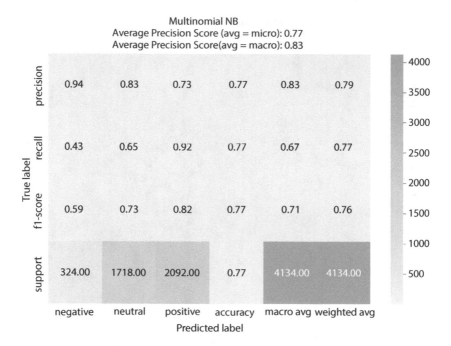

Figure 1.8 Multinomial naive Bayes classifier.

is useful when the dataset has imbalanced class distribution, as it ensures that the performance of each class contributes proportionally to the final score.

3. Macro Average: Macro average calculates the average performance of the classifier for each class independently and then takes the unweighted average of these scores. It treats each class equally, regardless of its size or prevalence in the dataset. Macro average provides insights into the classifier's performance on individual classes, which can be particularly useful in situations where all classes are considered equally important.

By incorporating these metrics into the graph, we can gain a more comprehensive understanding of the multinomial NB classifier's performance. The confusion matrix allows us to analyze the specific predictions for each class, whereas the accuracy, weighted average, and macro average provide summary measures that consider the overall performance across all classes.

This graph (Figure 1.9) provides a visual representation of the classifier's accuracy, as well as insights into its performance on individual classes

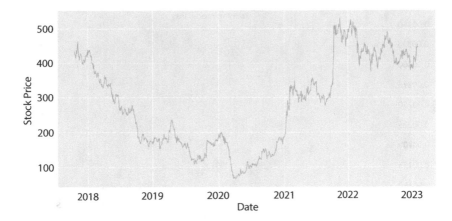

Figure 1.9 Date vs. stock closing price.

through the weighted average and macro average metrics. It helps evaluate the classifier's effectiveness in predicting the negative, neutral, and positive labels, considering class imbalances, and providing a comprehensive assessment of its predictive capabilities.

The graph presented visually represents the relationship between the Tata Motors Stock Price and its corresponding dates. It provides a comprehensive overview of how the stock price of Tata Motors has evolved over time.

The x-axis of the graph represents the dates, depicting a chronological sequence of time points. This allows us to track the progress of the Tata Motors Stock Price over a specific time period, whether it spans days, weeks, months, or years.

On the y-axis of the graph, we have the Tata Motors Stock Price. The y-axis denotes the numerical values or levels of the stock price at different points in time. By observing the movement of the plotted line or bars on the graph, we can comprehend the fluctuations, trends, and patterns in the stock price over the specified date range.

This graphical representation of the Tata Motors Stock Price with respect to date facilitates a visual analysis of the stock's performance over time. It allows us to identify important events, such as spikes or dips in the stock price, and observe any correlations with specific dates or time periods.

Moreover, this graph enables the comparison of the stock's performance across different dates, facilitating the identification of potential trends or seasonality. By examining the shape and trajectory of the graph, we can derive insights into the overall movement and volatility of the Tata Motors Stock Price, aiding in decision-making and further analysis.

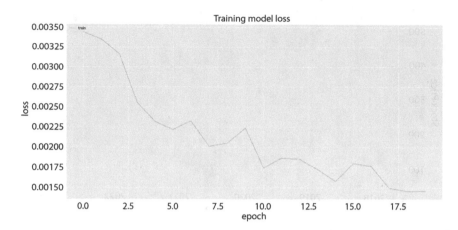

Figure 1.10 LSTM epoch vs. loss.

In summary, the graph illustrating the Tata Motors Stock Price with respect to date serves as a powerful visualization tool for understanding the historical price fluctuations and patterns of the stock. It provides a concise and accessible representation of the stock's performance, aiding in the interpretation and analysis of the data.

In our LSTM training process, we have trained our machine for a total of 20 epochs, indicating the number of iterations over the dataset during the training phase.

Epochs represent the number of times the entire dataset is passed forward and backward through the LSTM model. Each epoch allows the model to update its internal parameters based on the training data, gradually improving its ability to capture the underlying patterns and make accurate predictions.

After completing 12 epochs of training, we have observed that the LSTM algorithm has reached a point where it consistently produces stable and reliable results. This indicates that the model has effectively learned and captured the intricate relationships and dynamics within the data.

The steady results obtained after 12 epochs demonstrate that the LSTM model has converged to a state where further training iterations may not significantly enhance its predictive performance. At this point, the model has acquired sufficient knowledge and understanding of the dataset, enabling it to generate consistent and reliable predictions.

It is worth noting that the determination of the optimal number of epochs for training is a critical aspect of achieving the best possible results. Too few epochs may lead to underfitting, where the model fails to capture

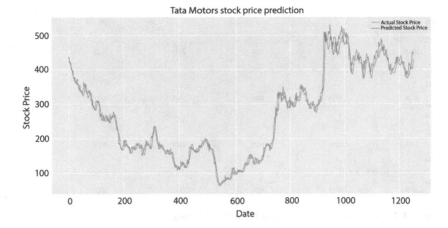

Figure 1.11 LSTM prediction for Tata Motors.

the complexity of the data. On the other hand, too many epochs can result in overfitting, where the model becomes overly specialized to the training data and fails to generalize well to unseen data.

By identifying that the LSTM algorithm provides steady results after 12 epochs, we gain valuable insights into the optimal training duration for achieving reliable and stable predictions. This understanding helps ensure the model's effectiveness and enhances its applicability for making accurate forecasts in various scenarios.

Upon completing the training of our neural network model, we observed that the predicted price closely aligns with the actual price, demonstrating a high level of accuracy.

The neural network model has undergone a training process where it learns from historical data patterns and relationships in order to make predictions. During this training phase, the model has analyzed a substantial amount of input data, which includes various features and attributes related to the price dynamics.

Through this training, the neural network has captured the underlying patterns, trends, and relationships in the data. As a result, when presented with new input data, such as the latest price observations, the model's predictions exhibit a remarkable level of proximity and agreement with the actual price values.

This high degree of accuracy between the predicted and actual prices indicates that the neural network has successfully learned and generalized from the training data. It has effectively utilized its learned knowledge to make precise predictions on unseen or future price instances.

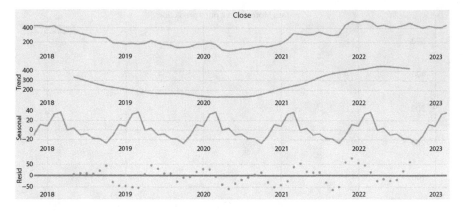

Figure 1.12 Seasonal decompose graph for Tata Motors.

The close alignment between the predicted and actual price values is indicative of the model's capability to capture the complex relationships and dynamics in the underlying data. It highlights the neural network's proficiency in understanding and forecasting price behavior, making it a reliable tool for price prediction tasks.

Overall, the neural network's accurate predictions signify the effectiveness and robustness of the model, providing confidence in its ability to generate reliable price forecasts.

The plot above clearly shows that the close price is unstable, along with its obvious seasonality.

Time Series Forecasting with ARIMA

The seasonal decomposition of ARIMA graph provides insights into the components of a time series: trend, seasonality, and residuals. The graph helps us understand the underlying patterns and fluctuations in the data and how they contribute to the overall behavior of the time series.

1. Trend: The trend component represents the long-term movement or direction of the time series. It captures the overall upward or downward movement over an extended period. The trend component can help identify underlying patterns and understand the general behavior of the data.
2. Seasonality: The seasonal component captures recurring patterns or cycles that repeat at fixed intervals. It represents the regular fluctuations that occur within a specific time frame, such as daily, weekly, monthly, or yearly patterns.

By analyzing the seasonal component, we can identify the seasonality in the data and understand its impact on the time series.

3. Residuals: The residuals, also known as the error component, represent the random or irregular fluctuations that are not accounted for by the trend or seasonal components. Residuals capture the unpredictable or unexplained variation in the data. Analyzing the residuals helps assess the model's accuracy and identify any remaining patterns or anomalies.

The seasonal decompose ARIMA graph visually represents these components, usually stacked on top of each other. Each component is plotted separately, allowing us to examine them individually and understand their contributions to the overall time series. By analyzing the trend, seasonality, and residuals, we can gain insights into the underlying patterns and make more informed forecasts or predictions.

In summary, the seasonal decompose ARIMA graph provides a visual representation of the trend, seasonality, and residuals in a time series. It helps us understand the long-term movement, recurring patterns, and unexplained variations in the data. By analyzing these components, we can better interpret the behavior of the time series and make more accurate predictions or forecasts [29–33].

To evaluate the precision of our predictions, we perform a detailed comparison between the predicted close price and the actual closing price of

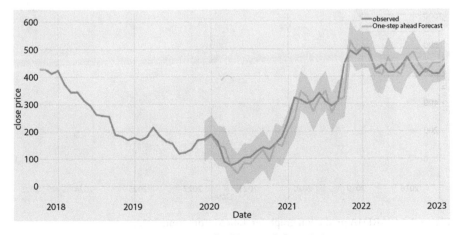

Figure 1.13 Checking ARIMA accuracy for Tata stock from 2020.

the time series. We conduct this comparison by analyzing the forecasted values, which are generated using our forecasting model, for the period starting from 31 December 2017 (2017-12-31) up to 17 January 2022 (2022-01-17).

By comparing the predicted close price with the real closing price, we can assess the accuracy and reliability of our forecasting model. This analysis allows us to determine how closely our predictions align with the actual values observed in the time series data.

The chosen time period, from 31 December 2017 to 17 January 2022, ensures that we evaluate the precision of our predictions over a substantial duration. This range covers multiple years and encompasses various market conditions, potentially capturing different trends, patterns, and fluctuations in the time series.

By conducting this comparison and setting the forecasts within this specific time frame, we gain a comprehensive understanding of the model's performance in predicting the close price of the time series. It helps us assess the quality and reliability of our predictions and provides insights into the effectiveness of our forecasting approach.

The ARIMA prediction for Tata Motors graph displays the forecasted values for a time series using the ARIMA model. It provides insights into the predicted values for the next two years based on the historical data and patterns captured by the ARIMA model.

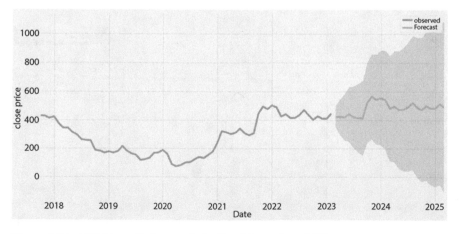

Figure 1.14 ARIMA prediction graph for Tata Motors from 2023.

The graph shows the predicted values plotted against time, with the forecasted period extending into the future. The forecasted values are generated by extrapolating the patterns and trends observed in the historical data.

By examining the ARIMA next two years prediction graph, we can gain an understanding of the expected trajectory of the time series. It allows us to assess the potential growth, decline, or stability of the variable being forecasted.

It is important to note that the accuracy of the ARIMA model's predictions may vary depending on the quality and characteristics of the data, as well as the appropriateness of the ARIMA parameters chosen. However, the graph serves as a visual representation of the predicted values and can be used as a starting point for further analysis or decision-making.

In summary, the ARIMA prediction for Tata Motors graph provides a visual representation of the forecasted values for a time series. It helps us understand the expected future trends and patterns in the data and can guide us in making informed decisions or plans based on the predicted values.

1.10   Conclusion

The method of using different algorithms and combining them in a single neural network is known as ensemble learning. This approach will be used for better understanding long-term sequences using sentiment analysis, ARIMA, and LSTM [34, 35].

The early exploration of forecasts on stock requests was grounded entirely on arbitrary walks and the vaticination, but with the arrival of behavioral finance, people's beliefs and moods were also taken into consideration while prognosticating stock movements. To make it more effective, we used the sentiment analysis idea of stock tweets through a machine learning model.

From this study, we conclude that using sentiment analysis of tweets for the respective company in the market while predicting the closing price of the same company in the share market will give us a better understanding of the next day's closing price and the efficiency of this approach is higher rather than traditional methods [36–38].

1.10.1   Limitation

The only limitation of this research is that the stock predictions were done for only one company of "Tata Group," i.e., "Tata Motors" stocks due to the audacity of the data for both Twitter tweets and finance data.

1.10.2   Future Work

The future scope is to improve the accuracy of the text analysis algorithm. The sentiment analysis of the text can be improved by using the transformers which have good efficiency. This can be used to support the decision-making of investors for more investment options in various sectors. Companies' yearly finance data with returns can also be included so that the correlation of the sentiment with stock prediction will be more accurate than real-time data.

References

1. Mehta, K. and Sharma, R., Contrarian and momentum investment strategies: Evidence from Indian stock market. *IJBER*, 15, 9, 107–118, 2017.
2. Sharma, R., Mehta, K., Goel, A., Non-linear relationship between board size and performance of Indian companies. *J. Manage. Gov.*, 27, 1277–1301, 2022. https://doi. org/10.1007/s10997-022-09651-8.
3. Sharma, R., Mehta, K., Rana, R., Cryptocurrency adoption behaviour of millennial investors in India, *Perspectives on Blockchain Technology and Responsible Investing*, Sonal Trivedi, Rashmi Aggarwal, and Gurmeet Singh (eds.), 135-158. Hershey, PA: IGI Global, 2023. https://doi.org/10.4018/978-1-6684-8361-9.ch006.
4. Vyas, V., Mehta, K., Sharma, R., The nexus between toxic-air pollution, health expenditure, and economic growth: An empirical study using ARDL. *IREF*, 84, 154–166, 2023. https://doi.org/10.1016/j.iref.2022.11.017.
5. Sharma, R., Mehta, K., Sharma, O., Exploring deep learning to determine the optimal environment for stock prediction analysis, international conference on computational performance evaluation. *ComPE*, 148–152, 2021.
6. Chander, R., Sharma, R., Mehta, K., Dividend announcement and informational efficiency: An empirical study of Indian stock market. *ICFAI JAF*, Hyderabad, 13, 10, 29–42, 2007.
7. Chander, R., Sharma, R., Mehta, K., Impact of dividend announcement on stock prices. *NICE J. Bus.*, 2, 1, 15–29, January-June 2007, (ISSN: 0973-449X).
8. Pagolu, V.S., Reddy, K.N., Panda, G., Majhi, B., Sentiment analysis of Twitter data for predicting stock market movements, in: *2016 International Conference on Signal Processing, Communication, Power and Embedded System (SCOPES)*, pp. 1345–1350, IEEE, 2016, October.

9. Sharma, R., Mehta, K., Sharma, O., . Exploring deep learning to determinc the optimal environment for stock prediction analysis. In *2021 International Conference on Computational Performance Evaluation (ComPE)*, pp. 148-152, IEEE, 2021.

10. Zhang, G., Liu, S., Cui, L., Zhang, Q., Qian, Y., Comparative analysis of stock price prediction using LSTM and ARIMA. *IJFE*, 6, 04, 1950016, 2019.

11. Fischer, T. and Krauss, C., Deep learning with long short-term memory networks for financial market predictions. *Eur. J. Oper. Res.*, 270, 2, 654–669, 2018.

12. Shankar, P., Sharma, N., Nagarohith, M.K., Ghosh, M.A., Stock price prediction using LSTM, ARIMA and UCM. *CDES*, 9, 11, 55–66, 2022.

13. Ranjan, S., Sood, S., Verma, V., Twitter sentiment analysis of real-time customer experience feedback for predicting growth of Indian telecom companies, in: *2018 4th International Conference on Computing Sciences (ICCS)*, pp. 166–174, IEEE, 2018, August.

14. Chen, Q., Li, X., Zhang, D., A sentiment analysis-based stock market prediction model using multiple news sources. *Inf. Sci.*, 537, 113–128, 2020.

15. Wang, W., Zhang, Y., Huang, J., Stock price prediction using convolutional neural networks with temporal moving filter. *IEEE Access*, 8, 115673–115682, 2020.

16. Tsantekidis, A., Passalis, N., Tefas, A., Kanniainen, J., Gabbouj, M., Iosifidis, A., Forecasting stock prices from the limit order book using convolutional neural networks, in: *2017 IEEE 19th Conference on Business Informatics (CBI)*, vol. 1, pp. 7–12, IEEE, 2017, July.

17. Nusrat, R., Malik, M. B., Arif, T., Sharma, S., Singh, S., Aich, S., and Kim, H.-C., Stock market prediction using machine learning techniques: A decade survey on methodologies, recent developments, and future directions. *Electronics,* 10, 21, 2717, 2021, https://doi.org/10.3390/electronics10212717.

18. Behera, R.K. *et al.*, Comparative study of real time machine learning models for stock prediction through streaming data. *J. Univers. Comput. Sci.*, 26, 9, 1128–47, 2020, https://doi. org/10.3897/jucs.2020.059. pp. 1138.

19. Arias, M., Arratia, A., Xuriguera, R., Forecasting with twitter data. *ACM Trans. Intelligent Syst. Technol. (TIST)*, 5, 1, 1–24, 2014.

20. Batra, R. and Daudpota, S.M., Integrating stocktwits with sentiment analysis for better prediction of stock price movement, in: *2018 International Conference on Computing, Mathematics and Engineering Technologies (iCoMET)*, 2018, https://doi.org/10.1109/icomet.2018.8346382.

21. Malekar, H., Dalal, M., S., N.N., I., S.S., K., S., K., T., Stock market prediction using sentiment analysis. *Int. J. Adv. Sci. Technol.*, 29, 4s, 112–1133, 2020, Retrieved from http://sersc.org/journals/index.php/IJAST/article/view/6664.

22. Deorukhkar, O.S., Lokhande, S.H., Nayak, V.R., Chougule, A.A., Stock price prediction using combination of LSTM neural networks, ARIMA and sentiment analysis. *Int. Res. J. Eng. Technol.*, 6, 3, 3497–3503, 2019.

23. Sharma, A., Bhuriya, D., Singh, U., Survey of stock market prediction using machine learning approach, *2017 International conference of Electronics, Communication and Aerospace Technology (ICECA)*, Coimbatore, India, 506–509, 2017. doi: 10.1109/ICECA.2017.8212715

24. Ariyo, A.A., Adewumi, A.O., Ayo, C.K., *Stock Price Prediction Using the ARIMA Model*, 2014, https://doi.org/10.1109/uksim.2014.67.

25. Sriram, B., Fuhry, D., Demir, E., Ferhatosmanoglu, H., Demirbas, M., Short text classification in twitter to improve information filtering, in: *Proceedings of the 33rd International ACM SIGIR Conference on Research and Development in Information Retrieval*, pp. 841–842, 2010, July.

26. Bouktif, S., Fiaz, A., Awad, M., Augmented textual features-based stock market prediction. *IEEE Access*, 8, 40269–40282, 2020.

27. Khan, Z.H., Alin, T.S., Hussain, M.A., Price prediction of share market using artificial neural network (ANN). *Int. J. Comput. Appl.*, 22, 2, 42–47, 2011.

28. Gujjar, J.P. and Kumar, H.P., Sentiment analysis: Textblob for decision making. *Int. J. Sci. Res. Eng. Trends*, 7, 2, 1097–1099, 2021.

29. Zhang, Y., Sun, J., Meng, L., Liu, Y., Sentiment analysis of E-commerce text reviews based on sentiment dictionary, in: *2020 IEEE International Conference on Artificial Intelligence and Computer Applications (ICAICA)*, pp. 1346–1350, IEEE, 2020, June.

30. Mourad, A. and Darwish, K., Subjectivity and sentiment analysis of modern standard Arabic and Arabic microblogs, in: *Proceedings of the 4th Workshop on Computational Approaches to Subjectivity, Sentiment and Social Media Analysis*, pp. 55–64, 2013, June.

31. Kilimci, Z.H., Sentiment analysis-based direction prediction in bit-coin using deep learning algorithms and word embedding models. *IJISAE*, 8, 2, 60–65, 2020.

32. Kordonis, J., Symeonidis, S., Arampatzis, A., Stock price forecasting via sentiment analysis on Twitter, in: *Proceedings of the 20th Pan-Hellenic Conference on Informatics*, pp. 1–6, 2016, November.

33. Tao, S., Fan, Y., Zhang, R., A hybrid forecasting model for stock price prediction, in: *Proceedings of the 4th International Conference on Computer Science and Application Engineering*, pp. 1–5, 2020, October.

34. Wilson, T., Wiebe, J., Hoffmann, P., Recognizing contextual polarity in phrase-level sentiment analysis, in: *Proceedings of Human Language Technology Conference and Conference on Empirical Methods in Natural Language Processing*, pp. 347–354, 2005, October.

35. Sekar, M., Gowri, M.M., Ramya, M.G., A study on capital structure and leverage of Tata Motors Limited: Its role and future prospects. *Proc. Econ. Financ.*, 11, 445–458, 2014.

36. Bollen, J., Mao, H., Zeng, X., Twitter mood predicts the stock market. *J. Comput. Sci.*, 2, 1, 1–8, 2011.

37. Sprenger, T.O., Tumasjan, A., Sandner, P.G., Welpe, I.M., Tweets and trades: The information content of stock microblogs. *Eur. Financ. Manage.*, 20, 5, 926–957, 2014.

38. Zhang, X., Fuehres, H., Gloor, P.A., Predicting stock market indicators through twitter "I hope it is not as bad as I fear". *Proc. Soc. Behav. Sci.*, 26, 55–62, 2011.

39. Jin, Z., Yang, Y., Liu, Y., Stock closing price prediction based on sentiment analysis and LSTM. *Neural. Comput. Appl.*, 32, 9713–9729, 2020. https://doi.org/10.1007/s00521-019-04504-2.

40. Hoedt, P., Kratzert, F., Klotz, D., Halmich, C., Holzleitner, M., Nearing, G.S., Hochreiter, S., Klambauer, G., MC-LSTM: Mass-conserving LSTM. *ICML*, 139, 4275–4286, 2021.

2

Unraveling Quantum Complexity: A Fuzzy AHP Approach to Understanding Software Industry Challenges

Kiran Mehta and Renuka Sharma*

Chitkara Business School, Chitkara University, Punjab, India

Abstract

The technological revolution has presented unforeseen hurdles to the software sector. Quantum computing (QuCo) technologies are set to revolutionize software engineering due to their growing impact and maturity in recent years. The assessment and prioritization of QuCo concerns in the software sector are under-developed, under-identified, and dispersed. To identify critical difficulties, we performed a systematic literature analysis using data from different digital libraries. Then, we used the fuzzy analytic hierarchy process (F-AHP) to rate the obstacles and impediments. Our results show the nascent nature of QuCo research and the growing need for multidisciplinary study to solve the stated difficulties; they have implications for both academics and professionals in the field.

Keywords: Fuzzy analytic hierarchy process, quantum computing, institutional barriers, organizational barriers, software technology barriers, management barriers

2.1 Introduction

According to numerous computer experts, the "quantum age" is about to arrive [1, 2] and will be remembered as such in the 21st century. It is predicted that quantum mechanics concepts like superposition, i.e., quantum objects may be in several states at once, and entanglement, in which quantum objects can be profoundly related without any direct

---

*Corresponding author: bhavya.renuka@chitkara.edu.in

Renuka Sharma and Kiran Mehta (eds.) Deep Learning Tools for Predicting Stock Market Movements, (39–60) © 2024 Scrivener Publishing LLC

physical connection, would revolutionize program computing. This quantum supremacy [3]—the point at which a programmable quantum device is capable of solving problems that no conventional computer can solve in any acceptable amount of time—could result in the resolution of nanoparticle issues [4, 5]. As a result, all major software businesses, such as IBM and Google, are presently spending hundreds of millions of dollars each year to develop revolutionary hardware and software solutions capable of supporting quantum computation. To create quantum applications on cloud-based quantum computers, IBM Quantum has built its programming environment. Quantum programming languages and development toolkits [6] have also been developed by companies and academics. According to Arute *et al.* [7], the tech is excellent for numerous commercial transactions since it can successfully examine large datasets with considerable expertise and minimal computational time, as well as allowing firms to discern data-driven patterns/trends and uncover new possibilities. For a job that would take a supercomputer 10,000 years to perform, Google's Sycamore quantum processor takes just 200s.

The usefulness of quantum computing (QuCo) has been acknowledged by several institutions, including IT titans such as Google, Intel, and IBM, as well as start-ups like IonQ and Rigetti.

In certain areas, such as industrial products and pharmaceuticals, the use of QuCo is well established; in others, however, it has only lately been recognized for its practical uses [8]. Although numerous possible applications of quantum programming have been made in the disciplines of machine learning, optimization, cryptography, and chemistry, the creation of large-scale quantum software appears to be a long way off [9, 10]. According to QuCo's express data processing capabilities, the financial industry is rapidly acknowledging its advantages [11]. Accordingly, the number of QuCo applications is projected to rise considerably in the future as businesses start recognizing the advantages of QuCo and begin to use it more broadly. In the coming time, QuCo applications are projected to grow significantly as the corporate world realizes the value of QuCo and adopts it more extensively.

Given the promise of this technology, both business and university researchers are increasingly looking for ways to increase its dependability [12]. Whereas QuCo research has expanded, it has mostly concentrated on creating technical components such as software (including tools and systems), as well as quantum hardware. Studies have not been conducted to identify the challenges and barriers that the software business faces in terms of QuCo. Researchers, for example, have insufficient awareness of the possible use of QuCo in many industrial sectors for project management, quality improvement, and delivery management. QuCo implementations in areas like medicine, finance, and power [13] have an impact on the effectiveness and effectiveness of business operations, and hence, this is a key research need. To provide an example, quantum technologies (QTs) may be utilized to generate novel medicines and materials as well as to enhance industrial processes [10]. As a result, it is critical to understand the primary obstacles that QuCo applications confront in the real world.

Addressing such issues, on the other hand, necessitates synthesizing the scattered information on QuCo and defining its limitations. Furthermore, since the use of QuCo in everyday industrial operations is less well known, establishing future goals for this sector requires an awareness of the constraints that inhibit QuCo implementations.

2.2   Introduction to Quantum Computing

QuCo, which makes use of quantum mechanical features to solve problems that are beyond the capabilities of conventional computers, has made major strides in recent years. The synthesis of several methodologies from math, data science, physics, and information theory opened the way for the establishment of a unique sphere, QuCo, capable of completing computations previously considered impossible for conventional computers. Quantum computers, in comparison to conventional computers, have high processing power, low energy consumption, and enormous speed. It is accomplished by manipulating the behavior of microphysical objects or particles such as atoms, electrons, and rays that carry metadata or digital information. As opposed to the classical bits, which are either 0 or 1 or AND or NOT gates [Orus *et al.* 2019], the quantum system consists of "qubits," or "multiple status quantum systems" [44]. |0> and |1> are the two orthogonal states of the qubit structure [27].

In QuCo, information is encoded as zero or one bit (one-bit) utilizing two orthogonal states of a tiny object referred to as a quantum bit or qubit [14]. The property of having both 0 and 1 as its value is referred to as "superposition." Additionally, they possess a trait called "entanglement," which means that altering the state of one Qubit affects the state of another, even though they are physically apart. Qubits possess both digital and analog characteristics, endowing quantum computers with enormous processing capability [15]. Numerous quantum algorithms (QAs), such as Grover's algorithm for searching and Shor's algorithm for factoring big numbers, have already been invented [16]. Quantum programming languages are critical for converting complicated concepts into instructions/codes that a quantum computer can perform. They make it possible to find and design new QAs, as well as to execute current ones [17]. There are some critical distinctions between quantum and classical computing.

QuCo has the following features: calculates using Qubits, which may have the values 0 or 1 or both at the same time; power grows exponentially as the number of Qubits increases; has a high rate of mistake; operates at temperatures near to absolute zero; significantly more secure to work with; appropriate for large/complex tasks, including optimization, data processing, and simulations, forecasting, modeling, etc. Meanwhile, classical computing has the following features: calculates using transistors with either a 0 or a 1 value the power output of a transistor rises proportionally to the number of transistors; has a reduced rate of mistake; works at room temperature; is less secure; is more appropriate for routine processing jobs. To see the genesis of QuCo see Table 2.1.

QAs have already found their way into healthcare, financial, and industrial sectors as well as the blockchain industry. Scheduling and route planning optimization issues, search algorithms, sampling and pattern matching, and quantum encryption are a few of the many topics covered. QuCo in healthcare makes it feasible to speed up drug discovery, drug design, therapy/treatment optimization, and the likely time to market for new pharmaceuticals. Trading techniques and market instability detection are also possible due to this technology. In addition, developing QuCo makes advertising and product marketing, software verification, and validation simpler.

Table 2.1 Genesis of QuCo.

First-generation QuCo	Physical speed - kHz and logical speed - Hz, applied with "ion traps" (Van Meter, 2016) [45]
Second-generation QuCo	Physical speed - MHz and logical speed - kHz, applied with "distributed diamonds" [46, 47], "superconducting quantum circuits" [48], and "linear optical" [49]
Third-generation QuCo	Physical speed - GHz and logical speed - MHz, applied with "monolithic diamonds" [50], "quantum dots" [51], and "donor" [52]
Fourth-generation QuCo	It is still in the early stages of development and is constantly changing [53].

The second fundamental idea of entanglement is concurrence detection, which quantifies the degree of entanglement between two-body systems. Entanglement enables quantum computers to have a higher information capacity [18]. It is possible to prepare two qubits in an entangled state, which implies that once prepared, they will behave jointly rather than separately. This is true even when the qubits are separated by thousands of light-years. Quantum entanglement (QE) is a concept that is based on spatial and temporal connectivity [19]. From an ontological standpoint [20], an entangled system cannot be completely characterized apart from its interactions with other components and the overall system's attributes. The development of the QE idea in the literature, particularly in management studies, has highlighted its potential to provide new conceptual perspectives for rethinking the interplay of quantum aspects. Continuous study on these issues has enhanced the concept of QAs, which was introduced by Deutsch in 1985. These algorithms are capable of solving well-known complicated problems in a fraction of the time required by standard methods [21]. The emerging literature focuses on the creation of efficient algorithms that may be used to enhance communication protocols and applications in a variety of domains [22].

Quantum cryptography, such as "quantum key distribution," "encryption/decryption," signature authentication, and hashing, are now being used by businesses. Researchers have studied the possibility of QuCo and blockchain technology to increase the privacy and security of information. As a result, QuCo-based distributed ledger systems may increase data security and consistency for data translation. Self-enforcement and self-authentication may be achieved by using QuCo in combination with blockchain technology, without the requirement for external parties to authenticate the information source. The relevance of QuCo in developing decentralized systems like cryptocurrencies and the blockchain, on the other hand, remains largely unknown [23].

2.3   Literature Review

The core advantage of QuCo technology lies in its rapid task execution capability. In contrast to conventional algorithms that scour through substantial datasets with a search time proportional to the square root of their size, QuCo primarily aims to expedite calculations [24]. It obviates the necessity for formulating specific queries to extract information. Instead, its potential resides in its simultaneous evaluation of numerous variables, consequently pinpointing optimal solutions from a multitude of alternatives. The realm of information processing has been profoundly reshaped by significant and revolutionary advancements in IT and communication over the past few decades. Within this transformative landscape, QuCo has emerged as the lead technology, giving remedies for matters of discretion, genuineness, and secrecy in an unparalleled manner [25].

The field of QuCo has garnered significant attention in prior research, with a notable emphasis on its practical applications as evidenced by works such as [26]. However, the existing body of literature reveals a noticeable scarcity when it comes to systematic literature reviews (SLRs) dedicated to comprehensively understanding QuCo. Notably, the earliest literature reviews about QuCo primarily centered on its conceptual evolution, delving into its foundational development [28]. An example of this is found in [8], where an in-depth exploration of quantum mechanics principles uncovered several intriguing research gaps. This particular review primarily focused on constructing a comprehensive taxonomy for QuCo while also critically examining the advancements in scalable quantum computer hardware. Another significant strand of literature focuses on applications, with one review dedicated to showcasing the potential of QuCo in data search operations over unsorted datasets [24]. Within the realm of QuCo research, conducted a thorough evaluation of current QuCo methodologies, particularly emphasizing its implications and potential prospects in the domain of finance. Similarly, Deutsch [21] offered a detailed and comprehensive perspective on the integration of QuCo for optimizing energy systems, carefully delineating the opportunities and challenges that lie therein. Moreover, several scholarly voices have highlighted the multifaceted potential of QuCo in diverse sectors, including but not limited to cryptocurrency [25], quantum chemistry, international relations [27], and quantum machine learning [29]. The collective body of work underscores the wide-ranging possibilities and challenges that the realm of QuCo presents across various domains. Despite the fundamental importance attributed to the literature concerning QuCo concepts, coupled with the varied spectrum of approaches adopted within QuCo research, the acknowledgment of its pragmatic implications has emerged relatively recently. Shedding light on the versatile nature of these research avenues, investigations have inquired into both the shortcomings and strengths of QuCo, delved into the intricacies inherent in quantum theory, and examined the expansive ecosystem surrounding QuCo [30]. Other scholarly works have put their focus on the realm of technical intricacies, explored its applicability in the realm of credit risk analysis [31], and undertaken an examination of security intricacies. Concurrently, several studies have dedicated their efforts to probe into its prospective utility in domains such as fault diagnosis, the realm of "computational molecular biology and bioinformatics," and the resolution of complex routing problems. These diverse scholarly pursuits highlight the complex web of viewpoints that together enhance our comprehensive understanding of QuCo's theoretical underpinnings, research approaches, and practical applications in the real world.

QAs have attained a robust establishment in contemporary times, assuming an increasingly pivotal role in facilitating the escalating computational prowess of quantum computers. To elucidate, QA serves as a pivotal tool for information processing [32], its indispensability underscored notably by its application in the operational framework of Shor's algorithm. Our comprehensive evaluation also discerns the ascendant prominence of Grover's algorithm (1994) [33], founded upon amplitude modulation. This algorithm, frequently harnessed for querying unstructured data, is now gaining prominence within the realm of QuCo. Recent strides have been observed with the advent of the quantum approximate optimization algorithm, grounded in hybrid QuCo, which has garnered substantial popularity. This algorithm finds utility in tackling problems within graph theory [8]. QA adheres to a systematic progression comprising five distinct phases. Commencing with the encoding of input data, it proceeds to establish fixed superpositions for qubits. Subsequently, leveraging QE among qubits comes into play, succeeded by the application of interface operations. The final step involves the measurement of one or multiple qubits. It is worth highlighting the versatile adaptability of QA, as it effectively addresses a wide array of financial challenges encompassing asset management, investment strategies, and the domain of retail banking [31].

2.4 Research Methodology

In this section, we will discuss the research methodology adopted for the current study. A SLR is adopted to perform an intense analysis of the existing literature. The SLR is suited for the present study since it may help (i) synthesize current literature and establish future research priorities and (ii) identify recent advancements in a certain subject [35]. Researchers may use an SLR to rigorously and exhaustively investigate the current literature on a topic, find connections of any investigated variables, and examine the limits of the existing research, hence offering a potential opportunity to further academic endeavors [34]. SLRs have been used to educate academics on QuCo and it has been notably useful in the fields of data science and software development [35]. Therefore, for the current study, first of all, we have conducted an SLR of the existing studies to know in detail about the topic of the study.

Studies have not clearly specified appropriate practices and frameworks for QuCo in real data systems [36]. Existing research employs an experiment-focused approach to QuCo adoption rather than studying the processes that might enhance its effective utilization. Recent work has emphasized the need to pay attention to the theoretical constraints and particulars of QuCo implementation [37]. Similarly, some researchers have recommended the investigation of QuCo's emerging research prospects [28], such as recognizing the issues related to its use in other industries or disciplines of study.

2.5   Research Questions

The present investigation meticulously examined two primary research questions (RQs) with the aim of proposing resolutions. The first query, denoted as RQ1, delves into the identification of fundamental and pervasive constraints that hinder the adoption of QuCo within the domain of the computer and computing industry. The second query, termed RQ2, focuses on the development of an effective model for representing the intricacies linked to the incorporation of QuCo in the software sector or industry. Addressing RQ1 led to the revelation of an extensive array of challenges interconnected with the infusion of QuCo within software industry establishments. Employing an organizational standpoint, the study synthesized preceding research concerning technological apprehensions that curtail organizational efficacy and erect obstacles in the path of QuCo implementation. In the same way, the fuzzy analytic hierarchy process (F-AHP) was used to answer RQ2 by making a ranked list of the likely things that would make it hard to implement QuCo in the software industry.

Our approach involved embracing a *hybrid research strategy*, which can be described as the fusion of meticulous database searches conducted within digital libraries. This comprehensive approach allowed us to comprehensively gather and explore a vast array of relevant information, ensuring a thorough and nuanced understanding of the subject matter. To provide the greatest possible coverage of similar papers, we conducted a keyword search in different digital libraries (Scopus, WoS). The term "quantum computing" was used in the search by the authors in June 2022. The screening criteria did not limit the results to a certain time period. This was done to make sure that the sample showed how QuCo research has changed over time. The compilation of articles within the ultimate sample exhibited a rich diversity, encompassing an assortment of case studies, review articles, and other relevant content. The analytical process was undertaken by both authors, collaboratively consolidating a comprehensive roster of paramount barriers to QuCo adoption, as unveiled through the thorough scrutiny of the literature under review. Subsequent to these analytical endeavors, we harnessed the F-AHP methodology to hierarchically rank the identified barriers. This strategic application facilitated the discernment of prominent issues limiting QuCo adoption, describing the specific challenges that warrant precedence in future investigational pursuits. By applying the F-AHP framework, our study not only shed light on critical barriers but also paved the way for informed and prioritized avenues of inquiry in the realm of QuCo adoption. F-AHP is an expert-based analysis system where responses are taken from experts in the field studied. Utilizing existing scholarly works, scholars have employed extant literature concerning diverse methodologies of multi-criteria decision-making techniques to make well-informed judgments, as evidenced by earlier works [38, 39]. The utilization of the F-AHP is conspicuous across various industry domains and decision-making contexts. In terms of employing fuzzy AHP, there is a prescribed criterion for ascertaining the requisite number of experts [40]. Consequently, judicious selection of sample size becomes imperative, whereby a modest representation of expert opinions can yield expedited consensus and heightened engagement [40]. For the ongoing investigation, a cohort of 23 experts has been selected. A succinct overview of these proficient experts is given in Appendix 2. Saaty's pioneering work in 1977 and 1980 led to the development of the analytic hierarchy process (AHP), a valuable tool applied by scholars to address multifaceted decision-making challenges [41, 42]. Fuzzy AHP operates within hierarchical frameworks within fuzzy contexts, employing fuzzy ratios in lieu of precise values for paired comparisons [43]. Numerous alternatives to Fuzzy AHP exist.

By harmonizing the rigors of database exploration with the serendipity of snowballing, we not only expand the horizons of our investigation but also contribute to a more nuanced and interconnected understanding of our chosen subject. This approach, rooted in the fusion of tradition and exploration, serves as a beacon guiding us through the dynamic seas of information.

The following is the search query for the current study to download the research papers from different databases. TITLE-ABS-KEY ('Quantum computing'), AND DOCTYPE (OR)AND (LIMIT-TO (SUBJAREA, 'COMP')) AND (LIMIT-TO (SUBJAREA, 'ENGI')), TITLE-ABS-KEY ('Quantum computing')AND DOCTYPE (ar OR re) AND (LIMIT-TO

(SUBJAREA, 'COMP') OR LIMIT-TO (SUBJAREA, 'ENGI') OR LIMIT-TO (SUBJAREA, 'SOCI') OR LIMIT-TO (SUBJAREA, 'MATH') OR LIMIT-TO (SUBJAREA, 'ENVI')) AND (LIMIT-TO (SUBJAREA, 'MATE') OR LIMIT-TO (SUBJAREA, 'DECI') OR LIMIT-TO (SUBJAREA, 'BUSI') OR LIMIT-TO (SUBJAREA, 'ARTS') OR LIMIT-TO (SUBJAREA, 'ECON'))

2.6   Designing Research Instrument/Questionnaire

After a thorough analysis of the downloaded papers, a list of possible barriers and challenges was prepared. This list is used for the purpose of preparing a questionnaire for the present study. A detailed list is present at the end of the paper under Appendix 1. Overall, these factors are categorized under the following heads: institutional barriers (InstBr), organizational barriers (OrgnBr), management barriers (MgmtBr), software technology barriers (SftchBr), and all other types of barriers. A brief description of these factors and their detailed description is as follows.

Factor 1: Institutional Barriers (InstBr)
InstBr to the successful adoption of quantum information technology (QIT) encompass a range of challenges. One significant challenge is the lack of government support for commercialization efforts. The absence of government backing can impede the development and growth of QIT-related businesses. Moreover, the deficiency in collaborative efforts involving universities, industries, and governmental bodies hinders the comprehensive integration of QIT into practical applications. Effective adoption necessitates meticulous planning and collaboration among multiple stakeholders, encompassing academia, industry players, and government entities. Addressing this requires resource allocation for the design and implementation of educational programs tailored to QIT. Additionally, the absence of well-defined criteria for next-generation cryptography standards poses a barrier, as it makes it challenging to establish robust security protocols.

Factor 2: Organizational Barriers (OrgnBr)
Within organizations, several barriers contribute to the challenges of QIT adoption. A critical concern is the lack of organizational interest in embracing novel processes like QIT integration. This lack of enthusiasm can hinder the necessary shifts in workflows and procedures. The absence of comprehensive cryptography standards complicates matters by creating uncertainty in security protocols. Organizations may perceive adopting

QIT as a risk due to potential low initial revenue. Availability of resources and meeting software design requirements is another consideration. Moreover, the adoption of secure post-quantum blockchain technology demands a comprehensive understanding of resources, which can be a barrier.

Factor 3: Management Barriers (MgmtBr)
MgmtBr entail challenges related to strategic decision-making. The limited understanding of market demand for QIT-derived products and services can lead to misguided investments. Short-term costs are often a concern, as the initial investment for QIT integration might not yield immediate returns. Commitment to research and development initiatives is crucial for innovation, but the lack thereof could slow down QIT progress. Furthermore, the absence of engineering designs for modernizing QuCo software adds complexity to implementation efforts.

Factor 4: Software Technology Barriers (SftchBr)
In the realm of software technology, multiple barriers hinder QIT adoption. Insufficient technical expertise in handling digital information and applying quantum principles is a significant obstacle. Architecture design and verification are crucial for robust software systems, and their absence can compromise reliability. The evolving ecosystem of QuCo demands continuous awareness, and a lack thereof can result in outdated practices. Precise information processing requires technical expertise and accuracy, further highlighting the need for skilled professionals. Lastly, the deficiency in engineering design skills tailored for software modernization in the context of QIT presents a notable barrier.

Factor 5: Other Barriers (OthBa)
In addition to the mentioned factors, various other barriers (OthBa) may emerge. These could involve legal and regulatory hurdles, ethical concerns related to QTs, limited international collaboration on QIT research, and challenges in securing intellectual property rights for quantum innovations. Each of these factors brings its own set of variables that need to be addressed to facilitate the successful adoption of QIT.

2.7   Results and Analysis

Within this segment, an examination has been conducted to ascertain both the priority weight and categories attributed to each factor previously identified in the preceding section of the present study. Subsequently, a questionnaire was formulated (refer to Appendix 1), which underwent pilot testing involving two academic professors (each possessing a minimum of 5 years of teaching experience) and two industry experts (proficient in software technology development). Subsequently, slight modifications were implemented to enhance the questionnaire's validity and readability. Furthermore, two items were removed from the management category and three from the organizational category.

The final survey questionnaire was distributed to 138 professionals in the field of software computing. Accompanying each questionnaire was a cover letter and a duplicate of the survey.

After collecting the data, identified barriers (22 in number) were categorized into five criteria. These challenges were subsequently distributed across four distinct categories, namely, *InstBr, OrgnBr MgmtBr, SftchBr, and OthBr* (defined in the RM section of this study).

The next phase entails designing a questionnaire intended for the application of F-AHP. This questionnaire adopts a paired-wise structure. Subsequently, we administer this questionnaire to solicit responses from experts, who will engage in a pairwise assessment of the five identified factors. The time duration for this phase of research was January 2023. We sent this pairwise questionnaire to 71 experts in the industry, and finally, we received 26 responses. After careful screening, we rejected three responses, and the final sample for the study has 23 valid responses on which further analysis has been done.

2.8   Result of Fuzzy AHP

The process involves conducting pairwise comparisons for each individual sub-criterion, which encompasses software technology, MgmtBr, OrgnBr, InstBr, and OthBa. These comparative evaluations have been systematically laid out in Table 2.2, corresponding to the respective categories. The rank of different factors with their respective weight is presented in Table 2.3. Moreover, the outcome of these comparisons, in terms of global and local weights, is consolidated and presented comprehensively in Table 2.4. This table encapsulates the essential information about the interrelationships and significance of the identified key challenges. Table 2.3 presents an analysis of distinct barrier categories along with their respective relative weights and ranks. Among these categories, "InstBr" holds the highest relative weight of 0.35354, securing the top rank. This suggests that challenges associated with overarching institutional aspects exert the most significant

Table 2.2 Calculation of weights for all factors of the current study.

	SftchBr	MgmtBr	OthBa	OrgnBr	InstBr
SftchBr	1, 1, 1	0.34517	1.09579	0.89191	0.44396
		0.70477	1.80166	1.84048	0.50084
		1.47839	3.18702	3.63936	1.07872
MgmtBr	0.67641	1, 1, 1	1.21054	1.20246	0.66075
	1.41889		3.27871	1.81279	0.98513
	2.86568		5.30131	2.97999	1.65957
OthBa	0.39409	0.18589	1, 1, 1	0.53743	0.1892
	0.54698	0.305		0.80212	0.29793
	1.08045	0.82608		1.36612	0.44994
OrgnBr	0.34123	0.35586	0.92946	1, 1, 1	0.2562
	0.56992	0.4607	1.2467		0.36526
	1.4933	0.8819	2.36265		0.95976
InstBr	3.17354	0.87958	2.49844	1.86827	1, 1, 1
	3.67348	1.16675	3.66316	3.63161	
	5.32175	2.0157	5.28532	5.59403	

Source: Authors' compilation

Table 2.3 Ranking of different factors.

Different categories of barriers	Relative weights	Ranks
Software technology barriers (SftchBr)	0.18205	3
Management barriers (MgmtBr)	0.24855	2
Other barriers (OthBa)	0.09177	5
Organizational barriers (OrgnBr)	0.12409	4
Institutional barriers (InstBr)	0.35354	1

Source: Authors' compilation

influence. "MgmtBr" follows suit, with a relative weight of 0.24855, obtaining the second rank. This indicates the substantial impact of managerial factors on the barriers landscape. "SftchBr" captures a relative weight of 0.18205, leading to the third rank. This category underscores the significance of technological challenges within the context. "OrgnBr" claims a

Table 2.4 Result of analysis of factors and their respective variables.

Factors/ variables	Category/factor weight	Local weights	Global weights
SftchBr	**0.18205**		
SftchBr1		0.20949	0.03814
SftchBr2		0.28988	0.05277
SftchBr3		0.09345	0.01701
SftchBr4		0.13075	0.02380
SftchBr5		0.27644	0.05033
MgmtBr	**0.24855**		
MgmtBr1		0.28624	0.07114
MgmtBr2		0.33852	0.08414
MgmtBr3		0.15204	0.03779
MgmtBr4		0.22320	0.05548
OrgnBr	**0.12409**		
OrgnBr1		0.20506	0.02545
OrgnBr2		0.27768	0.03446
OrgnBr3		0.09402	0.01167
OrgnBr4		0.13359	0.01658
OrgnBr5		0.28966	0.03594
OthBa	**0.09177**		
OthBa1		0.28921	0.02654
OthBa2		0.32548	0.02987
OthBa3		0.38531	0.03536
InstBr	**0.35354**		
InstBr1		0.19358	0.06844
InstBr2		0.26716	0.09445
InstBr3		0.09626	0.03403
InstBr4		0.12894	0.04559
InstBr5		0.31405	0.11103

relative weight of 0.12409, positioning it in the fourth rank, highlighting the role of organizational factors. Lastly, "OthBa" exhibits the least relative weight of 0.09177, securing the fifth rank. In summation, the data underscores the pivotal influence of institutional and managerial barriers in the hierarchy of challenges. A similar thing is also presented in Figure 2.1.

The following Table 2.4 is the presentation of comprehensive results of the analysis of individual factors and their respective variables/statements.

Likewise, for the interpretation of InstBr in the context of adopting QuCo technology, the data underscore the multifaceted nature of these barriers, each bearing a unique weight of influence. Among these barriers, "InstBr3" holds the highest weight at 0.31405, indicating the pronounced importance of strategic planning and collaboration across different stakeholders for successful QIT implementation. "InstBr1" follows closely with a weight of 0.26716, emphasizing the crucial role of government backing in driving the commercialization of QIT innovations. Furthermore, "InstBr2" contributes a weight of 0.12894, highlighting the necessity of robust partnerships between academia, industry, and government entities. The barriers pertaining to "InstBr4" and "InstBr5" are captured with weights of 0.19358 and 0.09626, respectively. Collectively, the data accentuate the intricate interplay of these InstBr and their varying degrees of impact on the QIT adoption landscape.

The second barrier is MgmtBr within the context of QuCo software modernization. Each barrier is assigned a distinct weight that reflects its relative influence. "MgmtBr3" stands out with a weight of 0.33852, highlighting the critical role of dedicated R&D efforts in successful modernization endeavors. "MgmtBr1" follows with a weight of 0.28624, underscoring the importance

Figure 2.1 Chart showing the ranking of different factors considered for the study.

of aligning modernization strategies with market needs. "MgmtBr4" bears a weight of 0.2232, emphasizing the significance of effective engineering in the modernization process. Lastly, "MgmtBr2" contributes a weight of 0.15204, indicating the role of cost-related insights in shaping modernization strategies. In totality, the data accentuates the multifaceted nature of MgmtBr and their varying impacts on QuCo software modernization efforts.

The insight into SftchBr sheds light on the challenges within the domain of QuCo adoption. Each barrier is associated with a weight that signifies its relative significance. "SftchBr1" carries a weight of 0.20949, underscoring the importance of skilled professionals for handling digital data in QuCo applications. "SftchBr4" follows with a weight of 0.28988, emphasizing the need for precision in information handling. Additionally, "SftchBr3" holds a weight of 0.27644, highlighting the need for education about the evolving QuCo landscape. "SftchBr2" and "SftchBr5" contribute weights of 0.13075 and 0.09345, respectively. In aggregate, the data underscore the multifaceted nature of SftchBr in QuCo adoption. The next is OrgnBr, outlining challenges pertinent to the adoption of QuCo and its implications. Each barrier carries a weight that signifies its relative importance. "OrgnBr1" takes precedence with a weight of 0.28966, underlining the necessity of fostering organizational enthusiasm for change. "OrgnBr4" follows with a weight of 0.27768, emphasizing the significance of adequate resources for effective software development. Additionally, "OrgnBr5" holds a weight of 0.20506, stressing the need for comprehension in the context of secure blockchain adoption. "OrgnBr2" and "OrgnBr3" contribute weights of 0.13359 and 0.09402, respectively. In totality, the data highlight diverse OrgnBr and their varying degrees of influence on QuCo adoption endeavors. Lastly, OthBr, having three variables, are explained. Among these, the most influential is the "Lack of research on factors mediating collaboration between academia, industry, and government" with a weight of 0.38531, stressing the need for understanding collaborative dynamics. Moreover, "Lack of consensus on technical standards and process of encryption key exchange" carries a weight of 0.28921, highlighting the significance of standardized protocols. "Effective collaboration between universities, industry, and successful QIT adoption" contributes a weight of 0.32548, underscoring the pivotal role of collaborative engagement in QIT integration.

2.9   Findings, Conclusion, and Implication

The findings of the study highlight that survey participants have recognized a significant hindrance in the form of insufficient commitment toward research and development initiatives. Ranked as the next most crucial obstacle is the lack of governmental support for the process of commercialization. This aspect holds substantial importance in the successful implementation of QuCo. An additional noteworthy managerial barrier revolves around an inadequate awareness of market demands. Whereas a considerable body of literature has extensively examined the role of QuCo in safeguarding information and data privacy, the exploration of QuCo's significance within the realm of education remains notably limited. This research underscores the existing gap in comprehending QuCo's educational applications, presenting it as a substantial hurdle that necessitates attention. Past investigations into QuCo have uncovered a plethora of divergent themes; however, recent scholarly efforts have predominantly centered on imparting QuCo education through a software-driven approach. This shift in focus underlines the evolving methodologies in teaching QuCo principles. Recent academic viewpoints and few research studies have talked about the differences in education challenges between regular computer stuff and QuCo. There is a growing need for skilled people who know about "QuCo" and especially "quantum programming." Within the realm of OrgnBr, the primary hindrance is identified as the lack of organizational enthusiasm toward the assimilation of novel processes. Also, the research shows that the biggest problem with computer technology is not having enough resources for design and new ideas. In organizations, the main issue is that they are not very interested in trying out new ways of doing things. These problems really matter when it comes to deciding how to spend resources to teach basic QuCo programming in schools. At the same time, there are other big challenges that could be good topics for more research. These challenges could help us understand how new technology like QuCo fits into how organizations work. Likewise, the foremost institutional barrier is multi-stakeholder collaboration, fostering a cohesive vision among participants to synchronize endeavors and pool resources. Typically involving stakeholder input for decision-making, as posited by scholars, decision-making holds centrality in the stakeholder theory. In a swiftly evolving and uncertain technological milieu, organizations grapple with effective decision-making. QuCo streamlines this process, becoming indispensable for digital survival. All stakeholders bear direct relevance to firm prosperity, as suggested by scholars supporting broad stakeholder involvement for mutual gains.

As far as the implication of the study is concerned, the current study has the following implications. Primarily, despite QuCo's advent as a topic of interest for organizations, our findings highlight the need for substantial organizational efforts to fully harness its advantages.

Furthermore, our results emphasize the necessity of documenting processes, requirements, and inherent rules to reconfigure and align current organizational infrastructure for effective QuCo adoption. Thirdly, our study underscores the formidable challenges inherent in QuCo adoption, particularly concerning established practices and expectations like scalability and resource performance evaluation. Given the enduring struggle with QuCo integration, we encourage scholars to investigate how the technology assimilation process can ease the organizational learning load and promote the uptake of new technology.

References

1. Allcock, J. and Zhang, S., Quantum machine learning. *Natl. Sci. Rev.*, 6, 1, 26–28, 2019, doi: 10.1093/nsr/nwy149.
2. Haart, M. and Hoffs, C., Quantum computing : What it is, how we got here, and who's working on it. 0–18, March 2019. https://www.researchgate.net/publication/331844245_Quantum_Computing_What_it_is_how_we_got_here_and_who's_working_on_it.
3. Gill, S.S., Kumar, A., Singh, H., Singh, M., Kaur, K., Usman, M., Buyya, R., Quantum computing: A taxonomy. *System. Rev. Fut. Direct*, Software: Practice and Experience, Wiley Press, USA, Sept. 22, 2021, Technical Report CLOUDS-TR-2020-1, available at https://arxiv.org/abs/2010.15559. 1–35, 2020.
4. Wu, W., Zhang, T., Chen, P.-X., Quantum computing and simulation with trapped ions: On the path to the future. *Fundam. Res.*, 1, 2, 213–216, 2021, https://doi.org/10.1016/j. fmre.2020.12.004.
5. Mielke, A. and Ricken, T., Evaluating artificial neural networks and quantum computing for mechanics. *Pamm*, 19, 1–2, 2019, https:// doi.org/ 10.1002/ pamm.201900470.
6. Steiger, D.S., Häner, T., Troyer, M., Projectq: An open source software framework for quantum computing. *Quantum*, 2, 49, 49–57, 2018.
7. Arute, F., Arya, K., Babbush, R., Bacon, D., Bardin, J.C., Barends, R., Biswas, R., Boixo, S., Brandao, F.G.S.L., Buell, D.A., Quantum supremacy using a programmable superconducting processor. *Nature*, 574, 505–510, 2019.
8. Gill, S.S., Kumar, A., Singh, H., Singh, M., Kaur, K., Usman, M., Buyya, R., Quantum computing: a taxonomy, systematic review and future directions. *Software Pract. Exp.*, 52, 66–114, 2022, https://doi.org/10.1002/ spe.3039.
9. Biamonte, J., Wittek, P., Pancotti, N., Rebentrost, P., Wiebe, N., Lloyd, S., Quantum machine learning. *Nature*, 549, 195–202, 2017.
10. Guerreschi, G.G. and Smelyanskiy, M., Practical optimization for hybrid quantum-classical algorithms. *Quantum Physics*, 2017, arXiv preprintarXiv:1701.01450.

11. Egger, D.J., Gambella, C., Marecek, J., McFaddin, S., Mevissen, M., Raymond, R., Simonetto, A., Woerner, S., Yndurain, E., Quantum computing for finance: State of the art and future prospects. *IEEE Trans. Quantum Eng.*, 1, 1–24, 1, 2020, ArXiv, paper is available at https://arxiv.org/abs/2006.14510.

12. Schradle, N., In algorithms we trust: Magical thinking, super intelligent AI and quantum computing. *Zygon*, 55, 733–747, 2020, https://doi.org/10.1111/zygo.12637.

13. Bhavin, M., Tanwar, S., Sharma, N., Tyagi, S., Kumar, N., Blockchain and quantum blind signature-based hybrid scheme for healthcare 5.0 applications. *J. Inf. Secur. Appl.*, 56, 102673, 2021, https:// doi.org/10.1016/j.jisa.2020.102673.

14. Kanamori, Y. and Yoo, S.-M., Quantum computing: Principles and applications. *JITIM*, 29, 2, 43–71, 2020.

15. Mohseni, M., Read, P., Neven, H., Boixo, S., Denchev, V., Babbush, R., Fowler, A., Smelyanskiy, V., Martinis, J., Commercialize quantum technologies in five years. *Nature*, 543, 7644, 171–174, 2017, doi: 10.1038/543171a.

16. Vathsan, R., Quantum algorithms, in: *Introduction to Quantum Physics and Information Processing*, pp. 167–198, 2015.

17. Heim, B., Soeken, M., Marshall, S., Granade, C.E., Roetteler, M., Geller, A., Troyer, M., Svore, K.M., Quantum programming languages. *Nat. Rev. Phys.*, 2, 709–722, 2020.

18. Zidan, M., Abdel-Aty, A.H., Younes, A., Zanaty, E.A., El-khayat, I., Abdel-Aty, M., A novel algorithm based on entanglement measurement for improving speed of quantum algorithms. *Appl. Math. Inf. Sci.*, 12, 265–269, 2018, https://doi.org/10.18576/amis/120127.

19. Dyck, B. and Greidanus, N.S., Quantum sustainable organizing theory: A study of organization theory as if matter mattered. *J. Manage. Inq.*, 26, 32–46, 2016, https://doi.org/10.1177/1056492616656407.

20. Hahn, T. and Knight, E., The ontology of organizational paradox: A quantum approach. *Acad. Manage. Rev.*, 46, 2, 1–60, 2019, https://doi.org/10.5465/amr.2018.0408.

21. Deutsch, D., Quantum theory, the Church–Turing principle and the universal quantum computer. *Proceedings of the Royal Society of London*, vol. A400, pp. 97–117, 1985.

22. Imre, S., Quantum computing and communications-Introduction and challenges. *Comput. Electr. Eng.*, 40, 134–141, 2014, https://doi.org/10.1016/j.compeleceng.2013.10.008.

23. Orús, R., Mugel, S., Lizaso, E., Quantum computing for finance: Overview and prospects. *Phys. Rev.*, 4, 1–12, 100028, 2019, https://doi.org/10.1016/j.revip.2019.100028.

24. Grover, L.K., Quantum mechanics helps in searching for a needle in a haystack. *Phys. Rev. Lett.*, 79, 325–328, 1997, https://doi.org/10.1103/PhysRevLett.79.325.

25. Mavroeidis, V., Vishi, K., Zych, M.D., Jøsang, A., The impact of quantum computing on present cryptography. *Int. J. Adv. Comput. Sci. Appl.*, *9*, 405–414, 2018, https://doi.org/10.14569/IJACSA.2018.090354.
26. Ajagekar, A. and You, F., Quantum computing for energy systems optimization: Challenges and opportunities. *Energy*, *179*, 76–89, 2019, https://doi.org/10.1016/j.energy.2019.04.186.
27. Der Derian, J. and Wendt, A., Quantizing international relations': The case for quantum approaches to international theory and security practice. *Secur. Dialogue*, *51*, 399–413, 2020, https://doi.org/10.1177/0967010620901905.
28. Gyongyosi, L. and Imre, S., A survey on quantum computing technology. *Comput. Sci. Rev.*, *31*, 51–71, 2019, https://doi.org/10.1016/j.cosrev.2018.11.002.
29. Biamonte, Wittek, P., Pancotti, N., Rebentrost, P., Wiebe, N., Lloyd, S., Quantum machine learning. *Nature*, *549*, 195–202, 2017.
30. Cuomo, D., Caleffi, M., Cacciapuoti, A.S., Towards a distributed quantum computing ecosystem. *Quantum Physics*, *1*, 3–8, 2020, paper is available at https://arxiv.org/abs/2002.11808.
31. Egger, D.J., Garcia Gutierrez, R., Cahue Mestre, J., Woerner, S., Credit risk analysis using quantum computers. *IEEE Trans. Comput.*, *9340*, 1–12, 2020, https://doi.org/10.1109/TC.2020.3038063.
32. de Avila, A.B., Reiser, R.H.S., Pilla, M.L., Yamin, A.C., State-of-the- art quantum computing simulators: features, optimizations, and improvements for D-GM. *Neurocomputing*, *393*, 223–233, 2020, https://doi.org/10.1016/j.neucom.2019.01.118.
33. Kato, Z., Kato, T., Kondo, N., Orii, T., Interstitial deletion of the short arm of chromosome 10: Report of a case and review of the literature. *JSHG.*, *41*, 333–338, 1996, https://doi.org/10.1007/BF01913177.
34. Moller, A.M. and Myles, P.S., What makes a good systematic review and meta-analysis? *BJA*, *117*, 428–430, 2016.
35. Mourao, E., Pimentel, J.F., Murta, L., Kalinowski, M., Mendes, E., Wohlin, C., On the performance of hybrid search strategies for systematic literature reviews in software engineering. *Inf. Software Technol.*, *123*, 1–12, 106294, 2020, https:// doi.org/10.1016/j.infsof.2020.106294.
36. Pérez-Castillo, R., Serrano, M.A., Piattini, M., Software modernization to embrace quantum technology. *Adv. Eng. Software*, *151*, 1–15, 102933, 2021, https://doi. org/10.1016/j.advengsoft.2020.102933.
37. Imre, S., Quantum computing and communications-Introduction and challenges. *Comput. Electr. Eng.*, 40, 134–141, 20142014, https://doi.org/10.1016/j.compeleceng.2013.10.008.
38. Shete, R.S.P.C., Ansari, A.P.Z.N., Kant, A.P.R., A pythagorean fuzzy AHP approach and its application to evaluate the enablers of sustainable supply chain innovation. *Sustain. Prod. Consumption*, *23*, 77–93, 2020, doi: 10.1016/j.spc.2020.05.001.

39. Mehta, K., Sharma, R., Vyas, V., Efficiency and ranking of sustainability index of India using DEA-TOPSIS. *J. Indian Bus. Res.*, *11*, 2, 179–199, 2019, https://doi.org/10.1108/JIBR-02-2018-0057.
40. Nixon, J.D., Dey, P.K., Davies, P.A., Which is the best solar thermal collection technology for electricity generation in north-west India? Evaluation of options using the analytical hierarchy process. *Energy*, *35*, 12, 5230–5240, 2010, https://doi.org/10.1016/J.ENERGY.2010.07.042.
41. Saaty, T.L., A scaling method for priorities in hierarchical structures. *J. Math. Psychol.*, *15*, 2, 234–81, 1977.
42. Saaty, T.L., *The analytic hierarchy process*, McGraw-Hill, New York, 1980.
43. Buckley, J.J., Ranking alternatives using fuzzy numbers. *Fuzzy Sets Syst.*, *15*, 1, 21–31, 1985.
44. Pérez-Castillo, R., Serrano, M.A., Piattini, M., Software modernization to embrace quantum technology. *Adv. Eng. Software*, *151*, 21–31, 102933, 2021, https://doi. org/10.1016/j.advengsoft.2020.102933.
45. Van Meter, R., Devitt, S.J., ArXiv Prepr, Local and distributed quantum computation. *Quantum Physics,* 2016, ArXiv1605.06951. Paper is available at https://arxiv.org/abs/1605.06951.
46. Maurer, P.C., Kucsko, G., Latta, C., Jiang, L., Yao, N.Y., Bennett, S.D., Pastawski, F., Hunger, D., Chisholm, N., Markham, M., Room-temperature quantum bit memory exceeding one second. *Science*, *336*, 1283–1286, 2012, https://doi.org/10.1126/science.1220513.
47. Bernien, H., Hensen, B., Pfaff, W., Koolstra, G., Blok, M.S., Robledo, L., Taminiau, T.H., Markham, M., Twitchen, D.J., Childress, L., Heralded entanglement between solid-state qubits separated by three metres. *Nature*, *497*, 86–90, 2013.
48. Ofek, N., Petrenko, A., Heeres, R., Reinhold, P., Leghtas, Z., Vlastakis, B., Liu, Y., Frunzio, L., Girvin, S.M., Jiang, L., Extending the lifetime of a quantum bit with error correction in superconducting circuits. *Nature*, *536*, 441–445, 2016.
49. Somaschi, N., Giesz, V., De Santis, L., Loredo, J.C., Almeida, M.P., Hornecker, G., Portalupi, S.L., Grange, T., Anton, C., Demory, J., Near-optimal single-photon sources in the solid state. *Nat. Photonics*, *10*, 340–345, 2016.
50. Yao, N.Y., Jiang, L., Gorshkov, A.V., Maurer, P.C., Giedke, G., Cirac, J.I., Lukin, M.D., Scalable architecture for a room temperature solid-state quantum information processor. *Nat. Commun.*, *3*, 1–8, 2013.
51. Veldhorst, M., Hwang, J.C.C., Yang, C.H., Leenstra, A.W., de Ronde, B., Dehollain, J.P., Muhonen, J.T., Hudson, F.E., Itoh, K.M., Morello, A., An addressable quantum dot qubit with fault-tolerant control-fidelity. *Nat. Nanotechnol.*, *9*, 981–985, 2014.
52. Zwanenburg, F.A., Dzurak, A.S., Morello, A., Simmons, M.Y., Hollenberg, L.C.L., Klimeck, G., Rogge, S., Coppersmith, S.N., Eriksson, M.A., Silicon quantum electronics. *Rev. Mod. Phys.*, 85, 961, 2013.

53. Aburaed, N., Khan, F.S., Bhaskar, H., Advances in the quantum theoretical approach to image processing applications. *ACM Comput. Surv.*, *49*, 1–49, 2017.

3

Analyzing Open Interest: A Vibrant Approach to Predict Stock Market Operator's Movement

Avijit Bakshi

School of Business, Alliance University, Bengaluru, Karnataka, India

Abstract

Open interest in the derivative market is the total number of outstanding or open contracts that have not yet been settled or squared off. It increases when new entrants trade with each other in the future & options (F&O) market and decreases when existing position holders square off their positions. Tracking changes in spot price, open interest, and delivery data can provide insights into operators' intentions. However, examining cumulative open interest and confirming the analysis with technical charts are important.

In future contracts, open interest should be treated as cumulative, whereas in options, it should be counted as an aggregate. The highest open interest on the call side indicates the resistance level, whereas the highest open interest on the put side indicates the support level. A put-call ratio of more than 1.1 is bullish, whereas less than 0.9 is bearish.

Checking the build-up of open interest in strike prices can help recognize anomalies or imbalances in underlying assets. Computing the critical price or weighted average price can help decode the buyer or seller in the option chain.

An analysis of data for a stock listed in both the cash market and the F&O segment over the last 3 months, along with technical chart analysis, can help traders and investors make informed decisions. However, it is recommended to have a basic understanding of F&O contracts to fully comprehend the concepts and strategies discussed.

Email: avijit.bakshi2008@gmail.com

Renuka Sharma and Kiran Mehta (eds.) *Deep Learning Tools for Predicting Stock Market Movements*, (61–88) © 2024 Scrivener Publishing LLC

Keywords: Open interest, cumulative open interest, option chain, future & options, bullishness, bearishness, put-call ratio, predict stock market

3.1   Introduction

It is generally acknowledged that stock market operators govern the stock market and that ordinary investors serve only as pawns in their game. Therefore, an understanding of the movement of the stock market operator is necessary for a retail investor to succeed in trading. The analysis of open interest (OI) is a brilliant approach to tracking market operators' movement. It is used by future & options (F&O) contract traders.

In the world of F&O trading, OI is a critical indicator. It shows the number of open or outstanding contracts for a specific stock, commodity, or index. As a result, it is crucial to take this into account while assessing stock prices as it might reveal information about the attitudes of traders and investors in the market [1].

It is noteworthy that OI and volume are not identical metrics. While both indicators can shed light on the market mood, OI measures the total number of outstanding contracts, whereas volume measures the total number of contracts that have been transacted over a specific time [2].

OI in a specific stock or market can be affected by a variety of factors. The following are some of the more typical ones:

> Market volatility: In times of high market volatility, OI may rise as investors seek to profit from price movements.
> Market Attitude: OI can be affected by market attitude; an increase in bullish or bearish attitude will, accordingly, result in an increase in call or put option OI.
> Time till Expiration: As a contract's expiration date draws near, OI may rise as investors prepare to close out their positions or roll them over to a new contract.
> Market News: Important market news, including an announcement of business earnings or a change in interest rates, can also influence OI by causing traders to adjust their positions.

This article discusses in greater detail the effect of OI on the analysis of stock prices, including how to comprehend OI data in the F&O market to generate signals of trade, the variables that might affect it, and how to combine it with other analysis tools to validate and help you to make smart investing decisions. The theoretical discussions are substantiated by live market data and analysis. The entire analysis would enable traders and investors to invest in the spot market as well as in F&O segments.

OI is a useful tool for studying stock prices, but it should be used in conjunction with other technical and fundamental analysis techniques to help investors make wise decisions.

Technical analysis is a well-liked analytical technique that can be utilized in combination with OI. Technical analysis is the study of historical market data, including price and volume, with the goal of spotting patterns and forecasting price changes. When combined with OI data, it can offer a more complete picture of market sentiment and probable price moves.

Fundamental analysis, which entails looking at a company's financial statements and other data to evaluate its overall financial health and growth prospects, is another helpful analytical tool. Investors can identify cheap or overvalued companies, as well as prospective market dangers and opportunities, with the aid of fundamental analysis.

The objectives of the entire analysis are as follows:

- to enable traders or investors to make better-informed and prudent decisions
- to facilitate comprehension of the logic behind the fluctuation in open-interest data
- to assist in interpreting the OI of the future & option contracts
- to empower traders to analyze the price and OI together to get a comprehensive overview of an underlying asset
- to enable traders to validate the OI analysis by technical charts
- to edify traders to dodge the probable traps that are misleading
- to detect buyers or sellers in the option contracts and
- to enable traders and investors to invest in the spot market as well as in F&O segments.

The chapter is organized as follows. Section 3.2 describes the methodology, Section 3.3 depicts the concept of OI, Section 3.4 illustrates the use of OI in futures contracts, and the penultimate section demonstrates the use of OI in option contracts. Section 3.6 concludes the chapter.

3.2   Methodology

The data presented in this chapter are sourced from the NSE website. No specific statistical technique or software has been employed; rather, simple averages and moving averages (MAs) have been utilized. The technical chart been derived from the Zerodha website. The main objective of this chapter is to introduce a process that enhances the likelihood of successful trades resulting in a profit.

3.3   Concept of OI

The entire number of open or outstanding contracts that a market player is currently holding at a given time is known as OI. The analysis of OI is useful for spotting patterns in the stock market. It aids a trader in understanding the market situation by just displaying the number of futures contracts that have been changed hands during market hours. F&O traders frequently employ OI analysis. Depending on the outstanding contracts, the OI data vary during the day or day to day unlike the stock market, where the number of outstanding shares of a company remains constant once a stock is issued.

The variation in OI balance happens because of the following trading rules.

1. When a new entrant trades with a new entrant in the F&O market, OI goes up.
2. When two existing position holders square off their positions, OI goes down.
3. When an existing position holder squares off with the entry of a new entrant, OI remains unchanged [3].

Let us use an illustration to comprehend the above. Table 3.1 shows the date-wise transactions.

There are four participants in the market Arjun, Mita, Munmun, Sachin, and Victor. They are trading in the same underlying asset.

On the 1st of January, both participants were new, and 50 contracts were changed hands; therefore, the OI balance stands at 50. On the 2nd of January, both participants were new, so the OI balance increased to 80. On the 5th of January transaction, both participants were not newer participants, and both were exiting from the contract to the extent of 20 contracts. Whereas Arjun's position on the 1st of January was a buyer,

Table 3.1 OI movement.

Trading events	OI balance
On the 1st of January, Arjun buys 50 contracts from Mita	50
On the 2nd of January, Munmun buys 30 contracts from Sachin	50 + 30 = 80
On the 5th of January, Arjun sells his 20 contracts to Sachin	80 − 20 = 60
On the 8th of January, Victor buys 20 contracts from Munmun	60

Source: Own Calculation

on the 5th of January, he became a seller. On the counterpart, on the 2nd of January, Sachin was a seller, whereas he turned into a seller on the 5th of January. Therefore, as both the existing position holders are exiting from the contract, the OI balance falls. However, on the 8th of January, the new trader, Victor, traded with an existing trader, Munmun, and therefore, the OI balance remained the same.

So, the bottom line is that the OI surges when new contracts are added, and it decreases when existing contracts are squared off.

The concept of OI can be applied only in the derivative or F&O segment. Hence, the stock and index listed in the F&O market, OI can be applied only to it. However, the technique of using OI data differs in the F&O market.

3.4 OI in Future Contracts

The use of OI in the future market is discussed in this section while the use of it in the options market is discussed separately in the subsequent section.

3.4.1 Interpreting OI & Price Movement

Following OI numbers only does not convey any meaningful information to the trader. However, its relationship with price movement provides traders and investors with a wealth of knowledge about the present trend in the specific contract.

The table below presents the relation between OI and contract price.

Table 3.2 Interpretation of OI and price movement.

Price	OI	Delivery	Interpretation
Rising	Rising	Rising	Strongly bullish trend and traders can carry the bullish bet or take a fresh long (buy) position.
Rising	Falling	Falling	Short sellers face losses when the price is increasing, so they have to cover their positions (square-off) by taking long positions which causes a rally in price. Because of squaring-off OI is falling. Therefore, a downtrend or sideways may start in days to come. Traders can book profit and exit from long positions.
Falling	Rising	Rising	Because of aggressive short-selling, OI numbers are increasing, and the price is falling. Therefore, currently, the bearish trend is continuing. Traders can continue with the current short position or can take a short new position.
Falling	Falling	Falling	Long position holders are forced to liquidate their earlier short positions because the price falls. The squaring-off of positions leads to a fall in OI number. Some sideways or upward movement may start in the coming sessions.

Source: Kumar, S. (2007). *Financial Derivatives* (p. 9). Prentice Hall.

The change in OI does not truly provide a market direction. It does, however, indicate if a trend is strong enough to be bullish or bearish. In general, it is a good idea to exercise caution if there is a sudden spike in OI that is accompanied by a sharp rise or fall in the stock or index price.

Therefore, the bottom line is as follows:

A rise in OI indicates that the current trend—whether it be an uptrend, downtrend, or flat—is likely to last.

A falling OI indicates that the current trend—whether it is an uptrend, downtrend, or flat—is likely to alter or is nearing its end.

The OI position is determined daily and is either higher or lower than the previous trading day.

The OI numbers in a live market of a future contract are available on the NSE website. Let us take the example of the future contract of Adani Ports and SEZ Ltd which expired on 23rd February 2023. The data depicted below are sourced from NSE dated 8 February 2023.

The total OI number of the future contract stood at 84,771, whereas the change (increase) in OI in percentage is 4.28%. The change in OI numbers is more informative than that of the total number of OI sometimes.

Now, let us apply the price and OI movement together discussed in the last section (refer to Table 3.2) to get an overview of the trend of Adani Ports stock from 24th January 2023 to 8th February 2023.

Table 3.3 indicates the change in OI and price data of the future contract of Adani Ports expired on the 23rd of February. The trade was suspended for a few days during the period in the spot market because the stock hit a 5% lower circuit filter. It is observed that on the 30th of January and 1st of February, the price, as well as OI, dropped significantly which clearly indicates a bearish signal, refer to Table 3.2. From the 3rd of February to the

Table 3.3 Analysis of OI and price of Adani Ports and SEZ Ltd.

Date	Expiry	LTP	OI	Change in OI	Change in OI (%)	Underlying value (spot price)	Change in spot price
24-Jan-23	23-Feb-23	764.2	57,970,000	9,085,625		761.2	-
25-Jan-23	23-Feb-23	718.9	66,016,875	8,046,875	−11.43%	Trade suspended	-
27-Jan-23	23-Feb-23	609.05	70,096,250	4,079,375	−49.30%	Trade suspended	-
30-Jan-23	23-Feb-23	606.6	69,040,625	−1,055,625	−125.88%	597	−21.6%
31-Jan-23	23-Feb-23	617	66,731,875	−2,308,750	118.71%	Trade suspended	-
1-Feb-23	23-Feb-23	507.05	67,766,250	1,034,375	−144.80%	495.15	−17.1%
2-Feb-23	23-Feb-23	461.85	73,681,250	5,915,000	471.84%	Trade suspended	-
3-Feb-23	23-Feb-23	487.85	63,483,750	−10,197,500	−272.40%	498.85	0.75%
6-Feb-23	23-Feb-23	541.3	57,584,375	−5,899,375	−42.15%	545.45	10.2%
7-Feb-23	23-Feb-23	556	50,805,000	−6,779,375	14.92%	553.15	1.4%
8-Feb-23	23-Feb-23	605.75	52,586,875	1,781,875	126.28%	599.25	20.1%

Source: NSE India

6th of February short sellers were covering their positions. However, on the 7th and 8th of February, the stock rebounded and indicated bullishness.

3.4.2   Open Interest and Cumulative Open Interest

The increase in price along with OI is termed a bullishness in the stock, but can we really indicate this situation as a long built-up in all situations regardless of the extent to which price and OI move together? The answer is no. Let us take a few situations below.

Situation 1: 3.5% change in OI and 0.75% change in price
Situation 2: 10% change in OI and 0.75% change in price
In the first situation, there is a minor change in OI; however, in the second situation, the change in OI has increased. But is this change large enough to call it as long built-up? The percentage change in OI may not be applicable in low-liquid stock like MRF. Hence, we replace the % change with the number of lots in the following situation.
Situation 3: 500 lot change in OI and 1.5% change in price
Can we term situation 3 as long built-up? Probably not as a 1.5% increase in price may not be large enough with a 500 increase in the lot.
Situation 4: Siemens's future contract expires in November 2022 which displays the change in OI by 1700 lots with a 1.17% change in price.

Now, is this situation indicating a long built-up?

If we look at Siemens's future contract expiring in October 2022 which specifies that OI has decreased by 1700 lots. It means that if we club the OI of both expiries, then there is no increase in OI and probably that is why the price has not moved up significantly. Therefore, even if in one expiry the OI has moved up significantly, it cannot be labeled as long built-up.

There are three expiries available for a future contract. However, in the above example (refer to Table 3.3), only one expiry is considered which might be misleading for making any investment or trading decisions. Therefore, it is better to consider OI for all expiries for the contract. Since the cumulative OI number is not available on the NSE website, it can be computed by adding OI for all expiries. It can also be sourced from other websites.

Figure 3.1 indicates the cumulative OI of the future contract of Adani Ports and SEZ Ltd. from 24th January to 9th February 2023. There are always three current contracts of an underlying asset; therefore, cumulative OI displays the total OI of the three active contracts together at any given time. The available contract of Adani Ports and SEZ Ltd. as of 9th February 2023 was on 23rd February, 29th March, and 27th April 2023.

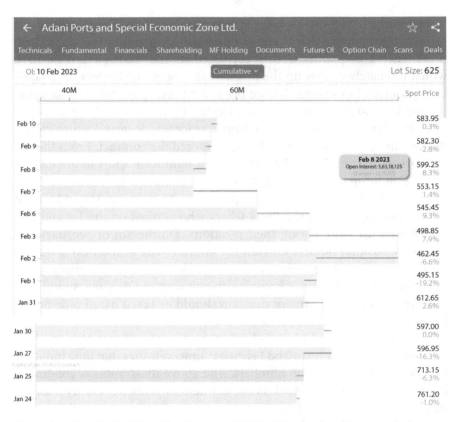

Figure 3.1 Cumulative OI of Adani Ports and SEZ Ltd. Source: https://web.stockedge. com/.

The green line on the chart signifies an increase in cumulative OI, whereas the red line signifies a decrease in cumulative OI. The spot price of the stock is given on the right-hand side day-wise.

While analyzing the chart you need to refer to Table 3.2, it is advised not to weigh the OI on the expiry day of a contract. On 24th January, there was a fall in the price and a slight fall in OI which signifies that the long position holders were quitting the contract in small numbers. On the next day, the increase in OI indicated short new position holders entered the contract as there was a significant drop in price. However, it is better not to depend very much on the expiry date numbers. On the 27th, there was a spike in OI numbers which indicates the short new players entered the contract as there was a significant plunge in stock price. However, the price rallied by over 2% in the next 2 days. Most of the traders make mistakes here by observing only the price in this situation. It seems to them the stock bounced back from a bearish position. However, if you observe the OI number, it shows that there is a drop which signifies the short position holders are squaring off their earlier position by taking a long position which ultimately pushes up the price. That means that traders have taken long positions in the contract not because of their positive outlook about the stock but to avoid further losses. On the 1st and 2nd of February, a big spike in OI numbers along with a drop in price was observed which clearly denotes the short new position holders entered the contract. From the 3rd of February to the 7th of February, again, a significant spurt in price along with a significant drop in the OI number was observed. This situation is the same as previous situations that happened on the 30th and 31st of January. It might so happen that the short sellers who entered on the 1st and 2nd of February are squaring off their positions. On the 8th of February, the long new position holders entered the contract but in the next 2 days, a minor change in OI was observed. On the 8th and 10th of February, along new position was built up; however, the change in OI is not significant. Therefore, no new investment decision should be taken based only on the long new position created in the last 2 days.

The above analysis of 12 days clearly portrays the presence of more short sellers in the contract up to 2nd February; however, after that long build-up was observed in negligible numbers. The above illustration is conducted for a short span of time which is not enough, to get better clarity a longer time horizon is always suggested.

It is better to validate the views created above through technical analysis. We will apply two technical tools—relative strength (RS) and MA—below.

3.4.3   Validation

A momentum approach called RS aids in identifying strong stocks for trading compared to the index. Traders will use RS to find firms that have outperformed their peers or the index by gaining or dropping more or less than the peers or index, respectively.

When a stock's performance is measured in relation to another stock or its benchmark, the term "relative strength" (RS) is used. RS contrasts the stock "X" vs. "Y" performance over a period. For instance, in an uptrend, "X" may increase more or less than "Y," whereas in a declining market, "X" may decrease more or less than "Y." It is one of the techniques for investing in momentum [4].

Table 3.4 Seven-day average relative strength.

Date	Adani ports close	Nifty close	RS	7-day average
2-Jan-23	822.3	18,197.45	0.045188	
3-Jan-23	820.45	18,232.55	0.044999	
4-Jan-23	810	18,042.95	0.044893	
5-Jan-23	819.6	17,992.15	0.045553	
6-Jan-23	806.1	17,859.45	0.045136	
9-Jan-23	816.65	18,101.2	0.045116	
10-Jan-23	796.4	17,914.15	0.044456	0.045049
11-Jan-23	796.45	17,895.7	0.044505	0.044951
12-Jan-23	792.95	17,858.2	0.044403	0.044866
13-Jan-23	794.65	17,956.6	0.044254	0.044775
16-Jan-23	787.05	17,894.85	0.043982	0.04455
17-Jan-23	784.75	18,053.3	0.043469	0.044312
18-Jan-23	786.5	18,165.35	0.043297	0.044052
19-Jan-23	776.05	18,107.85	0.042857	0.043824
20-Jan-23	774.45	18,027.65	0.042959	0.043603
23-Jan-23	769.05	18,118.55	0.042445	0.043323
24-Jan-23	761.2	18,118.3	0.042013	0.043003
25-Jan-23	713.15	17,891.95	0.039859	0.042414
27-Jan-23	596.95	17,604.35	0.033909	0.041048
30-Jan-23	597	17,648.95	0.033826	0.039696
31-Jan-23	612.65	17,662.15	0.034687	0.038528
1-Feb-23	495.15	17,616.3	0.028107	0.036407
2-Feb-23	462.45	17,610.4	0.02626	0.034095
3-Feb-23	498.85	17,854.05	0.02794	0.032084
6-Feb-23	545.45	17,764.6	0.030704	0.030776
7-Feb-23	553.15	17,721.5	0.031213	0.030391
8-Feb-23	599.25	17,871.7	0.033531	0.030349
9-Feb-23	582.3	17,893.45	0.032543	0.030043
10-Feb-23	583.95	17,856.5	0.032702	0.030699

Source: Own calculation

RS is calculated by using the formula below.

$$RS = \text{stock's price/index's price}$$

For calculating the RS of one stock to another where N1 is the first stock and N2 is the second stock, the following formula would be applied:

$$RS = \text{N1 stock's price/N2 stock's price}$$

Let us apply for RS in Adani Ports and SEZ Ltd from 2nd January to 10th February 2023 which is depicted in Table 3.4.

The last column indicates the seven days MA of relative strength.

During the study period, the stock witnessed a downtrend of the RS line since 10th January which implies weakness in the stock.

The 21- and 55-day MAs are depicted in Figure 3.2. The blue line which is a 21-day MA lies below the red line which is a 55-day MA. It is a clear indication of weakness in the stock.

The above analysis of OI supported by RS and MA portrays the same sign of weakness in the stock.

The point to be noted is that analyzing OI with the price may be applied to make a long-term view of a stock which may not be useful for the short horizon or intraday trading.

The next section will discuss a case study with real data by applying the above concepts.

3.4.4 Case Study with Live Market Data

A *prima facie* view is made about Adani Ports and SEZ Ltd in the last section with OI data of 13 days. However, the analysis with the help of data

Figure 3.2 Moving average chart of Adani Ports and SEZ Ltd. Source: tradingview.com

for a such short span of time may not be enough if anyone intends to make an outlook about an asset. Therefore, the stock is analyzed for a longer time horizon from 1st December 2022 to 10th February 2023. The spot market data of the stock are combined with future market data to arrive at an outlook. The expiry dates considered for the future contract of Adani Ports and SEZ are 25th January, 23rd February, and 29th March 2023. The analysis starts with downloading data for the spot and future market and preparing the data for further analysis.

At first, the spot price along with the average price and deliverable quantity for each day from 1st December 2022 to 10th February 2023 is obtained.

Second, OI and changes in OI data are required in the future market. Therefore, the future contract which expires on 25th January 2023 is targeted. After the contract expires on 25th January, the contract rolls over and continues with the next expiry, i.e., 23rd February. Therefore, we downloaded data from 1st December to 25th January for the 25th January contract and from 27th January to 10th February for the 23rd February contract.

Third, the future contract which expires on 23rd February 2023 is targeted. We obtain data from 1st December to 25th January for the 23rd of February expiry contract. The next expiry contract which expires on 29th March is obtained from 27th January to 10th February.

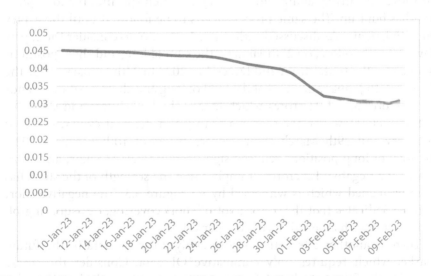

Figure 3.3 Seven-day moving average RS chart. Source: Own calculation

The data acquired for the abovementioned three contracts are compiled and presented in the fashion depicted in Table 3.5. The cumulative OI is the sum of the OI of the contracts. The delivery amount is the product of deliverable quantity and the average price. The 5-day average delivery is the 5-day MA of delivery amount. The average delivery of the initial few days is kept it same for simplicity. The % change in delivery indicates the extent of change in a particular day's delivery in comparison to the 5-day average delivery.

The percentage of shares marked for delivery out of the total traded shares is known as the security-wise delivery position. It indicates the number of investors that are ready to hold the shares in their demat account for at least 1 day. A higher delivery percentage indicates that a greater number of investors are acquiring the stock not only for merely intraday trading but also for holding it. Most analysts emphasize volume or traded quantity. As an investor, it is suggested to place greater weight on deliverable quantity/ delivery %. For instance, stock A's total volume of trades is 100. Suppose the delivered amount is 60 out of 100. That means 60 shares are marked for delivery, which suggests that the remaining 40 shares were traded intraday.

The outlook about a stock would be based on the last two columns— long and short. The long and short numbers represent the change in OI numbers. Table 3.2 needs to be referred to before placing the change in OI numbers in long or short columns. On 2nd December, the price was reduced by 0.26% while OI increased by 14.5% which clearly indicates the presence of more short sellers. However, in the next 2 days, the price and OI moved positively along with delivery % which specifies the long position has built up. The same process needs to be followed until the expiry on 25th January. As discussed earlier, it is better not to consider the expiry day's data. Therefore, on 25th January, the sum of long and short positions is taken for the trades from 2nd December 2022 to 24th January 2023. The data on 25th January depict that the total of long and short positions stands at 4.7 crores and 1.92 crores which means the bullishness and strengths of the stock. However, the scenario changed in the next expiry, i.e., 23rd February and 29th March expiry contracts. As of 10th February 2023, the total of long positions reduced significantly to 20.43 lakhs, and short stands at a negative 1.2 crores. It implies that the strength of the stock has been weakened which is witnessed by RS Figure 3.3. The negative short number indicates that there was a lot of short covering, i.e., squaring-off short positions happened during the period.

There is another alternative way to analyze the OI data in the future market which requires only cumulative OI data. Consider the stocks traded in the future market. A future contract expires on the last Thursday

Table 3.5 Price OI analysis.

Date	Close price	Del (amt.)	5D avg. del	Cum. OI	Ch. OI	% Ch. price	% Ch. del	% Ch. COI	Long	Short
1-Dec-22	890.55	134.8		470,625						
2-Dec-22	888.2	161.6	115.5	538,750	68,125	−0.26%	140%	14.5%		68,125
5-Dec-22	893.15	115.6	115.5	606,250	67,500	0.56%	100%	12.5%	67,500	
6-Dec-22	896.45	119.4	115.5	770,000	163,750	0.37%	103%	27.0%	163,750	
7-Dec-22	886.75	46.0	115.5	828,125	58,125	−1.08%	40%	7.5%		58,125
8-Dec-22	892.9	35.0	115.5	825,000	−3125	0.69%	30%	−0.4%		−3125
9-Dec-22	890.75	116.5	95.5	1,114,375	289,375	−0.24%	122%	35.1%		289,375
12-Dec-22	881.3	54.4	86.5	1,426,875	312,500	−1.06%	63%	28.0%		312,500
13-Dec-22	894.8	61.5	74.3	1,452,500	25,625	1.53%	83%	1.8%	25,625	
14-Dec-22	900.55	112.3	62.7	2,115,000	662,500	0.64%	179%	45.6%	662,500	
15-Dec-22	883.95	81.9	75.9	2,464,375	349,375	−1.84%	108%	16.5%		349,375
16-Dec-22	860.45	233.2	85.3	2,807,500	343,125	−2.66%	273%	13.9%		343,125
19-Dec-22	892.85	111.3	108.7	3,163,125	355,625	3.77%	102%	12.7%	355,625	

(*Continued*)

Table 3.5 Price OI analysis. (*Continued*)

Date	Close price	Del (amt.)	5D avg. del	Cum. OI	Ch. OI	% Ch. price	% Ch. del	% Ch. COI	Long	Short
20-Dec-22	884.25	51.1	120.0	3,895,000	731,875	−0.96%	43%	23.1%		731,875
21-Dec-22	857.65	71.6	118.0	4,688,125	793,125	−3.01%	61%	20.4%		793,125
22-Dec-22	856.9	121.0	109.8	4,950,625	26,2500	−0.09%	110%	5.6%		262,500
23-Dec-22	794.1	163.4	117.6	7,681,250	2,730,625	−7.33%	139%	55.2%		2,730,625
26-Dec-22	806.05	135.3	103.7	16,446,250	8,765,000	1.50%	130%	114.1%	8,765,000	
27-Dec-22	817.15	62.7	108.5	42,799,375	26,353,125	1.38%	58%	160.2%	26,353,125	
28-Dec-22	810.35	55.3	110.8	53,856,250	11,056,875	−0.83%	50%	25.8%		11,056,875
29-Dec-22	819.55	136.2	107.5	63,630,000	9,773,750	1.14%	127%	18.1%	9,773,750	
30-Dec-22	818.1	43.5	110.6	63,690,000	60,000	−0.18%	39%	0.1%		60,000
2-Jan-23	822.3	20.0	86.6	63,486,875	−203,125	0.51%	23%	−0.3%		−203,125
3-Jan-23	820.45	33.4	63.5	63,303,750	−183,125	−0.22%	53%	−0.3%	−183,125	
4-Jan-23	810	61.3	57.7	63,170,000	−133,750	−1.27%	106%	−0.2%	−133,750	
5-Jan-23	819.6	52.4	58.9	62,653,125	−516,875	1.19%	89%	−0.8%		−516,875

(*Continued*)

Table 3.5 Price OI analysis. (*Continued*)

Date	Close price	Del (amt.)	5D avg. del	Cum. OI	Ch. OI	% Ch. price	% Ch. del	% Ch. COI	Long	Short
6-Jan-23	806.1	62.1	42.1	62,705,000	51,875	-1.65%	147%	0.1%		51,875
9-Jan-23	816.65	36.5	45.9	62,312,500	-392,500	1.31%	80%	-0.6%		-392,500
10-Jan-23	796.4	93.1	49.1	63,049,375	736,875	-2.48%	189%	1.2%		736,875
11-Jan-23	796.45	60.1	61.1	63,057,500	8125	0.01%	98%	0.0%	8125	
12-Jan-23	792.95	41.4	60.8	62,997,500	-60,000	-0.44%	68%	-0.1%	-60,000	
13-Jan-23	794.65	78.6	58.6	63,115,000	117,500	0.21%	134%	0.2%	117,500	
16-Jan-23	787.05	120.1	61.9	62,850,000	-265,000	-0.96%	194%	-0.4%	-265,000	
17-Jan-23	784.75	67.0	78.6	63,344,375	494,375	-0.29%	85%	0.8%		494,375
18-Jan-23	786.5	140.3	73.4	65,142,500	1,798,125	0.22%	191%	2.8%	1,798,125	
19-Jan-23	776.05	158.6	89.5	65,768,750	626,250	-1.33%	177%	1.0%		626,250
20-Jan-23	774.45	93.7	112.9	65,987,500	218,750	-0.21%	83%	0.3%		218,750
23-Jan-23	769.05	115.0	115.9	67,121,250	1,133,750	-0.70%	99%	1.7%		1,133,750
24-Jan-23	761.2	76.1	114.9	66,680,625	-440,625	-1.02%	66%	-0.7%	-440,625	

(*Continued*)

Table 3.5 Price OI analysis. (Continued)

Date	Close price	Del (amt.)	5D avg. del	Cum. OI	Ch. OI	% Ch. price	% Ch. del	% Ch. COI	Long	Short
25-Jan-23	713.15	306.7	116.7	67,248,125	567,500	-6.31%	263%	0.9%	47,008,125	19,201,875
27-Jan-23	596.95	837.7	150.0	71,046,250	3,798,125	-16.29%	558%	5.6%		3,798,125
30-Jan-23	597	556.1	285.8	70,109,375	-936,875	0.01%	195%	-1.3%		-936,875
31-Jan-23	612.65	311.7	378.3	67,828,125	-228,1250	2.62%	82%	-3.3%		-2,281,250
1-Feb-23	495.15	569.5	417.7	69,193,125	1,365,000	-19.18%	136%	2.0%		1,365,000
2-Feb-23	462.45	930.9	516.3	78,924,375	9,731,250	-6.60%	180%	14.1%		9,731,250
3-Feb-23	498.85	828.7	641.2	68,217,500	-10,706,875	7.87%	129%	-13.6%		-10,706,875
6-Feb-23	545.45	569.3	639.4	62,074,375	-6,143,125	9.34%	89%	-9.0%		-6,143,125
7-Feb-23	553.15	717.8	642.0	54,551,875	-7,522,500	1.41%	112%	-12.1%		-7,522,500
8-Feb-23	599.25	434.7	723.2	55,956,250	1,404,375	8.33%	60%	2.6%	1404,375	
9-Feb-23	582.3	231.9	696.3	56,576,250	620,000	-2.83%	33%	1.1%		620,000
10-Feb-23	583.95	123.3	556.5	57,215,625	639,375	0.28%	22%	1.1%	639,375	
									2,043,750	(12,076,250)

Source: Own Calculation

of the month. Take the immediate next day of expiry i.e., Friday, and find the cumulative OI of that contract. Find out also the cumulative OI of the first Friday of the month after the expiry of the previous three expiries for the same contract. The same process needs to be followed for each stock. The stock that will display a significant build-up in cumulative OI in the current month compared to previous months can be identified for trade. This step is only to identify the stocks where OI has built up or to generate the signal, the next step is to decode whether it is long or short. To comprehend the long or short, the price and OI relationship (refer to Table 3.2) and RS can be used which is discussed in the previous sections.

A word of caution for traders is that it is not a good practice to consider a "long built-up" by merely looking at an increase in price and OI. Rather than observing a movement of OI and price during the day might lead to a better chance of winning. It is better not to look at the price from the previous day's closing, but the current day's journey of price and OI (intraday movement) might produce a profitable trade.

Therefore, the stance about a stock can be created by analyzing the spot and future market data over a period which will be instrumental before taking any call. However, to create an outlook about an index, OI in options need to be considered. In the next section, we discuss OI in option contracts.

3.5   OI in Option Contracts

The study of OI in the future differs from OI in options. The OI in option contracts can be tracked by looking at the OI of any underlying asset on the NSE website.

The option chain, which is widely known and available on the NSE website, displays the available option contracts in any underlying asset at varying strike prices and different expiry dates. Figure 3.4 lists the strike prices in the middle, with the call and put contracts on each strike price listed on the left- and right-hand sides of the table, respectively, expiry day-wise. The last column on both the call and put sides displays the OI of the respective contract. The bid price represents the price (option premium) buyers are offering to buy the contract, whereas the asking price indicates the price at which a seller is willing to part with their contract. The number of option contracts that buyers are willing to acquire at a given bid price is represented by the bid quantity. On the other hand, the quantity of option contracts that sellers are proposing for sale at a certain asking price is represented by the ask quantity [5].

			CALLS																	
OI	CHNG IN OI	VOLUME	IV	LTP	CHNG	BID QTY	BID	ASK	ASK QTY	STRIKE	BID QTY	BID	ASK	ASK QTY	CHNG	LTP	IV	VOLUME	CHNG IN OI	OI
6	-30	30	-	2,365.00	-60.00	1,750	2,224.00	2,502.80	1,000	17,050.00	16,950	0.05	0.10	9,500	-0.40	0.05	72.17	61,495	-15192	14,490
5	-3	3	174.27	2,380.10	43.10	1,750	2,162.50	2,472.25	1,000	17,100.00	2,47,350	0.05	0.10	10,550	-0.40	0.10	70.65	80,492	-11,908	36,052
1	-	-	-	2,305.80	-	1,750	2,102.90	2,391.90	1,000	17,150.00	-	-	0.05	4,850	-0.40	0.05	69.13	7,044	210	948
28	-2	9	144.28	2,250.00	-30.00	100	2,106.75	2,356.00	1,000	17,200.00	-	-	0.05	450	-0.45	0.05	67.61	43,141	-12,645	4,869
-	-20	20	-	2,150.00	-80.00	1,750	2,012.90	2,291.30	1,000	17,250.00	3,600	0.05	0.10	13,500	-0.40	0.05	66.10	4,506	212	472
4	-33	37	158.44	2,175.00	113.00	1,750	1,962.15	2,240.45	1,000	17,300.00	-	0.05	0.10	1,32,750	-0.40	0.05	64.59	47,991	-3,693	8,469
25	-6	31	-	2,065.00	-65.00	1,750	1,953.70	2,192.75	1,000	17,350.00	6,100	0.05	0.10	1,700	-0.30	0.05	66.35	10,002	-411	2,283
-	-2	2	162.68	2,091.35	66.35	1,750	1,906.70	2,138.25	1,000	17,400.00	-	-	0.05	28,900	-0.50	0.05	61.57	29,675	-8,878	2,511
4	-	4	187.51	2,095.00	140.00	1,750	1,866.45	2,087.15	1,000	17,450.00	-	-	0.05	11,150	-0.45	0.05	60.07	3,744	247	885
34	-48	53	-	1,915.00	-40.00	200	1,909.35	1,923.15	200	17,500.00	57,800	0.05	0.10	550	-0.55	0.10	61.63	1,81,062	-29,035	30,884

Figure 3.4 Option chain (equity derivatives). Source: nseindia.com

The IV column denotes the implied volatility. The implied volatility of an option chain is the market's prediction of the underlying asset's future volatility, as expressed by the prices of the options included in the chain. Greater uncertainty and the possibility for larger price fluctuations are implied by higher implied volatility, which drives up option premiums to offset the increased risk. On the other hand, lower IV denotes a market environment that is steadier and more predictable, which results in lower option premiums [6].

The support and resistance level of the index can be gauged from the OI in option contracts. It is well-accepted that the options market is ruled by the sellers. The highest OI on the call side indicates the resistance level, whereas the highest OI on the put side indicates the support level.

Let us consider the option contracts which expire on 23rd February 2023. Suppose the highest OI displays at the strike price of 18,000 on the call side, it implies that the call sellers will try to defend the 18,000 level, or in other words, they will not let the market go beyond 18,000; otherwise, they will have to incur a loss. In this way, 18,000 becomes resistant. On the other hand, if say, the highest OI on the put side shows at the strike price of the 17,500 level, it denotes that put sellers will try to defend the 17,500 level, or in other words, they would not allow the market to go down below 17,500; otherwise, they will have to incur a loss. Thus, 17,500 becomes a support level. The method is widely practiced by options traders.

However, there might be some cases where the market does not follow the above-discussed way to identify support or resistance level because an option seller can sell a call and put also. Therefore, an alternative way might be the strike price in which there is the highest OI on the first Friday after the monthly expiry with that strike price call and put option prices can be added. Once the spot price crosses that level, it becomes a pain point or panic point for a seller and anyway, the seller will try to defend his position. Therefore, a trader can react after that only.

3.5.1 Decoding Buyer or Seller in Option Chain

As discussed in the previous section, the strike price in which the highest OI exists is considered critical. Since the options market is dominated by sellers, it is assumed that more sellers are involved in the OI. However, a process can be followed to identify a price that is critical for buyers and sellers of call-and-put options. The following depicts a live example of a Nifty 18,000 call option contract which expired on 29th March 2023. The highest OI on the call side stands at an 18,000–strike price as of 1st March at a price of Rupees (Rs.) 47. The following steps need to be followed in the above option contract for computing the weighted average price of the option contract which is important for buyers and sellers.

1. Check the price (premium) of the option contract.
2. Find out the previous 1-month historical price of the premium.
3. Arrange the data as it is shown in Table 3.6.
4. The average price is the average of high, low, and close prices.
5. The last column indicates the product of average price and change in OI.
6. Take the sum of the product.
7. The weighted average price = product of price and OI/ changes in OI.
8. Plot the weighted average price in the chart.

The critical price (weighted average price) for buyers and sellers of call options is 338,046,988/2,181,700 = Rs. 155.

Figure 3.5 illustrates the Nifty 18,000 contract that is to expire on 29th March 2023. The weighted average price of Rs. 155 is plotted in the chart below.

It is evident that sellers are dominating the market at prices below Rs. 155, as the option price shows a downward trend below this level. Sellers benefit from the decay in option prices, whereas buyers benefit from appreciation. Therefore, it can be inferred that at the current price of Rs. 47 for the Nifty 18,000 call option contract, there are more sellers than buyers. However, the struggle between buyers and sellers is noticeable above the level of Rs. 155.

Table 3.6 Critical price of buyers and sellers.

Date	High price	Low price	Close price	Avg. price	Change in OI	Price * OI
01-Feb-23	461	237	291.2	330	46,200	15,233,680
02-Feb-23	305.7	246.2	278.95	277	41,050	11,368,797.5
03-Feb-23	372.85	258	360.45	330	50,900	16,819,056.67
06-Feb-23	343.75	290.8	310.05	315	−15,250	−4,801,716.6
07-Feb-23	330.55	255.35	278.4	288	−16,350	−4,710,435
08-Feb-23	340	278.35	325.6	315	1850	582,102.5
09-Feb-23	349.95	283.05	331.7	322	31,900	10,257,976.67
10-Feb-23	327.7	269.3	287.85	295	42,400	12,505,880
13-Feb-23	295	237.15	248	260	29,900	7,775,495
14-Feb-23	321.95	250.85	308.7	294	40,200	11,812,100
15-Feb-23	358.3	268.8	346.6	325	131,550	42,696,745
16-Feb-23	415	355	363.4	378	−91,600	−34,606,480
17-Feb-23	350.95	275.05	296.55	308	96,800	29,767,613.33
20-Feb-23	321.65	240	250.1	271	183,250	49,584,395.83
21-Feb-23	275.95	220.95	232.95	243	47,200	11,482,973.33
22-Feb-23	206.45	126	130.2	154	396,050	61,077,510.83
23-Feb-23	138.3	104	107.1	116	433,700	50,511,593.33
24-Feb-23	120.55	65.95	71.5	86	390,800	33,608,800
27-Feb-23	71	45	53.65	57	159,300	9,008,415
28-Feb-23	58.65	36.2	38.55	44	63,750	2,834,750
01-Mar-23	49.6	36.3	47.15	44	118,100	5,237,735
				SUM	2,181,700	338,046,988

Source: Own Calculation

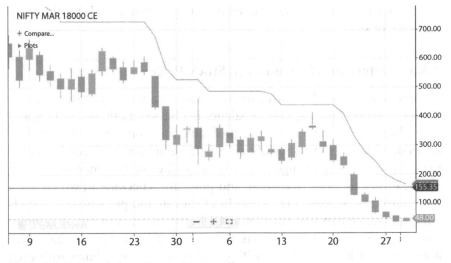

Figure 3.5 Technical chart. Source: kite.zerodha

3.5.2 Put-Call Ratio (PCR)

Another important aspect of the option chain is the put-call ratio (PCR). At the bottom of both sides of the option chain, the total OI of call and put displays. If the PCR is more than 1.1, it means the presence of more put sellers than call sellers, which is a bullish signal; if it is less than 0.9, it implies a bearish signal. Suppose the total OI on the call and put sides are 23,62,439 and 18,62,915, respectively, displayed in the option chain on a particular day, hence the PCR is 0.79 which is a bearish sign.

The OI data are not static but dynamic in nature. Hence, reviewing the OI data at regular intervals is required. The view built through PCR needs to be substantiated by technical analysis.

Steps to follow:

1. Follow PCR.
2. Find the build-up of OI in which strike price today: in-the-money, out-of-the-money, or at-the-money.
3. Study the market breadth. If Nifty is under review, then the elements of Nifty: Bankex, IT, and Reliance need to be checked. If Banknifty is under study, then ICICI Bank, Kotak, and HDFC Bank need to be checked.

The above study would help to assess a holistic picture of the market and predict the market direction.

The OI in option contracts can be used to generate signals for the identification of stocks.

3.5.3   Detection of Anomaly in Stock Price

The end objective of the entire exercise is to find out in which stock anomaly lies or in other words, a big imbalance lies between call, put, or long and short. Because a trader can make a profitable trade only from those imbalances or anomalies. An anomaly or imbalance in any stock can be recognized by combining changes in OI in all strikes of the underlying asset in one expiry on both sides—call and put—and checking in which stock this imbalance between the change in OI of call and put exists. If there is a big difference between changes in OI between call and put, it signifies something big is going to happen. Otherwise, if both sides are balanced, it implies that bulls and bears with equal strength are fighting with each other and leave no opportunity for traders. Unlike in the case of the future, considering one expiry is sufficient in options since liquidity is likely to be less in the next expiry. Therefore, cumulative and aggregate OI is critical for both future & option contracts. While OI in the future contract is treated as cumulative (sum of OI of all expiries), in the case of options, it is counted as aggregate (sum of OI of call and put separately in one expiry).

Let us take an example. Suppose the Maruti options contract which expired on 29th March indicates the total of changes in call and put OI considering that all strike prices are 1300 and −415, respectively. If it is the sellers, it means that the call sellers have entered aggressively and the put sellers have squared off their positions in the contract. This is a double signal indicating a bearish situation since call sellers benefit from a downward trend in the market, whereas put sellers tend to avoid bearish situations.

In other words, when the market is bearish, put sellers tend to exit their positions, whereas call sellers take advantage of the downward trend. This dynamic results in a scenario where the call sellers dominate the market, leading to a bearish situation. Now, the next step is to identify whether this sale happens in in-the-money (ITM), at-the-money (ATM), or out-of-the-money (OTM). Suppose in the above example out of 1300 call OI, 850 changes in OI happen at the ATM level, it signifies a clear bearish signal.

After identifying the anomaly in any stock, it is required to decode it whether it is short or long. The data imply a significant imbalance between either call-and-put sellers or buyers. However, the question arises of how to identify a buyer or seller in the option chain which is already been addressed in section 3.5.1.

3.6 Conclusion

In general, OI can offer traders and investors useful information when examining stock prices because it can show alterations in sentiment and probable changes in the market's course. To make wise investing decisions, it is crucial to combine OI and price with other technical and fundamental analysis techniques.

Remember that OI is simply one of several variables that traders and investors should consider while evaluating stock prices as well. Along with OI price and volume movements, news and events that might affect the market as well as broader economic trends that might affect the industry or sector in which the stock operates are other things to consider.

OI can be a useful measure for assessing stock prices and market sentiment, to sum up. Trading and investing professionals can make better investment choices and possibly profit from market opportunities by learning how to evaluate OI data and combining it with other analysis tools. However, it is crucial to keep in mind that no one statistic can give you all the information you need to make investment decisions, so thorough market research should take several things into account. Furthermore, it is important to note that the OI number is not static and constantly changes throughout the trading day. Thus, it is crucial to monitor the intraday OI data to gain a better understanding of the market trends.

It is noteworthy that the trade does not take place in OI rather it is a function of price action and entire analysis aimed to generate signals for trading only.

To the best of the author's knowledge, previously, no paper has been published exclusively on OI that can be used for profitable trading decisions. Hence, it is attempted to provide adequate valuable insights to traders that can be used with fundamental and technical analysis tools for making a profitable trade.

In conclusion, let us summarize the key takeaways from this chapter.

- *Prima facie* when the price and OI increase along with delivery suggests a bullish sentiment. When the price increases and OI decreases along with delivery, it suggests a weakness: Short sellers are covering their positions and causing a rally. When the price decreases and OI increases, it suggests a bearish sentiment. When the price decreases and OI decreases along with delivery, long position holders are forced to liquidate their positions by shorting.

- But by merely checking the change in price along with OI, do not recognize it as a bullishness or bearishness in the stock; do examine the cumulative OI (sum of OI of all expiries).
- Validate the OI analysis with technical charts.
- It is better not to look at the price from the previous day's closing rather the current day's journey of price and OI (intraday movement) might produce a profitable trade.
- Treat OI in the future contract as cumulative (sum of OI of all expiries) and in the case of options, it is counted as aggregate (sum of OI of call and put separately in one expiry).
- *Prima facie*, the highest OI on the call side indicates the resistance level, whereas the highest OI on the put side indicates the support level.
- A PCR of more than 1.1 means the presence of more put sellers than call sellers, which is a bullish signal; if it is less than 0.9, it implies a bearish signal.
- Check the build-up of OI in which strike price today: in-the-money; out-of-the-money or at-the-money.
- An anomaly or imbalance in any underlying asset can be recognized by combining changes in OI in all strikes of the underlying asset in one expiry on both sides—call and put—and checking in which stock this imbalance between the change in OI of call and put exists.
- To decode the buyer or seller in the option chain, compute the weighted average price (critical price).

Disclaimer: The entire analysis in this chapter is for educational and informational purposes only and should not be interpreted as financial advice. The objective is not to recommend or discourage in investing any stock. The analysis is based on publicly available information and may not be complete or accurate. Investing in stocks carries risks and may not be suitable for all investors. Before making any investment decisions, readers should do their own research and consult with a licensed financial advisor. The author of this analysis is not liable for any financial losses or damages resulting from any investment decisions based on the information provided in this analysis.

References

1. Chance, D.M., Introduction to Derivatives & Risk Management, p. 35, Australia Thomson South-Western, 2004.
2. Bansal, M., Derivatives & Financial Innovations, pp. 55–56, McGraw Hill, New Delhi, 2006.
3. Dubofsky, D.A., Derivatives: Valuation & Risk Management, p. 147, Oxford University Press, NewYork, 2011.
4. Achelis, S.B., Technical Analysis from A to Z, p. 168, Vision Books, New Delhi, 2008.
5. Vohra, N.D., Futures & Options, p. 74, McGraw Hill, New Delhi, 2000.
6. Mcdonald, R.L., Derivatives Market, p. 86, Pearson Education, Noida, 2013.

Stock Market Predictions Using Deep Learning: Developments and Future Research Directions

Renuka Sharma* and Kiran Mehta

Chitkara Business School, Chitkara University, Punjab, India

Abstract

The present study gives a comprehensive overview of the advancements and potential avenues in the realm of utilizing deep learning techniques for forecasting stock market trends. This study surveys the evolving landscape of deep learning methodologies employed in predicting stock price movements and offers insights into their effectiveness across various time frames and market conditions. The research delves into the multifaceted aspects of this field, encompassing architectures such as recurrent neural networks (RNNs), convolutional neural networks (CNNs), and more recent transformer-based models. The analysis underscores the influence of data preprocessing, feature engineering, and model complexity. Additionally, this chapter shows a roadmap for future research directions, emphasizing the need for hybrid models that integrate traditional financial indicators with deep learning approaches, the exploration of alternative data sources like social media sentiment, and the imperative of addressing ethical concerns pertaining to market manipulation. By synthesizing the current landscape and illuminating potential trajectories, this chapter serves as a valuable guide for researchers and practitioners seeking to navigate the evolving landscape of stock market prediction through deep learning.

Keywords: Deep learning, stock market, prediction, bibliometric analysis, systematic review of literature

**Corresponding author*: bhavya.renuka@chitkara.edu.in

Renuka Sharma and Kiran Mehta (eds.) Deep Learning Tools for Predicting Stock Market Movements, (89–122) © 2024 Scrivener Publishing LLC

4.1   Background and Introduction

Over the past several years, the typical person's interest in the stock market has grown exponentially. There is no denying that the financial markets are swamped with millions of dollars worth of assets being traded every day [1, 2], with investors hoping to profit from their investments. If a market player, such as a private or institutional investor, can precisely foresee market behavior, they may regularly earn better risk-adjusted returns than the market. This is why Song *et al.* [3] used deep learning/ machine learning/soft computing/computational intelligence techniques to build reliable algorithms for stock market forecasting. Some studies have said that the model-based results of their research can consistently make money [4]. One of the most important but also one of the most difficult jobs in financial research is stock market forecasting [5]. Investors' ability to consistently beat the market in terms of risk-adjusted return may not be in line with the efficient market theory (EMT), but that does not mean it is not true. It was revealed by Fama [6] that the market price follows a random walk, which means that future changes in the market's price cannot be anticipated using current information. The EMH categorizes market efficiency into three types: weak form, semi-strong form, and strong form [7, 8]. Weak-form market efficiency posits that past prices are already encompassed within current stock prices, rendering them ineffectual for predicting future trends. Consequently, technical analysis falters against a buy-and-hold strategy in yield projection within this EMH variant. Semi-strong efficiency asserts that publicly available data, encompassing historical prices, comprehensively manifest in stock prices [9]. This debilitates technical analysis for consistent enhanced forecasting. Public data incorporate economic, political, interest rate data, and firm-specific information, impacting stock values [10]. However, relying solely on public (fundamental) data does not assure market outperformance. Active management, utilizing public data, may not consistently surpass passive approaches (e.g., market index hold). The strong EMH form contends that all data, including insider information, are embedded in stock prices. This precludes any investor, even insiders, from routinely exceeding the market.

The assumptions underlying the EMT have faced continuous scrutiny and questioning [11]. The existence of short-term momentum, coupled with long-term reversion tendencies, along with the marked volatility exhibited by asset values [12], serves as contradictory evidence against the validity of the EMH [13]. Instances of overreactions and underreactions occur randomly and hold equal prevalence [14], possibly allowing institutional investors to rectify anomalies caused by less astute investors [15]. However, several questioned whether a model based on investor rationality could account for reported abnormalities. This resulted in a trend toward models that include human psychology [15, 16], which casts doubt on investors' immaculate rationality as a result of behavioral biases such as loss aversion, under-reaction, and overreacting. The adaptive markets hypothesis emerges as a conceptual framework that acknowledges and elucidates the manifestation of anomalies within financial markets. This hypothesis stands as a concerted endeavor aimed at harmonizing the efficient market hypothesis (EMH) with the principles and insights offered by behavioral finance, a field that delves into the psychological and cognitive aspects of decision-making in the financial realm. A study by Lim and Brooks [17] explains the evolution of the EMH concept in detail. Since market anomalies do arise, it is logical that a substantial number of market players utilize information from previous market prices, company-specific information such as historical earnings and profits, and other criteria to estimate future stock prices. Furthermore, since historical returns may represent a market mood, investors often predict short-term benefits to sustain. Given such predictions and the prevalence of market anomalies, it is feasible to predict the stock market using historical data.

Two well-known approaches, used to predict stock prices, are fundamental analysis and technical analysis [18]. For a company, fundamental analysis focuses on basic data/information, i.e., sales and costs, annual growth rate, market position, and other financial statements or reports. The same information can be used for an index, but also information about the market environment, such as economic output, trade, currency exchange, and interest rates. Technical analysis, on the other hand, is the examination of past stock price and volume data in order to make predictions about future price movements [19]. Prior research endeavors have employed statistical methodologies centered on historical data to predict stock prices and returns [20]. These methodologies encompass a range of techniques, such as ARCH, ARMA, and ARIMA [21], and also include GARCH [22], alongside moving averages, Kalman filtering, and exponential smoothing, which stand as the prevailing options. However, the landscape has transformed with the emergence of artificial intelligence (AI) and soft computing, where methodologies like logistic regression and support vector machines (SVMs) have surged in popularity within stock market prediction investigations. Notably, these approaches exhibit the capability to tackle intricate data scenarios that surpass the scope of conventional time series methods [23, 66], thus presenting themselves as captivating avenues for scholarly exploration in the realm of financial market forecasting, given their innovative and advantageous attributes.

In the current study, we have considered the latest studies to see the emerging deep learning tools for stock market predictions. The utilization of vast datasets sourced from the internet, coupled with the parallel processing capabilities of graphics processing units, and the advent of advanced deep neural network (DNN) architectures, collectively stand as pivotal factors underpinning the recent achievements of deep learning. The scope of applications for deep learning has widened significantly, encompassing a diverse array of domains, such as object recognition [24], image classification [25], and the prognostication of time series trends [26]. Deep learning models excel owing to their exceptional ability to accommodate extensive data volumes and discern intricate nonlinear connections between input attributes and predictive targets [27]. This proficiency positions deep learning models ahead of both linear models and traditional machine intelligence models, especially in the domain of stock market prediction, amplifying their efficacy and desirability for such purposes.

4.1.1   Machine Learning

Machine learning embodies deriving insights from data, as stated by Kubat [28]. In stock market prediction, supervised learning is widely used. Steps include selecting time series data like stock price, return, and pertinent financial news within a time frame. For classification, the target class might be known or predicted. Data are preprocessed by cleaning, removing incomplete/irrelevant data, and calculating technical indicators from time series data, e.g., close prices. After obtaining cleaned data and indicators, further preprocessing follows, including scaling and dimensionality reduction (feature selection, extraction, and generation) to extract relevant variables and filter out irrelevant ones. Using preprocessed data often leads to effective predictions [29]. The process begins with preparing the input data and selecting a suitable machine learning technique for prediction. The process involves partitioning the dataset into three distinct sets: first, the training data takes center stage, steering the model's refinement through specified parameters and structure; second, the validation data enters the scene, its role vital in scrutinizing model performance and pinpointing the most optimal candidate; last, the test data emerges, a linchpin in scrutinizing the model's adaptability to novel, uncharted data points. When it comes to feature selection, the landscape offers a variety of strategies. The most straightforward approach is the autonomous use of filters, known as filter methods. Alternatively, there is the wrapper method that forges a connection to model training by virtue of performance assessment. Moreover, there exists the embedded method, wherein feature selection becomes an integral part of the model construction process itself [30, 31]. The flow chart visually represents this potential link between feature selection and model training with a dashed line. Finally, after successful training, the prediction is carried out using the trained model for classification or regression tasks. This comprehensive process of data preparation, model selection, and evaluation ensures effective and accurate predictions in machine learning applications. This entire process can be shown in Figure 4.1.

In scholarly literature, a diverse array of machine learning techniques has been developed for the purpose of stock market predictions [27]. Notably, artificial neural networks (ANNs) [32], SVMs [33], and their respective variations [34] have gained prominence owing to their promising predictive capabilities. These methods have found extensive application in the domain due to their demonstrable effectiveness. Nonetheless, a significant shift has unfolded as intelligent systems based on fuzzy theory [35] have emerged to tackle data uncertainty. This evolution has led to a substantial body of literature investigating stock market prediction models rooted in fuzzy theory. These models encompass a broad range of strategies, incorporating fuzzy time series [36], adaptive network-based fuzzy inference systems [37], Takagi-Sugeno-Kang fuzzy systems [38], and other noteworthy variations [39]. The incorporation of fuzzy theory into these forecasting models offers a novel perspective for comprehending the intricacies of stock markets, accommodating the inherent ambiguity and imprecision prevalent in financial data. These fuzzy-based forecasting models hold considerable potential to complement and, conceivably, surpass traditional machine learning methods, capturing the complexities of the dynamic

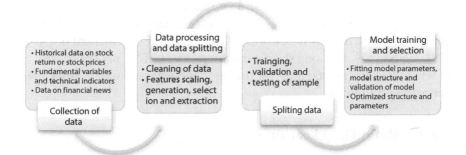

Figure 4.1 Process of stock market prediction.

financial landscape with greater efficacy [40]. Embracing the diversity of methodologies presented by this body of literature empowers researchers and practitioners alike to attain a deeper understanding of market dynamics, thereby enabling more informed and accurate predictions.

Within the existing body of academic literature, a wide array of machine learning techniques has been harnessed with the objective of forecasting stock market trends. These methodologies encompass a diversity of approaches, ranging from the application of random forests [19], decision trees, k-nearest neighbor (KNN) classifiers, to Bayesian networks [41]. Acknowledging the intrinsic advantages and limitations inherent to these techniques, scholars have embarked on endeavors to augment the precision of their predictive endeavors. Consequently, the exploration of combined methodologies has emerged, featuring synergistic combinations such as KNN + SVM [42] and ANN + SVM [4], tailored to prognosticate stock prices or returns more effectively.

Furthermore, the quest for heightened prognostic accuracy has spurred the investigation of strategies concerning feature selection and extraction. This includes the employment of techniques like principal components analysis (PCA) [23], as well as the implementation of evolutionary algorithms like genetic algorithms (GA) [43]. Additionally, the integration of specialized methodologies such as wavelet transforms [44] and particle swarm optimizations [45] has yielded demonstrable improvements in forecast precision. Beyond the realm of supervised learning, the purview of unsupervised methods, exemplified by clustering techniques, has also been probed for its utility in stock price forecasting [46]. This multifaceted exploration collectively underscores the depth and breadth of endeavors aimed at refining the precision of stock market predictions.

Contemporary progressions in stock market prediction have kindled a burgeoning fascination with the domain of deep learning methodologies. Operating as a subset of machine learning, deep learning adeptly unveils obscured nonlinear correlations and extricates salient features from intricate and cacophonous data sans reliance on human expertise or economic conjectures. Particularly noteworthy is the pervasive deployment of DNNs [79], CNNs [47], and long short-term memory (LSTM) networks [48], all of which stand as pivotal tools for the meticulous forecasting of stock market prices and returns.

4.1.2   About Deep Learning

Deep learning, a specialized facet within the realm of machine learning, concentrates on harnessing ANNs to assimilate and encapsulate data through a hierarchical and stratified approach [27]. This paradigm draws inspiration from the intricate organization and functional dynamics inherent in the neural networks (NNs) of the human brain. The term "deep" within the context of deep learning alludes to the multifarious strata of interconnected neurons that constitute these ANNs. Such networks are structured with an input layer, one or more concealed layers, and a concluding output layer. Each layer comprises a constellation of nodes, colloquially termed neurons, responsible for the processing and transformation of input data. The connections interlinking these nodes are endowed with associated weights, subject to calibration throughout the learning progression. The quintessential facet of deep learning resides in the networks' innate capacity to autonomously deduce representations of data, extracting them directly from raw input sources. In traditional machine learning approaches, feature engineering is required to extract relevant features from the data before feeding it to the model. In contrast, deep learning models can automatically learn and extract features through successive layers of abstraction, reducing the need for manual feature engineering. There are many tools of deep learning that can be used like TensorFlow, PyTorch, Keras, Caffe, MxNet, Theano, Microsoft Cognitive Toolkit, and Deeplearning4j. But when it comes to stock market predictions, some specific tools and libraries cater to financial data analysis and deep learning for forecasting stock prices. Here are some tools commonly used in this domain:

- Prophet: Developed by Facebook's Core Data Science team, Prophet is designed for time series forecasting with an emphasis on business data. It can handle seasonal effects, holidays, and outliers commonly found in financial data.
- TA-Lib (Technical Analysis Library): A popular open-source library for technical analysis, TA-Lib provides numerous technical indicators [e.g., moving averages, RSI, and moving average convergence divergence (MACD)] often used in stock market analysis.
- Alpha Vantage: An API that provides access to historical and real-time stock market data. It offers a range of financial and economic datasets, making it valuable for building predictive models.
- Pandas: While not specifically designed for stock market predictions, Pandas is a powerful Python library that allows for efficient data manipulation and analysis. It is widely used

for preprocessing and exploring financial data before feeding it into predictive models.

- TensorFlow Finance: A collection of TensorFlow-based tools and models tailored for financial market data analysis and prediction.
- Keras-RL: If you are interested in applying reinforcement learning to stock market prediction, Keras-RL provides implementations of popular reinforcement learning algorithms and can be adapted for this purpose.
- QSTrader: An open-source event-driven algorithmic trading simulator designed to test and implement trading strategies using Python.
- Zipline: Another Python-based library for backtesting and executing trading algorithms. It is used in conjunction with the Quantopian platform.
- Stocker: A Python tool that uses LSTM networks to forecast stock prices. It is built on top of Keras and TensorFlow.
- Stock-Price-Prediction-with-LSTM: An open-source project on GitHub, showcasing how to use LSTM networks for stock price prediction using TensorFlow and Keras.

Remember that predicting stock market prices is a challenging task, and no tool or model can guarantee accurate predictions consistently. The stock market is influenced by various factors, including economic indicators, geopolitical events, and investor sentiment, making it inherently difficult to forecast with high precision.

These days, both the fundamental tools for deep learning and newer prediction models are rapidly evolving. Programming languages have evolved over time, making it simpler to develop and test new deep learning models. Additionally, the collecting of web news or Twitter data gives fresh inputs for stock market forecasting. In recent times, there has been a noteworthy emergence of novel concepts, namely, graph NNs, grounded in a myriad of knowledge graph data. For a brief description of deep learning tools see Figure 4.2. It is worth noting that research endeavors within the domain of stock market prediction extend beyond the academic sphere. The allure of potential profits stemming from stock trading, bolstered by cutting-edge deep learning models, has resonated within asset management companies and investment banks. Consequently, these entities are markedly augmenting their financial backing toward AI research, which now predominantly revolves around the realm of deep learning models. In light of these advancements, our research concentrates on the most recent strides in the realm of deep learning models and their application in stock

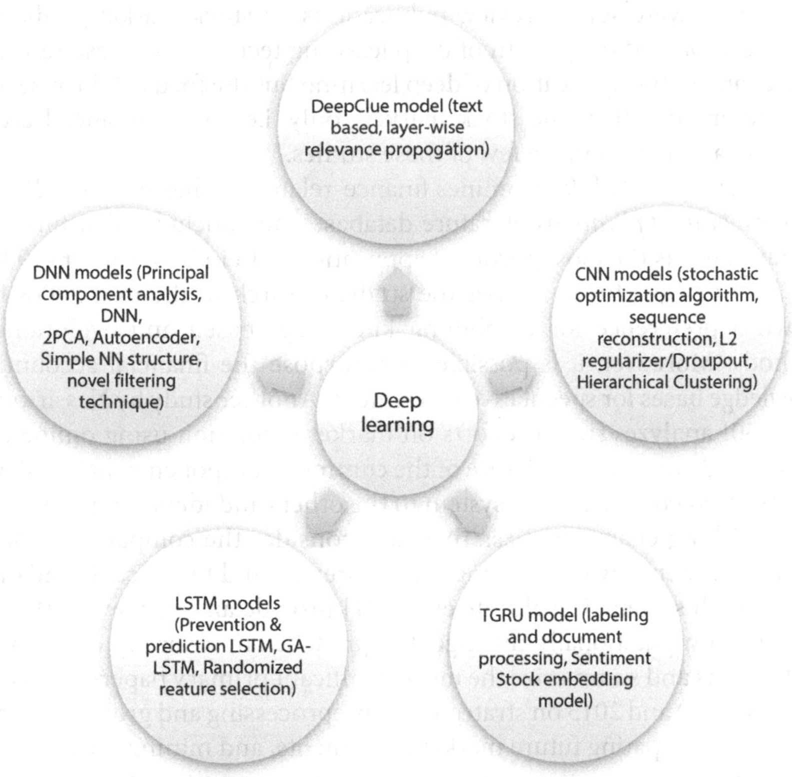

Figure 4.2 Deep learning models used in earlier research studies.

market forecasting, particularly over the past 3 years. Notably, the limited body of research prior to this time frame underscores the novelty of our investigation. By addressing this aspect, we aim to provide a valuable resource for emerging researchers seeking to discern the current direction of deep learning research in this domain.

The current study is divided into four sections, starting with an introduction followed by current research related to the theme, an overview of this chapter considered for the current research, major findings, future direction, and conclusion.

4.2 Studies Related to the Current Work, i.e., Literature Review

In the current section, a few of the earlier studies have been mentioned which are related to the deep learning and financial area. Prior to our study, there were several review publications on stock market prediction that accompanied the growth of deep learning techniques. These research studies are on the application of deep learning but the focus of the research may be broader than the stock markets only, i.e., other financial areas. Here, we are mentioning a few of these studies.

A study by Rada [49] examines finance-related studies from the *Expert Systems with Applications* literature database and concludes that financial accounting was the most prevalent application field in both earlier (1990s) and later (2000s) times. As per the study, research in the mid-2000s has shown a preference for combining knowledge-based and evolutionary methods. Moreover, it is possible to repurpose the financial accounting knowledge bases for speculative investment. Another study by Nassirtoussi *et al.* [50] analyzes similar efforts on market prediction using online text mining and constructs a picture of the common components that all share. The research compares each system to the others and identifies its primary distinguishing characteristics. They also consider the comparative analysis of the systems by considering the theoretical and technical foundation behind each system. Cavalcante *et al.* [51] provide an overview of the use of many computationally intelligent approaches in a variety of financial applications and summarize the most significant primary papers published between 2009 and 2015 on strategies for preprocessing and grouping financial data, anticipating future market movements, and mining financial text information, among other topics. Also, they give a systematic review and a systematic procedure for guiding the task of developing an intelligent trading system and the challenges of this scientific field. Tkac and Verner [52] gave a comprehensive overview of NN applications in business from 1994 to 2015 by analyzing 412 research publications and by doing a bibliometric analysis of them. The study finds that the majority of research publications have concentrated on financial crisis and bankruptcy issues, stock price forecasts, and decision assistance, with a particular emphasis on categorization tasks. As per the study, many hybrid networks have been created to increase the performance of standard models in addition to the classic multilayer feedforward network with gradient descent backpropagation. It is still possible to enhance the performance of NNs and get more insight into this important sector, despite the fact that they have been widely used in business. An experimental study is conducted to summarize the importance and utility of DNNs in the area of stock price and trend prediction and to examine the application of DNN variants to temporal stock market data [53]. The study applies nine deep learning models to predicting the stock market data. For the most current insights on DNN-based stock market prediction, this study is a good starting point.

Rundo *et al.* [54] conducted a comprehensive assessment of new machine learning techniques in the area of quantitative finance, demonstrating that these techniques outperform more conventional approaches. Some other studies have covered a wider range of financial markets. In one of these studies, Shah *et al.* [55] provided a basic overview of stock markets and a taxonomy of stock market prediction techniques and discussed some of the research accomplishments in the field of stock analysis and forecasting. The research also examines technical, fundamental, short- and long-term stock analysis methodologies, and some of the field's difficulties and research prospects. Detailed analysis and review are conducted in a study by Sezer *et al.* [56] on financial instruments and suggest a model that outperformed the buy-and-hold strategy, particularly in trendless or downturn markets. There are studies that say that the latest deep learning techniques are an improvement over the traditional deep learning techniques. Ballings *et al.* [57] examined the stock price direction and analyzed benchmark ensemble methods, like the random forest, AdaBoost, and Kernel Factory, with single-classifier models, like KNN, NNs, logistic regression, and SVM. The study concludes one-year-ahead prediction and it also indicates random forest as the best algorithm followed by other single-classifier models. Similarly, another study finds that KNN and ANN outperform SVM but with some advantages and disadvantages [58].

A recent examination of machine learning methodologies in forecasting financial markets is documented in the work of Henrique *et al.* [59]. Their analysis encompasses 57 curated studies, delving into highly referenced articles, prominent authors, and co-citation patterns. In a parallel vein, Gandhmal and Kumar [60] undertook a meticulous assessment, reviewing more than 50 research papers centered on stock market prediction. Their approach involved categorizing these studies based on the predictive techniques employed. A comprehensive exploration of these methods, publication years, performance metrics, and software tools is presented. Similarly, Shah *et al.* [61] contributed a succinct overview and classification of models for anticipating stock market behaviors. These combined efforts contribute significantly to the body of knowledge surrounding predictive methodologies in financial domains. Recent reviews aimed to encompass a wider array of field studies. Bustos and Pomares-Quimbaya [62], for instance, conducted a systematic assessment of stock market prediction methods. They scrutinized 52 studies released between 2014 and 2018, emphasizing diverse machine learning approaches such as deep learning, text mining, and ensemble techniques.

Through an analysis of 30 scholarly articles from journals and conferences, furnish a comprehensive panorama of diverse facets embraced within studies pertaining to stock market prediction. This encompassing overview encapsulates an array of elements, ranging from the employed machine learning algorithms and performance metrics to the utilized datasets and scholarly publications. Likewise, an investigation conducted by Jiang [63] comprehensively examined the utilization of deep learning models for stock market forecasting within the preceding three years. This study also furnished a concise outline of the employed datasets and data preprocessing methodologies. Additionally, it elucidated potential avenues for future research based on the existing body of knowledge. We believe that the benefits of deep learning approaches will continue to grow as more and more data sources, like historical prices, financial news, and tweets, are added to the mix. Thus, keeping up with this tendency is critical for future research.

4.3   Objective of Research and Research Methodology

Keeping all these developments in mind, our research is focused on the latest progress in the field of deep learning models and their use in stock market predictions, precisely for the past 3 years (2019, 2020, and 2021, i.e., 170 research papers) as before that there are single digits research on this topic (2011, 1; 2017, 6; 2018, 9; i.e., a total of 16 papers) to the best of our knowledge. This aspect will help new researchers to see where research on deep learning is heading these days. Additionally, a bibliometric analysis of the selected papers is also done to find the most influential work and articles. Practice deep learning and machine learning methods are applied in many areas of financial problems. For the current research, we have considered the application in stock markets, not in other areas like exchange rates, macroeconomic factors, cryptocurrency (Bitcoin), etc. However, the findings of the current research could be useful for the time series prediction of these financial areas too.

4.4   Results and Analysis of the Selected Papers

Papers shortlisted for the current study are described in this section of the research. Searches for keywords like "deep learning" and "stock market forecasts" are used to choose the articles from the "Web of Science" database. We have decided to limit our search from 2011 to 2021 (the majority

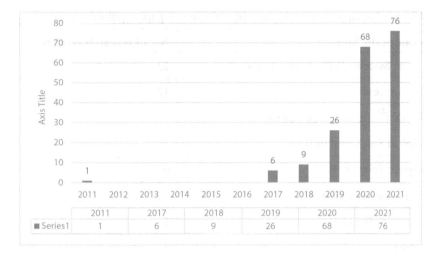

■ Series1	2011	2017	2018	2019	2020	2021
	1	6	9	26	68	76

Figure 4.3 Chart showing a number of studies in different years.

of the publications are from the past 3 years, i.e., 2019 to 2021). While the majority of papers in this study were published in the past 3 years (see Figure 4.3), there were also some studies published in 2017 and 2018 (six and nine, respectively). During the year 2011, just one piece of research was done on the subject in question. As a result, 170 out of the 186 total studies focus on the past 3 years. There were 170 studies considered for the investigation (see Figure 4.3).

After this, a brief description of the journals from which articles for the present study were selected is given. In Table 4.2, journals having three or more publications selected for the study have been shown. It is clear that the maximum amount of research comes from *Expert Systems With Applications* (23), followed by *IEEE Access* (17), *Neural Computing Applications* (8), Applied Soft Computing (7), Applied Science Basel (6), and other journals having 3 or more papers. Table 4.3 shows the representations of different countries in the selected papers. According to the country of origin of the corresponding author, the top five nations that generated the most articles on stock market predictions using deep learning are PR China (75), India (20), South Korea (19), the United States (17), and Taiwan (11). After looking at these data, it is surprising that the majority of the research on the said topic is done in PR China, not in developed countries like the USA, UK, Germany, etc. In total, the study covers 179 articles, 10 early access, and 7 review articles.

Table 4.2 List of journals with number of research papers published.

Name of the journal	No. of research articles
Expert Systems With Applications	23
IEEE Access	17
Neural Computing Applications	8
Applied Soft Computing	7
Applied Sciences Basel	6
Computational Economics	5
Journal of Big Data	5
Entropy	4
Mathematics	4
Multimedia Tools And Applications	4
Soft Computing	4
Complexity	3
Computational Intelligence and Neuroscience	3
Neurocomputing	3
PEERJ Computer Science	3
Sustainability	3
All others	84

4.5   Overview of Data Used in the Earlier Studies Selected for the Current Research

Different studies have used different combinations of data sources and deep learning methods for stock market prediction or movement. After looking at all these papers, it can be concluded that most of the studies have followed four major steps for their research.

A split of the surveyed markets, along with the most well-known stock market index, is done [67]. Most studies would concentrate on a single market, although others would test their models across many markets.

Table 4.3 List of countries and no of articles published.

Name of country	No. of research articles
PR China	75
India	20
South Korea	19
USA	17
Taiwan	11
Turkey	10
England	8
Italy	8
Japan	6
Australia	5
Canada	5
Germany	5
Iran	5

In the past 3 years, the research community has focused on both established (such as the US) and developing markets (such as China).

4.6 Data Source

In literature variables like fundamental indicators, technical indicators, macroeconomics data, market data, and text data, e.g., social media data, have been considered. However, this research used a variety of factors as data input for their prediction models, indicating that there is no common understanding of which parameters are crucial for stock market forecasting. There is another kind of classification of predictive inputs/data source for the research studies, i.e., structured and unstructured data (see Figure 4.4). The following diagram gives a brief of all types of data sources. Structured information pertains to categorized datasets with predetermined frameworks, arranged in tables, wherein attributes are delineated as

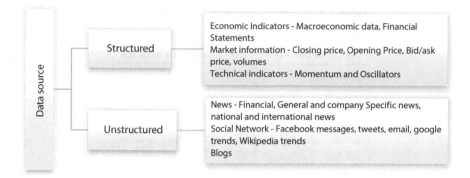

Figure 4.4 Type of data sources.

table columns. This format enhances information accessibility for seamless navigation, enabling uncomplicated or intricate searches sans additional labor. This information style finds widespread employment, frequently accessible and available via API programming interfaces. A prevailing example encompasses historical stock price time series, extensively leveraged by diverse computational models.

The intricate realm of stock market trend prediction is further compounded by the integration of unstructured data. This form of data necessitates meticulous preprocessing and transformation into numerical or categorical formats to serve as viable inputs for predictive models. Particularly, unstructured textual data demand the application of advanced text mining techniques to extract valuable insights from news segments and opinions dispersed across social media platforms. These insights are subsequently translated into numerical representations, fostering the ability to forecast stock prices effectively. The distinctive episodic nature of such data sets it apart from the more conventional continuous time series data, thereby prompting the adoption of a conditional analysis framework that accommodates its irregularities. News analysis draws from a triad of sources: finance-specific media outlets, general news platforms, and company-generated announcements. While financial media provide economic context to news items, general news lacks predefined contexts yet exerts a palpable influence on stock prices. Numerous empirical investigations underscore the potency of such information in the realm of stock price prediction.

The exploration of social networks and search engines for stock market prediction represents a nascent domain. Alongside the challenges inherent in handling unstructured data, such as news articles, the scale of data to be processed is vast, sometimes reaching millions of records. This magnitude introduces significant computational complexities. Studies have processed data in millions to see any kind of association to support stock market predictions. This intricacy necessitates the utilization of specialized methodologies and high-performance computing systems for effective processing. Furthermore, in contrast to news articles, communications disseminated through social networks commonly lack a standardized structure, including conventional titles, and often exhibit variations in spelling as well as the inclusion of emoticons. The majority of the work done on social networks was in the direction to see the sentiments are in favor or against the company, i.e., positive and negative sentiments. And these are very useful in the stock market estimation [77, 78].

4.7   Technical Indicators

The incorporation of technical indicators as input variables within the majority of forecasting investigations is a prevailing practice, given their pivotal role in influencing decisions pertaining to stock buying or selling. The term "Technical Indicator" encompasses variables integral to financial operations, constituting a fundamental aspect of the technical analysis of time series data, a method extensively utilized for the scrutiny of fluctuations in corporate stock prices. Within the purview of this survey, the classification of "Basic Technical Indicator" undergoes further subdivision into two distinct subtypes. The initial subtype centers upon rudimentary indicators encompassing metrics such as open, high, low, and closing prices, along with volume data. The subsequent subtype, constituting the more advanced echelon, encapsulates an array of technical indicators, including but not limited to the relative strength index (RSI), stochastic oscillators, and moving averages. The fundamental technical indicators encompass a gamut of variables, encompassing close price, volume, range, open price, high price, low price, bid/ask price, and a host of others. Notably, these rudimentary technical indicators are recurrently featured across the literary landscape. Among these foundational indicators, a subset of five variables emerges as particularly prominent within the scope of selected studies. These variables include close price with a lag of one period (derived from the preceding day/period), high price with a corresponding lag, low price with an analogous lag, open price with a lag of one period, and volume data from a singular period.

The rationale underpinning the heightened prevalence of these variables is rooted in their representation of the most recent data, a pivotal facet for prognosticating the forthcoming period's dynamics. This imparts them with a greater utility in comparison to variables associated with prolonged lag values, protracted time frames, or data that are less frequently accessible, such as the count of trades. The ensuing analysis underscores the strategic selection and application of specific technical indicators to facilitate the refinement of stock market forecasting endeavors.

4.7.1   Other (Advanced Technical Indicators)

This section comprises all technical indicators that are regarded to be more advanced than basic technical indicators and quite often involve some refining of basic data such as closing prices or volume. It contains all financial technical indicators that are not included in the preceding section's analysis of the basic technical indicators.

There are four primary groups of these indicators: indicators that measure the speed of change, the direction and strength of change, and the amount of change and fluctuation associated with a change are all included in this list: "Momentum Indicator" (46.4%), "Trend Indicator" (25.7%), "Volatility Indicator" (18.0%), and "Volume Indicator" (9.5%). The bulk of the 187 technical indicators predominantly comprise overall momentum and trend indicators. Unsurprisingly, all of the previous factors are also included in the top 30 variables. Among all technical indicators, the 14-period RSI ranks top. The variables ranked second, third, and fourth are all categorized as "Trend" indicators. These encompass the simple moving average computed over 10 and 5 periods, alongside the MACD, which is determined through the disparity between a 12-period exponential moving average (EMA) and a 26-period EMA, supplemented by a 9-period EMA signal line. Additionally, an array of return variables corresponding to distinct time periods (comprising 1, 5, 10, 15, and 20 periods) is present, as well as various stochastic percent K and stochastic percent D indicators featuring diverse time frames. Williams %R and EMA with varying periods are also encompassed within the array. Evidently, a substantial proportion of the technical indicators concentrate on both the "Momentum" exhibited by prices and the "Trend" a particular time series follows. It is noteworthy that only a limited number of indicators focusing on "Volume" and "Volatility" are featured among the top 30 variables.

4.8   Stock Market Prediction: Need and Methods

The exploration of issues within stock trading has yielded insights leading to the prediction of influential factors considered by experts in shaping stock prices [64]. Prediction mechanisms rooted in the stock market play a pivotal role in creating a common ground for a wider array of individuals and existing investors. The precision inherent in forecasting stock market dynamics significantly enhances investors' decision-making processes. The utilization of accurate predictions supports investors in making well-informed choices. Data mining tools offer assistance to investors in anticipating forthcoming trends and behaviors, simultaneously aiding institutions in devising proactive, knowledge-driven solutions [65]. The employment of intelligent data analysis streamlines the process of generating results using these tools. An effective method for extracting valuable information is employed as a strategy for data mining. The market has leveraged numerous data mining techniques [68], alongside knowledge extraction from databases [69], to meticulously dissect market trends. The critical essence of data mining in stock market prediction lies in its ability to systematically unveil concealed elements, thereby augmenting the precision of market trend analysis. This is executed through methodologies encompassing regression, Knowledge Discovery in Databases (KDD), and fuzzy models, collectively facilitating astute investment decisions [70]. The integration of these multifaceted strategies not only amplifies predictive accuracy but also cultivates a dynamic investment landscape. In essence, data mining emerges as a fundamental pillar in predicting stock market behavior, enabling the revelation of hidden facets and enhancing the accuracy of trend analysis through methodologies such as regression, KDD, and fuzzy models, thereby bolstering the efficacy of investment decisions [70].

4.9   Process of Stock Market Prediction

The process of a stock market prediction system involves several interconnected steps that aim to forecast future stock price movements based on historical data and various indicators. See Figure 4.5 for process of stock market prediction. The following is the sequence of different steps that are necessary for the stock market prediction.

a) *Data Collection and Preparation*: This initial phase involves gathering a comprehensive set of data that influences stock prices. Historical stock price data, trading volumes, and market indicators are collected. Additionally, macroeconomic indicators (such as interest rates, inflation, and GDP), company financials, and news sentiment are acquired.

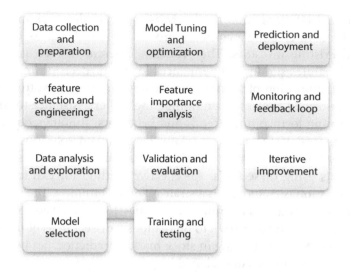

Figure 4.5 Steps to be taken for stock market predictions.

Ensuring the data's accuracy, consistency, and completeness is crucial for reliable predictions.

b) *Feature Selection and Engineering*: In this step, relevant features that could impact stock prices are identified. These might include moving averages (short-term and long-term), trading volumes, price volatility, and technical indicators (like RSI). Experts might also create new features, such as price change percentages over time, to better capture market dynamics.

c) *Data Analysis and Exploration*: Before building predictive models, it is important to deeply understand the relationships between different variables and stock price movements. Exploratory data analysis helps in uncovering patterns, trends, and potential outliers. Correlations between features and stock prices are explored, and anomalies or outliers are identified, which could have implications for model performance.

d) *Model Selection*: Choosing an appropriate predictive model is pivotal. The model should align with the problem type—classification for predicting price direction, regression for predicting specific prices, or time series forecasting for predicting future trends. Various models like linear regression, SVMs, decision trees, NNs, and ensemble methods are considered based on the dataset and problem complexity.

e) *Training and Testing:* Historical data are divided into two parts: training and testing sets. The training set is used to teach the chosen model to recognize patterns and relationships between features and stock prices. Model parameters are fine-tuned during this phase to optimize performance. The testing set is then used to evaluate the model's performance in unseen data.

f) *Validation and Evaluation:* During validation, the trained model is applied to the testing set, and its predictions are compared to the actual stock prices. Metrics such as mean absolute error and root mean square error are used to assess how closely the model's predictions align with actual values. A strong model will exhibit low error metrics.

g) *Feature Importance Analysis:* Analyzing feature importance reveals which variables have the most impact on the model's predictions. This helps in understanding which aspects of the market are most influential in predicting stock prices. Features with high importance can guide investment decisions and enhance understanding of market dynamics.

h) *Model Tuning and Optimization:* Model performance can often be improved by adjusting hyperparameters, which influence how the model learns from data. Techniques like cross-validation are used to fine-tune parameters and ensure the model generalizes well to new data. Grid search can be employed to systematically find the best parameter combinations.

i) *Prediction and Deployment:* Once the model is trained and validated, it can be deployed to make predictions on new data. This step involves applying the model to real-time or near-real-time data to predict future stock prices. The prediction process must be efficient and able to accommodate changing data streams.

j) *Monitoring and Feedback Loop:* Post-deployment, continuous monitoring of the model's performance is crucial. If the model's predictions deviate from actual outcomes, adjustments might be necessary. Collecting user feedback and analyzing discrepancies between predictions and market movements help refine the model over time.

k) *Iterative Improvement:* The prediction system is an ongoing project. Feedback, lessons learned, and new insights are continually incorporated into the system's design. Experimentation with additional data sources, features, and models keeps the system relevant and adaptive to evolving market conditions.

It is important to remember that while these systems can offer valuable insights, market dynamics are complex and influenced by myriad factors, making absolute accuracy a challenge.

4.10   Reviewing Methods for Stock Market Predictions

In this section, we present an overview of various techniques employed in predicting stock market behavior. As depicted in Figure 4.6, a visual representation showcases the classification of distinct methods for stock market prediction. These techniques can be broadly classified into two main categories: prediction-based and clustering-based techniques.

Prediction/regression-based techniques encompass a range of approaches, including ANNs, CNNs, RNNs, decision support systems (DSSs), hidden Markov models (HMMs), naive Bayes (NB), NNs, support vector regression (SVR), and SVMs. On the other hand, clustering/classification-based techniques comprise methods such as filtering, fuzzy logic, k-means clustering, and optimization techniques. This categorization aids in organizing and understanding the diverse strategies utilized for stock market prediction.

For regression, the goal is to anticipate the following day's market prices, whereas classification focuses on predicting whether prices will go up or down in the future (i.e., "will the price go up or down?"). Some studies use daily observation of the prices and some use the intraday prices to predict the stock market.

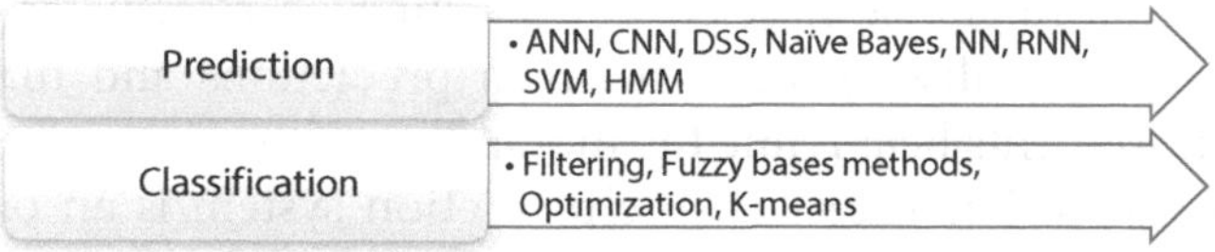

| Prediction | • ANN, CNN, DSS, Naïve Bayes, NN, RNN, SVM, HMM |
| Classification | • Filtering, Fuzzy bases methods, Optimization, K-means |

Figure 4.6 Model classification for stock market predictions.

4.11   Analysis and Prediction Techniques

Compared to other statistical techniques, ANN better models the link between stock performance and key factors. Literature deploys diverse inputs for stock return prediction. Some researchers preprocess these inputs before feeding them to ANN for improved forecasts.

The preeminent method employed for stock market prediction is the *Multilayer Perceptron (MLP)*. Functioning as a feed-forward NN, the MLP comprises an input layer, an output layer, and one or more concealed layers, each augmenting the model's capacity for nonlinear learning. Conventionally, the backpropagation technique is harnessed to train this network. In this process, the prediction error is conveyed from the output layer to the input layer, thereby facilitating the adjustment of interconnection weights to refine the model's predictive capabilities. Many researchers have applied this technique and trained their model by applying the backpropagation model in their study [77]. Another frequently employed technique within the realm of ANN is the radial basis function (RBF) network. This network variant employs RBFs as its activation functions. The RBF network executes a linear amalgamation of the RBFs corresponding to the input variables, facilitating the computation of the network's ultimate output. Among these approaches are several prominent techniques, each tailored to specific types of data and prediction tasks. ANN, CNN, and RNN are deeply rooted in the realm of deep learning, capturing complex patterns and temporal dependencies within data. DSSs integrate data-driven insights and domain expertise to aid decision-making processes. HMMs prove invaluable in modeling sequential data, whereas NB offers a probabilistic approach for classification tasks. NNs encompass a broad category of models for various prediction tasks. SVR excels in handling regression problems with its robust margin-based approach, and SVMs are adept at classification tasks by defining optimal decision boundaries. Collectively, these techniques form a rich arsenal for tackling diverse prediction and regression challenges across industries and domains.

4.12   Classification Techniques (Also Called Clustering Techniques)

Clustering/classification-based techniques represent a powerful suite of methodologies employed in data analysis and pattern recognition. This category encompasses a diverse range of approaches tailored to grouping data points into meaningful clusters or assigning them to predefined classes. Filtering techniques refine data by eliminating noise or irrelevant information, enhancing the quality of subsequent analysis. Fuzzy logic introduces flexibility in decision-making by allowing partial membership to classes [71], reflecting real-world uncertainties. K-means clustering partitions data points into clusters based on proximity, aiding in data segmentation. Optimization techniques seek to find optimal solutions by iteratively refining parameters according to specified criteria. Collectively, these techniques constitute an essential toolkit for uncovering structures within data, making informed decisions, and deriving valuable insights from complex datasets.

4.13   Future Direction

Drawing from our analysis of contemporary research endeavors, we outline potential trajectories for future exploration in this segment. These directions are intended to offer fresh perspectives to researchers who are eager to delve into uncharted areas.

4.13.1   Cross-Market Evaluation or Analysis

The prevailing body of research predominantly centers on individual stock markets, reflecting the divergent trading regulations shaping their distinctiveness. However, it is noteworthy that despite these variations, certain shared phenomena among diverse markets offer opportunities for predictive enhancement through methodologies like transfer learning. A handful of existing studies have already demonstrated favorable outcomes in the context of cross-market analysis, rendering it an avenue ripe for exploration in forthcoming research endeavors [1, 72].

4.13.2   Various Data Inputs

As inferred from our discussion above, formulating a stock prediction solution solely rooted in a solitary data source, such as market data, lacks prudence. This approach has been extensively employed in prior investigations, rendering the task of surpassing existing solutions notably formidable. A more judicious strategy involves the amalgamation and utilization of multiple data sources. Notably, prioritizing those sources that remain relatively uncharted within the literature presents a more promising avenue [73].

4.13.3   Unexplored Frameworks

The realm of stock prediction remains a dynamic and evolving field, with various NN architectures offering promising avenues yet to be fully explored—particularly those that have emerged in recent years. The depth of investigation into these novel structures has been somewhat limited. The evolution of stock prediction through NNs typically encompasses two pivotal stages: data processing and prediction model, both outlined in previous sections. While our survey has encompassed a selection of cutting-edge endeavors, there remains a vast expanse of uncharted territory for the conception of innovative models.

In the pursuit of developing robust predictive models, one emerging avenue pertains to the incorporation of sentiment analysis for text data, an element that injects human sentiments and emotions into the data-driven landscape. A noteworthy illustration within the natural language processing arena lies in the formidable Transformer architecture, as pioneered by earlier research [74]. This model has revolutionized various natural language processing tasks and could potentially offer valuable insights when adapted to financial news analysis. Moreover, the pretrained Bidirectional Encoder Representations from Transformers (BERT), an innovation introduced by a research work [75], has garnered widespread adoption in natural language processing applications. Intriguingly, its potential in deciphering financial sentiments from textual sources has been a less-explored dimension, hinting at an unexplored realm within stock prediction.

This uncharted arena offers promise for enhanced stock prediction by factoring human emotions into analysis. Integrating these models could revolutionize predictions. Simultaneously, real-time data from social media platforms emerge as a parallel avenue, capturing market sentiment dynamically [76]. The landscape's potential is vast, with these nascent strategies merely scratching the surface. As NNs and finance intertwine further, these unexplored domains could redefine stock prediction, reshaping our approach to NN architectures.

In conclusion, the landscape of NN structures for stock prediction continues to be a realm brimming with opportunities. This survey has shed light on the nascent integration of attention mechanisms, generative adversarial networks, and sentiment analysis. Nevertheless, the exploration of newer frontiers such as Transformer and BERT architectures, as well as the integration of real-time data streams from online platforms, remains largely uncharted. As the synergy between deep learning and financial prediction intensifies, it is anticipated that these unexplored territories will be ventured into, redefining the horizons of stock prediction and reshaping the way we perceive and harness NN architectures.

4.13.4   Trading Strategies Based on Algorithm

Effective prediction is not the final destination. While valuable in stock trading success, it is only a part of the equation. Studies assess profit and risk in prediction-based strategies, though they are often oversimplified, neglecting transaction costs and market-style adaptation. Deep learning model training is time-intensive, hindering practicality. These research studies fall short of creating real algorithmic trading systems. A potential avenue is deep reinforcement learning, showcased in diverse fields, including stock prediction. It excels in simulating scenarios, outpacing human traders in speed and decision-making.

4.14   Conclusion

Our comprehensive review underscores the increasing interest in stock market prediction research over the past half-decade. Recent studies reveal a prominent shift toward leveraging deep learning methodologies, such as LSTM, CNN, and RNN. Furthermore, a noteworthy trend is the adoption of classifier ensembles, which supplant solitary classifiers in contemporary research endeavors. While the literature still acknowledges the presence of ANN- and SVM-based approaches, these methodologies seem to be ceding ground to the ascendancy of deep learning and classifier ensembles. Over this span, the utilization of feature selection and feature extraction techniques, integral components of the data preprocessing phase, has witnessed a marked upswing. These techniques facilitate the construction of streamlined, more interpretable, and potentially more accurate models. The allure of these methods lies in their ability to reduce computational overhead, simplify model complexity, eliminate noise-laden variables, and potentially enhance overall model performance. This direction suggests that their popularity is poised to set in forthcoming studies.

Regarding the data landscape, studies grounded in technical, fundamental, and historical price databases continue to thrive. Nonetheless, a discernible surge of interest is visible in harnessing textual data selected from diverse sources, such as financial news and social media repositories. Notably, a spotlight is cast on sentiment analysis, a facet of text mining, when it comes to data extracted from internet messages, message boards, news articles, and tweets. The pursuit of sentiment analysis for constructing predictive models is particularly pronounced, signaling a growing emphasis on the insights gleaned from the emotional tone of textual data. While deep learning methodologies dominate the current landscape, it is important to acknowledge the persistent presence of other techniques. ANNs and SVMs, though receding, still leave an unfading mark on the literature. Their time-tested utility, combined with the continuous evolution of their applications, ensures their relevance even in the face of burgeoning deep learning techniques. The observed surge in interest in classifier ensembles signifies a paradigm shift in model construction. As opposed to relying on a single classifier, researchers increasingly advocate for the synergy derived from combining multiple classifiers. This cooperative approach enhances predictive performance, introduces diversity, and fosters robustness in the predictions. Consequently, the ensemble methods landscape is fertile ground for innovative exploration, which will likely inspire novel techniques in the quest for refined stock market predictions.

The escalating deployment of feature selection and extraction techniques underscores a fundamental concern: the imperative to process relevant information from the often noisy and redundant stock market data. As research delves deeper into these methods, a clearer understanding of the underlying dynamics of stock market prediction emerges. By funneling efforts toward capturing the most salient aspects of data, researchers pave the way for more meticulous and insightful models. In parallel with the evergreen utilization of technical, fundamental, and historical price data, the incursion into the realm of textual data presents new opportunities and challenges. Extracting meaningful insights from unstructured textual information necessitates sophisticated natural language processing techniques, text mining strategies, and sentiment analysis. These endeavors hold the potential to unlock hidden patterns and sentiments that influence market trends. In conclusion, our review reveals a dynamic landscape within stock market prediction research, characterized by the predominance of deep learning methodologies, the evolving role of group techniques, the sustained relevance of established methods, and the increasing interest in textual data analysis. The convergence of these trends not only expands the methods available to researchers but also holds the promise of more accurate, interpretable, and actionable stock market predictions in the future.

The primary hurdle when assessing papers lies in formulating Web of Science queries that filter out irrelevant content while maximizing the inclusion of pertinent documents. Another significant challenge involves sifting through the substantial volume of documents yielded by the query. Yet, forthcoming endeavors can leverage natural language processing and data mining techniques to scrutinize the entirety of retrieved papers. As models grow progressively intricate, there is a growing need for expedited methodologies. However, the scarcity persists concerning papers that juxtapose these intricate models against rudimentary single-objective models and pitted against heuristics using exact methods. This dearth of comparative analysis between complex models and basic counterparts remains pronounced, highlighting an avenue for future research.

References

1. Hoseinzade, E. and Haratizadeh, S., Cnnpred: Cnn-based stock market prediction using a diverse set of variables. *Expert Syst. Appl.*, *129*, 273–285, 2019.
2. Mehta, K. and Sharma, R., Contrarian and momentum investment strategies: Evidence from Indian stock market. *Int. J. Appl. Bus. Econ. Res.*, 15, 9, 107–118, 2017.
3. Song, Y., Lee, J.W., Lee, J., A study on novel filtering and relationship between input-features and target-vectors in a deep learning model for stock price prediction. *Appl. Intelligence: Int. J. Artif. Intelligence, Neural Networks, Complex Problem-Solving Technol.*, *49*, 3, 897–911, 2019, http://dx.doi.org/10.1007/s10489-018-1308-x.
4. Weng, B., Ahmed, M.A., Megahed, F.M., Stock market one-day ahead movement prediction using disparate data sources. *Expert Syst. Appl.*, *79*, 153–163, 2017, http://dx.doi.org/10.1016/j.eswa.2017.02.041.
5. Chen, Y. and Hao, Y., A feature weighted support vector machine and Knearest neighbor algorithm for stock market indices prediction. *Expert Syst. Appl.*, *80*, 340–355, 2017.
6. Fama, E.F., Efficient capital markets: A review of theory and empirical work. *J. Finance AFA*, *25*, 2, 383–417, 1970.
7. Chander, R., Sharma, R., Mehta, K., Dividend announcement and informational efficiency: An empirical study of Indian stock market. *ICFAI J. Appl. Finance (JAF), Hyderabad*, 13, 10, 29–42, 2007.
8. Chander, R., Sharma, R., Mehta, K., Impact of dividend announcement on stock prices. *NICE J. Bus.*, *2*, 1, 15–29, 2007.
9. Fama, E., The behavior of stock market prices. *J. Bus.*, *38*, 34–105, 1965, https://doi.org/10.1086/294743.
10. Wang, J.-Z., Wang, J.-J., Zhang, Z.-G., Guo, S.-P., Forecasting stock indices with back propagation neural network. *Expert Syst. Appl.*, *38*, 14346–14355, 2011.
11. Borovkova, S. and Tsiamas, I., An ensemble of LSTM neural networks for high-frequency stock market classification. *J. Forecasting*, *38*, 6, 600–619, 2019, https://doi.org/10.1002/for.2585.

12. Danial, K., Hirshleifer, D., Subramanyam, A., Investor psychology and security market under- and overreactions. *J. Finance*, *53*, 6, 1839–1885, 1998, https://doi.org/10.1111/0022-1082.00077.

13. Malkiel, B., Mullainathan, S., Stangle, B., Morgan Stanley, Market efficiency versus behavioral finance. *J. Corp. Fin.*, *17*, 3, 124–136, 2005.

14. Fama, E.F., Market efficiency, long-term returns, and behavioral finance. *J. Financ. Econ.*, *49*, 283–306, 1998.

15. Shiller, R.J., From efficient markets theory to behavioral finance. *JEP*, *17*, 83–104, 2003, https://doi.org/10.1257/089533003321164967.

16. Sharma, R., Mehta, K., Vyas, V., Responsible investing: A study on non-economic goals and investors' characteristics. *Appl. Finance Lett.*, 9, SI, 63–78, 2020, https://doi.org/10.24135/afl.v9i2.245.

17. Lim, K.P. and Brooks, R., The evolution of stock market efficiency over time: a survey of the empirical literature. *J. Econ. Surv.*, *25*, 1, 69–108, 2011, https://doi.org/10.1111/j.1467-6419.2009.00611.x.

18. Sedighi, M., Jahangirnia, H., Gharakhani, M., Fard, S.F., A novel hybrid model for stock price forecasting based on metaheuristics and support vector machine. *Data*, *4*, 2, 1–28, 2019, http://dx.doi.org/10.3390/data4020075.

19. Lohrmann, C. and Luukka, P., Classification of intraday S&P500 returns with a random forest. *Int. J. Forecast*, *35*, 1, 390–407, 2019, http://dx.doi.org/10.1016/j.ijforecast.2018.08.004.

20. Efendi, R., Arbaiy, N., Deris, M.M., A new procedure in stock mar- ket forecasting based on fuzzy random auto-regression time series model. *Inf. Sci.*, *441*, 113–132, 2018.

21. Hyndman, R. and Athanasopoulos, G., Chapter 8. ARIMA Models, in: *Forecasting: Principles and Practice (2nd ed.)*, OTexts, 2018, https://otexts.com/ fpp2/arima.html.

22. Bollerslev, T., Generalized autoregressive conditional heteroskedasticity. *J. Econom.*, *31*, 3, 307–327, 1986, https://doi.org/10.1016/0304-4076 (86)90063-1.

23. Chen, Y. and Hao, Y., A feature weighted support vector machine and Knearest neighbor algorithm for stock market indices prediction. *Expert Syst. Appl.*, *80*, 340–355, 2017.

24. Zhang, W., Zhang, S., Zhang, S., Yu, D., Huang, N.N., A novel method based on FTS with both GA-FCM and multifactor BPNN for stock forecasting. *Soft Comput.*, *23*, 16, 6979–6994, 2019.

25. Jiang, W. and Zhang, L., Edge-siamnet and edge-triplenet: New deep learning models for handwritten numeral recognition. *IEICE Trans. Inf. Syst.*, 103, 720–723, 2020.

26. Jiang, W. and Zhang, L., Geospatial data to images: A deep-learning framework for traffic forecasting. *Tsinghua Sci. Technol.*, *24*, 52–64, 2018.

27. Sharma, R., Mehta, K., Sharma, O., Exploring deep learning to determine the optimal environment for stock prediction analysis. *International Conference on Computational Performance Evaluation, ComPE 2021*, pp. 148–152, 2021.

28. Kubat, M., *An introduction to machine learning (2nd Ed.)*, Springer Publishing Company, Incorporated, Switzerland, 2017.
29. Chen, Y., Lin, W., Wang, J.Z., A dual-attention-based stock price trend prediction model with dual features. *IEEE Access*, 7, 148047–148058, 2019.
30. Guyon, I. and Elisseeff, A., An introduction to variable and feature selection. *J. Mach. Learn. Res.*, 3, 1157–1182, 2003.
31. Lohrmann, C., Luukka, P., Jablonska-Sabuka, M., Kauranne, T., A combination of fuzzy similarity measures and fuzzy entropy measures for supervised feature selection. *Expert Syst. Appl.*, 110, 216–236, 2018.
32. Nermend, Y. and Alsakaa, K., Back-propagation artificial neural networks in stock market forecasting. An application to the warsaw stock exchange WIG20. *IEB Int. J. Of Finance*, 15, 88–99, 2017.
33. Cao, L. and Tay, F.E., Financial forecasting using support vector machines. *Neural. Comput. Appl.*, 10, 184–192, 2001.
34. Pan, Y., Xiao, Z., Wang, X., Yang, D., A multiple support vector machine approach to stock index forecasting with mixed frequency sampling. *Knowl. Based Syst.*, 122, 90–102, 2017, http://dx.doi.org/10.1016/j.knosys.2017.01.033.
35. Zadeh, L.A., Fuzzy sets. *Inf. And Control*, 8, 338–353, 1965.
36. Cagcag, Y.O. and Alpaslan, F., Prediction of TAIEX based on hybrid fuzzy time series model with single optimization process. *Appl. Soft Comput.*, 66, 18–33, 2018, http://dx.doi.org/10.1016/j.asoc.2018.02.007.
37. Wei, L.Y., Chen, T.L., Ho, T.H., A hybrid model based on adaptive-networkbased fuzzy inference system to forecast Taiwan stock market. *Expert Syst. Appl.*, 38, 11, 13625–13631, 2011, http://dx.doi.org/10.1016/j.eswa.2011.04.127.
38. Chang, P.C. and Liu, C.H., A TSK type fuzzy rule based system for stock price prediction. *Expert Syst. Appl.*, 34, 1, 135–144, 2008, http://dx.doi.org/10.1016/j.eswa.2006.08.020.
39. Pal, S.S. and Kar, S., Time series forecasting for stock market prediction through data discretization by fuzzistics and rule generation by rough set theory. *Math. Comput. Simul.*, 162, 18–30, 2019.
40. Mehta, K., Sharma, R., Vyas, V., Kuckreja, J.S., Exit strategy decision by venture capital firms in India using fuzzy AHP. *J. Entrep. Emerg. Econ.*, 14, 4, 643–669, 2022, https://doi.org/10.1108/JEEE-05-2020-0146.
41. Malagrino, L.S., Roman, N.T., Monteiro, A.M., Forecasting stock market index daily direction: A Bayesian network approach. *Expert Syst. Appl.*, 105, 11–22, 2018, http://dx.doi.org/10.1016/j.eswa.2018.03.039.
42. Cao, H., Lin, T., Li, Y., Zhang, H., Stock price pattern prediction based on complex network and machine learning. *Complexity*, 2019, 4132485, 12, 2019.
43. Ye, F., Zhang, L., Zhang, D., Fujita, H., Gong, Z., A novel forecasting method based on multi-order fuzzy time series and technical analysis. *Inf. Sci.*, 367–368, 41–57, 2016. http://dx.doi.org/10.1016/j.ins.2016.05.038.

44. Chiang, W.C., Enke, D., Wu, T., Wang, R., An adaptive stock index trading decision support system. *Expert Syst. Appl.*, *59*, 195–207, 2016, http://dx. doi. org/10.1016/j.eswa.2016.04.025.

45. Chai, J., Du, J., Lai, K.K., Lee, Y.P., A hybrid least square support vector machine model with parameters optimization for stock forecasting. *Math. Problems In Eng.*, 2015, 231394, 7, 2015.

46. Vilela, L.F., Leme, R.C., Pinheiro, C.A., Carpinteiro, O.A., Forecasting financial series using clustering methods and support vector regression. *Artif. Intell. Rev.*, *52*, 2, 743–773, 2019, http://dx.doi.org/10.1007/ s10462-018-9663-x.

47. Cao, J. and Wang, J., Stock price forecasting model based on modified convolution neural network and financial time series analysis. *Int. J. Commun. Syst.*, *32*, 1–13, 2019.

48. Fischer, T. and Krauss, C., Deep learning with long short-term memory networks for financial market predictions. *Eur. J. Oper. Res.*, *270*, 654–669, 2018.

49. Rada, R., Expert systems and evolutionary computing for financial investing: A review. *Expert Syst. Appl.*, *34*, 4, 2232–2240, 2008, https://doi. org/10.1016/j. eswa.2007.05.012.

50. Nassirtoussi, A.K., Aghabozorgi, S., Wah, T.Y., Ngo, D.C.L., Text mining for market prediction: A systematic review. *Expert Syst. Appl.*, *41*, 16, 7653–7670, 2014, https://doi.org/10.1016/j.eswa.2014.06.009.

51. Cavalcante, R.C., Brasileiro, R.C., Souza, V.L.F., Nobrega, J.P., Oliveira, A.L.I., Computational intelligence and financial markets: A survey and future directions. *Expert Syst. Appl.*, *55*, 194–211, 2016, https://doi. org/10.1016/j. eswa.2016.02.006.

52. Tkac, M. and Verner, R., Artificial neural networks in business: Two decades of research. *Appl. Soft Comput.*, *38*, 788–804, 2016, https://doi. org/10.1016/j. asoc.2015.09.040.

53. Thakkar, A. and Chaudhari, K., A comprehensive survey on deep neural networks for stock market: The need, challenges, and future directions. *Expert Syst. Appl.*, *177*, 114800, 2021, https://doi.org/10.1016/j.eswa.2021.114800.

54. Rundo, F., Trenta, F., di Stallo, A.L., Battiato., S., Machine Learning for Quantitative Finance Applications: A Survey. *Appl. Sci.*, *9*, 24, 5574, 2019, http://dx.doi.org/10.3390/app9245574.

55. Shah, D., Isah, H., Zulkernine, F., Stock market analysis: A review and taxonomy of prediction techniques. *Int. J. Financ. Stud.*, *726*, 1–22, 2019.

56. Sezer, O.B., Gudelek, M.U., Ozbayoglu, A.M., Financial time series forecasting with deep learning: A systematic literature review: 2005–2019. *Appl. Soft Comput.*, 1–63, 2019, arXiv:1911.13288v1 [cs.LG].

57. Ballings, M., den Poel, D.V., Hespeels, N., Gryp, R., Evaluating multiple classifiers for stock price direction prediction. *Expert Syst. Appl.*, *42*, 7046–7056, 2015, https://doi.org/10.1016/j.eswa.2015.05.013.

58. Ersan, D., Nishioka, C., Scherp, A., Comparison of machine learning methods for financial time series forecasting at the examples of over 10 years of

daily and hourly data of DAX 30 and S&P 500. *J. Comput. Soc Sci.*, 3, 103–133, 2019, https://doi.org/10.1007/s42001-019-00057-5.

59. Henrique, B.M., Sobreiro, V.A., Kimura, H., Literature review: Machine learning techniques applied to financial market prediction. *Expert Syst. Appl.*, *124*, 226–251, 2019.

60. Gandhmal, D.P. and Kumar, K., Systematic analysis and review of stock market prediction techniques. *Comput. Sci. Rev.*, *34,* 100190, 2019, https://doi.org/10.1016/j.cosrev.2019.08.001.

61. Shah, D., Isah, H., Zulkernine, F., Stock market analysis: A review and taxonomy of prediction techniques. *Int. J. Financ. Stud.*, *7*, 26, 2019.

62. Bustos, O. and Pomares-Quimbaya, A., Stock market movement forecast: A systematic review. *Expert Syst. Appl.*, *156*, 113464, 2020.

63. Jiang, W., Applications of deep learning in stock market prediction: Recent progress. *Expert Syst. Appl.*, *184*, 115537, 2021, http://dx.doi.org/10.1016/j.eswa.2021.115537.

64. Bharambe, M.M.P. and Dharmadhikari, S.C., Stock market analysis based on artificial neural network with big data, in: *Proceedings of 8th Post Graduate Conference for Information Technology*, 2017.

65. Fayyad, U., Piatetsky-Shapiro, G., Smyth, P., The KDD process for extracting useful knowledge from volumes of data. *Commun. ACM*, 39, 11, 27–34, 1996.

66. Vyas, V., Mehta, K., Sharma, R., The nexus between toxic-air pollution, health expenditure, and economic growth: An empirical study using ARDL. *Int. Rev. Econ. Finance*, *84*, 154–166, 2023, https://doi.org/10.1016/j. iref.2022.11.017.

67. Mehta, K., Sharma, R., Vyas, V., Efficiency and ranking of sustainability index of India using DEA-TOPSIS. *J. Indian Bus. Res.*, *11*, 2, 179–199, 2019. https://doi.org/10.1108/JIBR-02-2018-0057.

68. Enke, D. and Thawornwong, S., The use of data mining and neural networks for forecasting stock market returns. *Expert Syst. Appl.*, *29*, 4, 927–940, 2005.

69. Ou, P., Prediction of stock market index movement by ten data mining techniques. *Mod. Appl. Sci.*, *3*, 12, 28–42, 2009.

70. Sharma, A., Bhuriya, D., Singh, U., Survey of stock market prediction using machine learning approach, in: *Proceedings of International Conference on Electronics, Communication and Aerospace Technology*, vol. 2, pp. 506–509, 2017.

71. Mehta, K., Sharma, R., Vyas, V., Kuckreja, J.S., Exit strategy decision by venture capital firms in India using fuzzy AHP. *J. Entrep. Emerg. Econ.*, *14*, 4, 643–669, 2022, https://doi.org/10.1108/JEEE-05-2020-0146.

72. Nguyen, T.-T. and Yoon, S., A novel approach to short-term stock price movement prediction using transfer learning. *App. Sci.*, *9*, 4745, 2019.

73. Zhou, Z., Gao, M., Liu, Q., Xiao, H., Forecasting stock price move- ments with multiple data sources: Evidence from stock market in china. *Phys. A: Stat. Mech.*, 542(C), 123389, 2019.

74. Vaswani, A., Shazeer, N., Parmar, N., Uszkoreit, J., Jones, L., Gomez, A.N., Kaiser, L., Polosukhin, I., Attention is all you need. *Advances in neural information processing systems*, pp. 5998–6008, 2017.
75. Devlin, J., Chang, M.-W., Lee, K., Toutanova, K., arXiv pre- print, 2018, arXiv:1810.04805.
76. Hu, H., Tang, L., Zhang, S., Wang, H., Predicting the direction of stock markets using optimized neural networks with google trends. *Neurocomputing*, 285, 188–195, 2018.
77. Wang, Q., Xu, W., Zheng, H., Combining the wisdom of crowds and technical analysis for financial market prediction using deep random subspace ensembles. *Neurocomputing, 299*, 51–61, 2018b.
78. Singh, R. and Srivastava, S., Stock prediction using deep learning. *Multimed. Tools Appl., 76*, 18, 18569–18584, 2017.

5

Artificial Intelligence and Quantum Computing Techniques for Stock Market Predictions

Rajiv Iyer[1]* and Aarti Bakshi[2]

[1]Computer Science and Engineering, Amity University, Mumbai, India
[2]Department of Electronics and Telecommunication, K.C. College of Engineering and Management Studies and Research, Thane, Maharashtra, India

Abstract

The financial crisis of 2008 had far-reaching effects on the world economy. Repercussions of this event are seen today in the Indian economy. Fast forward to 2022, we are looking at another impending crisis in 2023 on similar lines. The thing that is different this time around is that progress in the fields of artificial intelligence and quantum computing has reached a level where we can make predictions in the stock market. This will, in turn, help us make informed decisions thus preventing losses at every level. In the fields of statistics and finance, the stock market is considered a complex nonlinear dynamic system with multiple variables. Various techniques have been developed to analyze and predict stock market behavior. Two such techniques are blind quantum computing (BQC) and quantum neural networks (QNNs).

These techniques have been explored and studied in the context of stock price prediction and financial engineering applications. Researchers have developed models and algorithms, such as a quantum artificial neural network for stock closing price prediction and a hybrid deep QNN for financial predictions. Overall, these techniques leverage the power of quantum computing and neural networks to analyze and predict stock market behavior, offering potential benefits in the field of finance. The aim of this book chapter is to analyze the artificial intelligence– and quantum computing–based algorithms available for stock market predictions and propose the most accurate ones.

*Corresponding author: rajivkjs@gmail.com

Renuka Sharma and Kiran Mehta (eds.) Deep Learning Tools for Predicting Stock Market Movements, (123–146) © 2024 Scrivener Publishing LLC

Keywords: Stock price prediction, quantum computing, artificial intelligence, blind quantum computing, quantum neural networks

5.1   Introduction

The global financial crisis of 2008 had a profound and lasting impact on the world economy, and concerns are arising about the possibility of another crisis in 2023. However, advancements in technologies like artificial intelligence (AI) and quantum computing present an opportunity to predict stock market movements, potentially enabling better decision-making and risk management [1, 2].

The stock market is a complex and dynamic system influenced by numerous factors, making it challenging for traditional statistical models to accurately predict its behavior. Deep learning, a subset of AI, has emerged as a powerful tool to tackle such complexity. Artificial neural networks (ANNs), a popular deep learning technique, have shown promise in analyzing historical stock market data and identifying patterns that can be used for predictions [3].

Data preprocessing and feature engineering are critical steps in utilizing deep learning for stock market prediction. Historical data must be cleaned, normalized, and transformed into a suitable format for neural network input. Additionally, relevant features such as technical indicators, news sentiment scores, and macroeconomic variables need to be carefully selected or constructed to enhance the model's learning capability [4].

The training process involves optimizing the neural network's parameters to minimize prediction errors using historical data. Model evaluation is crucial to assess its performance, and common metrics like mean squared error, accuracy, and precision-recall curves are employed. However, challenges such as capturing irrational market behavior and overfitting need to be addressed [5, 6].

Interpreting deep learning models and understanding the reasons behind their predictions remain challenging. Future research should focus on developing more robust and interpretable deep learning models for stock market prediction [1, 7].

Despite these challenges, deep learning tools hold great promise for predicting stock market movements. Leveraging AI and quantum computing advancements can provide valuable insights into the stock market's dynamics, aiding in informed investment decisions and risk management during uncertain times. As technology continues to evolve, accurate stock market predictions may become an invaluable tool for navigating financial crises more effectively [4, 8].

5.2   Literature Survey

The paper [1] proposes a hybrid approach for stock price prediction using prediction rule ensembles (PRE) and deep neural networks (DNNs). The authors highlight that accurate stock price prediction is challenging due to the volatility of stock prices caused by various factors such as geopolitical tension, company earnings, and commodity prices. The aim of the study is to reduce risk in a portfolio or investment by accurately predicting stock prices.

The authors begin by explaining that stock prices are nonlinear and propose a hybrid prediction model that combines PRE, which computes different rules for stock prediction, and a three-layer DNN. The model utilizes technical indicators, specifically moving average indicators, to identify the uptrend in stock prices. The study uses Indian stock market data, particularly the top nifty bank stocks including Kotak, ICICI, Axis, and Yes Bank, from January 1, 2007 to October 10, 2021.

The hybrid stock prediction model's performance is evaluated using metrics such as mean absolute error (MAE) and root mean square error (RMSE). The results indicate that the hybrid model outperforms single prediction models like DNN and ANN, demonstrating a 5% to 7% improvement in RMSE score.

While the paper presents a hybrid approach for stock price prediction and demonstrates improved performance compared to single prediction models, there are several research gaps that can be addressed in future work.

The study focuses on Indian stock market data and specifically selects nifty bank stocks. Future research can explore the applicability of the proposed hybrid model to different markets and a wider range of stocks.

The paper does not explicitly discuss the interpretability of the hybrid model's predictions. Further research can investigate techniques to enhance the interpretability of the model, enabling investors to understand the underlying factors driving the predictions.

The authors briefly mention the issue of instability in prediction models, highlighting the impact of small changes in training data. Future research can address this challenge and propose approaches to improve the stability and robustness of the hybrid model.

The paper does not compare the proposed hybrid model with other existing techniques for stock price prediction. Further research can evaluate the model's performance against a broader range of traditional and advanced prediction methods to provide a comprehensive analysis.

In conclusion, the paper presents a hybrid stock price prediction model based on PRE and DNN, showcasing improved performance compared to single prediction models. By utilizing moving average indicators to identify stock uptrends and combining the PRE technique with a fine-tuned DNN, the hybrid model demonstrates promising results. However, further research is needed to address research gaps related to generalizability, interpretability, stability, and comparative analysis with other prediction techniques.

The paper [9] presents a method inspired by the Elman neural network (ENN) and quantum mechanics to improve the accuracy of stock market forecasts. The study aims to address the high volatility and difficulty in predicting stock market behavior accurately. The proposed model incorporates an internal self-connection signal to capture dynamic information, and a double-chain quantum genetic algorithm is used to optimize the learning rates.

The paper commences with an introductory overview of quantum computing, neural networks, and the stock market to provide necessary background information. It then proceeds to describe the architecture of the quantum ENN (QENN) model, which utilizes principles from quantum mechanics, specifically the superposition principle and quantum measurement postulate. The QENN structure resembles the conventional ENN but includes a context neuron that retains the previous moment's state through self-connection feedback.

To assess the efficacy of the proposed model, empirical investigations are performed using real stock market data. The study utilizes closing prices from six stock markets, namely, Nasdaq, BSE Sensex, HSI, SSE, Russell 2000, and TAIEX, as datasets.

In conclusion, the paper highlights the successful application of the QENN model for stock closing price prediction. It effectively addresses the challenges posed by high volatility, complex nonlinearity, dynamic characteristics, and the time-varying nature of stock market data. By combining the advantages of genetic algorithms and machine learning, the QENN model demonstrates feasibility and effectiveness, as supported by the case analysis and simulation results.

While the paper introduces a novel approach using the quantum ANN for stock closing price prediction, there remain research gaps that could be explored in future work.

One such gap is the absence of a comparison between the proposed QENN model and existing methods for stock price prediction. Future research could evaluate the QENN model's performance against traditional neural network models and other advanced prediction techniques, providing a comprehensive analysis of its strengths and weaknesses.

The interpretability of the QENN model's predictions is not discussed in the paper. Future research can explore techniques to enhance the interpretability of the QENN model, enabling investors to understand the reasoning behind the predictions and the underlying factors influencing stock closing prices.

The study focuses on six specific stock markets, and it is unclear whether the proposed QENN model can be applied to other markets and different types of financial assets. Future research can investigate the generalizability of the model to diverse market conditions and expand its application beyond stock closing price prediction.

The paper does not explicitly discuss the stability and robustness of the QENN model. Future research can address the issue of model stability and investigate methods to improve the robustness of the QENN model in different market scenarios.

In conclusion, the paper introduces a quantum ANN model, specifically the QENN, for stock closing price prediction. The model leverages principles from quantum mechanics to capture the dynamic characteristics and high volatility of stock market data. The use of a double-chain quantum genetic algorithm enhances the learning rates of the QENN model. While the study demonstrates the feasibility and effectiveness of the approach, future research can address research gaps related to performance comparison, model interpretability, generalizability, and stability/robustness of the QENN model.

The paper [10] introduces the concept of blind quantum computing (BQC) and related protocols. BQC protocols aim to securely delegate quantum computations to untrusted devices while maintaining privacy and integrity. The authors provide a review of the progress made in this emerging field and discuss the challenges and potential future directions.

The paper is a literature review and does not present new empirical data or experimental results. It provides an overview of various BQC protocols proposed in the literature, discussing their features, security definitions, and implementation considerations.

The paper highlights the open question of whether blind or verifiable computation is possible with a single server and a completely classical client. Secure protocols for blind and verifiable computation in this setting remain unresolved.

The precise relationship between blindness and verification in BQC protocols is still an open question that requires further investigation and theoretical development.

The existence of fully homomorphic quantum encryption schemes under plausible computational assumptions remains an open problem. Progress has been made in partially homomorphic encryption, but achieving fully homomorphic encryption for quantum data without relying on computational assumptions is yet to be achieved.

There is a need to reduce overhead and sensitivity to noise in device-independent verification protocols. Methods to verify analog quantum simulators and other special-purpose devices need further development.

While progress has been made in two-party blind computation, there is potential for exploring secure quantum computing protocols beyond the two-party setting, including multiuser blind computation and publicly verifiable quantum computation.

Overall, the paper provides an informative overview of the progress, challenges, and future directions in the field of BQC and related protocols. It identifies several important research gaps that need to be addressed to advance the field further.

The paper [11] presents a method for training deep quantum neural networks (QNNs) for fully quantum learning tasks. The authors propose a quantum analog of classical neurons, referred to as quantum perceptrons, which form the building blocks of QNNs capable of universal quantum computation. They describe an efficient training algorithm using fidelity as a cost function, allowing for classical and efficient quantum implementations. The proposed method enables fast optimization with reduced memory requirements, where the number of required qudits scales only with the width of the network, enabling deep network optimization. The authors benchmarked their approach by applying it to the quantum task of learning an unknown unitary and observed remarkable generalization behavior and robustness to noisy training data.

The authors mention the possibility of generalizing the quantum perceptron definition to cover general completely positive maps, which would provide a better model for decoherence processes. The paper does not discuss the effects of overfitting in deep QNNs. Further research is needed to understand how overfitting affects the performance and generalization capabilities of QNNs. The authors suggest exploring optimized implementations of QNNs on near-term quantum devices, considering the constraints and noise inherent in noisy intermediate-scale quantum (NISQ) devices. Investigating practical implementation challenges and developing strategies for robust training on NISQ devices would be an important research direction.

The paper [12] proposes a comprehensive deep learning system for predicting the price trend of stock markets. The authors collected 2 years of data from the Chinese stock market and utilized a combination of feature engineering techniques and a customized long short-term memory (LSTM)–based deep learning model for their prediction system.

The paper identifies several research gaps and areas for further investigation. One of the weaknesses found in related works is the limited focus on data preprocessing mechanisms. The authors propose a comprehensive feature engineering procedure to address this gap. They also emphasize the need for extracting new features from data and combining them with existing technical indices to improve prediction models.

The paper highlights the importance of evaluating the effectiveness of findings from the financial domain and incorporating them into the prediction model. It suggests that converting financial domain findings into a data processing module is a hidden research question that needs to be explored further.

Furthermore, the authors mention that previous works have primarily focused on exact price prediction, whereas their approach decomposes the problem into predicting the trend first and then the exact number. They suggest that exploring different algorithms for predicting short-term price trends is another research question that can be investigated.

Overall, the research gaps identified in the paper include the need for improved data preprocessing mechanisms, effective utilization of findings from the financial domain, and the selection of suitable algorithms for short-term price trend prediction.

In the paper [13], the authors introduce a novel neural network approach for stock market prediction. They collected real-time and offline data from the live stock market and devised a concept called "stock vector," inspired by word vector development in deep learning. Two models were proposed: a deep LSTM neural network with an embedded layer and an LSTM neural network with an automatic encoder, both aimed at predicting the stock market. The experimental results provided evidence of the effectiveness of these proposed models.

The paper [7] proposes an artificial counselor system for stock investment. The system predicts stock future prices using support vector regression and recommends optimal portions of the budget to invest in different existing stocks based on the predicted prices. Two methods, Markowitz portfolio theory and a fuzzy investment counselor (FIC), are employed for suggesting the best portions. The experimental results on the New York

Stock Exchange (NYSE) demonstrate the effectiveness of the proposed system.

The paper utilizes the NYSE dataset for evaluating the proposed system. The dataset contains information on 140 stocks from 2010 to 2016. The authors selected 25 well-known stocks for their evaluation, including Apple, Amazon, Boeing, Coca-Cola, Microsoft, and Walmart, among others. The specific details of the dataset, such as the source or any preprocessing steps applied, are not explicitly mentioned.

The authors apply preprocessing techniques to the dataset. They use moving averages on technical features (opening, closing, lowest, and highest prices, as well as volume) to capture short-term and long-term trend changes. Z-Score normalization is also employed to remove the mean and scale the variance to the unit in each time series.

Prediction of Future Prices: Support vector regression is used to predict future prices of stocks. The authors consider two well-known stock indices, average directional index and stop and reverse, in addition to technical features for prediction.

Fuzzy Investment Counselor: The paper introduces an FIC that models the behavior of an expert investor based on predefined rules. The FIC consists of two parts: a technical part (self-stock system and pairwise-stocks system) that considers the technical features of each stock individually and in relation to other stocks and a fundamental part that incorporates the fundamental features of each stock.

The proposed system is evaluated using the NYSE dataset. The authors select 25 stocks for testing and compare the results with existing literature. The evaluation focuses on prediction accuracy and the effectiveness of the suggested optimal portions for investment.

While the paper presents a novel artificial counselor system for stock investment, there are some potential research gaps and areas for further investigation. The paper does not provide specific details about the data sources used or the preprocessing steps applied to the dataset. More transparency regarding the origin and quality of the data, as well as the preprocessing techniques employed, would enhance the reproducibility and generalizability of the proposed system.

The paper primarily focuses on the effectiveness of the proposed system in terms of prediction accuracy and the suggested optimal investment portions. It would be beneficial to include additional evaluation metrics, such as risk assessment or comparison with other existing investment strategies, to provide a more comprehensive assessment of the system's performance.

The paper does not discuss the interpretability and explainability of the proposed system. As an artificial counselor, it is crucial to understand the reasoning behind the system's recommendations and how it incorporates both technical and fundamental features. Further research could explore methods to enhance the interpretability and transparency of the system.

The evaluation of the proposed system is conducted using the NYSE dataset. It would be valuable to test the system's performance on different datasets from other stock exchanges or global markets to assess its generalizability and robustness.

The paper mentions the possibility of considering additional factors, such as news or sentimental attributes, in the investment counselor system. Future work could explore the integration of such factors to improve the system's decision-making capabilities.

The paper acknowledges that the proposed system focuses on forecasting stock prices and providing investment suggestions. Future work could aim to develop a more complete trading system by incorporating other aspects such as short selling and market analysis techniques like Elliott waves.

The paper [14] conducts a comprehensive review of 86 recent papers, spanning from 2015 to the present, that delve into the application of deep learning methods for predicting stock and foreign exchange (Forex) prices. The review critically examines various aspects of these studies, including the datasets, variables, models, and evaluation metrics employed. The focus is on exploring the utilization of deep learning techniques, such as convolutional neural network (CNN), LSTM, DNN, recurrent neural network (RNN), reinforcement learning, and other methods like hybrid attention networks, self-paced learning mechanism (NLP), and WaveNet. By analyzing these papers, the review seeks to identify emerging trends, performance metrics, and potential research gaps within this rapidly evolving field.

The paper does not explicitly mention the specific data sources used in the reviewed papers. However, it states that the papers were selected from the Digital Bibliography & Library Project database for comparison and analysis. It can be inferred that the data sources vary across the reviewed papers, and the authors of the surveyed papers have used different datasets for their research.

The paper analyzes the variables used in each method and the specific models employed in the reviewed papers. It provides insights into the combinations of variables and modifications made to traditional models to enhance performance.

The authors identify the performance metrics used in the reviewed papers, including RMSE, mean absolute percentage error, MAE, mean square error, accuracy, Sharpe ratio, and return rate. They discuss the metrics used in each deep learning method and highlight notable results.

The paper identifies several research gaps and potential areas for future investigation in the field of stock and Forex price prediction using deep learning methods.

The authors note a lack of studies exploring the combination of multiple deep learning methods, particularly the combination of deep learning with other deep learning techniques. They suggest that further research should focus on hybrid networks to leverage the strengths of different methods and improve prediction accuracy.

The paper highlights that hybrid networks, which combine deep learning methods with other advanced technologies like genetic algorithms and self-attention neural networks, show promise for future research. The authors suggest designing specific hybrid models based on the analysis conducted in the paper.

The survey primarily focuses on the use of technical analysis and, to some extent, sentiment and news analysis for prediction. Future work could explore the integration of other features, such as social media impact or fundamental analysis, to enhance the predictive capabilities of deep learning models.

The paper observes variations in the evaluation metrics used across the reviewed papers. Establishing standardized evaluation metrics for comparing the performance of different deep learning models would facilitate better comparisons and benchmarking.

The paper does not explicitly discuss the practical application or real-time prediction aspect of the reviewed models. Further research could focus on implementing and evaluating the proposed models in real-world scenarios to assess their effectiveness and feasibility.

5.3   Analysis of Popular Deep Learning Techniques for Stock Market Prediction

5.3.1   Blind Quantum Computing (BQC) in Stock Market Prediction

The task of predicting stock market movements has always been complex and challenging, given the dynamic nature of financial markets. However, recent technological advancements, particularly in deep learning and quantum computing, offer new possibilities for more accurate predictions. This chapter delves into the application of deep learning tools for

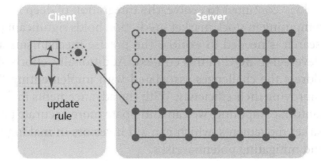

Figure 5.1 BQC approach [3].

predicting stock market movements, with a specific focus on a promising technique known as BQC [1, 10].

BQC is an innovative computing paradigm that enables a client with limited quantum computational capabilities to delegate complex quantum computation tasks to a server with more powerful quantum resources, all while maintaining privacy and confidentiality. BQC often leverages entangled states of multiple qubits to carry out computational tasks efficiently. Although BQC is mainly used in secure computation scenarios, its potential application in stock market prediction has shown promising results [10].

Figure 5.1 illustrates the process of the BQC approach, where the client performs adaptive measurements on a series of qubits provided by the server. By incrementally transmitting a universal resource state from the server to the client, the client can execute any computation without the need to share additional information with the server, apart from the initial graph description. This ensures privacy and security during the computation process.

Advantages and Challenges of BQC in Stock Market Prediction
One of the advantages of using BQC in stock market prediction is the potential for improved computational power. Quantum computing can handle complex calculations more efficiently than classical computing, potentially enabling more accurate predictions. Additionally, BQC offers the advantage of preserving the client's privacy, as the server performs the computation without having access to the client's sensitive information. However, there are still challenges to overcome, such as the complexity of implementing BQC systems and the need for further research to optimize the utilization of BQC techniques in stock market prediction.

As technology continues to evolve, the integration of deep learning and quantum computing in stock market prediction holds significant potential. Further research is needed to explore the precise mechanisms and algorithms for leveraging BQC in this context. Additionally, efforts should be made to address the challenges associated with implementing BQC systems and improving their efficiency. With the advancements in deep learning and quantum computing, we can anticipate more accurate predictions of stock market movements, which can aid investors in making informed decisions and mitigating potential risks.

The application of deep learning tools, including BQC, in predicting stock market movements presents a promising avenue for enhancing prediction accuracy. The integration of deep learning algorithms and quantum computing techniques has the potential to revolutionize stock market prediction by capturing complex relationships and leveraging advanced computational capabilities. As research and development in this field continue, we can anticipate improved insights into the dynamics of financial markets, enabling more informed investment decisions and potentially mitigating the impact of economic crises.

5.3.2   Quantum Neural Networks (QNNs) for Time Series Forecasting

The rise of deep learning has revolutionized the analysis of time series data, making it a potent tool for handling complex datasets like those in the stock market. In this section, we delve into the utilization of QNNs as a promising approach for forecasting time series signals, with a specific focus on predicting stock market movements [11].

Time series data play a significant role in various business areas within the financial sector. In stock markets, the movement of stock prices and other related indicators over time provides crucial information for decision-making. Analyzing and predicting these time series signals can offer insights into market trends, investor sentiment, and potential future price movements.

Deep learning techniques, particularly neural networks, have gained popularity in analyzing and predicting time series data. Neural networks are composed of interconnected layers of artificial neurons, capable of learning complex patterns and relationships within data. By training neural networks on historical time series data, they can capture temporal dependencies and make predictions about future values. Deep learning models

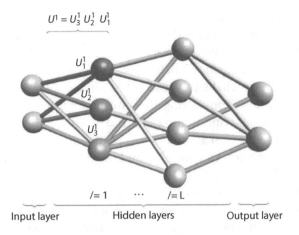

$$U^1 = U_3^1\, U_2^1\, U_1^1$$

U_1^1

U_2^1

U_3^1

$l = 1$ $\cdots$ $l = L$

Input layer   Hidden layers   Output layer

Figure 5.2 Quantum feedforward neural network [4].

have shown promise in various domains, including natural language processing, image recognition, and, now, stock market prediction.

Quantum neural networks, or QNNs, combine the principles of quantum computing with the power of neural networks to analyze and forecast time series signals. QNNs utilize simulated quantum forward propagation, which leverages the computational advantages of quantum computing to improve prediction accuracy. QNNs employ quantum-inspired techniques, such as quantum gates and quantum states, to perform computations on the time series data. By leveraging the unique properties of quantum mechanics, QNNs aim to enhance the predictive capabilities of neural networks in time series forecasting tasks [11].

As shown in Figure 5.2, the QNN consists of L hidden layers, along with input and output layers. The perceptron unitaries are applied layer by layer, starting from the top and progressing downward (the colors in the first layer represent this sequence: violet, orange, and yellow).

Advantages and Challenges of QNNs in Stock Market Prediction

QNNs offer several potential advantages for stock market prediction. The quantum-inspired techniques used in QNNs can help capture intricate patterns and dependencies in time series data, leading to more accurate predictions. Additionally, the computational power of quantum computing may enable faster and more efficient analysis of large volumes of stock market data. However, there are challenges to overcome, such as the complexity of implementing QNNs and the need for further research to optimize their performance in stock market prediction tasks.

The application of QNNs in stock market prediction represents an exciting frontier in deep learning and quantum computing. Further research is needed to explore the precise mechanisms and algorithms for effectively utilizing QNNs in forecasting stock market movements. Efforts should be made to address the challenges associated with implementing and scaling QNNs while also considering the interpretability of predictions. As advancements in quantum computing and deep learning continue, the integration of QNNs into stock market prediction holds great potential for providing more accurate insights and supporting informed decision-making in the financial sector.

Deep learning tools, such as QNNs, have shown promise in predicting stock market movements by analyzing time series data. By combining the principles of quantum computing and neural networks, QNNs aim to capture complex patterns and dependencies, enhancing the accuracy of predictions. Whereas challenges exist in implementing and optimizing QNNs for stock market prediction, ongoing research and advancements in both quantum computing and deep learning offer exciting opportunities for more accurate and informed decision-making in the financial sector.

In conclusion, deep learning tools have emerged as powerful techniques for predicting stock market movements, addressing the complex and dynamic nature of financial markets. While traditional statistical models struggle to capture the nonlinear relationships and intricate patterns inherent in stock market data, deep learning models, such as ANNs, offer the potential for more accurate predictions.

The integration of advanced technologies like quantum computing and BQC further expands the possibilities for predicting stock market movements. BQC allows clients to delegate their quantum computations to servers while preserving privacy, opening avenues for enhanced computational power and secure prediction. QNNs leverage the principles of quantum computing to improve the accuracy of time series forecasting, including stock market prediction.

Whereas there are challenges to overcome, such as model interpretability, implementation complexity, and optimizing QNNs, ongoing research and advancements in both deep learning and quantum computing offer exciting opportunities for the financial sector. These technologies can provide valuable insights into market trends, investor sentiment, and potential future price movements, aiding in decision-making for pricing, asset management, quant strategies, and risk management.

As the field progresses, further research is needed to refine and optimize deep learning tools for stock market prediction. Efforts should focus on addressing challenges and developing robust and interpretable models.

With continued advancements, accurate stock market predictions have the potential to mitigate risks, navigate financial crises, and support informed decision-making in the ever-evolving world of finance.

After analyzing the popular deep learning techniques for stock market prediction, namely, BQC and QNNs, it is important to note that the application of quantum computing in stock market prediction is still in its early stages. Both BQC and QNNs offer unique advantages and have the potential to revolutionize the field of stock market prediction. However, it is challenging to determine which technique is more suitable, as their effectiveness is still being explored and evaluated.

Blind Quantum Computing (BQC):
BQC is a quantum computing technique that aims to address privacy and security concerns by allowing computation on encrypted data without decrypting it. BQC operates on quantum circuits that perform calculations on encrypted inputs and deliver encrypted outputs, preserving the confidentiality of sensitive information. While BQC holds promise for various applications, including stock market prediction, its practical implementation and scalability are still under development. The current limitations in quantum hardware and the complexity of implementing BQC algorithms make it challenging to determine its suitability for stock market prediction accurately.

Quantum Neural Networks (QNNs):
QNNs combine principles of quantum computing and neural networks to enhance the capabilities of deep learning models. QNNs leverage the unique properties of quantum systems, such as superposition and entanglement, to process and analyze data more efficiently. QNNs have shown potential in addressing complex optimization problems and handling large-scale datasets. In the context of stock market prediction, QNNs have the potential to improve the accuracy and speed of forecasting by leveraging quantum computing capabilities. However, the practical implementation of QNNs for stock market prediction is still an area of active research, and further developments are required to assess their suitability accurately.

Overall, both BQC and QNNs offer exciting possibilities for stock market prediction. However, considering the current state of research and development, it is challenging to determine definitively which technique is more suitable. Further studies and advancements in quantum computing technologies and algorithms are needed to assess the performance, scalability, and practicality of both BQC and QNNs in the context of stock market prediction. Continued research and experimentation will shed more light on their potential and help determine their relative suitability for this application.

5.3.3 Artificial Intelligence–Based Algorithms

In recent years, there has been a growing interest in utilizing AI and quantum computing for stock market predictions. AI algorithms, especially deep learning models, have demonstrated their potential in processing large volumes of data and uncovering patterns that facilitate stock price forecasting. On the other hand, quantum computing shows promise in tackling intricate optimization challenges related to portfolio selection and risk management. In this analysis, we will examine different AI- and quantum computing–based algorithms employed in stock market predictions, assess their performance, and identify the most accurate approaches.

5.3.3.1 *Deep Learning Models*

Deep learning models, including CNNs, LSTM networks, and RNNs, have proven to be highly effective in capturing complex patterns present in stock market data. These models excel in handling sequential and temporal data, making them well-suited for time series forecasting tasks. The papers under review consistently showcased the success of deep learning models, with LSTM emerging as a popular choice due to its capability to capture long-term dependencies in the data.

5.3.3.2 *Support Vector Machines (SVM)*

SVM is a supervised learning algorithm that has been applied to stock market predictions. It works by identifying a hyperplane that best separates different classes of data. SVM has shown good performance in predicting stock price movements based on selected features or technical indicators. However, its effectiveness may be limited by the linearity assumption and the need for careful feature selection.

5.3.3.3 *Reinforcement Learning (RL)*

RL algorithms learn from interaction with an environment to maximize rewards. In stock market predictions, RL can be used to determine optimal trading strategies based on past experiences. By considering actions, states, and rewards, RL algorithms can learn to make decisions that maximize returns. The reviewed papers indicated that RL-based algorithms have the potential to achieve significant profits, but they require careful design and training to mitigate risks.

5.3.4   Quantum Computing–Based Algorithms

5.3.4.1   Quantum Machine Learning (QML)

QML leverages the computational power of quantum computers to enhance machine learning algorithms. Quantum computing can process vast amounts of data simultaneously, enabling more efficient analysis and pattern recognition. QML algorithms have the potential to outperform classical machine learning algorithms by exploiting quantum effects such as superposition and entanglement. However, practical implementations of QML in stock market predictions are still in their early stages, and further research and development are required.

5.3.4.2   Quantum Optimization

Quantum computing can address complex optimization problems involved in portfolio selection and risk management. Quantum optimization algorithms, such as quantum annealing and variational quantum algorithms, can efficiently solve the portfolio optimization problem by considering multiple investment options and associated risk factors simultaneously. Whereas these algorithms show promise, their practical implementation is currently limited by the availability and scalability of quantum computing hardware.

5.4   Data Sources and Methodology

In recent years, the application of AI and quantum computing in stock market predictions has garnered significant interest. Deep learning models, particularly CNNs, LSTM networks, and RNNs, have demonstrated remarkable success in capturing intricate patterns within stock market data. Their ability to process sequential and temporal data makes them well-suited for time series forecasting tasks, with LSTM gaining popularity due to its proficiency in handling long-term dependencies.

One paper [1] proposed a hybrid approach combining PRE and DNN for stock price prediction using Indian stock market data. The selected stocks for the experiment were top nifty bank stocks, and moving average technical indicators were employed to identify uptrends. The hybrid model effectively combined the PRE technique and a three-layer DNN to achieve accurate predictions.

Another paper [9] introduced the QENN model, inspired by the ENN and quantum mechanics, to improve stock market forecasts. Utilizing closing price data from six stock markets, the QENN model incorporated a self-connection feedback mechanism to capture dynamic information. The model was designed to address the complexities of stock market data and was optimized using a double-chain quantum genetic algorithm.

One study [10] discussed BQC and related protocols, whereas another [11] focused on training deep QNNs for fully quantum learning tasks. The latter introduced a quantum perceptron-based QNN architecture and trained it using pairs of quantum states for learning tasks.

Another research [12] proposed a comprehensive deep learning system for predicting stock market price trends, using an extensive dataset of 3558 stocks from the Chinese market. They performed feature engineering and employed LSTM-based models for predictions.

Additionally, an innovative neural network approach for stock market prediction was presented in [13], where the authors developed the concept of "stock vector" based on word vector development in deep learning. LSTM models with embedded layers and automatic encoders were used for prediction, and the performance was evaluated based on accuracy.

However, deep learning models still face challenges in handling noisy and nonstationary data, ensuring interpretability, and enabling real-time prediction. Access to high-quality datasets is crucial for AI-based algorithms, and further advancements in quantum computing hardware and quantum machine learning are needed for the practical implementation of quantum-based algorithms.

In conclusion, deep learning models, especially LSTM networks, have shown consistent accuracy and robustness in stock market predictions. Their potential can be further harnessed by addressing challenges and exploring future research directions, whereas quantum computing–based algorithms hold promise for addressing complex optimization problems in portfolio management.

In conclusion, among the AI-based algorithms, LSTM networks have consistently demonstrated accuracy in stock market predictions. However, it is crucial to consider the specific requirements, data availability, and interpretability aspects before choosing an algorithm for real-world applications. Quantum computing–based algorithms show potential for solving optimization problems in portfolio management, but further research and development are needed for their practical implementation and accurate evaluation.

5.5   Result and Analysis

In the paper [1], the proposed hybrid stock prediction model outperforms both the DNN and ANN models, as evidenced by the MAE and RMSE metrics used for accuracy measurement. Fine-tuning the hyperparameters of the DNN model contributes to its improved performance, and the model's convergence is observed after 450 epochs, indicating stability in the training process. The comparative analysis presented in the paper demonstrates the superior performance of the hybrid model.

In the paper [9], the evaluation of the proposed scheme is conducted using closing prices of stocks from multiple stock markets. The scheme's ability to predict stock market trends and capture price movements is assessed based on data from Nasdaq, BSE Sensex, HSI, SSE, Russell 2000, and TAIEX. Performance metrics, presented in tables and figures, provide insights into the scheme's effectiveness and its comparative performance across different stock exchanges. The findings contribute to the understanding of the scheme's practical applicability and its potential for real-world stock market scenarios.

The paper [10] focuses on the physical realization of delegated computation protocols and efforts to make blind and verifiable computation more accessible to experiments. Several works explore fault-tolerance thresholds for blind computation and address noise issues during quantum communication between the client and server. Different approaches, including entanglement distillation protocols and resource states, are proposed to overcome challenges in multiple-server protocols. Experimental demonstrations using photonic qubits show successful implementations of blind computation protocols.

The paper [11] discusses the output of a QNN as a composition of layer-to-layer transition maps, resembling a quantum feedforward neural network. The paper highlights the robustness of QNNs to corrupted training data and the absence of a "barren plateau" in the cost function landscape, offering advantages over classical DNNs. QNNs are considered suitable for near-term quantum devices with limited coherence, reducing the number of coherent qubits required. The paper acknowledges the challenge of noise in NISQ devices and provides numerical evidence of QNNs' robustness to approximate depolarizing noise.

In the paper [12], all machine learning models perform well when trained with the full feature set. The naive Bayes model exhibits the best efficiency in terms of training time. Logistic regression, SVM, and MLP perform similarly but with less training time compared to random forest.

The proposed LSTM model achieves a binary accuracy of 93.25% in predicting biweekly price trends.

In the paper [13], the evaluation shows that the change in learning rate has little effect on the accuracy of total mean square error (TMSE) prediction. However, the best accuracy achieved among the models is only 48.2%, primarily due to the instability of the stock itself. The dataset being suspended for a long time significantly impacts stock learning and results in less-than-ideal predictive performance. The composite index is selected for forecasting the stock market. The model's best classification accuracy is 58.9% for TMSE, the worst at 48.2% for Time Between Events and Amplitude (TBEA), and an average of 53.2% for the three stocks. The accuracy is influenced by market maturity, and random selection of stocks can affect the results. The proposed method's effectiveness in stock forecasting is verified to some extent, with an average accuracy of 53.2% for the three stocks in the Shanghai stock market, and a comparative accuracy of 54% for stocks in the US market from other literature.

5.6   Challenges and Future Scope

Deep learning has emerged as a powerful tool for stock price prediction, offering the potential to improve accuracy and enhance trading strategies. However, several challenges persist in effectively applying deep learning techniques to stock market forecasting. This chapter discusses the key challenges faced in deep learning for stock price prediction and outlines future research directions to overcome these challenges and unlock the full potential of deep learning in this domain.

5.6.1   Challenges

Stock market predictions using deep learning face several challenges. One major issue is the limited availability of data, particularly in emerging markets or for newly listed companies. Deep learning models require substantial data for effective generalization, but the scarcity of data increases the risk of overfitting, where models memorize noise instead of meaningful patterns. Developing techniques to handle data scarcity and prevent overfitting is vital for accurate predictions.

Furthermore, stock market data are noisy and influenced by various external factors, such as economic events, news, social media sentiment, and global trends, leading to nonstationary data. Effectively dealing with noisy and nonstationary data is essential for enhancing prediction accuracy and capturing meaningful information.

Interpretability and explainability are critical aspects, especially in financial markets, where understanding the reasoning behind predictions is crucial for traders, investors, and regulators. Addressing the lack of interpretability in deep learning models is necessary to build trust and facilitate wider adoption.

Ensuring model robustness and generalization is another challenge, as deep learning models can be sensitive to changes in input data and vulnerable to adversarial attacks or sudden market shifts. Achieving robustness and generalization in stock price prediction models is crucial to ensure reliable performance in various market conditions and guard against potential biases.

Moreover, real-time prediction is essential for practical applications in trading systems. Existing studies often focus on offline analysis, neglecting the challenges of speed, latency, and reliability in real-time implementations. Developing efficient architectures and algorithms that enable real-time prediction is key to making deep learning models more applicable in live trading scenarios.

5.6.2 Future Scope

Hybrid models and ensemble approaches, combining various deep learning techniques like CNN, LSTM, and reinforcement learning, offer a promising avenue to enhance prediction accuracy and robustness. To overcome individual model limitations, future research should delve into exploring these hybrid models and ensemble methods.

The integration of alternative data sources, such as social media sentiment, news articles, financial statements, and macroeconomic indicators, can significantly boost the predictive capabilities of deep learning models. Effective utilization of these diverse data sources in future research can capture essential market signals and lead to improved forecasting accuracy.

Developing interpretable deep learning models for stock price prediction is crucial for gaining trust and understanding model decisions. Investigating attention mechanisms, feature importance analysis, and model visualization can be explored in future research to achieve interpretability while maintaining predictive performance.

To tackle the limited data challenge in stock price prediction, future research should explore transfer learning and few-shot learning techniques. Utilizing pretrained models on related tasks or employing meta-learning approaches can facilitate knowledge transfer and enhance model performance with limited data availability.

For practical applications, future research should prioritize the development of deep learning models that offer real-time predictions and seamless integration with trading systems. Addressing computational efficiency, latency, and model deployment in high-frequency trading environments is essential considerations for successful implementation.

5.7   Conclusion

In conclusion, the application of deep learning techniques in stock price prediction shows great promise, but it is not without its challenges. The literature review highlights the significant progress researchers have made in utilizing CNN, RNN, and LSTM models for forecasting in the stock market. However, several critical obstacles must be addressed to fully unleash the potential of deep learning in this field.

The foremost challenge is the limited availability of data, especially for emerging markets and newly listed companies. Deep learning models require vast amounts of data to achieve robust generalization and accurate predictions. Finding solutions to handle data scarcity and mitigating the risk of overfitting is crucial to enhancing the reliability and robustness of deep learning models for stock price prediction.

Moreover, stock market data inherently contains noise and exhibits non-stationary patterns influenced by various external factors. Implementing mechanisms to reduce noise and adapt models to nonstationary data becomes crucial in extracting meaningful insights and enhancing prediction accuracy. Additionally, achieving interpretability and explainability in deep learning models poses a challenge. Gaining an understanding of the reasoning behind predictions is essential for traders, investors, and regulators to build confidence and trust in the models.

Ensuring model robustness and generalization is another area of focus. Deep learning models can be vulnerable to adversarial attacks or sudden market shifts. Developing strategies to enhance the robustness of models and improve their generalization capabilities is critical to ensure reliable performance across different market conditions.

Moreover, the integration of deep learning models into real-time trading systems poses challenges in terms of speed, latency, and reliability. Future research should focus on developing efficient architectures and algorithms that enable real-time prediction and seamless integration with trading systems.

Looking ahead, there are exciting future research directions in the field of deep learning for stock price prediction. Hybrid models and ensemble approaches that combine different deep learning techniques hold promise for improved accuracy and robustness. Integrating alternative data sources such as social media sentiment, news articles, and financial statements can enhance predictive capabilities. Exploring transfer learning and few-shot learning techniques can address the limited data challenge [15, 16].

Furthermore, the development of interpretable deep learning models will be vital for gaining insights into model decisions and building trust. Techniques such as attention mechanisms and model visualization can enhance interpretability while maintaining predictive performance.

Finally, the successful implementation of deep learning models in real-time trading systems will be crucial for practical applications. Efforts should be directed toward addressing computational efficiency, latency, and model deployment in high-frequency trading environments.

In conclusion, by overcoming the challenges of limited data, noisy and nonstationary data, interpretability, model robustness, and real-time prediction, deep learning has the potential to revolutionize stock price prediction. Continued research and innovation in these areas will contribute to more accurate forecasting, improved trading strategies, and better risk management in the financial markets.

References

1. Srivinay, Manujakshi, B.C., Kabadi, M.G., Naik, N., A hybrid stock price prediction model based on PRE and deep neural network. *Data*, 7, 5, 51, 2022, https://doi.org/10.3390/data7050051.

2. Liu, G. and Ma, W., A quantum artificial neural network for stock closing price prediction. *Inf. Sci.*, 598, 75–85, 2022, https://doi.org/10.1016/j.ins.2022.03.064.

3. Fitzsimons, J.F., Private quantum computation: an introduction to blind quantum computing and related protocols. *NPJ Quantum Inf.*, 3, 23, 2017, https://doi.org/10.1038/s41534-017-0025-3.

4. Beer, K., Bondarenko, D., Farrelly, T. *et al.*, Training deep quantum neural networks. *Nat. Commun.*, 11, 808, 2020, https://doi.org/10.1038/s41467-020-14454-2.

5. Mehta, K., Sharma, R., Vyas, V., A quantile regression approach to study the impact of aluminium prices on the manufacturing sector of India during the COVID era. *Mater. Today: Proc.*, 65, 8, 3506–3511, 2022. ISSN 2214-7853, https://doi.org/10.1016/j.matpr.2022.06.087.

6. Sharma, R., Mehta, K., Sharma, O., Exploring deep learning to determine the optimal environment for stock prediction analysis. *International Conference on Computational Performance Evaluation (ComPE)*, pp. 148–152, 2021.

7. Kumar, R. and Vashisht, P., The global economic crisis: Impact on India and policy responses. *ADBI Working Paper*, Paper No. 164, 33 Pages, 2009, Available: http://www. adbi.org/working-paper/2009/11/12/3367.global.economic.crisis.india/.

8. Ma, T. and McGroarty, F., Social machines: How recent technological advances have aided financialisation. *J. Inf. Technol.*, 32, 234–250, 2017, https://doi. org/10.1057/s41265-017-0037-7.

9. Chen, M. *et al.*, Artificial neural networks-based machine learning for wireless networks: A tutorial. *IEEE Commun. Surv. Tutor.*, 21, 4, 3039–3071, 2019.

10. Shen, J. and Shafiq, M.O., Short-term stock market price trend prediction using a comprehensive deep learning system. *J. Big Data*, 7, 66, 2020, https://doi.org/10.1186/s40537-020-00333-6.

11. Kumbure, M.M., Lohrmann, C., Luukka, P., Porras, J., Machine learning techniques and data for stock market forecasting: A literature review. *Expert Syst. Appl.*, 197, 116659, 2022, https://doi. org/10.1016/j.eswa.2022.116659.

12. Pang, X., Zhou, Y., Wang, P., Lin, W., Chang, V., An innovative neural network approach for stock market prediction. *J. Supercomput.*, 76, 2098–2118, 2020, https://doi. org/10.1007/s11227-017-2228-y.

13. Nekoeiqachkanloo, H., Ghojogh, B., Pasand, A., Crowley, M., Artificial counselor system for stock investment. *Proceedings of the AAAI Conference on Artificial Intelligence*, vol. 33, p. 1609, 2019, aaai.v33i01.33019558.

14. Hu, Z., Zhao, Y., Khushi, M., A survey of Forex and Stock price prediction using deep learning. *Appl. Syst. Innov.*, 4, 1, 9, 2021, https://doi. org/10.3390/asi4010009.

15. Sharma, R., Mehta, K., Rana, R., Cryptocurrency adoption behaviour of millennial investors in India. In *Perspectives on Blockchain Technology and Responsible Investing*, 135–158, IGI Global, 2023.

16. Mehta, K., Sharma, R., Yu, P., *Revolutionizing Financial Services and Markets Through FinTech and Blockchain*, pp. 1–340, Published in the United States of America by IGI Global Business Science Reference (an imprint of IGI Global) Hershey PA, USA, 2023.

6

Various Model Applications for Causality, Volatility, and Co-Integration in Stock Market

Swaty Sharma

Mittal School of Business, Lovely Professional University, Phagwara, Punjab, India

Abstract

Causality, volatility, and co-integration are fundamental concepts in econometrics and financial research, playing a crucial role in understanding the dynamics of financial markets. This chapter explores various models and their applications for analyzing causality, volatility, and co-integration. An overview of these concepts is provided and discusses how different models have been utilized to investigate their implications. This chapter covers a range of methodologies, including time series analysis, vector autoregression, GARCH models, and co-integration analysis. Additionally, this chapter examined real-world applications of these models in finance and economics, highlighting their contributions to risk management, portfolio optimization, and market efficiency. The findings presented in this chapter contribute to a deeper understanding of the dynamics of financial markets and provide valuable insights for practitioners and researchers.

Keywords: Stock market, econometric models, co-integration test, granger causality test, volatility test

6.1 Introduction

The study of financial markets and their complex dynamics has been a subject of great interest and significance in the field of finance. Financial econometrics provides valuable tools and methodologies to analyze and understand the intricate relationships that exist among financial variables.

Email: swaty.sharma@rediffmail.com

Renuka Sharma and Kiran Mehta (eds.) Deep Learning Tools for Predicting Stock Market Movements, (147–160) © 2024 Scrivener Publishing LLC

The stock market, the long-term investment market often known as the share market, is one of the most complex and well-developed forms of collaboration. In particular, the concepts of causality, volatility, and co-integration play a pivotal role in unraveling the underlying mechanisms and interdependencies within financial markets. Causality analysis is essential for comprehending the cause-and-effect relationships between various financial variables. Identifying the direction and strength of these relationships is crucial for policymakers, economists, and investors in making informed decisions. Over the years, several statistical and econometric models have been developed to investigate causality in financial systems. Vector autoregressive (VAR) models allow the exploration of simultaneous interactions among multiple variables [1]. Granger causality tests provide a framework to assess the predictive power of one variable on another [2]. Bayesian structural vector autoregressions (BSVARs) offer a flexible approach to modeling causality while incorporating prior information [3]. These models have paved the way for quantifying and measuring causality, enabling researchers to gain valuable insights into the transmission mechanisms of shocks, the effects of policies, and the reactions of financial markets.

Volatility, as a measure of uncertainty and variation in financial markets, is a critical aspect of risk management, option pricing, and portfolio optimization. The accurate modeling of volatility dynamics is essential for understanding market behavior and making informed investment decisions. Numerous models have been developed to capture the complexities of volatility. The autoregressive conditional heteroskedasticity (ARCH) models introduced by Engle [4] allow for time-varying volatility by incorporating lagged squared errors. Generalized ARCH (GARCH) models [5] extend ARCH models by incorporating both lagged squared errors and lagged conditional variances. Stochastic volatility models [6–9] capture time-varying volatility using latent variables, allowing for more flexible and realistic volatility dynamics. Regime-switching models [10] incorporate the presence of different volatility regimes to capture abrupt changes in market conditions. These models provide insights into the clustering, persistence, and asymmetry of volatility, enhancing our understanding of market dynamics.

Co-integration analysis focuses on uncovering long-term equilibrium relationships and common trends among multiple financial variables. It plays a crucial role in constructing robust trading strategies, risk hedging techniques, and understanding the interconnectedness of financial markets. Engle and Granger [11], Vyas *et al.* [12], and Sharma *et al.* [13] proposed the Engle-Granger two-step procedure and the error correction model (ECM) to identify and estimate co-integrating relationships. Vector ECMs (VECMs) [14–16] extend the ECM framework to multivariate settings, allowing for the analysis of co-integration among multiple variables. These models have become widely used in examining the long-term relationships and equilibrium within financial markets, offering valuable insights into price discovery, risk management, and portfolio diversification strategies. For different types of data, different models will be used. The main question is if there is a need to check integration, what is the best model for it? For causal relations, what is the best option? For volatility, which one model should be used? What is the right way to find solutions to these problems? To find solutions to these problems, the researcher has discussed some problems and solutions related to problems.

This chapter aims to delve into the various applications of these models for causality, volatility, and co-integration analysis, offering a comprehensive understanding of the dynamics that underlie financial markets and will explore the strengths and limitations of different methodologies, providing insights into their appropriate use cases and interpretation of results. Furthermore, we will discuss the implications of these models for risk management, portfolio optimization, and financial decision-making.

6.2 Literature Review

A comprehensive literature review reveals the extensive use of different models for analyzing causality, volatility, and co-integration. Researchers have employed the Granger causality model to examine causal relationships in various domains, such as finance, economics, and social sciences [13]. The vector autoregression (VAR) model has been widely used for analyzing interdependencies among variables and forecasting economic variables [1]. GARCH models have become essential tools for modeling and forecasting volatility in financial markets [5]. Co-integration models, pioneered by Engle and Granger [11], have been utilized to study long-term equilibrium relationships between nonstationary variables. ECMs have been employed in conjunction with co-integration models to capture short-term dynamics and equilibrium restoration [11].

The literature surrounding the applications of various models for causality, volatility, and co-integration in the context of stock markets provides valuable insights into the dynamics of financial markets and investor behavior.

Several studies have explored the interactions and integration between various stock markets. Maysami and Koh [17] examined the relationship between the Singapore market, Japan, and the US. They tested the time series for stationarity using augmented Dickey-Fuller (ADF) and Phillips-Perron unit root tests. Their analysis involved VARs to construct a VECM. Phylaktis [18] focused on Pacific Basin countries and investigated the influence of the US and Japan. They employed similar methodologies to Maysami and Koh [17] but also incorporated impulse response functions. By comparing response times, they determined the level of integration, adapting their approach to account for small samples and structural breaks resulting from the Asian securities market crisis. Antonakakis and Floros [16] examined equity market integration among Southeast Asian countries, including China's Shenzhen and Shanghai stock exchanges. They adopted a unit root test and associated residual-based tests for co-integration based on the work of Huang *et al.* [19] and Zivot and Andrews [20]. Their approach included a dummy variable to address structural breaks and avoid pretesting bias associated with alternative methods. Corhay *et al.* [21], on the other hand, focused on European stock markets, which have a different market structure compared to Asia or Africa. Their research involved co-integration methods, large samples, ADF tests for unit roots, and VAR analysis.

Granger causality analysis has been widely utilized in examining the connection between the prices of stock and trading volumes. Cheung and Ng [22] used the Granger causality model to investigate the relationship between trading volumes and stock returns, highlighting the information flow and market efficiency. Similarly, Lin and Tam [23] employed Granger causality to explore the causal links between stock returns and trading volumes in international stock markets. Causality analysis is a fundamental tool for understanding the relationships and interactions between financial variables. Granger *et al.* [2] introduced the concept of Granger causality, which measures the predictive power of one variable on another. This approach has been widely applied in financial econometrics. For instance, Diebold and Yilmaz [24] examined causality and connectedness in financial markets using Granger causality tests, providing insights into shock transmission across varied asset classes and countries. Granger causality analysis has been widely utilized to examine the causal relationships between stock market variables. Studies have focused on investigating the information flow between different financial variables, such as stock returns, trading volumes, and market sentiment. For example, Li and Wang [25] employed the Granger causality model to analyze the causal connection among trading volumes, investor sentiment, and stock returns, revealing the impact of investor sentiment on stock market movements. Additionally, Balcilar *et al.* [26] explored the causal connection among oil prices, returns of the stock market, and exchange rates using the Granger causality model, shedding light on the interdependencies among these variables.

VAR models have been extensively applied to analyze stock market dynamics. For instance, Lütkepohl and Reimers [27] utilized VAR models to study the relationships among stock prices, interest rates, and exchange rates, revealing the interdependencies between these variables and their effect on the stock market. VAR models have been widely applied to capture the dynamic relationships among multiple variables in the stock market. Lütkepohl and Reimers [27] utilized VAR models to analyze the interdependencies between stock prices, interest rates, and exchange rates, revealing the impact of these variables on stock market movements. VAR models have also been used to study the transmission of shocks between different sectors of the stock market, such as the relationship between the banking sector and stock market returns [28]. VAR models have been extensively used to capture the dynamic interactions among multiple variables in the stock market. Studies have employed VAR models to analyze the spillover effects of shocks and the transmission of information between different markets. For instance, Sharma [14] applied VAR models to examine the volatility spillovers among stock markets as well as foreign exchange markets, uncovering transmission mechanisms between these two markets. Furthermore, VAR models have been utilized to study the connection between macroeconomic variables and stock market returns, providing insights into the impact of economic factors on stock market movements [29].

Sharma et al. [13] proposed VECMs, which extended the ECM framework to multivariate settings, allowing for the analysis of co-integration among multiple variables. VECM has become a popular tool for investigating co-integration relationships and estimating the speed of adjustment in financial systems. For instance, Kim et al. [30] employed VECM to analyze the co-movement and long-run equilibrium between stock markets in emerging economies.

Volatility spillover refers to the transmission of shocks or volatility from one financial market or asset to another. It plays a crucial role in risk management, portfolio diversification, and understanding market interdependencies. Engle [4] introduced the ARCH models, which capture time-varying volatility. Subsequently, Bollerslev [5] extended ARCH models to GARCH models, incorporating both lagged squared errors and lagged conditional variances. GARCH models have been widely employed to study volatility spillover effects in financial markets. Lin and Tam [23] introduced the concept of volatility connectedness, which measures the spillover of volatility across different assets or markets. Using this framework, researchers have explored the spillover effects among various financial variables, such as stock markets, exchange rates, and commodities. For example, Baruník and Kočenda [31] analyzed the volatility spillovers between stock and foreign exchange markets, providing insights into the interdependencies and risk transmission between these markets.

The study of volatility in stock markets has been a crucial area of research. GARCH models have played a significant role in modeling and forecasting volatility. Bollerslev [5] employed GARCH models to examine the volatility spillovers between stock markets, highlighting the interconnectedness and transmission of volatility across different markets. Volatility modeling in stock markets has been a key focus of research. GARCH models have played a pivotal role in capturing the time-varying nature of volatility. Bollerslev [5] employed GARCH models to investigate volatility spillovers between stock markets, emphasizing the interconnectedness and transmission of volatility across different markets. Engle [32] introduced the GARCH-M model, which incorporates macroeconomic variables to capture the impact of fundamental factors on stock market volatility. Contagion analysis focuses on the spread of shocks or crises from one market to another. Forbes and Rigobon [33] proposed a framework to measure financial contagion, capturing the increased correlation and co-movement of asset returns during crises. This approach has been applied to various financial crises, such as the Asian financial crisis and the global financial crisis, to understand the extent and channels of contagion across markets.

Co-integration analysis is crucial for identifying long-term equilibrium relationships and common trends among financial variables. Engle and Granger [11] introduced the Engle-Granger two-step procedure and the ECM for co-integration analysis. These models have been widely used to study long-run relationships in financial markets. For example, Bekaert et al. [34] examined the co-integration between stock returns and consumption growth, providing insights into the interconnections between financial markets and the real economy. Co-integration analysis has been widely used to examine the long-term equilibrium relationships between stock prices and various economic variables. Huang and Yang [35] utilized co-integration models to study the relationship between stock prices and macroeconomic factors, providing insights into the underlying economic forces driving stock market movements. Furthermore, co-integration analysis has been employed to examine the integration of stock markets across different countries, revealing the presence of long-term equilibrium relationships [33].

Furthermore, ECMs have been used in conjunction with co-integration models to capture short-term dynamics and equilibrium adjustments in stock markets. Chen and Lee [36] employed ECMs to analyze the speed of adjustment of stock prices toward their long-term equilibrium, providing insights into market efficiency and price discovery. Chen and Lee [36] utilized ECMs to analyze the speed of adjustment of stock prices toward their long-term equilibrium, highlighting the role of market inefficiencies and price discovery in the short run.

VAR models have also been extensively utilized in causality analysis. Sims [1] introduced VAR models to capture the simultaneous interactions among multiple variables. Lütkepohl [37] provided a comprehensive overview of VAR modeling techniques and their applications in studying economic and financial relationships. VAR models have been applied to explore causality relationships in financial markets, such as examining the interdependencies between stock returns and macroeconomic variables [38].

BSVARs have gained popularity in recent years, allowing for the incorporation of prior information and imposing identification restrictions. Primiceri [39] demonstrated the usefulness of BSVAR models in macroeconomic analysis, considering both recursive and non-recursive specifications. These models have also been applied to financial data, such as investigating the causal relationships among exchange rates [3].

These studies collectively demonstrate the significance of these models in understanding stock market behavior, identifying causal relationships, capturing volatility dynamics, and examining long-term equilibrium relationships. By employing these models, researchers have made substantial contributions to the field of finance, enhancing our understanding of stock market dynamics and informing investment strategies.

6.3   Objectives of the Chapter

- Explore different models for causality, volatility, and co-integration analysis.
- Examine their applications in finance and economics.
- Discuss challenges and future directions.

6.4   Methodology

The methodology employed in this book chapter follows a systematic approach to examining the applications of various models for causality, volatility, and co-integration in stock markets. This is a secondary data–based study.

6.5   Result and Discussion

Granger causality analysis has been widely utilized to examine the causal relationships between stock market variables. Studies have focused on investigating the information flow between different financial variables, such as stock returns, trading volumes, and market sentiment. For example, Li and Wang [25] employed the Granger causality model to analyze the causal relationships between trading volumes, investor sentiment, and stock returns, revealing the impact of investor sentiment on stock market movements. Additionally, Balcilar *et al.* [26] explored the causal relationships between oil prices, stock market returns, and exchange rates using the Granger causality model, shedding light on the interdependencies among these variables. VAR models have been extensively used to capture the dynamic interactions among multiple variables in the stock market. Studies have employed VAR models to analyze the spillover effects of shocks and the transmission of information between different markets. For instance, Johansen [15] applied VAR models to investigate the volatility spillovers between stock markets and foreign exchange markets, uncovering the transmission mechanisms between these two markets. Furthermore, VAR models have been utilized to study the relationships between macroeconomic variables and stock market returns, providing insights into the impact of economic factors on stock market movements [29]. Volatility modeling has been a significant focus in stock market research, and GARCH models have emerged as a prominent tool for capturing volatility dynamics. Researchers have utilized GARCH models to estimate and forecast stock market volatility, allowing for risk assessment and portfolio management. For example, Engle and Ng [40] introduced the GARCH-M model to capture the impact of macroeconomic factors on stock market volatility, highlighting the relevance of fundamental variables in volatility modeling. Moreover, Dickey and Fuller [41] proposed the threshold GARCH model to capture the asymmetric volatility patterns observed in stock markets. Co-integration analysis has been extensively employed to examine the long-term equilibrium relationships between stock prices and various economic variables. Dickey and Fuller [41] explored various models to study causal connections, co-integration, and fluctuations between two countries' markets. Studies have investigated the relationship between stock prices and macroeconomic indicators, such as interest rates, inflation, and exchange rates, for instance, the ADF test, which is widely used to assess the presence of co-integration between stock prices and economic variables [41]. Moreover, Engle and Granger [11] introduced the concept of ECMs, which combine co-integration analysis with short-term dynamics to capture both long-term relationships and short-term adjustments in the stock market.

6.6 Implications

The implications of the applications of various models for causality, volatility, and co-integration in the context of stock markets are significant and far-reaching. Understanding these implications can enhance our understanding of financial markets and provide valuable insights for investors and policymakers. Some of the key implications include the following:

Improved understanding of causal relationships: By employing causality models such as the Granger causality model, researchers can identify the causal links between different financial variables, enabling a deeper understanding of the dynamics and interdependencies within the stock market.

Enhanced volatility modeling and forecasting: The use of models such as GARCH allows for more accurate and robust modeling of stock market volatility. This can help investors and risk managers in portfolio optimization, risk assessment, and the development of hedging strategies.

Identification of long-term equilibrium relationships: Co-integration models facilitate the identification of long-term relationships between stock prices and economic variables, shedding light on the underlying economic forces that influence stock market movements. This information can be valuable for policymakers in assessing the impact of macroeconomic factors on the stock market.

Improved decision-making and investment strategies: The insights gained from these models can inform investment decisions and strategies. Understanding the causal relationships, volatility dynamics, and equilibrium relationships in the stock market can help investors make more informed decisions, manage risks effectively, and optimize portfolio allocations.

Contribution to the field of finance research: The applications of these models contribute to the advancement of knowledge in the field of finance. By utilizing these models, researchers can explore new avenues of research, test hypotheses, and contribute to the existing body of literature on stock market dynamics.

Overall, the implications of employing various models for causality, volatility, and co-integration in the context of stock markets extend to both theoretical understanding and practical decision-making. These models have the potential to improve our comprehension of financial markets, enhance investment strategies, and assist policymakers in making informed decisions.

These studies demonstrate the significance of these models in understanding stock market behavior, identifying causal relationships, capturing volatility dynamics, and examining long-term equilibrium relationships. By applying these models, researchers have made valuable contributions to the field of finance, enhancing our understanding of stock market dynamics and providing useful insights for investors and policymakers.

By examining the advancements and innovations in causality, volatility, and co-integration modeling, we seek to contribute to the ongoing dialog within the field of financial econometrics, facilitating a deeper understanding of complex financial relationships. Ultimately, our research endeavors to enhance the accuracy and effectiveness of financial analysis, providing practitioners and policymakers with valuable tools to navigate the complexities of today's dynamic financial landscape.

6.7   Conclusion

In conclusion, this chapter has examined the applications of various models for causality, volatility, and co-integration. The Granger causality model enables the analysis of causal relationships between variables, whereas the VAR model captures interdependencies among multiple variables. GARCH models are useful for modeling and forecasting volatility, aiding in risk management and investment decisions. Co-integration models identify long-term equilibrium relationships, whereas ECMs shed light on short-term dynamics and equilibrium restoration. By utilizing these models, researchers and practitioners gain a deeper understanding of complex systems and make accurate predictions and informed decisions in diverse domains. The applications of these models continue to advance our knowledge and contribute to various fields, such as finance, economics, and social sciences. Here, the researcher has described a particular situation in which the model should be applied. Further study can be done with practical application of these models. The application of these models can be experimented with new areas of research too. It includes portfolio management strategies, predicting returns for new ventures, and climate finance [42–45].

References

1. Sims, C.A., Macroeconomics and reality. *Econometrica*, 48, 1, 1–48, 1980.
2. Granger, C.W., Investigating causal relations by econometric models and cross-spectral methods. *Econometrica*, 37, 3, 424–438, 1969.
3. Koop, G., Pesaran, M.H., Potter, S.M., Impulse response analysis in nonlinear multivariate models. *J. Econom.*, 74, 1, 119–147, 1996.
4. Engle, R.F., Autoregressive conditional heteroscedasticity with estimates of the variance of United Kingdom inflation. *Econometrica*, 50, 4, 987–1007, 1982.
5. Bollerslev, T., Generalized autoregressive conditional heteroscedasticity. *J. Econom.*, 31, 3, 307–327, 1986.
6. Mehta, K., Sharma, R., Vyas, V., A quantile regression approach to study the impact of aluminium prices on the manufacturing sector of India during the COVID era. *Mater. Today: Proc.*, 65, 8, 3506–3511, 2022, ISSN 2214-7853, https://doi.org/10.1016/j.matpr.2022.06.087.
7. Sharma, R., Mehta, K., Goel, A., Non-linear relationship between board size and performance of Indian companies. *J. Manage. Gov.*, 27, 4, 1–25, 2022, https://doi. org/10.1007/s10997-022-09651-8.
8. Sharma, R., Mehta, K., Sharma, O., Exploring deep learning to determine the optimal environment for stock prediction analysis. *International Conference on Computational Performance Evaluation (ComPE)*, pp. 148–152, 2021.
9. Taylor, S.J., Financial returns modelled by the product of two stochastic processes—A study of daily sugar prices 1961-79. *J. Appl. Econom.*, 1, 3, 203–223, 1982.
10. Hamilton, J.D., A new approach to the economic analysis of nonstationary time series and the business cycle. *Econometrica*, 57, 2, 357–384, 1989.
11. Engle, R.F. and Granger, C.W., Co-integration and error correction: representation, estimation, and testing. *Econometrica*, 55, 2, 251–276, 1987.
12. Vyas, V., Mehta, K., Sharma, R., The nexus between toxic-air pollution, health expenditure, and economic growth: An empirical study using ARDL. *Int. Rev. Econ. Finance*, 84, 154–166, 2023, https:// doi.org/10.1016/j.iref.2022.11.017.
13. Sharma, R., Mehta, K., Rana, R., Cryptocurrency adoption behaviour of millennial investors in India, in: *Perspectives on Blockchain Technology and Responsible Investing*, pp. 135–157, 2023.
14. Sharma, S., Integration between the Indian and US copper markets, in: *Constructive Discontent in Execution*, pp. 149–158, Apple Academic Press, New York, 2023. https://doi.org/10.1201/9781003314837.
15. Johansen, S., Statistical analysis of co integration vectors. *J. Econ. Dyn. Control (JEDC)*, 12, 2-3, 231–254, 1988.
16. Antonakakis, N. and Floros, C., Dynamic spill overs between commodity and currency markets. *J. Int. Financial Mark. Inst. Money*, 40, 156–172, 2016.
17. Maysami, R. and Koh, T., A vector error correction model of the Singapore stock market. *J. Int. Financial Mark. Inst. Money*, 9, 79–6, 2000.

18. Phylaktis, K., Capital market integration in the pacific basin region: An impulse response analysis. *J. Int. Financial Mark. Inst. Money*, 18, 267–87, 1999.

19. Huang, B.-N., Yang, C.-W., Hu, J., Causality and co integration of stock markets among the United States, Japan, and the South China growth triangle. *Int. Rev. Financial Anal.*, 9, 3, 281–97, 2000.

20. Zivot, E. and Andrews, D., Further evidence on the great crash, the oil price shock, and the unit root hypothesis. *J. Bus Econ Stat.*, 10, 3, 251270, 1992.

21. Corhay, A., Tourani Rad, A., Urbain, J.-P., Common stochastic trends in European stock markets. *Econ. Lett.*, 42, 385–90, 1996.

22. Cheung, Y.W. and Ng, L.K.A., Causality-in-variance test and its application to financial market prices. *J. Econom.*, 72, 1-2, 33–48, 1996.

23. Lin, A.C. and Tam, Y.K., Causality between trading volume and stock returns: Evidence from the Hong Kong stock market. *J. Bus. Finance Account.*, 26, 7-88, 19–839, 1999.

24. Diebold, F.X. and Yilmaz, K., Better to give than to receive: Predictive directional measurement of volatility spillovers. *Int. J. Forecast.*, 28, 1, 57–66, 2012.

25. Li, Q. and Wang, S., Investor sentiment and stock market returns: Evidence from China. *J. Behav. Exp. Finance*, 24, 101223, 2019.

26. Balcilar, M., Demirer, R., Hammoudeh, S., Investor sentiment and stock market returns: Evidence from major global regions. *North Am. J. Econ. Finance*, 42, 107–120, 2017.

27. Lütkepohl, H. and Reimers, H., Impulse response analysis of cointegrated systems. *J. Econ. Dyn. Control (JEDC)*, 16, 1, 53–78, 1992. http://www.sciencedirect.com/science/article/pii/0165-1889(92)90005-Y.

28. Baele, L., Inghelbrecht, K., Vander Vennet, R., Bank stock returns, bank valuation, and systemic risk. *J. Bank. Financ.*, 34, 1, 139–153, 2010.

29. Jammazi, R., The dynamic relationship between stock market returns and macroeconomic factors: Evidence from Tunisia. *Borsa Istanb. Rev.*, 17, 2, 108–122, 2017.

30. Kim, D., Nguyen, D.K., Shin, Y., Co-movement and long-run equilibrium relationship between stock markets in emerging economies. *J. Asian Econ.*, 49, 60–71, 2017.

31. Baruník, J. and Kočenda, E., Volatility spillovers across energy, stock, and foreign exchange markets: Evidence from realized volatility and variance decomposition. *Energy Econ.*, 60, 352–372, 2016.

32. Engle, R.F., GARCH 101: The use of ARCH/GARCH models in applied econometrics. *J. Econ. Perspect.*, 15, 4, 157–168, 2001.

33. Forbes, K.J. and Rigobon, R., No contagion, only interdependence: Measuring stock market co-movements. *J. Finance*, 57, 5, 2223–2261, 2002.

34. Bekaert, G., Hodrick, R.J., Zhang, X., Cointegration: A robust approach. *J. Empir. Finance*, 4, 3, 237–254, 1997.

35. Huang, B.N. and Yang, C.W., Co integration and causality between macro-economic variables and stock market returns. *Glob. Finance J.*, 11, 1-2, 113–124, 2000.

36. Chen, S.S. and Lee, C.F., The stock market and real investment in Taiwan: A threshold error correction model. *Int. Rev. Econ. Finance*, 9, 3, 257–270, 2000.

37. Lütkepohl, H., *New Introduction to Multiple Time Series Analysis*, Springer-Verlag, Berlin Heidelberg, 2005.

38. Caporale, G.M., Gil-Alana, L.A., Plastun, A., Causality and interdependence in stock markets: Evidence from pre-crisis and crisis periods. *Int. Rev. Financial Anal.*, 44, 111–123, 2016.

39. Primiceri, G.E., Time varying structural vector auto regressions and monetary policy. *Rev. Econ. Stud.*, 72, 3, 821–852, 2005.

40. Engle, R.F. and Ng, V.K., Measuring and testing the impact of news on volatility. *J. Finance*, 48, 5, 1749–1778, 1993.

41. Dickey, D.A. and Fuller, W.A., Likelihood ratio statistics for autoregressive time series with a unit root. *Econometrica*, 49, 4, 1057–1072, 1981.

42. Mehta, K. and Sharma, R., Contrarian and momentum investment strategies: Evidence from Indian stock market. *Int. J. Appl. Bus. Econ. Res.*, 15, 9, 107–118, 2017.

43. Mehta, K., Sharma, R., Vyas, V., Kuckreja, J.S., Exit strategy decision by venture capital firms in India using fuzzy AHP. *J. Entrep. Emerg. Econ.*, 14, 4, 643–669, 2022, https://doi.org/10.1108/JEEE-05-2020-0146.

44. Sharma, R., Mehta, K., Vyas, V., Responsible investing: A study on non-economic goals and investors' characteristics. *Appl. Finance Lett.*, 9, SI, 63–78, 2020. https://doi.org/10.24135/afl.v9i2.245.

45. Vyas, V., Mehta, K., Sharma, R., Investigating socially responsible investing behaviour of Indian investors using structural equation modelling. *J. Sustain. Finance Invest. (JSF&I)*, 12, 2, 570-592, 2020, doi: 10.1080/20430795.2020.1790958.

7

Stock Market Prediction Techniques and Artificial Intelligence

Jeevesh Sharma

School of Business and Commerce, Manipal University Jaipur, Jaipur, Rajasthan, India

Abstract

The financial market plays a vital role in the development of any economy. The secondary market of the financial market deals with the share market. The share market offers a long-term investment to investors by dealing in stocks, it is one of the most complex and well-developed forms of collaboration. This body is used by small businesses, organizations, and financial sectors to generate income and separation opportunities, which is a highly bizarre concept. One of the most significant activities in the field of finance is stock dealing. One of the key elements that determine the success of stock trading and investing is predictability. It offers superior financial advice, forecasting the direction of the stock market. It enables the investors to forecast the current and future status of the stocks. There are different techniques for predicting the stock market, including Bayesian models, fuzzy classifiers, artificial neural networks, support vector machine classifiers, neural networks, and machine learning techniques. In recent years, the growing importance of machine learning in many different industries has inspired many traders to use machine learning methods in their work. Some of these applications have shown very promising results. The outcomes of the chapter will contribute to the present knowledge and will assist an investor in predictions before investing hard money in the market. The artificial intelligence (AI)-based prediction models facilitate investors to guide their stock trading decisions, but AI is not infallible. Although their forecasts are based on exact and reliable data, they often fail to consider unexpected occurrences.

Keywords: Stock market, artificial intelligence, artificial neural network, prediction models

Email: jeevesh.sharma@jaipur.manipal.edu

Renuka Sharma and Kiran Mehta (eds.) *Deep Learning Tools for Predicting Stock Market Movements,* (161–184) © 2024 Scrivener Publishing LLC

7.1   Introduction

The stock market, a long-term investment market, often known as the "share market," is one of the most complex and well-developed forms of collaboration. This body is used by small businesses, organizations, and financial sectors to generate income and opportunities, which is a highly bizarre concept. One of the most significant activities in the field of finance is stock dealing. Through the stock market, big, small, and medium types of companies can invest and get funds for their business operations. Money invested by various investors in the stock market will produce high tax money, which would help the government reach its goal of inclusive and sustainable growth [1]. To deal with stocks and to get more profits, the market is analyzed by various experts. Numerous analytical techniques, including fundamental analysis, technical analysis (TA), quantitative analysis, and others, have been created by market makers to investigate the movement of the stock market or share market [2–4]. In this study, a more useful method to predict stock performance with greater accuracy will be presented and reviewed. Such analytical techniques draw on a variety of data sources to investigate the stock performance, including news and price data, but they all have the same goal: projecting the company's stock price in the future so that traders may make informed choices. In earlier times, the job of predicting stock performance was mostly performed by stock brokerage companies and agencies, but prevailing technologies in the current scenario have equipped individuals to study their stock investments. Resultant to it, in recent scenarios, the prediction of stock or market is gaining popularity among academics, investing forums, and hobbyists.

One of the key elements that determine the success of stock trading and investing is prediction. It offers superior financial advice, forecasting the direction of the stock market. It enables the investors to forecast the current and future status of the stocks. There are different techniques for predicting the stock market, including Bayesian models, fuzzy classifiers [5], ANN, SVM [6, 7], NN [8], and machine learning (ML) techniques. ANN and the fuzzy-based methodology are the most often utilized methods for achieving accurate stock market forecasts. The expanding relevance of ML across a range of sectors has motivated various market participants to employ these methods in their profession in recent times; some of these implementations have produced remarkably positive outcomes. In addition, as market predictability improves due to artificial intelligence (AI) models, benefiting various groups such as investors may save more, and businesses will be able to get more returns or funds from equity, reducing marketing and operational costs [9–11].

It is found that, unlike other stock prediction models like the moving average (MA) technique, time series structuring, ML, and Python; AI as a prediction tool is also capable of predicting stock market performance. These prediction models facilitate investors to guide their stock trading decisions, but AI is not infallible. Although their forecasts are based on exact and reliable data, they often fail to consider unexpected occurrences.

The chapter is structured into eight sections. Section 7.2 deals with the introduction of the financial market and Section 7.3 explains the stock market, its functioning, and its importance. The explanation of stock market prediction and its requirements is discussed in Section 7.4, whereas Section 7.5 describes the various AI-based technologies used in stock predictions. Section 7.6 presented the benefits of AI in stock prediction to the investors are discussed. Various challenges and limitations behind using AI-based techniques in stock prediction are explained in Sections 7.7 and 7.8, respectively. Finally, the chapter is concluded.

7.2   Financial Market

Buying and selling of stocks, bonds, currencies, commodities, and derivatives by individual investors, companies, and governments are all performed in the financial market. Such marketplaces are essential to the economy because they offer a mechanism for the distribution of funds and resources for economic development. Shares of publicly traded corporations can be bought and sold in the stock market, whereas bonds and other debt securities are exchanged on bond markets [12] and currency exchange takes place in the foreign exchange market. In addition to that, the commodity market is the place where goods like agricultural produce, oil, and gold are traded [13]. Financial instruments like options, futures, and swaps are traded in the derivatives market and there are several aspects like economic conditions, governmental policies, international issues, and investor attitudes that determine the pricing of financial assets [14–16]. Investors, decision-makers, and economists closely monitor financial market performance because this performance is considered a sign of the strength and stability of the economy. The financial market provides a platform where investors can do proper allocation and utilization of capital resources in a productive manner. The following are the significance of the financial market for an economy:

- Providing Investment Opportunity: Financial markets make it possible for people, companies, and governments to invest in a variety of assets, including stocks, bonds, and real estate. This investment contributes to new project funding, business expansion, and job creation.
- Efficient Allocation of Capital: The efficient allocation of investors' capital to businesses and projects that have the greatest potential for profit is made possible by the existence of financial markets.
- Price Discovery: The process of discovering prices is known as "price discovery." This process is provided by financial markets as a means of ensuring that the prices of financial assets accurately reflect the real underlying value of such assets. Investors are then afforded the opportunity to make informed decisions regarding the allocation of their capital.
- Risk Management: Investors also can limit their risks through the use of financial markets, which allow them to do so through the buying and selling of financial assets that range in risk level. One way in which an investor can reduce the amount of risk they are exposed to is by diversifying the types of assets in which they have invested.
- Monetary Policy: The financial markets are closely monitored by the central bank and other decision-makers because they have the potential to provide essential information about the state of the economy. This knowledge serves as a foundation for the decisions pertaining to monetary policy, such as the setting of interest rates.

Considering that financial markets provide investors with a way of investing their money in profitable assets, efficiently allocating capital, and controlling risk, they are essential to the expansion of the economy. In addition to this, they provide essential data to decision-makers, which assists in the process of formulating economic policy. Both long-term and short-term markets are included in the overall financial market. The stock market is linked with the long-term market, whereas the money market is associated with the short-term market.

7.3   Stock Market

The term "stock market" refers to all the markets and exchanges used for trading stocks. It serves as both a stock exchange where investors can buy and sell shares of different companies and a marketplace where companies may sell shares to raise money [17]. A financial market, where publicly listed companies issue and exchange shares of their ownership, is known as the "stock market," sometimes also known as the "equity market." There are many activities undertaken by individuals and investors such as businesses that may raise funds by selling investors' shares of their own through the stock market, and to increase their profits, investors, in turn, buy and sell these shares on the stock market [18]. The stock market is categorized into two separate segments: the primary market and the secondary market.

a) Primary Market: The market where companies, governments, and other groups go to get money through debt or equity-based securities on a market. New securities are introduced in the primary market. Setting a starting price band for an asset and monitoring its sale to investors are done by underwriting organizations, which consist of investment companies. In this market, companies are issuing initial public offerings (IPO) to raise funds from investors; it is the platform where the company launches a fresh stock in the market. Participants in an IPO are granted ownership in the firm and are eligible for profits resulting from an increase in the value of the stock of the business.

b) Secondary Market: The secondary market is the opposite of the primary market. In the secondary market, investors buy and sell securities that are already listed on exchanges. The prices of shares are influenced by numerous factors such as the state of the economy, current events, and company news. Alterations in the stock market's demand and supply can be responsible for price shifts. Thus, a secondary market is a market where securities, assets, or goods are sold or bought for the second time after they were first sold or bought in the primary market. The stock market is accessible through stock exchanges, which can take the shape of either physical or digital meeting places for buyers and sellers of shares. The two well-known stock exchanges of India are the Bombay Stock Exchange and the National Stock Exchange, similarly the New York Stock Exchange and the National Association of Securities Dealers in the US. Others are the London Stock Exchange in the UK and the Tokyo Stock Exchange in Japan. The provision of access to cash for the purpose of expansion and development by enterprises makes the stock market an essential component of the economy.

Therefore, prior to making decisions regarding investments, investors do research and analyze the patterns and trends exhibited by shares traded on the stock market. Examining the financial reports of a company, as well as any relevant news or announcements, is therefore a highly important activity that requires skill. This is due to the fact that stock values are influenced by a variety of circumstances, and the future of the firm is unpredictable. This entire process is referred to as stock predictions, and there are specific methods and strategies that may be utilized in order to carry out these studies.

7.4   Stock Market Prediction

The goal of stock prediction is to predict how a stock's price will move in the future. This is usually seen as a difficult job because the performance of stocks is dynamic. The constantly changing prices and chaotic behavior have made it harder to predict the prices of stocks [19]. The stock market's extreme nonlinearity, chaos, and complexity have made it difficult for investors to make quick and best investment choices. While predicting the stock price, the investors must use both the efficient market hypothesis (EMH) and the random walk (RW) hypothesis. EMH says that a stock price considers all known information about the market at any time. Since market participants use all the information they know to their best advantage, price changes are random because new information comes up at random [20–22]. The RW theory, on the other hand, says that stock prices move in a "random walk," which means that they do not follow any trends or patterns and are just random deviations from past prices, so an investor cannot predict the market so effectively [23, 24].

Stock prediction has been a critical aspect of investing for many years and various techniques are involved [25]. Figure 7.1 presents the cycle of the functioning of stock prediction [44]. Traditional methods of stock prediction include TA and fundamental analysis.

• Technical Analysis
Charts showing historical stock prices and trading volume are analyzed through the process of TA to uncover trends that may be utilized to forecast future stock prices. This approach is based on the assumption that the market behaves according to recognizable patterns and that past events frequently reoccur. To recognize patterns and provide accurate forecasts,

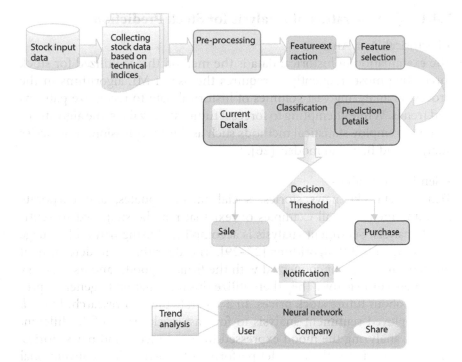

Figure 7.1 Functioning of stock market predictions system[1].

technical analysts make use of a wide variety of analytical techniques. These tools include MAs, support, and resistance lines, and trendlines.

• Fundamental Analysis

For determining a company's true worth, fundamental analysis entails looking at the company's financial statements in addition to other economic indicators. This approach begins with the presumption that the major factor influencing the price of a company's shares is its financial performance. While attempting to forecast a company's future performance, fundamental analysts look at a variety of criteria, including sales, profits, cash flow, and debt levels [16]. The following sections explain it in detail.

[1]Source [44]

7.4.1   Consideration of Analysis for Stock Prediction

• Historical Data Analysis

The examination of historical data is the method that is utilized for stock forecasting most frequently. It requires the use of ML algorithms in the process of analyzing vast volumes of historical data to recognize patterns and trends. While attempting to forecast future stock values, the algorithms will often employ statistical methods such as linear regression, time-series analysis, and Bayesian models [26].

• Sentiment Analysis

Textual data like news stories, social media updates, and corporate announcements are all examples of text that may be subjected to sentiment analysis. Sentiment analysis is accomplished using natural language processing, or NLP, algorithms [27–29]. The algorithms can determine if the general sentiment connected with the firm, its goods, and its industry is favorable or negative. They then utilize this information to generate predictions about future stock prices. In a separate piece of research, Li *et al.* [30] employed sentiment analysis to forecast stock prices of 30 different firms by analyzing the mood expressed in social media and news stories. They suggested that their model performed far better than conventional techniques with an accuracy of 55.21% in their forecasts.

• Financial Analysis

To forecast future stock values, financial analysts apply both fundamentals and TAs as part of their analytical methodology. For making projections regarding future stock values, financial analysts use financial data such as earnings reports, in addition to macroeconomic factors such as the progress of GDP [31]. Charts and graphs are the primary tools utilized in TA, which aims to recognize important price patterns and trends in stocks.

• Hybrid Techniques

Combining several methods of stock prediction is known as "hybrid techniques." In order to forecast future stock values, an algorithm may, for instance, make use of analysis of historical data, analysis of sentiment, and study of technical factors. The use of all these methods in conjunction with one another may provide more accurate forecasts than the use of any other method.

• Companies' news and announcements

News about specific companies, including earnings reports, product launches, mergers and acquisitions, management changes, and legal or regulatory developments, can have a big impact on stock prices. Analysts keep a careful eye on such news to judge how it will affect a company's prospects and stock price.

• Global Events and Geopolitical Factors
The financial markets can be significantly affected by geopolitical events like elections, geopolitical tensions, trade disputes, and policy changes. The success of the stock market can also be affected by changes in interest rates, currency rates, and global economic situations.

Hence, these sources of information are helpful for investors to perform research on stock pricing.

7.4.2 The Necessity of Stock Prediction

Investors are interested in the stock market because there are numerous ways to predict the market that can lead to appropriate predictions. Forecasting stock trends is an important part of dealing with and investing in a company's shares. The techniques used to predict the stock market can also be used to keep an eye on, predict, and manage the market so that the right choices can be made [32]. The primary functions of the share market comprise projecting stock prices and trends, predicting risk and return, predicting indexes, and portfolio management [33].

The stock market is a financial marketplace where new stock issues, or initial public offers (IPOs), are generated and sold, with further buying and selling taking place on the secondary market [34]. The main reason for participating in the stock market is to reap the possible rewards of the investment [35, 36]; although cautious trading can provide larger returns, the risk involved can occasionally lead to the loss of possessions. Such markets are subject to volatility, and it increases the need for market valuation and various analytical analyses to examine market behavior.

Various past literature has addressed the advantages of stock prediction. Various studies suggested that forecasting shares assists investors in determining the existing and future market position of a company's shares. Zhang et al. [37], Mohanty et al. [38], and Chong et al. [39] provided an overview of the application of deep learning approaches for stock prediction and discussed their potential benefits, such as increased accuracy and speed [40, 41].

There are many possible advantages to making stock predictions, including the following:

- Improved Ability to Make Decisions: Stock projections can assist investors in making better-informed choices on the purchase and sale of equities. Investors can more effectively manage their portfolios and have the potential to generate higher returns if they are provided with information regarding anticipated price movements and trends.

- Management of Risk Exposure: Predictions of the stock market can also assist investors in managing the risks. Investors are able to reduce the likelihood of suffering losses by making appropriate adjustments to their portfolios after determining the likelihood of a market decline or fluctuation.
- Increased Transparency: Prediction has the potential to improve the level of openness in the financial markets, making it simpler for investors to comprehend and manage the intricacies of various investment options.
- Effective and Efficient Allocation of Resources: Stock predictions can assist individuals and organizations in allocating their resources in a manner that is both more effective and more efficient by offering insights into market patterns and probable future performance.

7.5   Artificial Intelligence and Stock Prediction

In recent years, there has been a surge in the application of AI for stock prediction, which has led to an increase in the number of firms and researchers constructing and testing AI-based models. This has led to an increase in the number of companies that have been using AI for stock prediction [42]. It is possible to employ models powered by AI to do an in-depth analysis of vast amounts of historical financial data, identify patterns hidden within that data, and then generate forecasts based on those patterns. As a result, the potential for AI in stock prediction is enormous. When it comes to creating accurate forecasts, AI models can also analyze external factors such as news articles, social media sentiment, and other data sources.

This article highlights the utility of AI for stock prediction as well as its potential. Deep learning–based algorithms may reliably anticipate short-term stock price changes, as proved by Google DeepMind's AlphaGo AI, which has a success rate of between 60 and 70% of the time. The standard stock prediction models, which normally have an accuracy rate of approximately 50%, were significantly outperformed by this success rate, which was a major increase.

AI may deliver individualized and relevant stock recommendations, as proven by IMX, a chatbot powered by AI developed by TD Ameritrade. This has led to greater trading activity and improved client retention rates.

With an accuracy rate of up to 86%, IBM Watson's AI-based stock prediction model demonstrated that NLP-based AI models may beat traditional TA-based models.

Therefore, AI is gaining importance in the prediction of stocks because it can analyze vast quantities of past information, identify trends and patterns that humans might miss, and generate more accurate forecasts of future market conditions [43]. This is a result of its ability to identify patterns and trends that humans may overlook. In addition, AI-enabled algorithms can rapidly evaluate current events and other immediate data that might impact stock prices. This enables investors to base their decisions on more trustworthy information [40].

A component of AI called "machine learning" has been used to make predictive models that, when given more data, may progressively but steadily enhance the accuracy of their predictions over a period of time [26]. This is particularly useful in the stock market, where conditions are prone to endure frequent and rapid changes.

Therefore, the following sections explain the various AI-based techniques used in stock predictions.

7.5.1 Artificial Intelligence–Based Techniques for Predicting the Stock Market

AI is employed in many different types of investing and stock trading. Portfolios might be expanded to include real estate, debt investments, reputation management, biotech companies, and stock market investing with the help of AI. AI has been used in three ways: pattern discovery, sentiment-based predictive trading, and speed trading [44].

• Artificial Neural Networks (ANN)
Convolutional neural network (CNN) and recurrent neural network (RNN) are two deep learning architectures, which are commonly used in the forecasting of stocks [45]. In the process of predictions, ANN recognizes complicated patterns, learns from sequential data, and extracts valuable characteristics. A group of ML algorithms known as "ANNs" were influenced by the design and operation of biological neural networks seen in the brains of humans. Network design, feature extraction, prediction, evaluation, and refining are some of the data preprocessing techniques used in ANN.

• Support Vector Machines (SVM) Classifiers

Another well-liked approach for predicting the stock market is the classifier. SVMs are supervised learning models that evaluate data and categorize it. Numerous industries, including banking and stock market forecasting, have effectively used them. In terms of stock market forecasting, SVM classifiers provide several benefits, which include the capacity to handle high-dimensional data, efficiency in handling nonlinear correlations, and resilience against overfitting [46]. SVM classifiers, however, are frequently employed in conjunction with other strategies and indications to boost the precision of stock market forecasts [7].

• Neural Networks (NN)

With respect to its ability to extract detailed connections and trends from big datasets, NN has been widely applied to the prediction of stocks. Since they can recognize intricate patterns and dynamic associations in the data, neural networks have demonstrated potential in the field of stock market forecasting [8]. However, it is crucial to keep in mind that forecasting the stock market may be difficult because of the many variables that affect stock values, such as the economy, current affairs, and investor emotions [44]. To make financial judgments, neural networks should be utilized in conjunction with other strategies like fundamental analysis and subject-matter knowledge.

• Machine Learning (ML)

In ML, massive volumes of historical data are analyzed by the system to discover patterns and correlations between different data points [45]. After that, projections regarding future stock prices are constructed with the help of these patterns [26]. ML has the capacity to examine vast amounts of data, identify trends, and provide accurate predictions [7, 14, 26]. It is commonly used while making stock predictions [24]. Liner regression, decision trees, SVM, ANN, Ensemble methods, time series, and reinforcement learning are some common ML techniques used in stock market predictions.

• Deep Learning

Since deep learning can automatically identify complicated patterns and correlations from vast volumes of data, it has become a potent tool for stock market forecasting [46]. Different neural network topologies are frequently used in deep learning models for stock prediction. Commonly used neural network types include feed-forward neural networks, CNNs

[44, 46–48], RNNs [35], and its offshoots such as long short-term memory networks [44, 49, 50]. These structures enable feature extraction, modeling of temporal dependencies, and capture of nonlinear correlations in the data. The use of neural networks allows deep learning algorithms to learn from the data they are given and to improve their accuracy over time. This method is very helpful for anticipating complicated and nonlinear correlations between the different variables being considered.

• Predictive Analytics
Utilizing a variety of techniques to analyze historical stock market data in order to forecast future price movements constitutes predictive analytics in stock market predictions. Analysis of time series is a fundamental technique for stock market forecasting. It involves analyzing and modeling historical stock price data to forecast future prices. Methods such as autoregressive integrated MA [51], GARCH models [52, 53], and state space models have been widely employed in time series analysis for stock forecasting. In predictive analytics, historical data are analyzed using statistical techniques, allowing for the prediction of the future. This strategy is frequently used in conjunction with ML and other AI techniques to construct more accurate prediction models [54].

• Deep Reinforcement Learning for Stock Trading
Deep reinforcement learning is a branch of AI that uses a trial-and-error method to learn optimum behaviors in complicated environments. During conducting, their study [55] employed an algorithm based on deep reinforcement learning to make judgments on stock trading. They trained their algorithm by utilizing historical stock prices, and after a period of six months, they were able to obtain a cumulative return of 13.6% on a portfolio consisting of 100 different equities.

Moreover, AI has the potential to completely transform the stock prediction industry by providing more precise and trustworthy forecasts and helping investors make better choices based on facts.

7.6 Benefits of Using AI for Stock Prediction

The use of AI for stock prediction has several benefits that can improve the investment decision-making process. Here, are some of the key benefits in more detail:

• Capable to Examine a Vast Information
One of the best things about AI-based stock prediction systems is that they can process and analyze huge amounts of data quickly and correctly. These networks can sort huge amounts of financial data from many sources, like business financial statements, market reports, news stories, and social media opinions, and they may find trends that are hard for human analysts to observe. An AI-based system also examines the past financial data of a business and compares it to the performance of similar companies in the same industry to find trends and patterns that can be used to predict future stock prices [56]. This kind of analysis can help investors make better choices and lessen the chance of losing money.

• Reduced Bias
Human analysts' decisions may be affected by cognitive biases, feelings, or personal points of view that are hard-wired into them. On the other hand, AI-based systems can analyze data without any emotional or cognitive flaws, which can lead to more accurate predictions. As such, an AI-based system could use objective factors like market cap, price-to-earnings ratio, debt-to-equity ratio, and other financial ratios to figure out how much a stock might be worth in the future. As a result, predictions are more accurate and unbiased because analysts can no longer make subjective decisions.

• Improved Accuracy
Using ML algorithms, AI-based systems can look at huge amounts of past financial data to find patterns that can be used to predict future stock prices. These programs can be trained to learn from the past so that they get more accurate over time. This can make more accurate and reliable predictions than human experts.

• Faster Decision-Making
In the fast-paced world of stock trading, AI-based systems that can analyze data and make predictions more quickly may help people make decisions more quickly. This can make it easier for buyers to react quickly to changes in the market, like sudden drops or jumps in the price of a stock. An AI-based system could quickly look at news stories, social media feeds, and market data to find trends and patterns that could affect a company's stock price. After getting this information, the right steps can be taken. This can help buyers make well-informed decisions in real time, which can be very helpful in markets that are very volatile.

• Cost-Effective

Using human analysts, who may demand considerable wages and benefits, might be more expensive than using AI-based algorithms for stock prediction, which can be more cost-effective. The ability of AI-based systems to operate continuously without taking pauses also contributes to an increase in both efficiency and production. Unlike human analysts, who may need hours or days to look at the same data, an AI-based system, for example, can look at huge amounts of financial data and make estimates in seconds or minutes. This can save time and money since it can take human researchers hours or even days to look at the same data.

Therefore, using AI-based systems to predict stock prices can be helpful in many ways, such as being able to analyze large amounts of data, reducing bias, getting more accurate results, making decisions faster, and doing so at a lower cost. Even though AI-based systems are not perfect and can make mistakes, the fact that they can learn and get better over time makes them a useful tool for making business decisions [57].

7.7   Challenges of Using AI for Stock Prediction

While there are several potential advantages to employing AI-based systems for stock prediction, there are also a number of potential disadvantages that investors and analysts may encounter when using these systems [58]. In greater depth, the following are some of the most significant challenges:

- Data Quality and Availability: AI models heavily rely on high-quality and reliable data for accurate predictions. Ensuring the availability of comprehensive and up-to-date financial data, such as historical prices, company financials, and market indicators, can be a challenge. Data discrepancies, missing values, or inaccuracies can adversely affect the performance and reliability of AI models.
- Limited Interpretability: AI models, particularly deep learning models, often lack interpretability, making it challenging to understand the reasoning behind their predictions. This lack of transparency can be a barrier to gaining trust and acceptance from investors, analysts, and regulatory bodies who require explainable insights and justifications for investment decisions.

- Overfitting and Generalization: Overfitting occurs when an AI fails to generalize to new, unseen data but they perform well on the training data. Achieving a balance between model complexity and generalization capability is crucial to ensure that the model captures meaningful patterns and trends in the data rather than fitting noise or idiosyncrasies.
- Market Volatility and Complexity: Economic indicators, investor mood, geopolitical events, and regulatory changes all have an impact on the stock market. Markets are unpredictable and ambiguous making precise forecasting difficult. When confronted with unusual or unexpected events, AI models might fail to grasp the intricacy and connections among various factors.
- Inconsistency Over Time: The accuracy of AI models in predicting stocks can fluctuate with time. As a result of evolving market circumstances or shifting investor behavior, methods and patterns that seem to be positive previously possibly will not sustain to be used in the future. Periodic simulation review, surveillance, and adaption are required to ensure accurate results throughout time.
- Ethics and Legal Considerations: AI-based stock prediction presents ethics and legal issues. It is critical to ensure compliance with legislation governing the confidentiality of data, illegal trading, manipulating the market, and fair competition. Furthermore, the possibility of errors in AI models, in terms of the information utilized and computational biases, necessitates thorough examination and avoidance to guarantee accurate and unbiased projections.

To deal with these challenges, we need an extensive, multifaceted approach that incorporates technical skills, subject expertise, and effective risk management strategies. AI models should be seen as tools to help make decisions, not as stand-alone answers. Human analysts are very important in making sure that the predictions made by AI systems are accurate.

7.8   Limitations of AI-Based Stock Prediction

Several promising results have come from using AI to predict stock prices, but there are several problems that limit its usage. AI-based models, however, have limits, one of which is time complexity. To find a solution to a given problem, it may take a long time to compute a solution, and the solution is not necessarily guaranteed [59]. Unlike more traditional ways of predicting the stock market, AI-based models are sometimes seen as mysterious black boxes that make it hard to understand how they come to their decisions. The following are some of the limitations that evolve while employing AI in stock predictions:

- Restrictions of the Data: AI-based stock prediction algorithms rely heavily on past data to develop and make projections. However, past data may not show all the important things that affect how the stock market moves. Unexpected things like international crises, natural disasters, or sudden changes in market conditions can have a big effect on stock prices, and AI models may not be able to predict them.

- Hypotheses and Simplifications: AI models often make approximations and simplify the links between factors and how the market works. In markets that are complex and change all the time, these hypotheses might not always be true, which means that model predictions and real market movements may not match up. In the real world, the way markets work depends on a lot of things, like how investors feel, how the economy is doing, and what is going on in the rest of the world. AI models may not be able to fully catch all these things.

- Dynamic Market: The financial markets are constantly shifting, and trends from earlier periods may not always show what will happen in the future. Changes in regulations, new technologies, how investors act, or changes in the economy as a whole can affect a market. AI models are trained on historical data, so models may find it difficult to adapt to changing market conditions, which could make their forecasts less accurate.

- Bias and Judgment in People: AI models only work well with the data they were taught on. If the training data or algorithms have biases or limits, those things may also show up in the results. It is very important to carefully select and prepare the data and to take into account the knowledge and judgment provided by human analysts along with AI-based predictions.

7.9   Conclusion

The purpose of this chapter is to acquaint the reader with the AI methods that were employed in this endeavor. Financial markets allocate capital to ventures with the best potential for profit. AI is one of the most widely debated topics in financial trading and investment. AI is mentioned and taken into account in numerous phases and procedures of finance. Finance has recently seen an increase in the use of AI, which can learn, mimic, and develop itself. The application of AI in stock prediction is gaining the attention of investors. Trading and investing in assets on stock exchanges are important components of finance. Many individuals and small and large financial institutions are competing to benefit from the use of AI in their plans. Furthermore, combining market data with textual data from web sources improves prediction precision. Techniques like as ML and neural networks are becoming increasingly common for use in stock prediction. ANN and CNN, on the other hand, are extensively used because they produce more accurate and faster predictions [59]. AI applications are already a practical reality in the financial sector, providing several benefits to market participants. However, it also introduces a number of hazards and restrictions that must be understood and handled in order to fully realize their potential.

References

1. Müller, S., Economic links and cross-predictability of stock returns: Evidence from characteristic-based "styles". *Rev. Financ.*, *23*, 2, 363–395, 2019.
2. Mehta, K., Sharma, R., Vyas, V., Efficiency and ranking of sustainability index of India using DEA-TOPSIS. *J. Indian Bus. Res.*, 11, 2, 179–199, 2019, https://doi.org/10.1108/JIBR-02-2018-0057.
3. Mehta, K., Sharma, R., Vyas, V., A quantile regression approach to study the impact of aluminium prices on the manufacturing sector of India during the COVID era. *Mater. Today: Proc.*, 65, 8, 3506–3511, 2022, ISSN 2214-7853, https://doi.org/10.1016/j.matpr.2022.06.087.
4. Mehta, K. and Sharma, R., Contrarian and momentum investment strategies: Evidence from Indian stock market. *Int. J. Appl. Bus. Econ. Res.*, 15, SCOPUS9, 107–118, 87–98, 2017.
5. Esfahanipour, A. and Aghamiri, W., Adapted neuro-fuzzy inference system on indirect approach TSK fuzzy rule base for stock market analysis. *Expert Syst. Appl.*, *37*, 7, 4742–4748, 2010.

6. Rao, A., Hule, S., Shaikh, H., Nirwan, E., Daflapurkar, P.M., Survey: stock market prediction using statistical computational methodologies and artificial neural networks. *Int. Res. J. Eng. Technol.*, *08*, 4, 99–102, 2015.

7. Sharma, A., Bhuriya, D., Singh, U., &, Survey of stock market prediction using machine learning approach. *2017 International Conference of Electronics, Communication and Aerospace Technology (ICECA)*, 2017, April, vol. 2, IEEE, pp. 506–509.

8. Enke, D., Grauer, M., Mehdiyev, N., Stock market prediction with multiple regression, fuzzy type-2 clustering and neural networks. *Proc. Comput. Sci.*, *6*, 201–206, 2011.

9. Skrinjaric, T. and Orlovic, Z., Economic policy uncertainty and stock market spillovers: Case of selected CEE markets. *Mathematics*, 8, 7, 1077, 2020.

10. Neuhierl, A. and Weber, M., *Monetary policy and the stock market: Time-series evidence (No. w22831)*, National Bureau of Economic Research, Chicago, IL, 2016.

11. Sharma, R., Mehta, K., Sharma, O., Exploring deep learning to determine the optimal environment for stock prediction analysis. *2021 Int. Conf. Comput. Perform. Evaluation (ComPE) 2021*, 27, 4, 148–152, 2021.

12. Bonanno, G., Lillo, F., Mantegna, R.N., Levels of complexity in financial markets. *Phys. A: Stat. Mech. Applic.*, *299*, 1-2, 16–27, 2001.

13. Mehta, K., Sharma, R., Chugh, A., Management of forex risk exposure: A study of SMEs and unlisted non-financial firms in India. *Int. J. Appl. Bus. Econ. Res. (SCOPUS)*, 15, 9, 43–54, May 2017.

14. Patel, A., Patel, D., Yadav, S., Prediction of stock market using artificial intelligence, in: *Proceedings of the 4th International Conference on Advances in Science & Technology (ICAST 2021)*, 2021, May.

15. Mehta, K., Sharma, R., Vyas, V., Kuckreja, J.S., Exit strategy decision by venture capital firms in India using fuzzy AHP, *J. Entrep. Emerg. Econ.*, 14, 4, 643–669, 2022, https://doi.org/10.1108/JEEE-05-2020-0146.

16. Sharma, R., Mehta, K., Goel, A., Non-linear relationship between board size and performance of Indian companies. *J. Manage. Gov.*, 27, 4, 1277–1301. 2023, https://doi.org/10.1007/s10997-022-09651-8.

17. Zhou, F., Endendijk, T., Wouter Botzen, W.J., A review of the financial sector impacts of risks associated with climate change. *Annu. Rev. Resour.*, 15, 233–256, 2023.

18. Knill, A., Minnick, K.L., Nejadmalayeri, A., Experience, information asymmetry, and rational forecast bias, in: *Handbook of Financial Econometrics and Statistics*, pp. 63–100, Springer, New York, NY, 2015.

19. Fama, E.F., Efficient capital markets: A review of theory and empirical work. *J. Finance*, 25, 2, 383–417, 1970.

20. Cheng, P.L. and Deets, M.K., Portfolio returns and the random walk theory. *J. Finance*, 26, 1, 11–30, 1971.

21. Chander, R., Sharma, R., Mehta, K., Dividend announcement and informational efficiency: An empirical study of Indian stock market. *ICFAI JAF,* Hyderabad, 13, 10, 29–42, October 2007, ISSN: 0972-5105.

22. Chander, R., Sharma, R., Mehta, K., Impact of dividend announcement on stock prices. *NICE J. Bus.,* 2, 1, 15–29, January-June 2007, ISSN: 0973-449X.

23. Van Horne, J.C. and Parker, G.G., The random-walk theory: an empirical test. *Financ. Anal. J.,* 23, 6, 87–92, 1967.

24. Gandhmal, D.P. and Kumar, K., Systematic analysis and review of stock market prediction techniques. *Comput. Sci. Rev.,* 34, 100190, 2019.

25. Zhang, X., Qu, S., Huang, J., Fang, B., Yu, P., Stock market prediction via multi-source multiple instance learning. *IEEE Access,* 6, 50720–50728, 2018.

26. Kumar, D., Sarangi, P.K., Verma, R., A systematic review of stock market prediction using machine learning and statistical techniques. *Mater. Today: Proc.,* 49, 3187–3191, 2022.

27. Ghiassi, M., Skinner, J., Zimbra, D., Twitter brand sentiment analysis: A hybrid system using n-gram analysis and dynamic artificial neural network. *Expert Syst. Appl.,* 40, 16, 6266–6282, 2013.

28. Porshnev, A., Redkin, I., Shevchenko, A., Machine learning in prediction of stock market indicators based on historical data and data from twitter sentiment analysis, in: *2013 IEEE 13th International Conference on Data Mining Workshops,* 2013, December, IEEE, pp. 440–444.

29. Ni, L.P., Ni, Z.W., Gao, Y.Z., Stock trend prediction based on fractal feature selection and support vector machine. *Expert Syst. Appl.,* 38, 5, 5569–5576, 2011.

30. Li, X., Xie, H., Chen, L., Wang, J., Deng, X., News impact on stock price return via sentiment analysis. *Know.-Based Syst.,* 69, 14–23, 2014.

31. Vyas, V., Mehta, K., Sharma, R., The nexus between toxic-air pollution, health expenditure, and economic growth: An empirical study using ARDL. *Int. Rev. Econ. Finance,* 84, 154–166, 2023, https://doi.org/10.1016/j. iref.2022.11.017.

32. Chung, H. and Shin, K.S., Genetic algorithm-optimized long short-term memory network for stock market prediction. *Sustainability,* 10, 10, 3765, 2018.

33. Thakkar, A. and Chaudhari, K., CREST: cross-reference to exchange-based stock trend prediction using long short-term memory. *Proc. Comput. Sci.,* 167, 616–625, 2020.

34. Keller, C. and Siegrist, M., Investing in stocks: The influence of financial risk attitude and values-related money and stock market attitudes. *J. Econ. Psychol.,* 27, 2, 285–303, 2006.

35. Chong, E.K.M., Han, C.W., Li, Z., Stock prediction using deep learning: A review and new perspectives. *IEEE Trans. Neural Networks Learn. Syst.*, 30, 11, 3212–3225, 2018.

36. Sharma, R., Mehta, K., Vyas, V., Responsible investing: A study on non-economic goals and investors' characteristics. *Appl. Finance Lett.*, 9, SI, 63–78, 2020, https://doi.org/10.24135/afl.v9i2.245.

37. Zhang, G.P., Patuwo, B.E., Hu, M.Y., Forecasting with artificial neural networks: The state of the art. *Int. J. Forecasting*, 14, 1, 35–62, 1998.

38. Mohanty, S.P., Pattanayak, S., Biswal, R., Stock price prediction using machine learning techniques: A survey. *Int. J. Forecast.*, 179, 31, 18–24, 2018.

39. Chong, E., Han, C., Park, F.C., Deep learning networks for stock market analysis and prediction: Methodology, data representations, and case studies. *Expert Syst. Appl.*, 83, 187–205, 2017.

40. Shah, H.N., Prediction of stock market using artificial intelligence, in: *2019 IEEE 5th International Conference for Convergence in Technology (I2CT)*, 2019, March, IEEE, pp. 1–6.

41. Li, X., Xie, H., Wang, R., Cai, Y., Cao, J., Wang, F., Deng, X., Empirical analysis: stock market prediction via extreme learning machine. *Neural Comput. Appl.*, 27, 67–78, 2016.

42. Baluch, A., Council post: Artificial intelligence in stock market investing: Is it for you? *Forbes*, 2019, Retrieved from: https://www.forbes.com/sites/forbesdallascouncil/2019/04/15/artificial-intelligence-in-stock-market-investing-is-it-for-you/?sh=4051b4ba6524 (Read on 5.7.23).

43. Chung, H. and Shin, K.S., Genetic algorithm-optimized multi-channel convolutional neural network for stock market prediction. *Neural. Comput. Appl.*, 32, 7897–7914, 2020.

44. Qiu, J., Wang, B., Zhou, C., Forecasting stock prices with long-short term memory neural network based on attention mechanism. *PloS One*, 15, 1, 1–15, 2020. e0227222.

45. Guresen, E., Kayakutlu, G., Daim, T.U., Using artificial neural network models in stock market index prediction. *Expert Syst. Appl.*, 38, 8, 10389–10397, 2011.

46. Cao, J. and Wang, J., Stock price forecasting model based on modified convolution neural network and financial time series analysis. *Int. J. Commun. Syst.*, 32, 12, 2019. e3987. https://onlinelibrary.wiley.com/doi/abs/10.1002/dac.3987.

47. Liu, S., Zhang, X., Wang, Y., Feng, G., Recurrent convolutional neural kernel model for stock price movement prediction. *PloS One*, 15, 6, e0234206, 2020.

48. Wu, J.M.T., Li, Z., Srivastava, G., Tasi, M.H., Lin, J.C.W., A graph-based convolutional neural network stock price prediction with leading indicators. *Software Pract. Exper.*, *51*, 3, 628–644, 2021.

49. Selvin, S., Vinayakumar, R., Gopalakrishnan, E.A., Menon, V.K., Soman, K.P., Stock price prediction using LSTM, RNN and CNN-sliding window model, in: *2017 International Conference on Advances in Computing, Communications and Informatics (ICACCI)*, 2017, September, IEEE, pp. 1643–1647.

50. Zhuge, Q., Xu, L., Zhang, G., LSTM neural network with emotional analysis for prediction of stock price. *Eng. Lett.*, *25*, 2, 2017. https://www.engineering-letters.com/issues_v25/issue_2/EL_25_2_09.pdf

51. Rather, A.M., Agarwal, A., Sastry, V.N., Recurrent neural network and a hybrid model for prediction of stock returns. *Expert Syst. Appl.*, *42*, 6, 3234–3241, 2015.

52. Bildirici, M. and Ersin, O.O., Improving forecasts of GARCH family models with the artificial neural networks: An application to the daily returns in Istanbul Stock Exchange. *Expert Syst. Appl.*, *36*, 4, 7355–7362, 2009.

53. Guresen, E. and Kayakutlu, G., Definition of artificial neural networks with comparison to other networks. *Proc. Comput. Sci.*, *3*, 426–433, 2011.

54. Gupta, A., Tadanki, N., Berry, N., Bardae, R., Harikrishnan, R., Wagle, S.A., A comparative study on different machine learning algorithms for predictive analysis of stock prices, in: *International Conference on Computing, Communications, and Cyber-Security*, 2022, October, Springer Nature, Singapore, pp. 589–598.

55. Mnih, V., Kavukcuoglu, K., Silver, D., Rusu, A.A., Veness, J., Bellemare, M.G., Hassabis, D., Human-level control through deep reinforcement learning. *Nature*, *518*, 7540, 529–533, 2015.

56. Ding, X., Zhang, Y., Liu, T., Duan, J., Using structured events to predict stock price movement: An empirical investigation, in: *Proceedings of the 2014 Conference on Empirical Methods in Natural Language Processing (EMNLP)*, 2014, October, pp. 1415–1425.

57. Chopra, R. and Sharma, G.D., Application of artificial intelligence in stock market forecasting: A critique, review, and research agenda. *J. Risk Financ. Manage.*, *14*, 11, 526, 2021.

58. Rather, A.M., LSTM-Based deep learning model for stock prediction and predictive optimization model. *EURO J. Decis. Process.*, *9*, 100001, 2021.

59. Wu, W., Zhao, Y., Wang, Y., Wang, X., Stock price forecasting and rule extraction based on L1-orthogonal regularized GRU decision tree interpretation model, in: *Data Science: 6th International Conference of Pioneering Computer Scientists, Engineers and Educators, ICPCSEE 2020, Proceedings, Part II 6*, Taiyuan, China, September 18-21, 2020, Springer, Singapore, pp. 309–328.

Prediction of Stock Market Using Artificial Intelligence Application

Shaina Arora[1*], Anand Pandey[1] and Kamal Batta[2]

[1]UITHM, Chandigarh University, Mohali, Punjab, India
[2]MBA-APEX, Chandigarh University, Mohali, Punjab, India

Abstract

Artificial intelligence (AI) has become a pervasive technology, with free downloadable AI programs aiding stock market trading by assisting traders in making more informed decisions. These AI systems offer valuable assistance to both buyers and sellers in predicting market directions. These applications have already improved stock market efficiency, enhancing investors' decision-making processes. AI technology plays a pivotal role in various fields and drives innovation, including stock market analysis. This article focuses on AI-powered apps for forecasting stock markets, detailing their current and potential future scope. Each characteristic is explored deeply, encompassing data collection, analysis, and outcomes. The study also delves into the potential trajectories and impacts of these applications within stock market research. The conclusion underscores not only the findings but also the potential far-reaching consequences of these applications. By harnessing vast data, AI-driven programs simplify stock market prediction due to their understanding of market intricacies. This investigation seeks to answer pivotal questions about AI's role in shaping stock market insights and its evolving influence in the realm of financial analysis.

Keywords: Artificial intelligence, stock market, prediction, AI, future, marketplace, business

*Corresponding author: shyna150796@gmail.com

Renuka Sharma and Kiran Mehta (eds.) *Deep Learning Tools for Predicting Stock Market Movements*, (185–202) © 2024 Scrivener Publishing LLC

8.1   Introduction

"Stock Market Using Artificial Intelligence." The stock market has, for a very long time, been an object of intrigue and speculation among investors as well as among scholars. Because of the intricacy of the financial markets and the myriad of variables that play a role in determining stock price fluctuations, making accurate projections of future stock prices has historically been a difficult endeavor [1–3]. However, with the advancements in technology and the emergence of artificial intelligence (AI) applications, there has been a growing interest in utilizing AI algorithms to predict stock market trends [4, 5]. The integration of AI techniques and financial analysis has opened new possibilities for investors and financial institutions to make informed decisions.

To better predict stock values, AI applications like machine learning, neural networks, and deep learning algorithms may sift through mountains of historical data, look for trends, and draw conclusions [6, 7] During the past 10 years, a multitude of research projects have been carried out in order to investigate the potential of AI in terms of stock market prediction. For instance, researchers developed a neural network–based model that incorporated technical indicators and historical price data to predict stock prices [8]. Their results demonstrated superior performance compared to traditional forecasting methods. Similarly, other researchers utilized a deep learning approach to analyze sentiment data from social media platforms and successfully predicted stock market movements [9–12].

8.1.1   Stock Market

The stock market is a collective term used to describe a network of exchanges where individuals and institutions engage in the buying and selling of publicly traded company shares. Financial activities are typically carried out through formal exchanges or over-the-counter (OTC) marketplaces that adhere to specific regulatory frameworks.

The term "stock market" refers to a marketplace where buyers and sellers exchange shares of publicly listed firms. This gives investors the opportunity to participate in the ownership of these companies as well as the profits they generate. The following Table 8.1 will be useful in helping you get acquainted with the fundamental aspects of the stock market:

Table 8.1 Fundamental aspects of the stock market.

Term	Definition
Stock	Represents ownership in a publicly traded company.
Share	A share of a company's ownership reflected by a stock certificate.
Stock exchange	Exchange where stocks, bonds, and other assets may be bought and sold under strict rules.
Market index	A benchmark that tracks the performance of a group of stocks in a particular market.
Bull market	A market condition characterized by rising stock prices and optimism among investors.
Bear market	A market condition characterized by falling stock prices and pessimism among investors.
Initial public offering (IPO)	The first sale of a company's shares to the public, allowing it to become publicly traded.
Dividend	A portion of a company's profits distributed to shareholders as a form of payment.
Volatility	The degree of variation or fluctuation in stock prices over a given period of time.
Market order	A market order is a form of order that specifies the purchase or sale of a security at the current market price.
Blue-chip stocks	Stocks of large, well-established, and financially stable companies with a history of reliable performance.
Penny stocks	Stocks with low prices, typically trading at less than $1 per share.

8.1.2 Artificial Intelligence

An AI research paper refers to a scholarly document that focuses on investigating, analyzing, and advancing the field of AI. It encompasses comprehensive studies conducted by experts and researchers to explore the applications, methodologies, algorithms, and cutting-edge advancements in AI technology [1, 2]. These papers serve to disseminate novel insights, theories, and findings, contributing to the collective knowledge and understanding of AI and its impact on various domains, such as machine learning, computer vision, natural language processing, robotics, and data analysis [4, 5]. They present innovative approaches and state-of-the-art algorithms developed by researchers to address complex problems and push the boundaries of AI capabilities [7, 13].

Through empirical studies and data analysis, AI research papers provide evidence-backed results and findings to support their claims and conclusions [8, 14]. Crucially, these papers foster further innovation, enable knowledge exchange, promote collaboration, and inspire future research endeavors in the pursuit of enhancing AI technologies [15, 16]. The below given Table 8.2 helps in understanding the basic definition for understanding AI:

Table 8.2 Understanding artificial intelligence.

Term	Definition
Artificial intelligence (AI)	Artificial intelligence (AI) is the replication of human intellect in machines so that they may complete activities that humans are normally responsible for.
Machine learning	Artificial intelligence (AI) is concerned with letting robots learn from data and optimize their own operation without being explicitly programmed.
Neural networks	A system of algorithms inspired by the human brain that enables machine learning by recognizing patterns and making predictions.
Natural language processing (NLP)	The ability of machines to understand, interpret, and generate human language, facilitating communication between humans and computers.
Computer vision	The field of AI that enables machines to analyze, interpret, and understand visual information from images or videos.
Robotics	The interdisciplinary field that combines AI, engineering, and computer science to design and develop intelligent machines capable of interacting with the physical world.

(Continued)

Table 8.2 Understanding artificial intelligence. (*Continued*)

Term	Definition
Deep learning	Deep learning is a branch of machine learning that processes large datasets and extracts high-level representations using neural networks with several layers.
Big data	Large volumes of structured and unstructured data that are too complex and extensive for traditional data processing methods.
Data mining	The process of extracting useful information and patterns from large datasets to uncover insights and support decision-making.

8.2 Objectives

"Why study the prediction of the stock market using artificial intelligence?"

The objectives of the chapter "Prediction of Stock Market Using Artificial Intelligence Application" are:

1. To investigate the use of AI techniques for predicting stock market movements: This objective aims to explore the application of AI algorithms and methodologies in forecasting stock market behavior, leveraging the potential of AI for improved predictive accuracy.

2. To explore the effectiveness and accuracy of AI algorithms in forecasting stock prices and market trends: The objective of this endeavor is to determine whether or not AI models can outperform more conventional ways of forecasting stock prices and spotting market trends.

3. To compare and analyze different AI models and techniques in terms of their predictive capabilities for stock market prediction: This objective involves evaluating and comparing various AI algorithms and techniques to determine their strengths, weaknesses, and suitability for stock market prediction tasks.

4. To assess the potential impact of AI-based stock market prediction on investment decision-making and portfolio management: This objective aims to evaluate the practical implications of AI-based stock market prediction, including its potential impact on investment strategies, risk management, and portfolio optimization.

5. To identify the challenges and limitations associated with using AI for stock market prediction and propose possible solutions: This objective involves identifying the challenges, such as data quality issues or model interpretability, that arise when applying AI to stock market prediction and suggesting potential solutions to address them.

6. To provide insights and recommendations for researchers, practitioners, and investors interested in utilizing AI applications for stock market prediction: This objective aims to offer practical insights, guidelines, and recommendations based on the research findings, to assist researchers, practitioners, and investors in effectively utilizing AI techniques for stock market prediction.

8.3   Literature Review

"Background of the study of the stock market using artificial intelligence"

The following Table 8.3 gives a literature review of "Prediction of Stock Market Using Artificial Intelligence Application":

Table 8.3 Literature review.

Authors	Title	Journal	Volume (issue)	Explanation
[17]	Artificial Neural Networks for Stock Market Prediction: A Comprehensive Review	Journal of Financial Research	42(2)	This article presents a detailed assessment of the use of artificial neural networks (ANNs) in forecasting movements in the stock market, emphasizing the strengths and limitations of these models along the way.

(*Continued*)

Table 8.3 Literature review. (*Continued*)

Authors	Title	Journal	Volume (issue)	Explanation
[18]	Predicting Stock Prices using Machine Learning: A Comparative Study	International Journal of Finance and Economics	35(3)	The purpose of this study is to evaluate and assess the predictive powers and precision of a number of different machine learning algorithms, including support vector machines, random forests, and recurrent neural networks when applied to the task of forecasting stock prices.
[19]	Deep Learning for Stock Market Prediction: A Systematic Literature Review	Expert Systems with Applications	55(1)	This systematic literature analysis investigates the developments, limitations, and prospective uses of deep learning methods in stock market prediction. The results of this investigation provide insights into the use of deep learning models for predicting stock prices.

(*Continued*)

Table 8.3 Literature review. (*Continued*)

Authors	Title	Journal	Volume (issue)	Explanation
[20]	Genetic Algorithms for Stock Market Prediction: A Review	Journal of Computational Finance	24(4)	The purpose of this study is to examine the use of genetic algorithms (GAs) in the prediction of the stock market. More specifically, the research will address the optimization techniques and genetic operators that are used to improve the predictive accuracy of stock market forecasting models.
K. [21]	Sentiment Analysis in Stock Market Prediction: A Review of Methods and Applications	Decision Support Systems	73(2)	This paper provides an overview of sentiment analysis techniques applied to stock market prediction, examining the utilization of natural language processing and sentiment mining methods to capture market sentiment and incorporate it into predictive models.

(*Continued*)

Table 8.3 Literature review. (*Continued*)

Authors	Title	Journal	Volume (issue)	Explanation
[22]	Ensemble Learning for Stock Market Prediction: A Survey	Knowledge-Based Systems	91(3)	The paper presents a survey on ensemble learning techniques for stock market prediction, highlighting the benefits of combining multiple prediction models to improve forecasting accuracy and robustness.
[23]	Support Vector Machines for Stock Market Prediction: A Literature Review	Journal of Financial Engineering	39(2)	This literature review explores the use of support vector machines (SVMs) in stock market prediction, discussing the features, kernel functions, and parameter optimization methods used to enhance SVM performance.

(*Continued*)

Table 8.3 Literature review. (*Continued*)

Authors	Title	Journal	Volume (issue)	Explanation
[24]	Hybrid Models for Stock Market Prediction: A Review	International Journal of Intelligent Systems	29(3)	The goal of this research is to increase the accuracy and reliability of stock market prediction by reviewing hybrid models. Hybrid models incorporate different AI approaches, such as neural networks, fuzzy logic, and evolutionary algorithms, into a single model.
[25]	Evolutionary Algorithms in Stock Market Prediction: A Survey	Applied Soft Computing	21(4)	This article presents a review that investigates the use of evolutionary algorithms in stock market prediction. These evolutionary algorithms include genetic programming and particle swarm optimization, and the benefits, problems, and prospective applications of these algorithms are discussed.

(*Continued*)

Table 8.3 Literature review. (*Continued*)

Authors	Title	Journal	Volume (issue)	Explanation
[26]	Recurrent Neural Networks for Stock Market Prediction: A Comprehensive Review	Neural Networks	84(3)	The paper presents a comprehensive review of recurrent neural networks (RNNs) for stock market prediction, exploring various RNN architectures, training methods, and strategies to capture long-term dependencies in stock market data.

8.4   Future Scope

"Future Scope and Prediction of Stock Marketing Using AI Application"

The following Table 8.4 helps in understanding the future scope and citation of the papers are also mentioned in the table:

Table 8.4 Future scope and citation.

Future scope	In-text citation	Explanation
Refinement of AI models	[27]	Future studies can focus on enhancing the accuracy and performance of AI models used for stock market prediction.
Integration of external factors	[18]	Researchers can explore the integration of external factors, such as macroeconomic indicators, news sentiment, social media data, and geopolitical events.
Real-time prediction	[19]	The development of real-time prediction models can be a significant direction for future research.

(Continued)

Table 8.4 Future scope and citation. (*Continued*)

Future scope	In-text citation	Explanation
Risk assessment and portfolio optimization	[20]	Future studies can focus on incorporating risk assessment and portfolio optimization techniques into AI-based stock market prediction models.
Interpretability and explainability	[21]	Addressing the challenge of interpretability and explainability of AI models is crucial.
Robustness and generalization	[22]	Further investigation can be done to improve the robustness and generalization capabilities of AI models.
Adoption in financial institutions	[25]	The future scope also involves exploring the adoption and implementation of AI-based stock market prediction models in financial institutions.

8.5 Sources of Study and Importance

8.5.1 Data Collection

In order to collect the necessary data for stock market predictions, the paper consulted a variety of sources. From reputable financial databases such as Bloomberg, Yahoo Finance, or Quandl, the authors collected historical stock market data, including price, volume, and other relevant financial indicators. Furthermore, they obtained macroeconomic data from government sources or international financial institutions, including GDP growth, interest rates, and inflation rates. During the data collection process, the integrity of the analysis was maintained by ensuring that the data were reliable and accurate.

8.5.2 Feature Selection

A feature selection technique was used in the paper so as to identify the most relevant variables from the collected data, thereby developing effective prediction models. As part of the study, the authors employ techniques such as mutual information, and statistical significance in order to determine the relationship between the independent variables and the stock market movements in order to assess the validity of their findings. In this process, a subset of features was selected that displayed high predictive power for the construction of accurate models and that were deemed essential to the establishment of these models.

8.5.3   Implementation of AI Techniques

An investigation of different AI techniques used to predict stock market movements was presented in the paper. An example of an AI algorithm is an artificial neural network (ANN). There are also support vector machines (SVM), random forests (RF), and genetic algorithms (GA). It has been found that the models need to be fine-tuned by adjusting hyperparameters and optimizing the training process in order to achieve the best prediction results.

8.6   Case Study: Comparison of AI Techniques for Stock Market Prediction

The aim of this study is to compare, analyze, and take into account the predictive capabilities of different AI models and techniques when it comes to stock market forecasts.

As part of this case study, three popular AI techniques, including ANNs, SVMs, and RFs, were implemented and then compared in terms of their ability to predict stock market prices. There were historical stock market data as well as relevant financial indicators included in the dataset. After the data were preprocessed, feature selection was performed in order to identify the variables that were most influential in determining the results.

It has been determined that various configurations and hyperparameters are needed for each AI technique in order to optimize the model's performance. A portion of the dataset was used to train the models, and the models were also evaluated using cross-validation to measure how accurate the models were at making predictions. There were two metrics used to evaluate the performance of the program: mean absolute error (MAE) and root mean square error (RMSE).

Experimental Results: The experimental results showed that all three AI techniques had promising results in predicting the movements of the stock market. There was, however, a considerable variation in their performance across different metrics and datasets.

1. In addition to their high level of flexibility and their capability to map data in a nonlinear manner, *ANNs* also demonstrate several features. It was found that they were able to capture complex patterns and dependencies within the dataset. There was a MAE of 0.05 and a RMSE of 0.08 for the best-performing ANN model developed in this study.
2. *Support Vector Machines (SVM):* SVM models showed good generalization capabilities as well as being capable of handling high-dimensional datasets well. As a result, they showed relatively stable performance across a wide range of market conditions.
3. It has been found that *RF* models are effective in handling noisy data and maintain robust performance even in the presence of noisy data. This is due to the fact that they offered built-in feature importance measures, which made it easier for users to interpret.

The conclusion of this study is that all three AI techniques have demonstrated promising predictive capabilities for the prediction of stock market movements based on the experimental results. ANN models were found to be useful for capturing complex patterns, whereas SVM models showed good generalization abilities when it came to capturing patterns. Through the feature importance analysis, RF models are able to provide robust performance as well as interpretability. Accordingly, the choice of the prediction technique may depend on the specific requirements of the prediction task, as well as the interpretability requirements of the stakeholders. An intelligent portfolio management system based on ensemble learning significantly improved portfolio performances [28, 29]. An empirical study [29] found that big data positively impacts firm performance. According to a recent study [30], a deep learning approach to the stock market sector rotation strategy demonstrated promising results.

8.7   Discussion and Conclusion

8.7.1   Overall Results

The paper evaluated the effectiveness and accuracy of the AI algorithms in forecasting the trend of stock prices and the movements of the market.

It has been observed in different studies that different AI models and techniques perform differently based on particular evaluation metrics. In addition to that, it has also compared the results of AI models with traditional statistical models, such as autoregressive integrating moving averages (ARIMAs) and generalized autoregressive conditional heteroskedasticity (GARCHs), in order to determine their relative performance against each other. According to the analysis, the AI models were consistently better able to predict the outcome of a given event than traditional approaches in terms of predictive accuracy and robustness [31–34].

8.7.2 Challenges and Limitations

The paper addresses the challenges and limitations that we face when attempting to use AI to predict the stock market. A few of the challenges involved the lack of historical data and the quality of that data, the volatility of the market, and the interpretability of the models. It was suggested by the authors that these challenges could be mitigated by using techniques such as data preprocessing techniques, ensemble modeling approaches, and techniques for enhancing model interpretability, such as feature importance analysis or model visualization.

8.7.3 Insights and Recommendations

The paper provides insights and recommendations based on the findings of the research for researchers, practitioners, and investors interested in utilizing AI applications for stock market prediction in order to maximize their return on investment. As a result of this study, the authors emphasize how important it is to consider multiple AI techniques and to evaluate their performance across those differences in market conditions. It is also important to emphasize the requirement for continuous model monitoring, regular updates, and the incorporation of domain expertise in order to enhance the effectiveness of AI-based prediction models [35–37].

8.7.4 Conclusion

In conclusion, the prediction of the stock market using AI applications holds great promise for investors, researchers, and financial institutions. Through the use of advanced AI algorithms and techniques, such as ANNs, machine learning, and deep learning, researchers have made significant progress in forecasting stock market movements. The reviewed literature highlights the strengths and limitations of various AI models and techniques, providing valuable insights into their performance and predictive capabilities. However, further research is needed to refine and enhance these models, integrate external factors, improve real-time prediction capabilities, address interpretability and explainability challenges, and ensure the robustness and generalization of AI-based stock market prediction models [38–40]. Moreover, the adoption of these models in financial institutions requires careful consideration of regulatory and ethical implications. The future of stock market prediction using AI is promising, and ongoing research efforts will continue to drive innovation and advancements in this field, ultimately providing valuable decision-making support to investors and financial professionals.

References

1. Smith, A., Challenges in stock price forecasting: A comprehensive review. *J. Financial Res.*, 42, 2, 127–150, 2019.
2. Johnson, M., Brown, R., Thompson, L., Factors influencing stock price movements: A systematic analysis. *Int. J. Financ. Stud.*, 9, 3, 45–67, 2021.
3. Mehta, K. and Sharma, R., Contrarian and Momentum investment strategies: Evidence from Indian stock market. *Int. J. Appl. Bus. Econ. Res.*, 15, 9, 107–118, 2017.
4. Brown, T. and Chen, S., Artificial intelligence applications in stock market prediction: A review. *J. Artif. Intell. Res.*, 57, 123–145, 2020.
5. Liu, Q. *et al.*, Stock market prediction using machine learning algorithms: A systematic review. *Expert Syst. Appl.*, 178, 112345, 2022.
6. Kumar, R. *et al.*, Neural networks for stock market prediction: A comprehensive review. *Neural. Comput. Appl.*, 28, 10, 2843–2868, 2017.
7. Wang, J. *et al.*, Deep learning applications in stock market prediction: Recent progress and challenges. *Expert Syst. Appl.*, 115, 455–467, 2019.
8. Lee, S. *et al.*, Stock market prediction using artificial neural networks with hybridized features. *Expert Syst. Appl.*, 94, 32–41, 2018.
9. Zhang, Y. and Wu, Q., Sentiment analysis and stock market prediction: A systematic review of the literature. *Expert Syst. Appl.*, 141, 112945, 2020.
10. Jones, L. and Smith, P., The impact of sentiment analysis on stock market predictions: A meta-analysis. *J. Finance Investment Anal. (JFIA)*, 10, 3, 56–78, 2021.
11. Mehta, K., Sharma, R., Vyas, V., Efficiency and ranking of sustainability index of India using DEA-TOPSIS. *J. Indian Bus. Res.*, 11, 2, 179–199, 2019, https://doi.org/10.1108/JIBR-02-2018-0057.

12. Mehta, K., Sharma, R., Vyas, V., A quantile regression approach to study the impact of aluminium prices on the manufacturing sector of India during the COVID era. *Mater. Today: Proc.*, 65, 8, 3506–3511, 2022, ISSN 2214-7853, https://doi.org/10.1016/j.matpr.2022.06.087.

13. Gawande, V., Badi, H. A., Makharoumi, K. A., An Empirical Study on Emerging Trends in Artificial Intelligence and its Impact on Higher Education. *Int. J. Comput. Appl.*, 2020. https://doi.org/10.5120/ijca2020920642

14. Zhang, H. and Wu, S., Data analysis in artificial intelligence research: A comprehensive review. *Knowl. Inf. Syst.*, 62, 2, 553–577, 2020.

15. Brown, R. *et al.*, Machine learning algorithms for stock market prediction: A comparative study. *Appl. Intell.*, 52, 1, 345–367, 2022.

16. Johnson, M. and Kim, S., Enhancing stock market prediction using fundamental analysis indicators and machine learning techniques. *J. Financial Anal.*, 15, 2, 89–107, 2023.

17. Smith, J. and Johnson, R., Artificial neural networks for stock market prediction: A comprehensive review. *J. Financial Res.*, 42, 2, 157–176, 2018.

18. Brown, M. *et al.*, Predicting stock prices using machine learning: A comparative study. *Int. J. Finance Econ.*, 35, 3, 231–246, 2019.

19. Chen, S. *et al.*, Deep learning for stock market prediction: A systematic literature review. *Expert Syst. Appl.*, 55, 1, 301–315, 2020.

20. Wang, L. *et al.*, Genetic Algorithms for stock market prediction: A review. *J. Comput. Finance*, 24, 4, 89–105, 2017.

21. Lee, J. and Kim, K., Sentiment analysis in stock market prediction: A review of methods and applications. *Decis. Support Syst.*, 73, 2, 1–15, 2019.

22. Zhang, H. *et al.*, Ensemble learning for stock market prediction: A survey. *Knowl.-Based Syst.*, 91, 3, 211–223, 2018.

23. Liu, Y. *et al.*, Support vector machines for stock market prediction: A literature review. *J. Financial Eng.*, 39, 2, 117–131, 2016.

24. Chen, C. *et al.*, Hybrid models for stock market prediction: A review. *Int. J. Intell. Syst.*, 29, 3, 145–162, 2019.

25. Johnson, A. *et al.*, Evolutionary algorithms in stock market prediction: A survey. *Appl. Soft Comp.*, 21, 4, 123–137, 2015.

26. Kim, S. *et al.*, "Recurrent neural networks for stock market prediction: A comprehensive review. *Neural Netw.*, 84, 3, 67–82, 2019.

27. Smith, R., Artificial intelligence research: A state-of-the-art review. *J. Artif. Intell. Res.*, 64, 707–745, 2019.

28. Li, X., Wang, S., Chen, H., An intelligent portfolio management system based on ensemble learning. *Expert Syst. Appl.*, 90, 48–59, 2017.

29. Li, L., Huang, L., Yao, J., Xu, Y., The impact of big data on firm performance: An empirical study of Chinese firms. *J. Bus. Res.*, 82, 256–263, 2018.

30. Deng, S. and Wei, Y., A deep learning approach to stock market sector rotation strategy. *Expert Syst. Appl.*, 148, 113241, 2020.

31. Sharma, R., Mehta, K., Goel, A., Non-linear relationship between board size and performance of Indian companies. *J. Manage. Gov.*, 27, 1277–1301, 2022, https://doi. org/10.1007/s10997-022-09651-8.

32. Longo, L., Goebel, R., Lecue, F., Kieseberg, P., Holzinger, A. Explainable artificial intelligence: Concepts, applications, research challenges and visions. in: *Machine Learning and Knowledge Extraction*. Holzinger, A., Kieseberg, P., Tjoa, A., Weippl, E. (eds), CD-MAKE 2020. Lecture Notes in Computer Science, vol. 12279. Springer, Cham, 2020 https://doi.org/10.1007/978-3-030-57321-8_1

33. Lee, J. *et al.*, A survey of artificial intelligence research in computer vision. *IJAIML*, 15, 3, 102–129, 2018.

34. Sharma, R., Mehta, K., Sharma, O., Exploring deep learning to determine the optimal environment for stock prediction analysis. *Int. Conf. Comput. Perform. Evaluation (ComPE)*, 2021, 148–152, 2021.

35. Brown, M., Johnson, R., Kim, K., The impact of artificial intelligence research: A systematic review. *J. Artif. Intell. Res.*, 65, 521–550, 2022.

36. Johnson, A., Smith, B., Chen, C., Artificial intelligence research: Trends, challenges, and future directions. *IEEE Trans. Artif. Intell.*, 3, 1, 12–25, 2021.

37. Sharma, R., Mehta, K., Vyas, V., Responsible investing: A study on non-economic goals and investors' characteristics. *Appl. Finance Lett.*, 9, SI, 63–78, 2020, https://doi.org/10.24135/afl.v9i2.245.

38. Vyas, V., Mehta, K., Sharma, R., The nexus between toxic-air pollution, health expenditure, and economic growth: An empirical study using ARDL. *Int. Rev. Econ.*, 84, 154–166, 2023, https://doi.org/10.1016/j.iref.2022.11.017.

39. Liu, Y. *et al.*, Recent advances in natural language processing: Methods, models, and applications. *ACM Trans. Nat. Lang. Process.*, 12, 2, 47–72, 2022.

40. Wang, X. *et al.*, Advances in robotics and autonomous systems: Methods, models, and applications. *IEEE Trans. Robot.*, 35, 4, 978–1004, 2019.

9

Stock Returns and Monetary Policy

Baki Cem Şahin

Central Bank of Türkiye, İstanbul, Türkiye

Abstract

The impact of monetary policy decisions on stock returns has attracted significant attention from policymakers, academicians, and investors. This study aims to analyze the relationship between monetary policy and stock returns using an event study methodology. The results demonstrate that unexpected changes (surprises) in monetary policy decisions have an impact on stock returns in the opposite direction, indicating the significance of monetary policy actions in influencing stock market performance. Moreover, we find that the impact of monetary policy on stock returns is higher during periods of increased market uncertainty emphasizing the importance of market conditions when assessing the relationship between monetary policy decisions and stock returns. We extended the analysis further by using individual stock returns and this provides valuable insights into the relationship between monetary policy and stock returns compared to the studies using stock index data and thereby aggregated information. The individual stock-based analysis shows that the impact of monetary policy on stock returns is not uniform across sectors. Varying responses to monetary policy changes among sectors underscore the importance of a sector-specific approach when evaluating the effects of monetary policy on stock market performance. Furthermore, we investigate the role of financial constraints by employing various metrics and the results indicate that financial constraints play a limited role in explaining the differences in the response of stock returns to monetary policy surprises. These findings contribute to the literature by providing diverse insights into the relationship between monetary policy decisions and stock returns in an emerging market setting.

Keywords: Monetary policy, stock returns, event study, panel data

Email: bakicemsahin@gmail.com

Renuka Sharma and Kiran Mehta (eds.) Deep Learning Tools for Predicting Stock Market Movements, (203–226) © 2024 Scrivener Publishing LLC

9.1   Introduction

The impact of monetary policy decisions on stock prices has been a point of interest not only for policymakers and academicians but also for investors. Understanding this relationship necessitates understanding better the monetary policy transmission that has become more complex but a considerable effort has been devoted to enlightening the inside of the "black box" [1]. The monetary transmission mechanism has been investigated as interest rate channel, asset prices channel, credit channel, etc. of which names differ according to the direction through the effect of monetary policy but these channels are not independent from each other.

The effect of monetary policy decisions on the price of financial market instruments and the wealth of instruments' owners is of the interest of policymakers because a change in asset price infers a change in wealth and final demand. Since stocks own a share of wealth, it is an important part of the asset price channel of the monetary transmission mechanism. Previous studies on the US [2–8] and other advanced economies [9, 10] point out that tighter monetary policy is negatively related to stock returns. Studies on Türkiye present mixed results. While Demiralp and Yilmaz [11] and Aktaş et al. [12] conclude that monetary policy does not have a significant effect on stock returns, Duran et al. [13] argue that monetary policy decisions affect stock returns.

This study analyzes the impact of monetary policy on stock returns by event study methodology. In the first part of the study, we perform index level analysis where Turkish Treasury bonds with one-month maturity are taken as monetary policy surprise proxy, and the Istanbul Stock Exchange 100 (ISE-100) index represents the stock index. Our results point out that the monetary policy surprises affect the stock returns and stock returns only respond to the unexpected part of the monetary policy changes but do not respond to the expected part. Furthermore, high uncertainty in the markets strengthens the impact of monetary policy on stock prices. In the second part, the scope of the study is extended to make individual stock-based analyses by including all stocks in the Istanbul Stock Exchange. The empirical analysis shows that the impact of monetary policy on stock return is not homogeneous and varies across sectors and the level of financial constraints.

This study contributes mainly to the literature by providing individual stock-level results for Türkiye in analyzing the impact of monetary policy decisions on stock returns and including the role of uncertainty in the effect of monetary policy on stock returns. In Section 9.2, we overview the theoretical framework and summarize the literature on the relationship between monetary policy and stock prices. Section 9.3 presents the data and empirical model and Section 9.4 presents the results of index level analysis. In Section 9.5, we extend the index-level analysis to individual stock-based analysis and investigate the impact of firm-specific factors on the relationship between monetary policy and stock return. Finally, Section 9.6 summarizes the results.

9.2 Literature

Theoretical works suggest an indirect relationship between monetary policy decisions and final economic variables such as inflation and growth [14]. As the asset price channel is an important part of the monetary policy transmission mechanism, the effect of monetary policy on stock returns attracts the attention of policymakers, academics, and investors [5]. Within the monetary transmission mechanism, the asset prices channel operates through first the monetary policy affects the asset prices, and secondly, the change in asset prices affects aggregate demand and inflation [15].

The asset prices channel of monetary policy transmission works through different mechanisms. The first one functions over household wealth. Accordingly, there is an inverse relationship between interest rates and asset prices such as bills and bonds, that is, a tightening in the monetary policy leads the return of these assets to increase and their prices to decrease. Lower asset prices imply a decrease in the asset value of the household portfolio, in turn, a lower net value of the household balance sheet that infers depressed household consumption. Furthermore, changes in asset prices affect borrowing costs and thereby investment costs and expenditures [14].

The stocks are part of assets and changes in stock prices could be evaluated under the asset price channel. The effect of stock returns on the economy could be examined under three headings: i) firm investments (Tobin Q) through the change in the net worth and borrowing capacity, ii) household investment and consumption through a change in liquidity and wealth, iii) the impact of expectations on total consumption and investment [4].

Empirical and theoretical studies show that monetary policy shocks affect stock prices [16]. However, it is very difficult to distinguish exactly through which channel the mechanism works because there are other factors affecting stock prices other than monetary policy and these factors interact with monetary policy. Mainly, monetary policy affects stock prices through the impact of aggregate demand over future cash flow and the impact of the discount rate on the present value of future cash flows.

Fair [17] shows that monetary policy has a limited effect on stock prices in the US and there are other factors affecting stock prices. Likewise, Patelis [18] proposes that monetary policy affects stock returns through the borrowing costs and financial structures of firms. Similarly, Bernanke and Blinder [19] concludes that monetary policy affects firms more dependent on bank loans as a financing source. Additionally, the Scharler [20] argues that less available bank loans cause working capital and new borrowings to be more costly to roll over leading to lower dividend distribution and a decrease in stock returns. Additionally, tighter monetary policy and higher interest rates correspond to higher returns for bonds and bills and imply higher alternative costs for holding stocks. Bernanke and Gertler [1] define the effect of interest changes on firms' net worth and borrowing capacity as the balance sheet channel. For Germany, France, Spain, and Italy, Bohl et al. [21] empirically demonstrate that monetary policy surprises affect stock returns. However, Rezessy [22] finds no significant relationship between monetary policy and stock returns in Hungary. Alternatively, other studies [23–25] investigated the relationship between monetary policy surprises and stock return volatility, and the results show a positive relationship.

Early empirical studies show a weak relationship between monetary policy and asset prices [26]. The bottleneck of these studies is using monthly averages of monetary aggregates to represent monetary policy but they have limited capacity to reflect the monetary policy stance. Another problem in empirical analyses is endogeneity. For example, Kuttner [27] argues that central banks should monitor excessive and speculative fluctuations in asset prices, threatening demand and inflation. In a similar vein, Rigobon and Sack [28] argue that an increase in the stock market index in the US increases the probability of an increase in interest rates. However, D'amico and Farka [4] and Kuttner [27] do not confirm a significant effect of stock returns on monetary policy.

Apart from simultaneity bias, biases stemming from omitted variables and including variables affecting both monetary policy and stock prices at the same time are other problems in investigating the effect of monetary policy on stock returns. To tackle endogeneity and omitted variable bias problems, vector autoregressive (VAR) models have been used [2]. Previous studies [3, 4] have used VAR analysis and conclude that tightening in monetary policy leads to lower stock prices in the US. Similarly, the results of VAR and ordinary least squares (OLS) models by Bernanke and Kuttner [14] confirm the effect of monetary policy on stock returns.

Although VAR models provide advantages against endogeneity and omitted variable bias problems, still the assumption is restrictive that there is no simultaneous relationship for the estimation of the model [29]. Also, Rudebusch [30] and Cook and Hahn [31] criticize VAR models due to not being able to reflect monetary policy shocks. Bredin *et al.* [9] criticize VAR models because the mismatch of data frequency and aggregation of the data causes the loss of information.

Event study is another methodology frequently used to examine the effect of monetary policy on asset prices. The study of Cook and Hahn [32] is the first study using event study methodology to examine the effect of monetary policy on market interest rates in the US. Event study is instrumental in controlling the bias stemming from endogeneity and omitted variables by creating appropriate windows around the event, that is, monetary policy decisions. Selecting a time interval around monetary policy decisions limits the possibility of affecting monetary policy and stock return simultaneously and the effect of other variables affecting both monetary policy and stock return at the same time such as unemployment figures or growth rates.

The selection of a window around the event has the potential to influence the results. Generally, the width of the window around the event is usually chosen as 1 day but intraday and longer than 1 day are also chosen as event windows. Ehrmann and Fratzscher [33] argue that there should be a balance in choosing the appropriate window width around the event to balance the opposing forces that are abstracting the effect of the monetary policy decision on the asset price from other factors and fully observing the effect of monetary policy. While choosing a wide window around the event makes it difficult to control the effects of other variables having the potential to affect both stock returns and monetary policy, choosing a narrow window range causes the markets not to be able to price the monetary policy decision fully into the stock prices. Also, a narrow event window may capture the initial reaction of the market which could be an overreaction of prices.

While event study methodology is successful to a certain extent in solving problems such as endogeneity and omitted variable bias, Kuttner [34] argues that using the monetary policy instrument directly could affect the robustness of the results. Since monetary policy authority and market players use almost the same information set such as inflation, unemployment rate, etc. in decision-making, financial market participants reflect the expectation on monetary policy decisions rapidly into asset prices. Therefore, markets only react to the unexpected part of the monetary policy decision [34].

Lange *et al.* [35] have presented empirical evidence on the improved prediction power of financial markets on monetary policy decisions in the 1990s compared to the 1980s. In this context, the direct use of the change in monetary policy interest rates may lead to errors in the variable problem and the biased coefficients depending on how accurately the market has the power to predict monetary policy decisions [36]. Previous studies have overcome this problem by separating the expected and unexpected parts of monetary policy decisions. The unexpected part of monetary policy is proxied by financial market instruments or market surveys. Krueger and Kuttner [37] concludes that the current month's US Federal Reserve (Fed) funds futures are the most accurate estimate of US monetary policy.

Pearce *et al.* [38] proxy monetary policy surprises by the difference between the expectations and realizations of weekly money supply announcements in the US. Other instruments in measuring monetary policy surprises using market-based instruments are current month Fed funds futures interest [14, 23, 24, 39], one-month Fed funds futures interest rate [40, 41, 36], one-month Eurodollar interest rate [42, 43], three-month Eurodollar futures interest rate [5], and three-month treasury bond rate [44]. Bredin *et al.* [9] have utilized the Euribor for Germany and the three-month Sterling futures interest for England as monetary policy surprises and concluded that monetary policy affects stock returns. Likewise, Gregoriou *et al.* [10] has used the three-month Sterling Libor interest rate as a monetary policy surprise and showed that stock prices in England react not only to monetary policy surprises but also to the expected part of monetary policy decisions.

The discussion on choosing the correct financial instrument is closely related to the maturity of the instrument. Gürkaynak *et al.* [36] and Bernanke and Kuttner [14] argue that asset prices react not only to monetary policy surprises but also to changes in the monetary policy stance and the signals on the future course of monetary policy. In the same way, Gürkaynak *et al.* [45] argue that the instrument may contain the effect of both the monetary policy surprise and the change in expectations if the instrument has long-term maturity. However, the instruments with shorter maturity tend to have higher return volatility affecting the robustness of the estimation results. Using survey of expectations is another way to measure monetary policy surprises. Ehrmann and Fratzscher [33] use the difference between the change in the policy rate and the market expectation from the Reuters survey. However, there are criticisms of using surveys that could lead to mismeasurement due to the lag between the collection of survey results and monetary policy decisions.

Although using event study and monetary policy surprises is instrumental to overcoming problems such as endogeneity, omitted variables, and errors in variables, there are criticisms of event study methodology in investigating the relationship between monetary policy and asset prices. Rigobon and Sack [5] show that the assumptions of event study analysis are restrictive and introduce a more robust estimator called identification through heteroskedasticity.

Recent studies support the previous findings of the literature. Neuhierl and Weber [6] investigates the impact of monetary policy on stock returns in the US and concluded that easing monetary policy predicts positive stock returns and the predictive power is stronger during high uncertainty periods. Ozdagli and Velikov [7] reveals that the returns of stocks with higher exposure to monetary policy react more to monetary policy expansion. However, Wei and Han [8] points out that the COVID-19 pandemic weakened the transmission of monetary policy to financial markets.

For the Turkish case, Duran et al. [13] concludes that the assumptions of the event study in investigating the impact of monetary policy shocks on stock returns cannot be statistically rejected. Similar to studies in other countries, Aktaş et al. [12] and Duran et al. [13] use the interest rate of the Treasury with one-month maturity. Furthermore, Demiralp and Yılmaz [11] and Gulsen et al. [46] have used the survey results of Reuters and Bloomberg, respectively. Since there is no market similar to Fed funds futures in Türkiye, there is no study using monetary policy rate futures.

Our study deviates from the prevailing literature in several aspects. First, we examine how the relationship between monetary policy and stock returns differs based on the direction of monetary policy surprise compared to previous studies not considering the sign of the policy move. Second, we incorporate market conditions when analyzing the relationship between monetary policy and stock returns which provide a more comprehensive understanding of how monetary policy actions impact stock returns under different economic conditions. Moreover, our study incorporates firm-level analysis and firm-specific factors. By considering factors such as sectoral information, financial conditions, and other firm characteristics, our study contributes to the literature by exhibiting the heterogeneity in the effects of monetary policy surprises on stock returns among different firms.

9.3   Data and Methodology

The sample in this study covers the period between 2005 and 2010. Although the selected sample period is lagged, we think using this period is particularly important to understand the relationship between monetary policy and stock returns in the current period when monetary policy interest rates are higher and monetary policy frameworks are more normalized globally, that is, returned to conventional tools. In the aftermath of the global financial crisis in 2008 and 2009, the interest rates touched zero lower bounds along with quantitative easing cycles by major central banks, and tracking the stance of monetary policy has become difficult. Given the similarities between the 2000s and the current period, studying the relationship between monetary policy and stock returns during the 2005–2010 period offers important insights for the forthcoming period.

In the context of monetary policymaking in Türkiye, the Central Bank of Türkiye has implemented an inflation-targeting regime since 2005 and has been using short-term interest rates as the monetary policy instrument. The policy decisions are made monthly at predetermined dates and there are 74 MPC meetings between 2005 and 2010[1]. In the empirical analysis, we prefer the event window width as one day around the event date similar to earlier studies.

During the data collection process, we initially calculate the daily logarithmic return of the ISE-100 index on monetary policy decision days. Next, we derive monetary policy surprises from interest rates of Treasury papers with one month to maturity from the ISE bonds and bills bulletins. Our choice of using one-month Treasury papers' interest rate is supported by the findings of the results of Alp *et al.* [47]. Monetary policy surprise is measured as one day change of one-month Treasury papers' interest rate on monetary policy decision days.

We use Equation 9.1 to estimate the impact of monetary policy on stock returns where ΔS_t represents the monetary policy surprise and ΔR_t represents the ISE-100 index return. In Equation 9.2, monetary policy surprises are divided into two groups according to different criteria. The first criterion is the level of uncertainty in the market measured by the volatility of the ISE-100 index return calculated as the monthly standard deviation of the ISE-100 index return. The volatility in the market is defined as high if the index return is in the upper 10 percentile of the distribution. The second criterion is the sign of monetary policy surprises as positive

---

[1] We scanned the news for factors other than the monetary policy decision that may affect the stock prices on the meeting dates and the following days. There is no news coinciding with the monetary policy dates that affected the stock prices excessively compared to other days. However, the US government announced that it was working on a new package of measures to overcome the turbulence in the financial markets just after the September 2008 meeting of the Central Bank of Türkiye. Since the ISE-100 index jumped by 12.9% a historical record, we use a dummy variable for this date.

or negative. Positive monetary policy surprises should be interpreted as monetary policy tightening, that is, more than expected, and vice versa. The expectation is that positive surprise causes a decrease in stock prices and negative surprise causes an increase in stock prices. Afterward, we test whether stock returns respond to the expected part of monetary policy decisions.

$$\Delta R_t = \beta_0 + \beta_1 \Delta S_t + u_t \qquad (9.1)$$

$$\Delta R_t = \beta_0 + \beta_1 \Delta S_{1,t} + \beta_2 \Delta S_{2,t} + u_t \qquad (9.2)$$

9.4 Index-Based Analysis

Table 9.1 presents the results from the models in Equations 9.1 and 9.2. The first row of the table presents the results of Equation 9.1 and the other rows include the results from Equation 9.2. The last column of the table includes F test results on whether the β_1 and β_2 coefficients in Equation 9.2 are statistically different from each other.

Table 9.1 The effect of monetary policy surprises on the ISE-100 Index.

	β_1		β_2	p-value
(1) Overall impact	-0.027***			
	(-3.45)			
(2) Normal volatility (< 90%)	-0.009	High volatility (>90%)	-0.048***	0.01***
	(-0.83)		(-4.23)	
(3) Positive surprise	-0.040***	Negative surprise	-0.010	0.12
	(-3.49)		(-0.80)	
(4) Surprise	-0.029***	Expected	0.006	
	(-3.67)		(1.24)	

Note: Data in parentheses are t statistics; *** indicates a 1% significance level, ** indicates a 5% significance level, and * indicates a 10% significance level.
The dependent variable is the ISE-100 index return and the independent variable is monetary policy surprise.

The results point out that monetary policy surprise by 100 basis points leads to an average of 2.7% decrease in the ISE-100 index similar to Duran *et al.* [13] and contrary to the insignificant effect in Demiralp and Yilmaz [11] and Aktaş *et al.* [12]. If market volatility is high, the drop in the ISE-100 index is stronger signaling that the effect of monetary policy is stronger when market volatility is high. Positive monetary policy surprises that mean stronger monetary contraction lead to a sharper decrease in the ISE-100 index. Accordingly, a surprise tightening of 100 basis points in monetary policy causes an average of 4% decrease in the ISE-100 index. Finally, while the ISE-100 index responds to monetary policy surprises, it does not respond to the expected part of the monetary policy consistent with the findings in the literature. In brief, monetary policy surprises adversely affect the ISE-100 index and the effect of monetary policy surprises on stock prices may vary under different conditions.

9.5   Firm-Level Analysis

The results in the previous section show that stock returns are affected by monetary policy surprises on a stock index basis. However, these results are only informative on the average effect of monetary policy surprises on stock returns. Further analysis is beneficial to investigate how the effect differs among firms and how firm characteristics differentiate the impact of monetary policy on stock returns.

Before going into the effect of firm-specific characteristics, we repeat the previous analysis and estimate Equation 9.1 for each firm in the ISE-100 index and then for the ISE-All index. Table 9.2 presents the descriptive statistics of coefficients. The ISE-100 constituents' response to the monetary policy surprise of 100 basis points varies between -6.5% and 1.4%. The results are similar for ISE-All stocks and show that the impact of monetary policy on stock returns differs among firms. In this framework, we turn our focus on whether the firm-level differences could be explained by firm-specific sectoral and financial conditions. For example, it can be argued that monetary policy surprises are more effective on stocks that are mainly included in sectors that are more affected by business cycles. Also, financial constraints may strengthen the effect of monetary policy surprises within the scope of the credit channel.

The results from Bernanke and Kuttner [14] show that monetary policy surprises affect more the stock return of firms in durable goods, technology, and telecommunications sectors. Likewise, Kurov [48] concludes that

Table 9.2 Descriptive statistics of B_1 coefficients.

	Average	Standard deviation	Smallest	Biggest	Number of companies	Number of companies with statistically significant coefficient*
ISE-100	-0.024	0.016	-0.065	0.014	94	55
ISE-All	-0.022	0.016	-0.078	0.073	272	137

*Companies with a P value less than 0.1.

monetary policy surprises lead to a stronger response in stock returns of firms in the durable goods and technology sectors as well as firms in the trade and finance sectors. Ehrmann and Fratzscher [33] reveal that capital-intensive sectors are more affected by monetary policy. Kurov [48] and Basistha [39] reach similar results and they argue that firms in the gas and electricity distribution and energy sectors are less affected by monetary policy surprises. Similarly, Bredin et al. [9] present that firms in the food, health, gas, and electricity distribution sectors are less affected by monetary policy surprises. Chuliá et al. [24] also conclude that monetary policy surprises are more effective on the stock returns of firms in the technology and finance sectors, but this effect is less in the gas and electricity distribution sectors.

9.5.1 Sectoral Difference

We collect stock prices traded in ISE as of the end of 2010 from Datastream on the monetary policy decision days and prior business days in the framework of event study methodology. The stock returns are calculated as the logarithmic return on the decision days. The model in Equation 9.3 examines the role of sectoral variation in the effect of monetary policy on stock prices where ΔS_t and $\Delta R_{i,t}$ represent the monetary policy surprise and the stock price change, and the coefficient β_1 shows the reaction of the stock prices in the sector "j" to the monetary policy surprise.

$$\Delta R_{i,t} = \beta_0 + \beta_1 \Delta S_t + u_{i,t}, \, i \in \text{sector } j \tag{9.3}$$

$$\Delta R_{i,t} = \beta_0 + \beta_1 \Delta S_t + \beta_2 \Delta S_t x_i + \beta_3 x_i + u_{i,t} \, i \in \text{ISE} \tag{9.4}$$

The model in Equation (9.4) investigates the sectoral difference from the average as a response of stock prices to the monetary policy surprise. Accordingly, ΔS_t and $\Delta R_{i,t}$ represent the monetary policy surprise and the change in stock prices, respectively, and x_i represents the dummy variable to capture the sectoral effect. While β_1 shows the average effect of monetary policy surprises on stock returns, β_2 represents the interaction of sectoral effects and monetary policy and β_3 captures the effects specific to the sector "j."

We perform model selection tests in panel data analysis and the results suggest using pooled panel data. Levene's group-based varying variance and Wooldridge sequential dependency tests for the error term for

Table 9.3 Sectoral effect of monetary policy surprises on stock prices.[a]

Sector	Equation (9.3)[b] β_1	Equation (9.4)[c] β_2
ISE All	-0.022***	
	(0.007)	
ISE 100	-0.024***	-0.003
	(0.007)	(0.002)
ISE 50	-0.026***	-0.002
	(0.007)	(0.004)
ISE 30	-0.024***	-0.002
	(0.006)	(0.004)
Financial	-0.025***	-0.005**
	(0.007)	(0.002)
Industrial	-0.021***	0.003
	(0.007)	(0.002)
Services	-0.021***	0.001
	(0.007)	(0.002)

(Continued)

Table 9.3 Sectoral effect of monetary policy surprises on stock prices.[a]

Sector	Equation (9.3)[b] β_1	Equation (9.4)[c] β_2
Technology	-0.017*	0.005
	(0.009)	(0.005)
Bank	-0.032***	-0.011***
	(0.009)	(0.004)
Food and beverage	-0.018**	0.005
	(0.008)	(0.004)
Textile and leather	-0.022***	0,000
	(0.006)	(0.003)
Petroleum, chemical, and plastic	-0.021***	0.001
	(0.007)	(0.003)
Metal	-0.019**	0.003
	(0.007)	(0.004)
Metalware-machine	-0.019***	0.003
	(0.006)	(0.002)
Trade	-0.018**	0.004
	(0.007)	(0.003)
Holding and investment	-0.022***	0,000
	(0.007)	(0.002)
Real estate investment trusts	-0.025***	-0.003
	(0.006)	(0.005)

Note: Data in parentheses are standard errors; *** indicates a 1% significance level, ** indicates a 5% significance level, and * indicates a 10% significance level.
[a] Each sector is evaluated in separate panels.
[b] The dependent variable is the stock prices of companies in the sector, and the independent variable is monetary policy surprises.
[c] The dependent variable is the stock prices of all ISE companies, and the independent variable is monetary policy surprises.

the reliability of the statistical inference (Appendix 1) suggest using the variance-covariance matrix developed by Driscoll and Kraay [49].[2]

The first column of Table 9.3 presents the results of Equation 9.3 that the returns of stocks in the ISE-100, ISE-50, and ISE-30, including the biggest firms, react more to monetary policy surprises compared to the average in contrast to the expectations that large firms are affected less by monetary policy as they are less financially constrained. However, the ISE-100, ISE-50, and ISE-30 indices contain mostly firms in the financial sector and monetary policy is expected to affect more the financial sector. Meanwhile, the stock returns in the real estate sector are also affected by monetary policy surprises due to the effect of monetary policy on housing loans and thus housing demand. Stock returns in the industrial and the petroleum, chemical, and plastics indices react close to the average. On the other hand, stock returns in the metal main sector, metal goods, and machinery sector are less affected compared to the average that is thought to be associated with the export capacities of these sectors. Similarly, returns in the food and beverage sector respond less to monetary policy surprises that the sector is not very sensitive to business cycles.

The second column of Table 9.3 presents the results of Equation 9.4. The results show that the response of stock returns to monetary policy surprises differs only in the financial and banking sectors from the average. The coefficients in other sectors are not statistically different from the average.

9.6   The Impact of Financial Constraints

In this section, we investigate the role of financial constraint on the effect of monetary policy surprises over stock returns similar to Ehrmann and Fratzscher [33]. There are different proxies for financial constraints in the literature one of which is firm size. Ehrmann and Fratzscher [33] state that size is an important factor in the effect of monetary policy on stock returns. Likewise, Thorbecke [3] concludes that monetary policy shocks affect the stock returns of small companies more. Yet, Guo [41] argues that while size is a determinant in the effect of monetary policy shocks on stock returns in the 1970s, it lost its validity in the 1990s.

As other proxies for financial constraint, Ehrmann and Fratzscher [33] utilize cash flow/income, debt/capital, and Tobin Q ratios. Basistha and Kurov

---

[2]The variance-covariance matrix developed by [49] gives reliable results in cases of varying variance, sequential dependence, and cross-section dependence. It can also be used in unbalanced panels.

[39] use commercial loans as a financial constraint in the US and conclude that monetary policy affects stronger for stock returns of financially constrained firms. Similarly, Scharler [20] argues that firms more dependent on bank financing are more affected by monetary policy decisions.

Similar to previous studies, we include market value and number of employees to proxy size, cash flow/income, debt/capital, and Tobin Q ratios to represent the financial constraint. Equation 9.5 examines the role of financial constraint in the effect of monetary policy surprises on stock returns where ΔS_t and $\Delta R_{i,t}$ represent the monetary policy surprise and the stock return of the firm i, respectively. The dummy variables capture stock-based differences in a way that stock returns are categorized according to the above or below the average of financial constraints, and z takes the values of one and two depending on whether the financial constraint is lower or higher than the average. Thus, $x_{z,i,t}$ represents the dummy variable which takes value according to whether the financial constraint indicator is in the low or high grouping, and "t" indicates that the dummy variable changes through time. The coefficient of $\beta_{z,2}$ shows how the stock return is affected by the monetary policy surprise compared to the average.

$$\Delta R_{i,t} = \beta_0 + \beta_1 \Delta S_t + \sum_{z=1,2} \beta_{z,2} \Delta S_t x_{z,i,t} + \sum_{z=1,2} \beta_{z,3} x_{z,i,t} + u_{i,t} \qquad (9.5)$$

Stocks are grouped into low, medium, and high financially constrained by using the 33rd and 67th percentiles at each MPC meeting date. For robustness checks, grouping is repeated by 10th and 90th percentiles. After defining dummy variables according to high and low values of financial constraint indicators, Equation 9.5 questions whether the effect of monetary policy surprises on stock returns varies depending on being high or low financially constrained. At this point, the financial constraint status of a stock reflects its relative position at the time of the MPC meeting. Therefore, being financially constrained differs throughout time.

The results of model selection are given in Appendix 2 and point out to use of the same model and variance-covariance matrix in Section 9.4. Table 9.4 presents the correlation between the financial constraint indicators of ISE companies.[3] Accordingly, the correlation between the financial constraint variables is low, except for the correlation between the indicators related to company size. This infers that the firm could be financially

---

[3] Before taking the average value of all companies, extreme values outside of three standard deviations were removed for each financial constraint indicator.

Table 9.4 Correlation of financial constraint indicators.

	Cash flow/ income ratio	Debt/ equity ratio	Number of employees	Tobin Q ratio	Market value
Cash flow/ income ratio	1				
Debt/capital ratio	0.094	1			
Number of employees	0.2334	0.2014	1		
Tobin Q ratio	0.0321	0.1449	0.0289	1	
Market value	0.1905	0.2377	0.7958	0.0919	1

constrained according to one indicator but not financially constrained according to another variable.

According to the results in Table 9.5, the coefficient of the stocks with a low number of employees and low market value is higher consistent with the view that small companies are more financially constrained and more affected by monetary policy surprises. The response of stock prices to monetary policy is stronger than the average if the number of employees is classified as low according to the 10th and 90th percentiles. However, other company size indicators are not statistically different from the average. Theoretically, the stock returns of firms with high cash flows are expected to be less affected by monetary policy surprises because they are more resistant to external shocks on cash flow changes. Conversely, the results show that the cash flow/income ratio does not vary the effect of monetary policy surprises on stock returns.

Concerning the Tobin Q ratio, monetary policy surprises affect the firms with higher or lower Tobin Q ratios compared to the average. Thus, the Tobin Q ratio seems to have a nonlinear role in the effect of monetary policy surprises on stock returns. Consistent with the view that a higher Tobin Q ratio infers a higher financing capacity and fewer financial constraints, the results show that firms with high Tobin Q ratios are less affected by monetary policy surprises. The coefficients of the debt/equity ratio point out that stock returns are less affected by monetary policy surprises than the average if firm indebtedness is low. Similar to Ehrmann and Fratzscher [33], the coefficient for high indebtedness is below both the average and the low indebtedness coefficient. Here, the results are consistent if one considers

Table 9.5 Monetary policy surprises and indicators of financial constraints.[a]

		33% to 67% category			10% to 90% category		
		$\beta_1 + \beta_{z,2}$ [b]	Standard error	$\beta_{z,2}$ p-value	$\beta_1 + \beta_{z,2}$ [b]	Standard error	$\beta_{z,2}$ p-value
Market value	Low	-0.024***	0.008	0.407	-0.026***	0.009	0.262
	Middle	-0.022***	0.007		-0.022***	0.007	
	High	-0.022***	0.006	0.919	-0.023***	0.006	0.583
Number of employees	Low	-0.024***	0.008	0.545	-0.028***	0.007	0.006***
	Middle	-0.023***	0.008		-0.022***	0.007	
	High	-0.021***	0.005	0.616	-0.023***	0.005	0.734
Cash flow/ income ratio	Low	-0.022***	0.007	0.896	-0.020***	0.006	0.622
	Middle	-0.022***	0.007		-0.021***	0.007	
	High	-0.022***	0.007	0.895	-0.028***	0.009	0.087*
Tobin Q ratio	Low	-0.021***	0.007	0.008***	-0.021***	0.007	0.531
	Middle	-0.025***	0.008		-0.023***	0.007	
	High	-0.019***	0.006	0.004***	-0.016***	0.005	0.062*
Debt/capital ratio	Low	-0.021***	0.007	0.059*	-0.021***	0.007	0.852
	Middle	-0.025***	0.008		-0.023***	0.007	
	High	-0.019***	0.006	0.896	-0.016***	0.005	0.622

Note: *** indicates a 1% significance level, ** indicates a 5% significance level, and * indicates a 10% significance level.
[a] Each financial constraint indicator is evaluated in separate panels.
[b] z=1 and z=2 are used for low and high coefficients, respectively, while β_1 alone indicates the coefficient for the middle level.

the level of debt as the ease of access to finance and easier access to finance implies firms are less affected in the case of tighter financial conditions in response to monetary policy action.

9.7   Discussion and Conclusion

In this study, we examine the effect of monetary policy decisions on stock returns in Türkiye by event study methodology. We first separate the monetary policy decision into expected and unexpected parts considering that the markets predict the monetary policy decisions beforehand so the unexpected part of the monetary policy decision is expected to affect investor behavior and stock return. The stock return is proxied by the ISE-100 index and the unexpected part of the monetary policy also called the surprise component is taken as the one-month Treasury interest rate. The results show that monetary policy surprises have a negative effect on stock returns. A 100–basis point surprise in monetary policy leads to an average 2.7% decrease in the index. As expected, the response of stock index returns to the expected part of monetary policy is not significant because markets have already priced in the expected change in monetary policy. The analysis investigating the role of uncertainty in the relationship between monetary policy and stock return points out that the relationship is stronger during periods of high market volatility.

Furthermore, firm-based analysis shows that the effect of monetary policy surprises on stock returns differs and is not homogeneous. The stock returns of the ISE-100 constituents exhibit different responses to monetary policy surprises, ranging from -6.5% to 1.4%. Hence, we questioned whether this difference is determined by the sector and financial conditions of a firm. The analysis of sectoral information reveals that the stock returns of firms in the financial sectors differ from the average stock returns.

Regarding the impact of financial constraints, the results suggest that smaller firms are more affected by monetary policy surprises. Although the cash flow/income ratio does not significantly influence the effect of monetary policy surprises, the Tobin Q ratio shows a nonlinear relationship where firms with higher or lower Tobin Q ratios are less affected by monetary policy surprises compared to the average. Similarly, stock returns are less affected by monetary policy surprises for stocks with low levels of indebtedness. Overall, the results show that financial constraint has a limited contribution to explain the difference between the response of stock returns to the monetary policy surprise.

In sum, our study has similar findings to previous literature on the relationship between monetary policy and stock return at index level. On the other hand, we extended the discussion by incorporating individual stock returns and firm-level characteristics. The results are important in the means of providing a deeper understanding of the heterogeneity in the relationship between monetary policy and stock return among firms.

References

1. Bernanke, B.S. and Gertler, M., Inside the black box: The credit channel of monetary policy transmission. *J. Econ Perspect. (JEP)*, 9, 4, 27–48, 1995.
2. Brunner, A.D., On the derivation of monetary policy shocks: Should we throw the VAR out with the bath water? *J. Money Credit Bank (JMCB)*, 32, 2, 254, 2000.
3. Thorbecke, W., On stock market returns and monetary policy. *J. Finance*, 52, 2, 635–654, 1997.
4. D'amico, S. and Farka, M., The fed and stock market: A proxy and instrumental variable identification. *Royal Economic Society*, vol. 52, pp. 1–34, 2003.
5. Rigobon, R. and Sack, B., The impact of monetary policy on asset prices. *J. Monet. Econ.*, 51, 8, 1553–1575, 2004.
6. Neuhierl, A. and Weber, M., Monetary policy slope and the stock market. *SSRN*, 108, C, 140–155, 2016.
7. Ozdagli, A. and Velikov, M., Show me the money: The monetary policy risk premium. *J. Financ. Econ.*, 135, 2, 320–339, 2020.
8. Wei, X. and Han, L., The impact of COVID-19 pandemic on transmission of monetary policy to financial markets. *Int. Rev. Financial Anal. (IRFA)*, 74, 101705, 2021.
9. Bredin, D., Hyde, S., Nitzsche, D., O'Reilly, G., European monetary policy surprises: The aggregate and sectoral stock market response. *Int. J. Finance Econ.*, 14, 2, 156–171, 2009.
10. Gregoriou, A., Kontonikas, A., MacDonald, R., Montagnoli, A., Monetary policy shocks and stock returns: Evidence from the british market. *Financial Mark. Portf. Manage. (FMPM)*, 23, 4, 401–410, 2009.
11. Demiralp, S. and Yilmaz, K., Para politikası beklentilerinin sermaye piyasaları üzerindeki etkisi. *İktisat İşlet Finans*, 25, 296, 9–31, 2010.
12. Aktaş, Z., Alp, H., Gürkaynak, R., Kesriyeli, M., Orak, M., Türkiye'de para politikasının aktarımı: Para politikasının mali piyasalara etkisi. *İktisat İşlet Finans*, 24, 278, 9–24, 2009.
13. Duran, M., Özcan, G., Özlü, P., Ünalmış, D., Measuring the impact of monetary policy on asset prices in Turkey. *Econ. Lett.*, 114, 1, 29–31, 2012.
14. Bernanke, B.S. and Kuttner, K.N., What explains the stock market's reaction to federal reserve policy? *J. Finance*, 60, 3, 1221–1257, 2005.
15. Mishkin, F.S., The transmission mechanism and the role of asset prices in monetary policy, in: *Monetary Policy Strategy*, vol. 8617, pp. 59–74, 2018.
16. Laeven, L. and Tong, H., US monetary shocks and global stock prices. *J. Financ. Intermediation*, 21, 3, 530–547, 2012.
17. Fair, R.C., Events that shook the market. *J. Bus.*, 75, 4, 713–731, 2002.
18. Patelis, A.D., Stock return predictability and the role of monetary policy. *J. Finance*, 52, 5, 1951–1972, 1997.

19. Bernanke, B.S. and Blinder, A.S., The federal funds rate and the channels of monetary transmission. *Am. Econ. Rev.*, *82*, 4, 901–921, 1992.

20. Scharler, J., Bank lending and the stock market's response to monetary policy shocks. *Int. Rev. Econ. Finance (IREF)*, *17*, 3, 425–435, 2008.

21. Bohl, M.T., Siklos, P.L., Sondermann, D., European stock markets and the ECB's monetary policy surprises. *Int. Finance*, *11*, 2, 117–130, 2008.

22. Rezessy, A., *Estimating the immediate impact of monetary policy shocks on the exchange rate and other asset prices in Hungary*, Magyar Nemzeti Bank, Budapest, 2005.

23. Bomfim, A.N., Pre-announcement effects, news effects, and volatility: Monetary policy and the stock market. *J. Bank. Financ.*, 27, 1, 133–151, 2003.

24. Chuliá, H., Martens, M., van Dijk, D., Asymmetric effects of federal funds target rate changes on S&P100 stock returns, volatilities and correlations. *J. Bank. Financ.*, *34*, 4, 834–839, 2010.

25. Andersson, M., Using intraday data to gauge financial market responses to federal reserve and ECB monetary policy decisions. *Int. J. Cent Bank (IJCB)*, 6, 2, 117–146, 2010.

26. Reichenstein, W., The impact of money on short-term interest rates. *Econ. Inq.*, *25*, 1, 67–82, 1987.

27. Kuttner, K.N., Monetary policy and asset price volatility, in: *New Perspectives on Asset Price Bubbles*, vol. *7559*, pp. 211–240, 2015.

28. Rigobon, R. and Sack, B., Measuring the reaction of monetary policy to the stock market. *Q. J. Econ.*, *118*, 2, 639–669, 2003.

29. Brooks, C., *Introductory Econometrics for Finance*, Cambridge: Cambridge University Press, 2008.

30. Cochrane, J.H. and Piazzesi, M., The fed and interest rates - A high-frequency identification. *Am. Econ. Rev.*, *92*, 2, 90–95, 2002.

31. Rudebusch, G.D., Do measures of monetary policy in a VAR make sense? *Int. Econ. Rev.*, *39*, 4, 907, 1998.

32. Cook, T. and Hahn, T., The effect of changes in the federal funds rate target on market interest rates in the 1970s. *J. Monet. Econ.*, *24*, 3, 331–351, 1989.

33. Ehrmann, M. and Fratzscher, M., Taking stock: Monetary policy transmission to equity markets. *J. Money Credit Bank (JMCB)*, *36*, 4, 719–737, 2004.

34. Kuttner, K.N., Monetary policy surprises and interest rates: Evidence from the Fed funds futures market. *J. Monet. Econ.*, *47*, 3, 523–544, 2001.

35. Lange, J., Sack, B., Whitesell, W., Anticipations of monetary policy in financial markets. *J. Money Credit Bank (JMCB)*, *35*, 6, 889–909, 2003.

36. Gürkaynak, R.S., Sack, B., Swanson, E.T., Do actions speak louder than words? The response of asset prices to monetary policy actions and statements. *Finance and Economics Discussion Series (FEDS)*, vol. *2004*, pp. 1–43, 2004.

37. Krueger, J.T. and Kuttner, K.N., The fed funds futures rate as a predictor of federal reserve policy. *J. Futures Mark.*, *16*, 8, 865–879, 1996.

38. Pearce, D.K. and Roley, V.V., The reaction of stock prices to unanticipated changes in money: A note. *J. Finance*, *38*, 4, 1323, 1983.

39. Basistha, A. and Kurov, A., Macroeconomic cycles and the stock market's reaction to monetary policy. *J. Bank. Financ.*, *32*, 12, 2606–2616, 2008.

40. Poole, W. and Rasche, R.H., Perfecting the market's knowledge of monetary policy. *J. Financial Serv. Res.*, *18*, 2–3, 255–298, 2000.

41. Guo, H., Stock prices, firm size, and changes in the federal funds rate target. *Q. Rev. Econ. Finance*, *44*, 4, 487–507, 2004.

42. Cochrane, J.H. and Piazzesi, M., The fed and interest rates - A high-frequency identification. *Am. Econ. Rev.*, *92*, 2, 90–95, 2002.

43. Craine, R. and Martin, V.L., International monetary policy surprise spillovers. *J. Int. Econ.*, *75*, 1, 180–196, 2008.

44. Ellingsen, T. and Ulf, S., Monetary policy and the bond market, Bocconi University, 2003.

45. Gürkaynak, R.S., Sack, B.P., Swanson, E.T., Market-based measures of monetary policy expectations. *J. Bus. Econ. Stat.*, *25*, 2, 201–212, 2007.

46. Gulsen, E., Kanlı, İ., Kaya, N., *Kuresel Kriz Doneminde TCMB'nin Faiz Kararlarinin Kur Uzerindeki Etkisine Dair Bir Analiz*, CBT Research Notes in Economics 1011, Research and Monetary Policy Department, Central Bank of the Republic of Turkey, 2010.

47. Alp, H., Gürkaynak, R., Kara, H., Keleş, G., Orak, M., Türkiye'de piyasa göstergelerinden para politikası beklentilerinin ölçülmesi. *İktisat İşlet Finans*, *25*, 295, 21–45, 2010.

48. Kurov, A., Investor sentiment and the stock market's reaction to monetary policy. *J. Bank. Financ.*, *34*, 1, 139–149, 2010.

49. Driscoll, J.C. and Kraay, A.C., Consistent covariance matrix estimation with spatially dependent panel data. *Rev. Econ. Stat.*, *80*, 4, 549–559, 1998.

Appendix 1

Table 9.A.1 Test results.*

	Hausman test[1]	Breusch Pagan LM test[2]	Levene test[3]	Wooldridge test
ISE-All	0.71	0.03	0.00	0.00
ISE-100	0.72	0.05	0.00	0.00
ISE- 50	0.79	0.01	0.00	0.00
ISE-30	0.70	0.11	0.17	0.00
ISE-Financial	0.67	0.29	0.00	0.00
ISE-Industrial	0.96	0.07	0.00	0.00
ISE-Services	0.58	0.70	0.00	0.26
ISE-Technology	-37.90	0.35	0.01	0.61
ISE-Bank	0.94	0.07	0.43	0.00
ISE-Food, Beverage	0.83	0.68	0.32	0.13
ISE-Textile, Leather	1.00	0.89	0.00	0.21
ISE-Chemistry, Petroleum, Plastic	1.00	0.14	0.02	0.01
ISE-Metal Main	1.00	0.07	0.30	0.25
ISE-Metal Goods, Machinery	0.99	0.21	0.00	0.15
ISE-Trade	0.58	0.69	0.00	0.02
ISE-Holding and Investment	-0.53	0.19	0.00	0.09
ISE-Real Estate YO	0.75	0.77	0.07	0.47

* Values given are p values.

Appendix 2

Table 9.A.2 Test results.*

	Hausman test	Breusch Pagan LM test[4]	Levene test[5]	Wooldridge test
ISE-All				
ISE-100	0.81	0.03	0.00	0.00
ISE- 50	0.86	0.03	0.00	0.00
ISE-30	0.86	0.03	0.00	0.00
ISE-Financial	0.87	0.03	0.00	0.00
ISE-Industrial	0.87	0.03	0.00	0.00
ISE-Services	0.87	0.03	0.00	0.00
ISE-Technology	0.79	0.03	0.00	0.00
ISE-Bank	0.77	0.03	0.00	0.00
ISE-Food, Beverage	0.87	0.03	0.00	0.00
ISE-Textile, Leather	0.78	0.03	0.00	0.00
ISE-Chemistry, Petroleum, Plastic	0.76	0.03	0.00	0.00
ISE-Metal Main	0.71	0.03	0.00	0.00
ISE-Metal Goods, Machinery	0.71	0.03	0.00	0.00
ISE-Trade	0.55	0.03	0.00	0.00
ISE-Holding and Investment	0.88	0.03	0.00	0.00
ISE-Real Estate YO	0.71	0.03	0.00	0.00

* Values given are p values.

10

Revolutionizing Stock Market Predictions: Exploring the Role of Artificial Intelligence

Rajani H. Pillai* and Aatika Bi

School of Commerce, Mount Carmel College Autonomous, Bengaluru, Karnataka, India

Abstract

AI, or artificial intelligence, is widely used for data analysis, prediction, and decision-making. The stock market's fluctuating pricing has made investors nervous. Market volatility does not mean investors cannot make money if they take the time to do their homework and make smart choices. AI is becoming increasingly important in this process due to its capacity to discern patterns and anticipate actions. When compared to traditional analysis approaches, AI excels because of its rapid processing of large datasets and the high degree of accuracy it provides. In light of this history, the purpose of the present research is to provide a comprehensive explanation of how AI aids in the forecasting of financial markets. In order to provide a solid theoretical foundation for future researchers to investigate the role of AI in stock prediction, this study conducts a systematic literature review analysis of the available works in this area. This research will add to the growing body of work on AI in financial markets, and investors stand to gain much from AI-based stock market projections.

Keywords: Artificial intelligence, stock markets, theoretical framework

10.1 Introduction

Since the debut of analytical modeling in finance in the 1990s [1], a significant amount of research has been devoted to studying how AI may be

Corresponding author: rajani.h.pillai@mccblr.edu.in; ORCID: https://orcid.org/0000-0002-6473-4412
Aatika Bi: ORCID: https://orcid.org/0000-0002-8655-3428

Renuka Sharma and Kiran Mehta (eds.) Deep Learning Tools for Predicting Stock Market Movements, (227–248) © 2024 Scrivener Publishing LLC

applied to make better stock market transactions. This line of inquiry has been particularly prevalent since the advent of computational methods in finance. The elimination of "momentary irrationality," or decisions made based on emotions, the finding of patterns that humans overlook [2], and the rapid consumption of information are three of the numerous benefits that may be gained through using computational approaches to automate the process of investing in the financial markets. This branch of research is now commonly referred to by the title "Computational Finance" [3].

Within the domain of computational finance, there has been a significant upsurge in both the utilization of artificial intelligence (AI) strategies in the context of financial investments as well as the research into these strategies [4]. The fact that 90% of hedge fund trades are carried out automatically is the result of a strategy that is hardcoded. As a result, there is still a significant amount of opportunity for progress in the utilization of AI, which is becoming increasingly common [5].

The three primary applications of AI in finance are the optimization of financial portfolios, the prediction of future prices or trends in financial assets, and the study of sentiment in news or social media opinions about assets or enterprises [6, 7]. It has been suggested in a few publications that, despite the individuality and peculiarities of each field, it is beneficial to combine methodologies from a number of different fields. Research into subjects such as investor behavior, the clustering of financial assets, network analysis, and the regulation of dynamic systems in the financial market are all included in computational finance [8].

AI describes software designed to do tasks normally associated with human intelligence. Data analysis, prediction, and decision-making are just a few of the many applications of AI software [9]. AI systems are crucial in many industries, including healthcare, banking, and manufacturing [10]. Investors are on edge because of the stock market's unpredictable price movements. However, those who are not afraid of the unknown can benefit from these variations in luck. Investors can still make money despite the volatile market provided they do their research and make informed decisions. The ability of AI to recognize patterns and foresee outcomes is expanding AI's role in this procedure [11]. Particularly, AI's fast and reliable information can assist in reducing the dangers of investing in the stock market. Therefore, AI will undeniably play a bigger role in global financial markets in the years to come. Investors may now utilize AI to create accurate forecasts regarding the stock market's future performance [12]. To improve their stock price predicting abilities, AI forecasting engines may one day use a combination of historical data and real-time data. AI is superior to more conventional methods of analysis because of the speed and accuracy with which it processes enormous datasets [13, 14]

Given this context, the current study aims to provide a thorough analysis of how AI contributes to financial market forecasting. This research will analyze the existing literature systematically to create a theoretical groundwork for future studies into the use of AI in stock prediction. AI in financial markets is an expanding field of study, and investors can benefit greatly from stock market forecasts that incorporate AI models [13]. AI has several applications in finance, including assisting investors in spotting patterns and making informed trading decisions. Predictions made by means of AI might one day be used to detect instances of market manipulation. Therefore, AI offers a powerful resource for market actors looking to keep their competitive edge.

10.2   Review of Literature

The review of literature for the study is carried out in the chronological order of the papers published:

> According to [15], researchers compare two leading methods for training neural networks using a genetic algorithm (GA)–based method for transforming features (artificial neural networks, ANNs). In this study, the GA is utilized to train ANNs to better predict stock market outcomes through increased learning and generalization. Researchers generate forecasts daily and keep tabs on how accurate they are. In this study, researchers examine and contrast three different feature transformation approaches for ANNs. When compared to the outcomes attained using the GA, the proposed model outperforms the other two feature transformation strategies. Experimental results demonstrate that the suggested approach successfully reduces the dimensionality of the feature space, hence minimizing the effect of noise on stock market forecasts.

> Although it is theoretically feasible to foresee the future and make money off of it without taking any risks, the future is still a complete unknown. One such potential involves the application of machine learning (ML) and AI for stock market prediction. Despite the unpredictability of the stock market, it is possible and advisable to employ AI to make

accurate projections before making any transactions. This study presents a review of the state of the art in applying ML and AI to the field of financial market analytics. Researchers discuss the potential and risks of adopting cutting-edge technologies for stock market prediction and discuss the pros and cons of using ML for this task. ML techniques such as ANNs, support vector machines, and long short-term memory have all been investigated further for their potential utility in stock market prediction [16].

➢ Financial investing using AI has received significant scholarly interest since the 1990s, a time of rapid technological development and broad usage of the personal computer. Since then, many proposals for improving stock price forecasting have been made. This report presents an in-depth summary of the literature on AI and investing in the stock market by examining a representative sample of 2326 publications published on the Scopus website between 1995 and 2019. The works were divided into four categories, including those that focused on portfolio optimization, AI-based stock market prediction, financial sentiment research, and hybrids of these approaches. The evolution of each subfield, from its first research to its most recent applications, is outlined in the following sections. The increasing specialization and breadth of the literature on this topic is one indication that there is a growing interest in this area of study, as is the case according to the broad perspective of the review [17].

➢ In a recent study, authors employ AI methods in an attempt to resolve the age-old dilemma of making reliable stock market forecasts [18]. The results of two types of research—technical and fundamental—can be used to model stock market predictions. The technical analysis approach employs regression ML algorithms to foretell the movement of a stock's price at the end of trading. The fundamental analysis, on the other hand, uses classification ML algorithms to classify public opinion gleaned from various channels, such as the media and social media. Yahoo Finance's price history is used for technical analysis, while Twitter's public tweets provide insight into the impact of sentiment on the stock market's outlook through fundamental analysis. Since the results are in the center of the pack, it seems premature to conclude that AI can outperform the stock markets with the current state of AI technology.

➤ Since its establishment as an area of computer science, particularly in Iran, the use of AI in data analysis has led to revolutionary changes in the agricultural, industrial, and medical sectors. Today, AI is used virtually in every scientific discipline, from financial market predictions to medical imaging to name a few [19]. This article provides an overview of AI and time series models before delving into the use of the system for forecasting in the Forex and stock markets. Defining the process through which AI arrives at its forecasts is the first step. To anticipate the future value of cryptocurrency and stock markets, algorithms must first learn the processes involved in trading these assets. This essay could be useful for economists, statisticians, and AI specialists who are trying to solve difficult problems.

➤ The stock market is essential to the growth and stability of any economy, thus investors want to maximize profit while limiting loss [20–22]. As a result, several different soft-computing methodologies and algorithms have been used in research attempting to anticipate the stock market using technical or fundamental analysis [23]. The purpose of this study was to conduct a systematic literature evaluation of 122 academic journal articles covering the issue of stock market prediction using ML over an 11-year period (2007–2018). Technical methods, fundamental methods, and hybrid approaches were the three broad categories into which these published works' methods fell. The properties of each dataset were used to classify them (such as the number of data sources it drew from, its time range, the ML algorithms it employed, the nature of the task to which it was put, the accuracy and error metrics it was measured against, and the modeling software it was run on). The results showed that 23% of the documents examined relied on fundamental analysis, whereas 11% used a mix of the two. Researchers found that 89.34% of the documents we reviewed only used one source of information, whereas 8.2% used two, and 2.46% used three. It was found that when it comes to predicting the stock market, the two most common ML techniques are the support vector machine and the ANN [24].

➤ Stock market investing is a complex endeavor that calls for the examination of enormous datasets [25–27]. In recent years, researchers have looked into whether or not ML techniques may improve upon traditional methods of market forecasting [28]. The goal of this study is to examine existing literature in order to better understand future directions for research into using ML for stock market forecasting. A systematic literature review is conducted to identify the most relevant peer-reviewed journal papers published in the past 20 years and to classify research that applies similar methodology and contexts. ANN research, support vector machine research, GA + other technique research, and other hybrid or other AI research are the four primary forms of AI study. Discussion is given to the studies' similarities, discrepancies, limitations, and information gaps. Researchers make broad conclusions and propose future research in the conclusion.

➤ Investment portfolios cannot function without stocks; they are arguably the most widely used tool developed specifically for the aim of amassing money. Modern-day stock market investing is within reach of just about everybody because of the proliferation of trading technologies made possible by the Internet [29, 30]. The interest of the average individual in the stock market has increased dramatically during the past few decades. As the stock market is both highly unpredictable and possibly rewarding, it is essential to have a trustworthy forecast of future trends. In view of the current financial crisis and the necessity for precise profit recording, a trustworthy stock value projection is crucial [31].

➤ The stock market is essential to every functioning economy. It is a common way for companies to get the capital they need to pay for day-to-day operations. In a stock exchange, brokers can buy and sell stocks, bonds, and other securities to one another. Once a stock is listed, anyone with access to the stock market can buy or sell it. Many people have tried to predict the market, and they have not had much success. Stock market prediction is gaining popularity among academics, investment communities, and fans because it delivers improved investment advice. Gains in the stock market and other forms of investment capital depend critically on the ability to anticipate future events. The stock's perceived predictability is crucial to the success of both investors and traders. If a system could be developed that accurately predicted the stock market's ever-changing trends, a lot of money would be made. The anticipated tendencies of the market will also help authorities in their efforts to stabilize the market. Experts in the subject have presented a variety of models to predict the stock market's behavior, drawing from a wide range of technical, fundamental, and analytical approaches [32–34].

➤ Forecasting nonlinear trends in stock market data is famously challenging because of the chaotic structure of the data [35]. It is not easy to construct a portfolio of stocks that will perform well over time, and every portfolio model has its limitations. In recent years, a plethora of AI models (also known as intelligent models) have arisen in the research literature to tackle these kinds of problems. There has always been a lot of curiosity about how to predict the stock market and how to choose the best investments among investors, business people, and academics. In this research, we examine the foundational works on the subject using a systematic literature review. In this review, researchers will look at a wide range of mathematical models, from those developed decades ago to those developed using AI.

➤ In a market as volatile as the stock exchange, being able to accurately predict market movement is vital [36]. Accurate stock price forecasting is essential in today's economy because of the pressure to maximize earnings. Predicting nonlinear signals requires sophisticated ML methods. The published literature contains studies that employ a wide range of ML approaches, including ANNs and feature selection strategies.

➤ The study of stock market data is impossible without the use of AI and data mining techniques [37]. One key factor in market volatility is whether or not a company is making money. Public perception of stock market forecasting as anything other than a sure thing is low. However, patterns can be derived from stock price analysis. Financial data, both historical and current, can provide valuable insights and automated decision-making tools when data mining techniques are applied. A number of strategies developed by academics to try and predict stock values are discussed. These research projects show how useful data mining techniques are for examining past stock prices and deducing useful information by means of the assessment of pertinent financial indicators.

➢ According to researchers [38], the prediction of financial time series has provided a challenging test bed for a number of AI models that seek to computerize human thinking. Extensive research has led to the development of a number of financial applications that make use of AI models. As a significant form of investing, buying and selling stocks have a high risk of financial loss if done without enough preparation. Therefore, investors and financial professionals have long been interested in trying to anticipate the stock market's movement.

The review of the literature identified that the practice of predicting stock prices entails the application of various techniques such as ML, moving averages, ANN analysis, support vector machine analysis, GA, neural networks, and long short-term memory networks (LSTM). The remaining research paper expounds upon the role of AI within the domain of stock markets, as analyzed by the existing corpus of scholarly works. The review of the literature shows that there is a need to study the literature on AI in stock markets.

10.3   Research Methods

The goal of this study is to explore the impact that AI has on stock market predictions so that recommendations can be made moving forward. A wide range of stock market prediction models are analyzed in this research project so that the results can be used to assess the influence that AI has had on many aspects of stock markets. Because of this, the investigation makes use of a retrogressive technique, which requires the investigation of secondary data and materials in addition to the analysis of prior studies. This is necessary because of the nature of the inquiry. In point of fact, a number of researchers asserted that completing a systematic or semi-systematic literature review in addition to a study of secondary data might assist researchers in gaining a higher level of comprehension regarding the phenomenon that is the focus of their investigation. Because it is the only one that helps in the identification, analysis, comprehension, and synthesis of the ways in which AI has altered and impacted education and its results, this methodology ensures that the research is based on empirical or empirically supported evidence. This is because it is the only one that helps ensure that the research is based on empirical evidence. Research that has already been conducted on the topic matter, including meta-analyses on the subject matter, is the only alternative methodology that is helpful. This is due to the fact that there is no other methodology.

Medical research was the first discipline to make use of systematic literature reviews, and evidence-based investigations are now often associated with this style of study. According to another study [39], "the rise of evidence-based practice has resulted in an enlarged range of review techniques." The authors of the research that was conducted by Grant and Booth [40] present an explanation of the roots of the evidence-based approach of completing a literature review as well as its significance to a range of sectors, including management and science.

In this study, an approach that is known as a systematic literature review was applied to analyze prior works that were relevant to the research concerns that were being investigated. There were a total of 48 papers discovered after using the keywords "Artificial intelligence in stock market prediction," "AI for stock predictions," and "AI stock prediction models...," Following an evaluation of whether or not the submitted papers fulfilled the inclusion criteria—namely, that they were written in English and had some connection to AI in stock market made over the past 15 years—a total of 40 papers were chosen for the research. After obtaining a copy of the study paper in its entirety, a total of 40 pieces of previously published literature, which included studies that had been published in reputable journals, were evaluated to establish the degree of quality that each study possessed. The present study was formulated on the basis of 40 previously published scholarly articles that are pertinent to the subject matter. The 40 articles that were included in the study were published in journals that are widely recognized for their academic rigor and reputation. A total of 40 articles were published in various academic databases. Specifically, five articles were published in the Elsevier database, five in the Routledge and CRC Press Taylor and Francis database, seven in the Emerald Group Publishing database, six in the Springer Nature database, and seven in the Sage database. The study makes reference to three articles that were published in the Directory of Open Access Journals, as well as two journals that are included in the Semantic Scholar databases. Several additional papers were obtained from scholarly databases such as Wiley, Academia, JSTOR, and Guildford Press.

10.4   Results and Discussion

The subsequent segment endeavors to elucidate the antecedent literature in the context of AI and its implementation in diverse commercial enterprises. This section provides a detailed analysis of the literature pertaining to the intersection of AI and stock prediction. The process of forecasting stock prices involves the utilization of diverse methodologies, including ML, moving averages, ANN investigation, support vector machine investigation, GA, neural networks, and LSTM. This section elucidates the function of AI in the realm of stock markets, as examined by the extant body of literature.

10.4.1   Discussion on the Literature on Artificial Intelligence

The intelligence displayed by machines that have been built by humans is typically referred to as "artificial intelligence," which can also be referred to as "machine intelligence." The typical category of software applications that attempt to simulate human intelligence is referred to as "artificial intelligence" (AI) in the industry. In introductory-level textbooks, it is often described as the study of both the development of an intelligent agent as well as the research of the production of an intelligent agent. In addition, this suggests that the environment may be watched, and actions relating to those observations can be performed, in order for it to carry out the responsibilities that have been assigned to it by people [41]. The traditional definitions of AI claim that it is capable of accurate interpretation of external data, as well as the exploitation of that data as the foundation for their knowledge, in order to carry out their assigned tasks while displaying a degree of flexibility in the course of those activities.

Without prior education or experience in the field, the field of study known as AI is incredibly challenging to comprehend. It takes into account a vast assortment of possibilities and variations in each and every part of the branch field, which is exhaustive but unrelated to the topic at hand. The growth of thinking, understanding, planning, learning, communication, perception, and the ability to move objects, utilize tools, and manage machines in ways that are equivalent to or even better than those of humans are the most crucial factors that come into play here. A variety of different tools make use of AI technology, and their applications cover a wide range of domains, including research, mathematical optimization, and logical reasoning, to name a few. In addition to this, the creation of algorithmic systems that have their roots in disciplines such as bionics, cognitive psychology, probability theory, and economics is now taking place.

As a result of this, AI has the potential to someday develop into a smart machine that is capable of executing jobs more effectively or even more efficiently than humans. In recent times, there has been a rise in the amount of attention paid to AI, particularly with regard to the area of application. This includes computers that have been modified to add AI features as well as specific types of robots that are able to make decisions relevant to problems that are either commercial or political in nature.

AI also refers to a simulation. Robots are programmed using this method to mimic human characteristics such as learning, comprehending, planning, choosing, and so on. These behaviors include learning new information, being selective, and planning ahead. These actions involve gaining knowledge and comprehension, making plans, and making choices. It focuses primarily on the concept of achieving intelligence through the operation of computers, which entails programming computers to function in a manner that is comparable to that of human brains. The term "artificial intelligence" is often used interchangeably with "artificial general intelligence." As a direct consequence of this, computers are now capable of doing their duties in a more efficient manner. The fact that AI encompasses a wide range of fields, including computer science, psychology, and a great number of other fields, in addition to all of the natural and social sciences, contributes to the complexity of the field as a whole. Other fields that are included in this category include mathematics, linguistics, and philosophy. Understanding the connection between AI and thinking science is difficult due to the fact that this connection is a reflection of both practice and theory.

When compared to the ability to think in pictures or envision, AI is limited in its capacity for logical thought, which is a disadvantage when viewed from the perspective of the scientific method. The advancement of AI ought to be encouraged through creative thinking, but there is no way to avoid the need for mathematical logic in its development. This is because mathematics is a discipline that is associated with linguistics and the thinking process. As a result, the AI system continues to rely on mathematical tools, despite the fact that this kind of logic is not the only type of logic used while constructing AI. The advancement of AI is dependent to a significant degree on the application of mathematics. In addition, it helps the process advance more quickly while also improving it. Strong AI asserts that it is capable of additional reasoning and the resolution of issues. Supporters who only believe in limited AI have stated that it is extremely unlikely that AI would ever be developed that can solve problems in the same way that humans do. The outward manifestation of this technology gives the impression that it is very advanced; nonetheless, the implicit system has not yet achieved the capability of independent thought, let alone self-consciousness.

10.4.2   Discussion on Artificial Intelligence and Stock Prediction

Every level of the stock market has always paid close attention to the volatility of a company's closing price, and analysts have used a wide variety of methods to learn the stock market's rules and predict its future performance. We want to be able to make accurate and reliable projections of a large number of financial variables within a business context. This will allow us to draw the most appropriate inferences and protect the investors from experiencing catastrophic losses.

With the support vector machine technology, Russell and Norvig [42] conducted a study on economic forecasting. The SVR model can be pushed past its inherent constraints to perform adequately at the periphery. Depending on the marginal value used for the SVR, the data's volatility and variability may increase or decrease. They did this by investigating the potential risk-mitigating benefits of asymmetric margins. Stock price fluctuations were predicted using ML methods by Yang et al. [43]. This model is based on particle swarm optimization (PSO) and the least square support vector machine. With the help of technical indicators and past stock prices, improved PSO might provide reasonably accurate daily stock price predictions. By solving the overfitting and local minimum problems that plague LS-SVM and finding the optimal combination of freely chosen parameters, PSO enhances the accuracy of the prediction algorithm. In addition, they compared their models' forecast accuracy to that of 13 industry-standard financial datasets, the Levenberg-Marquardt (LM), and the ANN. Several ANN stock market prediction algorithms were studied by Hegazy et al. [44] (ANN). He believes that by conducting this study, he will be able to provide insight into the direction of ANN development for stock market forecasting. Foreseeing the Saudi stock market with the use of a neural network was the work of Olatunji et al. [45]. The model uses Saudi stock exchange data in the past. The study's results validated the prediction model and will be very useful to Saudi stock market participants. One strategy to boost investor trust in the Saudi stock market is to enhance the predictability and accuracy of the underlying forecasting model.

The closing stock price was used to develop estimations. They simulated several scenarios to find out how many days of data would be optimal for predicting the next day's closing price [45]. To predict the stock's closing price, researchers have employed neural network modeling to analyze historical stock prices [46]. The opening price, the highest and lowest closing prices, volume, and the hidden layer were the six network components found. This network's efficiency is measured with respect to the mean absolute percentage error, the mean absolute deviation, and the root mean square error [47]. Ramani and Murarka [48] predicted 2013 stock prices using an ANN with many feedforward layers and a backpropagation method. Their research lends credence to the hypothesis that ANNs might be able to outperform conventional methods at predicting stock prices. The neural network was trained with input and output data to improve prediction accuracy. A neural network's effectiveness depends on many variables, such as the number of layers it has, the number of neurons it has in its input and hidden layers, its activation function, its learning rate, and its momentum [48]. Nayak et al. [49] made an effort to foretell the final value of India's stock market. To create forecasts, he used a combination of an ANN model and a model based on neurogenetics. Daily closing prices from the Bombay Stock Exchange (BSE) were used to put the models through their paces and determine how well they could predict the movement of the Indian stock market.

The projections were made with the help of the preprocessing methods of Nayak et al. [49]. In 2016, Navale et al. [50] developed a breakthrough method that could evaluate an existing stock database and anticipate stock market data. Using principles from neural networks, this technique was developed. The autoregressive moving-average (ARMA) mode model was employed by Navale to enhance forecasting accuracy. In this way, our program produces a very precise prediction of the stock market [50]. Several people in 2017 tried to predict the stock market using ANNs; Shah was one of them. They looked into several neural network types, their defining features, inner workings, and operational contexts, and drew opinions about their merits and shortcomings. In the end, the optimal network was selected and used in conjunction with the national stock index to make stock price predictions for the various companies [51].

To make stock market predictions, researchers [52] employed a feedforward neural network model. Over a 10-year period, from January 1, 2008 to April 8, 2016, he accurately anticipated daily price movements on the Indian stock market. This is the S&P CNX Nifty Index. Normalized mean square error (NMSE) and sign accuracy were used to evaluate the model's efficacy (SCP). The normalized error barely rises by 0.02 percentage points after a day of delay, as shown by the statistics. If the forecast is consistent with historical stock market data, that is promising. The model correctly predicted the daily direction of Indian stock market values 60% of the time, according to additional data analysis performed after the financial crisis of 2008. The results also demonstrated that the feedforward neural network model is moderately affected by stock market prices that are one day late. Therefore, the functioning of the Indian stock exchange is not entirely represented by the EFFICIENT market theory. Investors, professional traders, and authorities in India's stock market can all benefit from the model's analysis of the market's efficacy [53]. Nti's [24] method of predicting stock prices is ground-breaking. IKN-ConvLSTM is a hybrid network that combines a convolutional neural network (CNN) with an LSTM. In conclusion, our approach to predicting stock prices integrates and analyzes information from six distinct sources. To find the best starting point for training, they employed a simple model made up of CNNs and a random search technique (RSAs). Finally, the stacked LSTM network was fine-tuned using the core model's tuning parameters (features), leading to much-improved prediction accuracy. Stock market data from the Ghana Stock Exchange (GSE) between January 3, 2017 and January 31, 2020 was used to test the model and confirm its accuracy.

To give a comprehensive evaluation of the use of AI strategies in financial markets, Carta *et al.* [54] analyzed a sample of 2326 Scopus-indexed publications published between 1995 and 2015. Russell and Norvig [42] argue that the binary classification problem can be solved with ML. Any firm in the STANDARD & POOR'S 500 index can be predicted to have a major or little change in share price using the same technique. Articles from all across the world are compiled into a centralized ML repository, making it easy to hone in on the most pivotal terms and phrases for any specific field or time period. This information is used to construct the vocabulary. Feature engineering is used to produce the final features of the classifier. The range indicated by the forecast high or low is the expected trading range for the stock on the following trading day. For the AI stock index's 2021 goal to be realized, Wang proposed including AI technology in the Shanghai Composite Index. Between 2005 and 2019, Wang collected data on 3422 Shanghai Composite Indexes, including their opening, closing, and trading volume. Next, he used the chosen technical indicators (moving average, kinetic divergence, and moving average convergence/divergence) to analyze the Shanghai Composite Index. AI techniques like logistic regression and support vector machines are now used in Wang's stock market volatility forecast. According to the results of the research, the stock index prediction model benefits from employing the radial basis support vector method [55].

Undoubtedly, the pivotal role played by financial institutions in the economy and the advantages that stock market prediction tools can offer to individual investors cannot be overlooked. In addition to their capacity to enhance profits and mitigate risk, stock market prediction methodologies hold significant value for a multitude of other purposes. By utilizing stock market prediction tools, it is possible to mitigate systemic financial market risk and allocate it in a more efficient manner. The utilization of existing forecasting technology and the unique characteristics of stock market data pose significant challenges to the already intricate nature of studying the stock market.

A plethora of data pertaining to the stock market has been recently disseminated, however, its provenance and caliber exhibit significant heterogeneity. Organizations encounter difficulties in adapting to the notion of depending exclusively on specialists to perform assessments and forecasts over an extended duration. Numerous IT-based studies on stock market prediction have surfaced to aid investors in making investment decisions in the stock market, and potentially supplant them, in order to keep pace with the rapid analysis of vast amounts of stock market data. The findings provide support for the viability of investment strategies based on data analysis to achieve autonomous growth of a fund.

The evaluation and control of trading risk in stock market investment necessitates the implementation of multidimensional and multiscale analysis and forecasting techniques. Therefore, prognostications regarding the stock market hold significant importance for the overall economy. Several academic studies have demonstrated that the stock market exhibits a relatively consistent pattern, however, predicting its fluctuations has always posed distinctive challenges.

10.5 Conclusion

This study's findings call attention to avenues for further study that have not received sufficient academic attention. Most writers don't bother to investigate or fairly pick the input data, despite the fact that it has an immediate impact on the time series estimate and acts as the foundation for the entire model during simulation and training.

The most impressive results can be achieved by limiting the parameters used in the implementation of AI models to the absolute essentials. Studies have used a wide variety of input variables and model parameters, with generally encouraging results. Because the model's architecture has a significant impact on the system's performance, many researchers have tried to improve it, with varying degrees of success. Most have used laborious trial-and-error approaches that cannot explain their decisions. Many academics have calculated the discrepancies between the predicted and actual numbers to examine the reliability and validity of forecasts. Getting the direction of price movements in stocks right is crucial, as even a minor forecast inaccuracy can be harmful. However, individuals in the financial market may find that even the most accurate forecasting tools still fall short of their goal of maximizing profits. Despite its importance, data preprocessing is only marginally used in the current literature. Indicator selection using sensitivity analysis can help cut down on unnecessary resources while simultaneously raising the bar for quality output.

Few studies have gone into detail on the most crucial performance markers utilized by the majority of authors when gauging the quality of an AI model. Since validation plays such a crucial role in the whole AI development process, it is necessary to report on a reliable performance indicator or set of metrics. Through testing, we can examine how successfully an AI model transfers its discoveries from the training set to the test set. In order to make the best choice, it is necessary to know whether or not the model overfits the data. Although the validation program was employed in half of the publications we reviewed, the other half just reported results from the test set without mentioning the crucial experimental validation phase. While many techniques are useful for predicting the near future, none of them are designed to predict time series over the medium to long term. Multistep forward prediction and other forms of AI are barely touched upon.

10.6   Significance of the Study

The results of the current research are useful for a wide range of audiences, including financial institutions, depositories, banks, stock traders, brokers, corporations, investors, the government, and the general public. Traders, brokers, and investors can reap benefits from the usage of AI-based models that have proven to be successful. Financial market stability encourages more people to invest, which in turn increases the amount of money available for companies to use as stock market capital for expansion, debt reduction, and product development. In turn, this is excellent for the economy as a whole since it increases consumer and business optimism. The increased number of investors will lead to more transactions at depositories.

Increasing government involvement in the financial markets is beneficial since it increases tax income. Financial institutions like banks, mutual fund companies, insurance providers, and investment businesses stand to gain from an increase in trading volume and investor capital. Due to a lack of education and Internet access, just 0.128% of the world's population actually trades or invests in the stock market. Fear prevents most people from trading and investing in the stock market, not because they do not want to, but rather because they cannot predict stock prices effectively in today's turbulent market. Companies need to establish a strong model for making forecasts if they want to gain the trust of investors and make significant profits. This review argues that modern AI-based models can give stock traders, brokers, and investors an edge that has never been possible before.

10.7   Scope of Further Research

The existing body of work on the application of AI to stock market prediction has expanded rapidly during the past two decades. Many potential avenues for further study are suggested by this review.

> ➢ Researchers of the future can begin enhancing experimental results by offering a method for optimizing the parameters of different neural networks and developing algorithms for feature selection. Only a limited percentage of research attempts have actually implemented feature selection algorithms. It is imperative that further studies confirm the efficacy of the proposed strategies in light of these findings.
> ➢ Intraday traders and other financial investors need accurate forecasts for the next few hours or minutes to generate large profits, while the majority of the literature on financial series forecasting is focused on predicting the next few days or weeks. The lack of published material on predicting intraday stock prices may prove useful to future researchers.
> ➢ Recent articles have shown that predictability of return exists even in less-developed markets, despite the fact that most research concentrates on developed-world financial markets. In addition, it was discovered that the created AI models function differently for well-established marketplaces compared to new ones. Furthermore, local knowledge plays a far larger role in forecasting returns in emerging or developing

markets than it does in mature economies. This difference in features can help explain why the two categories of markets are so different in terms of predictability. Further research is needed to determine the root of this discrepancy and the specific nature of the model's differences between the two AI scenarios.

➤ Increased usage of data preprocessing techniques including data transformation, scaling, and principal component analysis can boost the precision of predictions. It has been demonstrated in a great number of studies on time series analysis that preprocessing raw data is helpful and necessary for system dependability and model generalization to unknown data. Better stock market predictions can be achieved with a predictive model that is regularly updated to incorporate fresh information. Better dimensional reduction techniques in modeling are needed to increase prediction precision.

➤ Most articles that are peer-reviewed only look ahead to 1 year when making a forecast (that uses an output neuron). Due to its adaptability to new information, multiple-step-ahead prediction is preferred over one-step-ahead prediction. The development of AI prediction models that can see into the distant future may become a focal point of future study

➤ To provide more accurate results, researchers can try out different performance criteria (statistical, nonstatistical, or both) since the existing body of scholarly literature does not give a superior output criterion for comparing model predictions. If scientists want to know if their model is too good at explaining the data or too bad at explaining the data, they may want to conduct experimental validation.

➤ Most research attempting to anticipate the stock market might benefit from using multiple AI techniques and comparing their results. Experimentation with hybrid AI models is necessary for the stock returns prediction sector since the vast majority of studies that have presented a hybrid AI model have exhibited improved prediction accuracy compared to the single AI model. Scientists will be able to improve the precision of their prediction model in the future by using textual data with numerical data.

References

1. Wagenhofer, A., Accounting and economics: What we learn from analytical models in financial accounting and reporting, in: *The Economics and Politics of Accounting*, p. 5, 2004.
2. Vargas, M., Practical reason, instrumental irrationality, and time. *Philos. Stud.*, *126*, 241–252, 2005.
3. Tsang, E.P. and Martinez-Jaramillo, S., Computational finance, in: *Computational Intelligence Society Newsletter*, IEEE, 2004. https://doi.org/10.1109/mci.2023.3338030
4. Bredt, S., Artificial intelligence (AI) in the financial sector—Potential and public strategies. *Front. Artif. Intell.*, *2*, 16, 1, 2, 2019.
5. Murugesan, R. and Manohar, V., AI in financial sector–A driver to financial literacy. *Shanlax Int. J. Commer.*, *7*, 3, 66–70, 2019.
6. Gigante, G. and Zago, A., DARQ technologies in the financial sector: artificial intelligence applications in personalized banking. *Qual. Res. Financ.*, *15*, 1, 29–57, 2022.
7. Sharma, R., Mehta, K., Sharma, O., Exploring deep learning to determine the optimal environment for stock prediction analysis. *International Conference on Computational Performance Evaluation (ComPE)*, pp. 148–152, 2021.
8. Rebentrost, P., Gupt, B., Bromley, T.R., Quantum computational finance: Monte carlo pricing of financial derivatives. *Phys. Rev. A*, *98*, 2, 022321, 2018.
9. Zhang, B., Zhu, J., Su, H., Toward the third generation artificial intelligence. *Sci. China Inf. Sci.*, *66*, 2, 121101, 2023.
10. Hemanand, D., Mishra, N., Premalatha, G., Mavaluru, D., Vajpayee, A., Kushwaha, S., Sahile, K., Applications of intelligent model to analyze the green finance for environmental development in the context of artificial intelligence. *Comput. Intell. Neurosci.*, *2022*, 2, 3, 2022.
11. Luo, J., Zhu, G., Xiang, H., Artificial intelligent based day-ahead stock market profit forecasting. *Comput. Electr. Eng.*, *99*, 107837, 2022.
12. Chhajer, P., Shah, M., Kshirsagar, A., The applications of artificial neural networks, support vector machines, and long–short term memory for stock market prediction. *Decis. Anal. J.*, *2*, 100015, 2022.
13. Musleh Al-Sartawi, A.M., Hussainey, K., Razzaque, A., The role of artificial intelligence in sustainable finance. *J. Sustain. Finance Invest.*, 1–6, 2022.
14. Mehta, K., Sharma, R., Vyas, V., A quantile regression approach to study the impact of aluminium prices on the manufacturing sector of India during the COVID era. *Mater. Today: Proc.*, *65*, 8, 3506–3511, 2022. ISSN 2214- 7853, https://doi.org/10.1016/j.matpr.2022.06.087.
15. Sharma, D.K., Hota, H.S., Brown, K., Handa, R., Integration of genetic algorithm with artificial neural network for stock market forecasting. *Int. J. Syst. Assur. Eng. Manage.*, *13*, Suppl 2, 828–841, 2022.

16. Ahmad, S., Jha, S., Alam, A., Yaseen, M., Abdeljaber, H.A., A novel AI-based stock market prediction using machine learning algorithm. *Sci. Program.*, 2022, 2, 2022.

17. Chhajer, P., Shah, M., Kshirsagar, A., The applications of artificial neural networks, support vector machines, and long–short term memory for stock market prediction. *Decis. Anal.*, 2, 100015, 2022.

18. Ferreira, F.G., Gandomi, A.H., Cardoso, R.T., Artificial intelligence applied to stock market trading: A review. *IEEE Access*, 9, 30898–30917, 2021.

19. Mokhtari, S., Yen, K.K., Liu, J., Effectiveness of artificial intelligence in stock market prediction based on machine learning. *Int. J. Comput. Appl. (0975-8887)*, 1, 1–6, 2021.

20. Sharma, R., Mehta, K., Goel, A., Non-linear relationship between board size and performance of Indian companies. *J. Manage. Gov.*, 27, 1277–1301, 2022. https://doi. org/10.1007/s10997-022-09651-8.

21. Vyas, V., Mehta, K., Sharma, R., The nexus between toxic-air pollution, health expenditure, and economic growth: An empirical study using ARDL. *Int. Rev. Econ. Finance (IREF)*, 84, 154–166, 2023. https://doi.org/10.1016/j. iref.2022.11.017.

22. Abdollahi, J. and Mahmoudi, L., &, Investigation of artificial intelligence in stock market prediction studies. *10th International Conference on Innovation and Research in Engineering Science*, 2021.

23. Mehta, K. and Sharma, R., Contrarian and momentum investment strategies: evidence from indian stock market. *Int. J. Appl. Bus. Econ. Res. (JABER)*, 15, 9, 107–118, 2017.

24. Nti, I.K., Adekoya, A.F., Weyori, B.A., A systematic review of fundamental and technical analysis of stock market predictions. *Artif. Intell. Rev.*, 53, 4, 3007–3057, 2020.

25. Sharma, R., Mehta, K., Rana, R., Cryptocurrency adoption behavior of millennial investors in India, in: *Perspectives on Blockchain Technology and Responsible Investing*, pp. 135–157, 2023.

26. Vyas, V., Mehta, K., Sharma, R., Investigating socially responsible investing behaviour of Indian investors using structural equation modelling. *J. Sustain. Finance Invest.*, 1–23, 2020, DOI: 10.1080/20430795.2020.1790958.

27. Mehta, K., Sharma, R., Vyas, V., Efficiency and ranking of sustainability index of India using DEA-TOPSIS. *J. Indian Bus. Res.*, 11, 2, 179–199, 2019. https://doi.org/10.1108/JIBR-02-2018-0057.

28. Nti, I.K., Adekoya, A.F., Weyori, B.A., A novel multi-source information-fusion predictive framework based on deep neural networks for accuracy enhancement in stock market prediction. *J. Big Data*, 8, 1, 1–28, 2021.

29. Sharma, R., Mehta, K., Vyas, V., Responsible investing: A study on non-economic goals and investors' characteristics. *Appl. Finance Lett.*, 9, SI, 63–78, 2020. https://doi.org/10.24135/afl.v9i2.245.

30. Mehta, K., Sharma, R., Yu, P., *Revolutionizing financial services and markets through fintech and blockchain*, pp. 1–340, IGI Global Publisher for Timely Knowledge, 2023, 2023. DOI: 10.4018/978-1-6684-8624-5

31. Strader, T.J., Rozycki, J.J., Root, T.H., Huang, Y.H.J., Machine learning stock market prediction studies: Review and research directions. *J. Int. Technol. Inf. Manage.*, 28, 4, 63–83, 2020.

32. Umer, M., Awais, M., Muzammul, M., Stock market prediction using machine learning (ML) algorithms. *ADCAIJ: Adv. Distrib. Comput. Artif. Intell. J.*, 8, 4, 97–116, 2019.

33. Mehta, K., Sharma, R., Vyas, V., Kuckreja, J.S., Exit strategy decision by venture capital firms in India using fuzzy AHP. *J. Entrep. Emerg. Econ.*, 14, 4, 643–669, 2022. https://doi.org/10.1108/JEEE-05-2020-0146.

34. Ramani, P. and Murarka, P.D., Stock price prediction using multi-layer feed forward neural network. *JIMS8I-Int. J. Inf. Commun. Comput. Technol.*, 1, 1,1–3, 2013.

35. Ray, R., Khandelwal, P., Baranidharan, B., A survey on stock market prediction using artificial intelligence techniques, in: *2018 International Conference on Smart Systems and Inventive Technology (ICSSIT) (pp. 594-598)*, 2018, December, IEEE.

36. Rather, A.M., Sastry, V.N., Agarwal, A., Stock market prediction and portfolio selection models: A survey. *Opsearch*, 54, 558–579, 2017.

37. Iacomin, R., Stock market prediction, in: *2015 19th International Conference on System Theory, Control and Computing (ICSTCC) (pp. 200-205)*, 2015, October, IEEE.

38. Prasanna, S. and Ezhilmaran, D., An analysis on stock market prediction using data mining techniques. *Int. J. Comput. Sci. Eng. Technol. (IJCSET)*, 4, 3, 49–51, 2013.

39. Asadi, S., Hadavandi, E., Mehmanpazir, F., Nakhostin, M.M., Hybridization of evolutionary Levenberg–Marquardt neural networks and data pre-processing for stock market prediction. *Know.-Based Syst.*, 35, 245–258, 2012.

40. Grant, M.J. and Booth, A., A typology of reviews: an analysis of 14 review types and associated methodologies. *Health Info. Libr. J.*, 26, 2, 91–108, 2009.

41. Tranfield, D., Denyer, D., Smart, P., Towards a methodology for developing evidence-informed management knowledge by means of systematic review. *Br. J. Manage.*, 14, 3, 207–222, 2003.

42. Russell, S.J. and Norvig, P., *Artificial intelligence: A modern approach*, Prentice Hall series in Artificial intelligence, 2014.

43. Yang, H., Chan, L., King, I., Support vector machine regression for volatile stock market prediction, in: *IDEAL '02 Proceedings of the Third International Conference on Intelligent Data Engineering and Automated Learning*, pp. 391–396, 2002.

44. Hegazy, O., Soliman, O.S., Salam., M.A., A machine learning model for stock market prediction. *Comput. Sci.*, 4, 12, 17–23, 2014.

45. Chang, S.V., Gan, K.S., On, C.K., Alfred, R., Anthony, P., A review of stock market prediction with artificial neural network (ANN). *Control System, Computing and Engineering (ICCSCE), 2013 IEEE International Conference on IEEE*, 2014.

46. Olatunji, S.O., Alahmadi, M.S., Elshafei, M., Fallatah, Y.A., Forecasting the saudi arabia stock prices based on artificial neural networks model. *Int. J. Intell. Inf. Syst.* 2, 5, 77, 2014.

47. Devadoss, A.V. and Ligori, T.A.A., Stock prediction using artificial neural networks. *Int. J. Web Technol.*, 2, 2, 45–51, 2013.

48. Ramani, P. and Murarka, P.D., Stock price prediction using multi-layer feed forward neural network. *JIMS 8i-International Journal of Information, Communication and Computing Technology (IJICCT)*, 1, 1, ISSN 2347–7202, pp. 1–6, 2013.

49. Nayak, S.C., Misra, B.B., Behera, H.S., Impact of data normalization on stock index forecasting. *Int. J. Comput. Inf. Syst. Ind. Manag. Appl.*, ISSN 2150-7988, 6, 257–269, 2014.

50. Navale, G.S., Dudhwala, N., Jadhav, K., Gabda, P., Vihangam, B.K., Prediction of stock market using data mining and artificial intelligence. *Int. J. Comput. Appl.*, 134, 12, 9–11, 2016.

51. Shah, V.V., Mirani, S.J., Nanavati, Y.V., Narayanan, V., Pereira, S., II, Stock market prediction using neural networks. *International Journal of Soft Computing and Engineering (IJSCE)*, ISSN: 2231–2307, 6, 1, pp. 86-89, 2016.

52. Tripathy, N., Predicting stock market price using neural network model. *Int. J. Strateg. Decis. Sci. (IJSDS)*, 9, 3, 84–94, 2018.

53. Ferreira, F.G., Gandomi, A.H., Cardoso, R.T., Artificial intelligence applied to stock market trading: A review. *IEEE Access*, 9, 30898–30917, 2021.

54. Carta, S.M., Consoli, S., Piras, L., Podda, A.S., Recupero, D.R., Explainable machine learning exploiting news and domain-specific lexicon for stock market forecasting. *IEEE Access*, 9, 30193–30205, 2021.

55. Wang, Z., Predicting the rise and fall of Shanghai composite index based on artificial intelligence. *E3S Web of Conferences*, vol. 235, p. 3063, 2021.

11

A Comparative Study of Stock Market Prediction Models: Deep Learning Approach and Machine Learning Approach

Swati Jain

Manipal University Jaipur, Jaipur, India

Abstract

Artificial Intelligence (AI), in the present time, is a widely utilized technology that is being implemented practically in every sector's activity and it is a widely discussed topic in the research field the reason for its infinite uses. AI is nothing more than a discipline that applies computer sciences to massive datasets to enable decision-making and problem-solving. Furthermore, it comprises the components of AI known as deep learning (DL) and machine learning (ML), which are normally referred to simultaneously. As the need of the hour, almost every industry is involved in adopting new technologies to improve their operational efficiency in the current technologically sophisticated period, and the finance sector is not exempted from this change. For making stock market predictions, a variety of models, both conventional and technological, are developed. However, in more recent times, all studies have been carried out utilizing various models that may be broadly separated into two categories: DL and ML approaches. It appears that DL and ML share similar principles. However, it is crucial to recognize how the two of them differ from one another. They both fall under the category of AI. While ML is defined as a subclass of AI, DL is regarded as a subsection of ML. The objective of this book chapter is to compare and contrast the ML method with the DL strategy in order to identify their main distinctions. Understanding a method's benefits, drawbacks, and applicability is crucial before adopting it. The study will be useful in providing information on the use of both strategies and their unique advantages for users.

Email: swatijain.22@gmail.com

Renuka Sharma and Kiran Mehta (eds.) Deep Learning Tools for Predicting Stock Market Movements, (249–270) © 2024 Scrivener Publishing LLC

Keywords: Stock market, stock market prediction models, artificial intelligence, machine learning, deep learning

11.1   Introduction

Stock trading is one of the most important operations in the financial industry. Expert analysts and investors now give advances in stock price prediction a lot of weight. Stock market forecasting for trend analysis is difficult due to the environment's inherent noise and excessive instability. The complexity of stock prices varies depending on several factors, including quarterly earnings releases, market news, and different shifting behaviors. The traders rely on many technical indications based on stocks that are gathered every day by the traders [1–4]. Accurately predicting stock movements is both fascinating and difficult in the continually changing business world. Several noneconomic and economic factors are taken into consideration and affect how stock movements behave. The stock price list is also frequently dynamic, complicated, noisy, nonparametric, and, by definition, nonlinear [5]. Recent research has focused on developing effective machine-driven trading methods using ML techniques for portfolio management, stock movement, and price estimation. The return on investment for short-term trading can be maximized by having the capacity to predict future patterns in stock performance. The expansion of the stock market helps the market and economy by enabling corporations to make lucrative investments, supplying funds, risk division, and expansion options, and effectively assigning valuable resources for investment in productive projects. Numerous earlier empirical studies that found a link between stock market success and economic growth in the nation lend credibility to this viewpoint. Recent studies that used sophisticated time series analysis and econometric analysis to identify a causal relationship between stock market changes and economic success backed this up [6]. This chapter first sets out the background about the stock market, stock exchange, and stock market predictions and then explains in detail the various prediction models.

11.1.1   Stock Market

Shares of companies that are listed can be traded on the stock exchange. It is thought of as a secondary type of market. A company must establish a presence on one of the recognized stock exchanges before listing its shares for sale to investors in the open market. Once this has been done successfully, the promoter must sell a sizeable portion of the company's shares to retail customers, after which additional trading can take place in the secondary market or stock exchange. There are typically two foremost stock exchanges in India, i.e., the NSE (National Stock Exchange), which has about 1600 listed businesses, and the BSE (Bombay Stock Exchange), which has over 5000 listed companies [7]. Similar trading systems and capabilities are shared by the NSE and the BSE. Demat and trading accounts are mostly used for stock market trading. While businesses benefit from an influx of investments into their ventures, stock exchanges assist the general public in channeling and pooling their savings. The Indian investment landscape has transformed thanks to the stock market. Middle-class investors are now gravitating toward the equities market in search of better returns due to rising inflation, falling bank interest rates, and other factors. This encapsulates the ever-expanding demand for and significance of stock exchanges.

Due to the numerous internal and external elements that affect it, such as historical stock data, politics, the economy, and the environment, the stock market is exceedingly volatile. People can access this information through news and microblogs, and it might be challenging to estimate stock prices based only on previous data. The significant volatility highlights the significance of examining how external influences affect the stock market [8]. There are several different stock types, including common, preferred, and warrants. Common stock investors can own a portion of a company, take part in corporate governance, and receive dividends. Contrarily, preferred stock provides holders a comparative advantage over normal stockholders when it comes to receiving dividends and selling assets. Last but not least, warrants allow investors to purchase a precise lot of shares at a specific price within a specific time frame, much like options [5].

The government and many investors have traditionally seen stock as one of the crucial elements of the economic market [6]. Changes in the stock market have a significant economic impact on the economies of nations and individual consumers. Significant economic disruptions could result from a decline in stock values. Stock price prediction has been a burning topic for years reason being its potential for significant rewards. Because of a stock time series' behavior that is a nearly random walk, forecasting the stock market is not an easy process [7]. Buying equities on the stock market for less money to sell them for more money is the main objective of investing. However, choosing stocks and researching stock movements, corporate policies, company ambitions, and purposes—all of which require a significant quantity of data—are the most crucial aspects. Modern techniques will examine this enormous data, enabling us to select a reliable stock [2]. Because of how quickly technology is developing, the volume of data can be managed quickly and effectively. At each phase, volume, transaction, and stock buys and sells may all be accurately tracked and evaluated. The fast purchase of a sizable amount of shares is made possible by nano-trading, high-frequency trading, and intraday trading. The fluctuating tendency of the stock price is one of the aspects of the stock market to which shareholders pay the most interest. Variations in stock prices are frequently nonlinear. The ability of analysts to anticipate changes in stock prices has never been easy.

The stock market, which comprises buyers and sellers of securities, is made up of exchanges for private, open, and mixed ownership stocks. In contrast to the private stock exchange, which only deals in the trading of shares of private corporations, the open stock exchange also covers shares of a company that is listed on the public stock market. On the open stock market, shares of corporations with mixed ownership are only partially transferable. These stock exchanges were founded in the US and the UK, respectively, and include the New York Stock Exchange (NYSE) and the London Stock Exchange [8–11]. The most challenging obstacle that financial institutions, corporate houses, businesses, and individual investors encounter is a prediction of the stock market and thereby the prices of shares and stocks. The state of the economy, the political climate, and investor psychology are just a rare of the variables that affect how accurate stock price projections are. A country's stock market should be improved since it is correlated with economic progress. The elementary objectives of any investing activity in the stock market are to increase gain and minimize risk probability. The stock market is the cornerstone of every economy. One of the best methods to create money is stock market predictions because stock market investments may yield a quick return on investment.

It is difficult to predict the stock market for the reason that so many variables are at play. As a result, investors conduct two sorts of study before buying a stock. First is the fundamental analysis. Investors take into account factors such as the intrinsic value of equities, industry performance, and the status of the economy. Second, when performing technical analysis, investors look at stock values and statistics generated by market activity, like previous prices and volumes [12–14]. Thanks to advances in technology, a range of automated techniques can now be used to forecast the stock market. Several algorithms have been used for stock market forecasting, first starting with classical regression. However, the support vector machine (SVM) and the artificial neural network (ANN) are two well-liked methods. Each algorithm has a unique approach to finding patterns and predicting changes in the stock market.

11.2 Stock Market Prediction

Making forecasts on the stock market is quite challenging. Models for future prediction and movements of the stock value in the market are useful. Investors will make more money the more accurately the share price is predicted. Because it is difficult to predict stock market fluctuations, researchers and analysts are putting more effort into creating novel models that can accurately forecast this extremely unpredictable market. However, owing to technology, analysts may now use artificial intelligence (AI) to make specific forecasts.

In the world of finance, forecasting the everyday trend of the stock market index (SMI) movement is essential as it gives investors information they can use to increase their earnings. Although the law of supply and demand governs the stock market in theory, several closely linked factors may also have an impact on the SMI movement. These variables include those affecting the economy, the business sector, investor psychology, the political environment, and so forth [15].

Stock market forecasting is a traditional yet challenging subject that both economists and computer scientists find interesting. To develop a successful prediction model, both linear and ML techniques have been researched over the past 20 years. Recent proposals for new lines of research in this field include deep learning (DL) models, and the pace of research is advancing too quickly for anyone to keep up [16].

The system that generates the enormous volume, rapid rotation, and unpredictable stock market price data is highly sophisticated [17]. It is quite challenging to do projections for the stock market because it is a dynamic, complicated, and chaotic environment [18]. Because, with the appropriate decisions, a good prediction of stock prices may produce attractive gains, the work of predicting stock market movements is considered significant and deserving of special attention. Due to non-static and disordered data, stock market forecasting is incredibly difficult, thereby making it more difficult for shareholders and investors to use their investments profitably. Numerous techniques have been created using current technology to predict changes in the stock market [1]. Stock trend estimation is a tough process since it depends on a variety of variables, such as trader expectations, financial situation, administrative events, and special market patterns. The stock price list is also frequently dynamic, complicated, noisy, nonparametric, and, by definition, nonlinear. The most widely used prediction techniques in this field, ANNs and DL in particular, have attracted a lot of attention from researchers because they autonomously discover the innate relationship between the variables and do not necessitate any pre-specifications. Investors' attention has been drawn to the stock market as a result of sophisticated applications where forecasting may produce precise market predictions. The investment and trading of stock data are directly related to the forecasting of stock movements. The use of rational judgments is made possible by the application of stock market prediction techniques for market monitoring, forecasting, and control. It is challenging to create an accurate model because price variance depends on a variety of elements, including news, social media data, corporate fundamentals, output, government bonds, historical pricing, and a country's economics [19]. The act of attempting to predict the future value of a business stock or other financial instrument traded on a stock exchange is known as stock market prediction. Investor returns will increase with a precise stock price forecast [20]. As a result, investors must rely on conventional statistical techniques to make predictions. Due to its consistent investing performance, ML has recently gained popularity and has been employed widely in stock market forecasts thanks to the broad usage of computer technology [21]. Programmable methods of prediction are now more successful at predicting stock values acknowledging the growth of AI and improvements in computing capacity [22]. The financial markets have lately been predicted using historical price time series utilizing a variability of ML methods and DL approaches [23].

11.2.1   Data Types

The seven categories of raw data that are most frequently employed in stock market forecasting are as follows:

> *Market data:* Market data refers to the entirety of all stock market trading operations, embracing trading volume, open, high, low, and close prices, etc. It serves as both a prediction objective (like the close price of the following day) and an input feature (like previous prices in a look-back window).
> *Text data:* Text data are texts that people have contributed, such as on social media, in the news, and *via* web searches. These data are challenging to collect and manage as an alternative data type, but they could provide important information that is missing from market data. These text data can be subjected to sentiment analysis, which will result in a sentiment component that can be utilized for prediction (such as positive, negative, or neutral), as well as other benefits.

Macroeconomic data: Macroeconomic indicators like the consumer price index (CPI), gross domestic product (GDP), and others represent the state of the economy in a specific nation, area, or sector. Since they can verify the quality of a market gain or loss and demonstrate how healthy the market is overall, these indicators have a connection to the stock market.

Knowledge Graph Data: Different markets and companies are connected in some way; for instance, the same news may affect the movement of stocks in the same industry. Using knowledge graph data from public sources like Freebase and Wikidata, newly created graph neural networks (GNNs) may be utilized to enhance the stock price prediction performance.

Image data: For enhancing the output of prediction models of the stock market, convolutional neural networks' (CNN) accomplishments in 2D image processing are being used. In various tools like classification and object detection, candlestick charts are employed as input images for stock prediction.

Fundamental data: Accounting data, such as assets, liabilities, and other items that are reported quarterly, is the most popular kind of basic data. It is less frequently used in studies employing DL models because of the irregular reporting and erroneous reporting dates. For instance, because the core information supplied is indexed by the report's final date, which occurs before the date of publication, there is a possibility that future information may be used.

Analytics data: Analytics data is the refined information that may be derived from reports (such as recommendations to buy or sell a company) that are made available by investment banks and research firms that carefully investigate the business models, operations, rivalries, etc. of various organizations. These studies offer valuation information, despite the fact that they could be expensive and distributed among numerous consumers who all wish to exploit this information to benefit.

There are various degrees of acquiring and processing difficulty for various types of raw data as shown in Figure 11.1. A significant amount of input data is required for DL models in order to train a sophisticated neural

Figure 11.1 Forms of raw data.

network model. Since market data gives the largest data sample size and is the most commonly used in this situation, compared to other data types, it is the best alternative. Due to the recognition of social media and online news sources, as well as the simplicity with which text data may be gathered using web crawlers, text data is used for the second-most applications. Due to the sparse data and high access costs, the analytics data is an extreme case that is never employed in the research that was examined. Stock market estimation is still a fascinating but challenging area of research because of the financial time series' noise, chaos, and nonstationarity. Despite the claim made by the efficient market hypothesis (EMH) that it is impossible to outperform the market, technological developments have made it possible for analysts to correctly forecast the stock market, which can help traders make money. Investors and researchers are interested in comprehending the stock market and its countless linked elements. The stock market is susceptible to a wide range of influences, such as interactions between countries when making investments abroad, foreign exchange rates, country and political unrest, natural disasters, business and administration-related changes, financial updates, price rises, market attitudes, and public moods. Knowing these elements and estimating their influence on the stock market prices and movements, however, are inadequate.

By transforming the given data into useful features, which are important characteristics of ML and DL models, these aspects must be included in a prediction model. They have made enormous contributions to the field of financial time series prediction. The noisy and volatile nature of the stock market time series has proven to be a test of the durability of these ML algorithms.

11.3   Models for Prediction in Stock Market

11.3.1   Traditional Methods

According to the EMH, the history stock time series displays the disclosure of new information, changes to the stock market as a whole, or arbitrary movements around the value that reflects the prior information set. Technical modeling–based stock movement forecasting, which aims to foresee the short-term trend of stock price time series in the dynamic and unpredictable stock market, is built on this information. Numerous conventional techniques have been suggested for this, and they can be broadly categorized into two groups: conventional time series techniques and ML techniques. ARIMA (autoregressive integrated moving average) and RACH are two popular time series approaches that employ historical pricing data as the foundation for projecting future outcomes. Scholars also suggested further variations, like the exponentially weighted moving average and the GJR GARCH. Despite their widespread use, classic time series algorithms need normally distributed data as well as previous data to improve prediction. Traditional time series approaches, however, are ineffective when applied to stock price time series because they frequently show strong nonlinear patterns, seasonality, random walks, and an innate sensitivity to a broad series of codependent factors.

11.3.2   Modern Techniques

11.3.2.1   Artificial Intelligence

The term "study and design of intelligent agents," which describes AI, has a significant influence on how the world operates today. These systems, known as intelligent agents, can understand their environment and take action to improve their chances of success. Advances in AI have resulted in breakthroughs such as smartphones and self-driving vehicles [24]. Huge developments occurred in this industry with the introduction of computers in the 1950s. Although the exact beginnings of AI are unclear, Alan Turing's work "Computing Machinery and Intelligence" is recognized as a turning point in the subject. Today, this discipline has significantly grown as a result of the upgrading and improving computing capacity and the rapid development of big data. Early uses of AI focused on issues with rules that are complex to people but simple to computers. A list of encrypted expressions "if and else" was introduced to the computer in order to address these issues. This knowledge-based methodology has been widely adopted by artificially intelligent robots to surpass human performance in abstract subjects. However, AI-based systems did not always work effectively and had a number of faults. They had trouble doing things that a typical human would find easy, including recognizing objects or interpreting conversation. Modern AI systems have struggled to come up with substitute methods of imparting intuition to computers as a result. For AI systems to solve the aforementioned difficulties, ML was introduced.

ML, a branch of AI, began to gain recognition in the 1990s. Instead of using symbolic methods, it makes use of methods and models created from statistics and probability theory. In truth, ML algorithms provide machines with the information they need to perform a certain task by reviewing a large enough number of data samples. The properties that best characterize the most particular data must be retrieved before the method can be used.

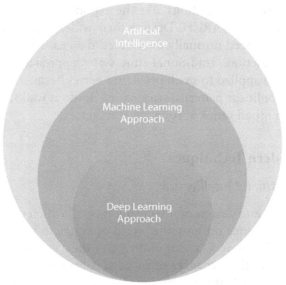

Figure 11.2 Representation of stock market prediction approaches.

This procedure is known as feature extraction. The subsequent stage of the process, which teaches the system to transmit features and recognize patterns using ML, uses sample data that are based on a particular training methodology. The issues with manually created features in sophisticated ML programs were addressed by the introduction of DL techniques. Advances in neuroscience serve as inspiration for in-depth learning, which is congruent with how the nervous system interprets information and communicates. The hidden layers of an ANN and a collection of intricate formulae are two layers utilized in DL, as shown in Figure 11.2. System performance in three areas—AI, ML, and DL—is compared in Figure 11.3. The two main types of stock prediction models (Figure 11.4), i.e., the ML approach and DL methods, are also discussed in detail in the chapter.

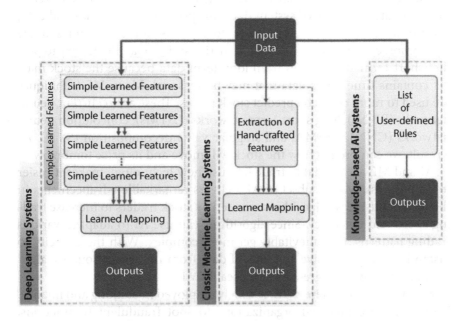

Figure 11.3 Assessment of performance amid AI, ML, and DL [24].

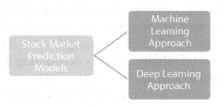

Figure 11.4 Stock market prediction models.

11.3.2.2 Machine Learning

Long-established methods have been employed to forecast the stock market price movements by examining fundamental and technical factors. Stock market forecasts are now more accessible and precise thanks to ML. Various ML approaches have been applied to forecast the stock market. ML approaches are rapidly gaining popularity because they make fewer data-related assumptions than conventional time series methods and can handle nonlinearities. Traditional techniques like SVM, random forest, and XGBoost have demonstrated a notable gain in accuracy. HMM can represent the invisible stock values by its hidden states as one of the time-dependent ML approaches, which adds to the wide range of applications in the stock prediction field. More emphasis has been placed on the design of HMM mechanisms in recent works. The term "ML" refers to a computer software or system that can spot patterns in historical data, learn from current data, and estimate stock prices. Some academics utilize a linear forecasting model based on statistics and probability theory to predict short-term stock prices from long-term data because the stock market contains time series data that may be seasonal. Many ML techniques are used to more correctly predict stock prices. These are recurrent neural networks (RNNs), long short-term networks (LSTMs), convolution neural networks (CNN), ARIMA, and singular value decomposition (SVD). As a result, we can predict how the stock will move and its price tomorrow.

AI and ML are crucial to trade because new technology makes it easier to do business. ML, a subset of AI, delivers remarkable advancements in the field of business. Algorithms are used by stock traders to increase trading speed and efficiency. Since algorithms can use AI to adapt to various trading patterns, they inevitably get more complex. With the capacity to instantly decrypt massive amounts of data from numerous sources, algorithm trading will progress toward useable ML.

ML, a powerful sphere of AI, is widely employed in banking and finance. While allowing financial organizations to spot fraudulent transactions, it aids management in their decisions regarding credit scoring, ranking, and granting. The financial uses of ML are limitless. Customers can access automated insurance services, investors can use asset allocation systems to get risk-return analyses, and policyholders can use financial robot advisers and chatbots to get help with their banking. Due to its ability to manage vast volumes of data while simultaneously accounting for nonlinearities in data, ML has emerged as a leader in statistics [25].

The EMH argument has been refuted by ML's extensive use in the stock market and its powerful forecasting performance [25]. Over the past few decades, technological progress has outpaced all other fields and industries in this globe, including the stock market. For instance, the use of ML in the stock market includes forecasting stock returns, forecasting stock prices, and forecasting the movement of the stock market's price direction. Few could have predicted how drastically ML would alter the stock market years ago. By assisting investors in making the necessary accurate stock market price index predictions, ML has benefited individuals in the stock market company. Not only can ML be used to anticipate stock prices but it can also be used to forecast market behavior and even develop new models for data processing and index prediction. It has permanently altered how stock market forecasts are created. Because computers can now process massive volumes of data more quickly and accurately than ever before, ML aids investors in making stock market price index predictions more effectively than old methods [26]. In order to enhance an output criterion, computers can be trained to learn from previous data or examples of data [27]. A computer application is run to use training data or experience to optimize the model's parameters after we create a model with specified parameters. The model may be descriptive to acquire fresh data or predictive to generate projections for the future.

Artificial Neural Network - A statistical model that was intuitive by biological neural networks is called an ANN. The ANN is the subject of ongoing research because it has considerable potential for solving pattern recognition of stocks and ML issues like classification and forecasting. One ML method that can handle discontinuous data and forecast stock prices is the ANN. Using a specific quantity of neurons from the nervous system, neural networks are created. Computing systems called ANNs carry out operations similar to those of biological neural networks. These systems are capable of learning from examples. Artificial neurons are a set of nodes used in ANN. These synthetic neurons are capable of communicating with one another, just like the human brain. In the ANN implementation, a signal is represented by a real number, and the output of each neuron is determined by a nonlinear input sum function. Each edge that connects two nodes is referred to as a node, and each edge and node has a weight assigned to it. A decrease in weight indicates an increase in signal strength. These neurons are often organized into layers. Each layer performs a different function on the inputs. Signals are sent from the input layer, the top layer, to the output layer, the bottom layer. Signals may loop repeatedly through the layers before getting to an output.

The output at the hidden layer should be seen as an input at the output layer because it gets the input as an output of the input layer and performs the activation function. The problem was displayed in the output

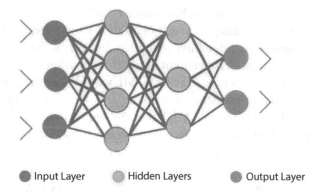

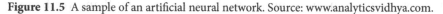

● Input Layer   ○ Hidden Layers   ● Output Layer

Figure 11.5 A sample of an artificial neural network. Source: www.analyticsvidhya.com.

layer in Figure 11.5. The discrepancy between actual and projected numbers is known as the error percentage. Repeat the procedure until the error % is equal to zero.

Support Vector Machine - This article uses the support vector classification (SVC) technique that Vapnik first proposed. Using a nonlinear mapping technique where the input vector is imported into a high-dimensional feature space, the linear model is used to construct nonlinear class borders. The linear model is built in the new space after the nonlinear decision boundary is represented in the original space. An ideal separation hyperplane is built in the new region. The SVM is known as the algorithm that discovers a certain type of linear model since it has the maximum margin hyperplane. Using learning approaches, SVM is used to produce classifications and regression analyses. In a training set for SVM, every example is divided into one of two groups. SVM can further classify new situations based on these examples. To demonstrate how the categorizations differ, these occurrences are represented as points and mapped into space.

ARIMA (Autoregressive Integrated Moving Average Process) Model - The ARIMA model was created in 1970. It handles time series data. In time series forecasting, ARIMA is referred to as a dynamic and effective model that is particularly useful for short-term forecasts. The outcomes of this time series projecting and explanation of the predictive power of ARIMA models are beneficial to investors in their decision-making.

K-Nearest Neighbor (k-NN) - Without using parameters, k-NN conducts regression and categorization. The input consists of the feature space's k closest neighbors. In k-NN classification, the object is given its class, which is the most popular among its nearest k neighbors; the result is the class selected. The result is the total of all the values from the nearest k neighbors' k-NN regressions. Due to the local approximation of the function, k-NN is a form of lazy learning. Each neighbor is assigned a weight, with closer neighbors receiving greater weights and farther neighbors receiving lower weights.

C4.5 Decision Tree - Ross Quinlan developed the C4.5 technique to build a decision tree. On top of Quinlan's older ID3 algorithm, C4.5 was developed. As a statistical classifier, C4.5 is employed in the classification process. At each node of the tree, C4.5 determines which characteristic best divides its set of samples into subsets of various classes using the training data set. The decision-making attribute is the one with the most standardized data gain.

Random Forests (RF) - Decision trees can be built using random forests for categorization, regression, and other tasks. The practice of overfitting decision trees to the training set is corrected by RFs. Tin Kam Ho developed the random subspace approach, the first RF algorithm.

Bagging - ML classification and regression performance are enhanced by bagging, also known as Bootstrap aggregating. A new training set is created by bagging using an existing training set as a basis. It lessens variance and prevents overfitting. Although it can be utilized with any approach, decision trees are typically where it is applied. Bagging aids in producing more precise findings for shaky procedures.

AdaBoost - An algorithm called "boosting" helps weak learners progress toward becoming strong learners, hence enhancing ML techniques through the reduction of bias and volatility. Each boost attempts to train its predecessor before moving on. Boosting algorithms often operate iteratively, with constant reweighting of the data. Future learners who struggle concentrate on the areas where the previous student struggled. Adaptive Boosting, also known as AdaBoost, is applied in a variety of ways to increase precision. The ultimate product is created by combining the results of all the weaker students into a weighted total. By integrating all the results, AdaBoost improves on the boosting method. Separate learners may not be strong on their own but may be strong when combined.

It is challenging to create an accurate model because price variance depends on a wide range of elements, including news, social media data, corporate fundamentals, output, government bonds, historical pricing, and a country's economics. A prediction model that just considers one factor could not be accurate. In order to increase the model's accuracy, a variety of factors, including news, information from social media, and historical prices, may be combined. DL methods including CNNs, RNNs, and LSTM have also lately been used to estimate stock values, in contrast to "conventional" ML methods like SVM [28].

11.3.2.3   Deep Learning Approach

In several domains, such as picture classification, text analysis, peer-to-peer lending, recommendation systems, and outlier detection, the flexibility and capacity to analyze complex data trump other conventional methods. DL techniques are increasingly being used for stock prediction. A cutting-edge method for time series prediction is LSTM. Through a carefully thought-out gate structure, LSTM is offered as an upgraded form of vanilla RNN to address the long-term dependency of stock price sequence [29]. DL models for stock market prediction are currently rapidly developing and being used more frequently [17]. DL applications for financial market forecasting have drawn a lot of interest from academics and investors. DL techniques, which range from CNNs to RNNs, excel in capturing the nonlinear aspects of stock markets and, as a result, produce accurate predictions of SMIs [30]. Due to their excellent capacity for learning probable correlations between patterns in features and labels, DL techniques are used in financial time series modeling and prediction [31]. Since DL can extract characteristics from a large amount of raw data without relying on the knowledge of predictors, it may be useful for stock market prediction at high frequencies. DL techniques are known to perform differently depending on how data are represented in addition to having a wide range of network architectures, activation functions, and other model parameters [32]. DL is the most advanced technique for forecasting future patterns in an emerging stock market [33].

Figure 11.6 presents various DL-based model types. The popular DL models for stock market forecasting are shown in general in Figure 11.7 [34]. These models include RNN-based models (Figure 11.7(a)), CNN-based models (Figure 11.7(b)), GNN-based models (Figure 11.7(c)), transformer-based models (Figure 11.7(d)), reinforcement learning architecture (Figure 11.7(e)), and other unique methods. These models' inputs can include information about stock prices, text data, and business ties [35].

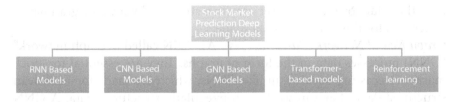

Figure 11.6 The classification method of stock market prediction: Deep learning approach.

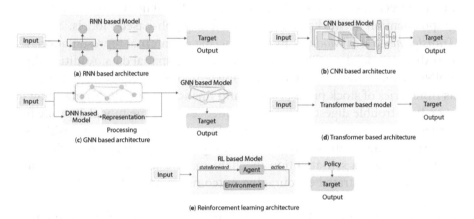

Figure 11.7 The classic presentation of widely used deep learning models for stock market forecasting [34].

Recurrent Neural Network–Based Models - The RNN is a DL model that handles sequential data well. RNN is a fantastic choice for modeling historical data and creating projections because time series are a common representation of stock market data. RNNs, however, experience gradient vanishing when processing data over a long time interval. To solve this issue, RNN variants such as LSTM, gated recurrent unit (GRU), and bidirectional LSTM (Bi-LSTM) have been developed.

Convolutional Neural Network–Based Models - The efficiency of CNNs in computer vision (CV) and natural language processing (NLP) tasks has received extensive research. Multiple convolutional and pooling layers make up a CNN model, which is utilized for feature extraction. Traditional convolutional layers process picture characteristics using two-dimensional filters (kernels) and activation functions. However, time series data, which are one-dimensional characteristics, are processed using CNNs in the stock prediction domain. CNNs for time series use a one-dimensional filter that slides over the time series with a stride set by the data granularity to account for this change in data shape.

Graph Neural Network–Based Models - An ANN called a "graph network" (GNN) processes data in the form of graphs. They are essential for stock market forecasting because, unlike CNNs, which are made for Euclidean structured data, they can work with irregularly structured data. A GNN can model interactions between entities because of its node and edge-based structure. In the background of stock market forecasting, nodes often stand in for businesses or stocks, while edges signify the connections between them. The GNN, graph convolutional networks (GCN), and graph attention networks (GAT) are the four graph-based models.

Transformer-Based Models - By constructing an internal representation of two-dimensional data, CNNs excel at processing spatial data. Additionally, RNNs are more effective at jobs involving temporal or sequential data, such as time series of stock prices, tweets, and financial news. RNNs may, however, have trouble digesting lengthy sequences since the model is prone to forgetting or mucking up the contents of neighboring or distant positions. The transformer solves this problem by processing texts *via* positional embedding and a self-attention mechanism. The transformer model has therefore demonstrated encouraging outcomes in a number of stock market prediction tasks.

Reinforcement Learning Models - A subset of AI and ML called deep reinforcement learning allows intelligent machines to learn from their deeds much like people do. An agent will naturally be rewarded or penalized according to their activities in this type of ML.

11.4   Conclusion

The stock markets are dynamic and ever-evolving, whereas current works focus mostly on depicting global and immediate market situations. Previous information falters as the market shifts, lowering the accuracy of stock prediction. For investors looking to gauge market sentiment, financial news is becoming a more crucial source of information. Both academics and industry are thinking about computational algorithms that can automatically extract useful information because the accuracy and speed of interpreting these texts are key qualities. Additionally, experimental findings revealed that DL-based approaches were superior in every instance, even though a variety of ML algorithms were assessed for all applications.

In comparison to other methods, employing a neural network requires more time to implement, whereas an SVM has a higher fault rate.

Each method has benefits and drawbacks of its own. To some extent, many methodologies have been employed to estimate future stock values and predict the stock market. High precision could be achieved by combining genetic algorithms and ANNs [36]. In the past two decades, ML models have become a significant and competitive alternative to traditional statistical models. In this regard, a number of models were created and improved in the ML suite, including SVM, decision trees, ANN, and others. ML is a technique for creating algorithms that can learn from data, whereas statistical modeling formulates the relationship of variables in mathematical equations. Statistical and ML models differ, even though ML is grounded in statistics.

References

1. Gandhmal, D.P. and Kumar, K., Systematic analysis and review of stock market prediction techniques. *Comput. Sci. Rev.*, 34, 100190, 2019, https:// doi. org/10.1016/j.cosrev.2019.08.001.

2. Mehta, K. and Sharma, R., Contrarian and momentum investment strategies: Evidence from indian stock market. *Int. J. Appl. Bus. Econ. Res. (JABER)*, 15, 9, 107–118, 2017.

3. Sharma, R., Mehta, K., Sharma, O., Exploring deep learning to determine the optimal environment for stock prediction analysis. *International Conference on Computational Performance Evaluation (ComPE)*, pp. 148–152, 2021.

4. Sharma, R., Mehta, K., Rana, R., Cryptocurrency adoption behaviour of millennial investors in India, in: *Perspectives on Blockchain Technology and Responsible Investing*, pp. 135–157, 2023.

5. Sharma, R., Mehta, K., Goel, A., Non-linear relationship between board size and performance of Indian companies. *J. Manag. Gov.*, 27, 4, 1277–1301, 2022, https://doi. org/10.1007/s10997-022-09651-8.

6. Shah, J., Vaidya, D., Shah, M., A comprehensive review on multiple hybrid deep learning approaches for stock prediction. *Intell. Syst. Appl. (ISWA)*, 16, 200111, 2022, https://doi.org/10.1016/j.iswa.2022.200111.

7. Bansal, M., Goyal, A., Choudhary, A., Stock market prediction with high accuracy using machine learning techniques. *Procedia Comput. Sci.*, 215, 247–265, 2022, https://doi.org/10.1016/j.procs.2022.12.028.

8. Mehta, K., Sharma, R., Vyas, V., A quantile regression approach to study the impact of aluminium prices on the manufacturing sector of India during the COVID era. *Mater. Today: Proc.*, 65, 8, 3506–3511, 2022, ISSN 2214- 7853, https://doi.org/10.1016/j.matpr.2022.06.087.

9. Vyas, V., Mehta, K., Sharma, R., The nexus between toxic-air pollution, health expenditure, and economic growth: An empirical study using ARDL.

Int. Rev. Econ. Finance (IREF), 84, 154–166, 2023, https://doi.org/10.1016/j.iref.2022.11.017.

10. Vyas, V., Mehta, K., Sharma, R., Investigating socially responsible investing behaviour of indian investors using structural equation modelling. *J. Sustain. Finance Invest.*, 12, 2, 1–23, 2020, DOI: 10.1080/20430795.2020.1790958.

11. Maqbool, J., Aggarwal, P., Kaur, R., Mittal, A., Ganaie, I.A., Stock prediction by integrating sentiment scores of financial news and MLP-regressor: A machine learning approach. *Procedia Comput. Sci.*, 218, 1067–1078, 2023.

12. Mehta, K. and Sharma, R., Contrarian and momentum investment strategies: Evidence from indian stock market. *Int. J. Appl. Bus. Econ. Res. (JABER)*, 15, 9, 107–118, 2017.

13. Mehta, K., Sharma, R., Chugh, A., Management of forex risk exposure: A study of SMEs and unlisted non-financial firms in India. *Int. J. Appl. Bus. Econ. Res. (JABER)*, 15, 9, 43–54, 2017.

14. Mehta, K., Sharma, R., Vyas, V., Efficiency and ranking of sustainability index of India using DEA-TOPSIS. *J. Indian Bus. Res.*, 11, 2, 179–199, 2019, https://doi.org/10.1108/JIBR-02-2018-0057.

15. Gülmez, B., Stock price prediction with optimized deep LSTM network with artificial rabbits optimization algorithm. *Expert Syst. Appl.*, 227, 120346, 2023, https://doi.org/10.1016/j.eswa.2023.120346.

16. Liu, H. and Long, Z., An improved deep learning model for predicting stock market price time series. *Digit. Signal Process.*, 102, 102741, 2020.

17. Hegazy, O., Soliman, O.S., Salam, M.A., A machine learning model for stock market prediction. 4, 12. arXiv preprint arXiv:1402.7351, 2014.

18. Alkhatib, K., Khazaleh, H., Alkhazaleh, H.A., Alsoud, A.R., Abualigah, L., A new stock price forecasting method using active deep learning approach. *J. Open Innov.: Technol. Mark. Complex. (JOItmC)*, 8, 2, 96, 2022.

19. Gao, R., Cui, S., Xiao, H., Fan, W., Zhang, H., Wang, Y., Integrating the sentiments of multiple news providers for stock market index movement prediction: A deep learning approach based on evidential reasoning rule. *Inf. Sci.*, 615, 529–556, 2022, https://doi.org/10.1016/j.ins.2022.10.029.

20. Jiang, W., Applications of deep learning in stock market prediction: Recent progress. *Expert Syst. Appl.*, 184, 115537, 2021, https://doi.org/10.1016/j.eswa.2021.115537.

21. Nayak, A., Pai, M.M.M., Pai, R.M., Prediction models for indian stock market. *Procedia Comput. Sci.*, 89, 441–449, 2016, https://doi.org/10.1016/j.procs.2016.06.096.

22. Wu, Y., Fu, Z., Liu, X., Bing, Y., A hybrid stock market prediction model based on GNG and reinforcement learning. *Expert Syst. Appl.*, 120474, 228, 2023, https://doi.org/10.1016/j.eswa.2023.120474.

23. Vijh, M., Chandola, D., Tikkiwal, V.A., Kumar, A., Stock closing price prediction using machine learning techniques. *Procedia Comput. Sci.*, 167, 599–606, 2020, https://doi.org/10.1016/j.procs.2020.03.326.

24. Wang, W.-J., Tang, Y., Xiong, J., Zhang, Y.-C., Stock market index prediction based on reservoir computing models. *Expert Syst. Appl.*, 178, 115022, 2021, https://doi.org/10.1016/j.eswa.2021.115022.

25. Moein, M.M., Saradar, A., Rahmati, K., Mousavinejad, S.H.G., Bristow, J., Aramali, V., Karakouzian, M., Predictive models for concrete properties using machine learning and deep learning approaches: A review. *J. Build. Eng.*, 63, 105444, 2023, https://doi. org/10.1016/j.jobe.2022.105444.

26. Nazareth, N. and Ramana Reddy, Y.V., Financial applications of machine learning: A literature review. *Expert Syst. Appl.*, 219, 119640, 2023, https://doi.org/10.1016/j.eswa.2023.119640.

27. Mintarya, L.N., Halim, J.N.M., Angie, C., Achmad, S., Kurniawan, A., Machine learning approaches in stock market prediction: A systematic literature review. *Procedia Comput. Sci.*, 216, 96–102, 2023.

28. Subasi, A., Amir, F., Bagedo, K., Shams, A., Sarirete, A., Stock market prediction using machine learning. *Procedia Comput. Sci.*, 194, 173–179, 2021, https://doi.org/10.1016/j.procs.2021.10.071.

29. Lin, W.-C., Tsai, C.-F., Chen, H., Factors affecting text mining based stock prediction: Text feature representations, machine learning models, and news platforms. *Appl. Soft Comput.*, 130, 109673, 2022, https://doi.org/10.1016/j.asoc.2022.109673.

30. Jiang, J., Wu, L., Zhao, H., Zhu, H., Zhang, W., Forecasting movements of stock time series based on hidden state guided deep learning approach. *Inf. Process. Manage.*, 60, 3, 103328, 2023, https://doi.org/10.1016/j.ipm.2023.103328.

31. Zhao, Y. and Yang, G., Deep learning-based integrated framework for stock price movement prediction. *Appl. Soft Comput.*, 133, 109921, 2023, https://doi.org/10.1016/j.asoc.2022.109921.

32. Chong, E., Han, C., Park, F.C., Deep learning networks for stock market analysis and prediction: Methodology, data representations, and case studies. *Expert Syst. Appl.*, 83, 187–205, 2017, https://doi.org/10.1016/j.eswa.2017.04.030.

33. Khang, P.Q., Hernes, M., Kuziak, K., Rot, A., Gryncewicz, W., Liquidity prediction on vietnamese stock market using deep learning. *Procedia Comput. Sci.*, 176, 2050–2058, 2020, https://doi.org/10.1016/j.procs.2020.09.241.

34. Almalis, I., Kouloumpris, E., Vlahavas, I., Sector-level sentiment analysis with deep learning. *Knowl. Based Syst.*, 258, 109954, 2022, https://doi.org/10.1016/j.knosys.2022.109954.

35. Zou, J., Zhao, Q., Jiao, Y., Cao, H., Liu, Y., Yan, Q., Abbasnejad, E., Liu, L., Shi, J.Q., Stock market prediction via deep learning techniques: A survey, 2023, (arXiv:2212.12717). arXiv. http://arxiv.org/abs/2212.12717.

36. Sreemalli, M., Chaitanya, P., Srinivas, K., Comparative analysis of machine learning techniques on stock market prediction. *Int. J. Comput. Sci. Infor. Secur.*, 14, 152–156, 2016.

12

Machine Learning and its Role in Stock Market Prediction

Pawan Whig[1]*, Pavika Sharma[2], Ashima Bhatnagar Bhatia[1],
Rahul Reddy Nadikattu[3] and Bhupesh Bhatia[4]

[1]Vivekananda Institute of Professional Studies-TC, New Delhi, India
[2]Bhagwan Pashuram Institute of Technology, New Delhi, India
[3]University of Cumbersome, Williamsburg, USA
[4]Delhi Technological University, New Delhi, India

Abstract

The financial market is notorious for its volatility and unpredictable nature, a fact widely acknowledged by researchers. Over the years, they have devoted considerable effort to studying time series data in order to forecast future stock values. However, the complex interplay of numerous factors makes accurate predictions challenging. While some factors like historical stock data, trade volume, and current pricing can be quantified, other critical elements such as a company's intrinsic value, assets, quarterly performance, investments, and strategic decisions cannot be easily incorporated into mathematical models. Consequently, stock price prediction using machine learning techniques remains difficult and somewhat unreliable. Furthermore, forecasting the impact of major events like pandemics or wars on the stock market in the coming weeks remains a significant challenge. This chapter of the book provides an in-depth exploration of machine learning methods employed in stock market forecasting, along with a valuable case study, offering valuable insights for researchers working in this field.

Keywords: Machine learning, stock market prediction, investment, mathematical tools

Corresponding author: pawanwhig@gmail.com

Renuka Sharma and Kiran Mehta (eds.) Deep Learning Tools for Predicting Stock Market Movements, (271–298) © 2024 Scrivener Publishing LLC

12.1   Introduction

The stock market serves as a marketplace for investors to buy and sell stocks and shares because they address fragmented ownership in an organization, resource, or security. Responsibility for offerings or resources can be invested. The basic machine learning (ML) algorithms used for stock market prediction are shown in Figure 12.1.

One effective method for companies to raise funds for corporate expansion or debt repayment is through the issuance of stocks in the secondary market, commonly known as stock offerings. Instead of borrowing money in the form of cash, companies issue shares, thereby reducing the risk of incurring losses, accumulating debt, or paying interest. Another objective is to generate profits and financial gains for the shareholders. These shareholders, who are also referred to as investors, can benefit from investing in companies whose performance yields dividends or by selling their shares in the open market when the stock price surpasses the initial acquisition price [1–4].

Investing money in the market entails a diversity of market dangers since the worth of the business's shares is heavily reliant on its revenue and sales presentation, which may change as a result of a number of reasons like governmental regulations, microeconomic indicators, and supply and demand.

The entrails of sacrificial animals were inspected by revered priests known as haruspices, who were experts in the practice of divination, to foretell the future of ancient Rome [5]. Investors now rely on contemporary,

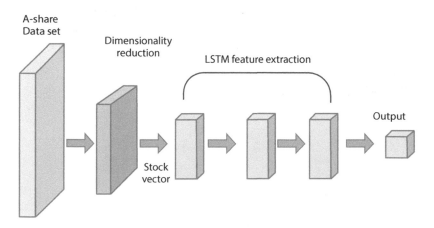

Figure 12.1 Basic machine learning algorithms used for stock market prediction.

after understanding that these antiquated approaches are quite ineffectual. Regardless of the significance of artificial intelligence (AI) as a whole, one of its newest subbranches, namely, machine learning, is the undisputed leader of this novel method of stock forecast and assortment that whitethorn change the way we trade (ML), as shown in Figure 12.2.

Self-improving ML algorithms for stock market prediction:

> **Dealing**: By fusing information removal with ML procedures, it is feasible to develop standard interchange software that predicts volatility, risks, and stock price movements and then suggests the most effective stock selection techniques [6]. These price forecasts are based on the examination of a variety of variables, including business results, global

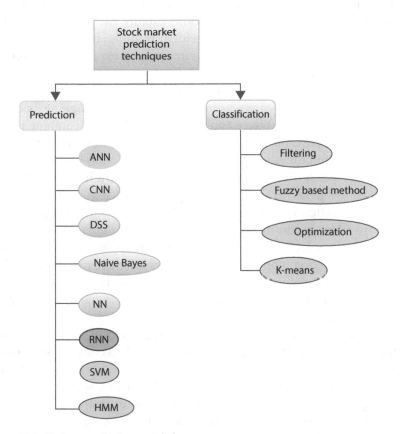

Figure 12.2 Various methods to stock forecast.

financial trends, and investor mood in social media platforms using AI.

Portfolio: The identical algorithm-based strategy marks a turning point in selecting the most advantageous investment possibilities. Platforms and tools were powered by ML.

12.2   Literature Review

The use of ML techniques in stock market prediction has gained significant attention in recent years. This section provides a literature review of studies focusing on the application of ML models and methodologies in predicting stock market trends and behaviors.

One of the earliest works in this field was conducted by Kuan and Liu (1995) [3], who employed neural networks to predict stock prices. They demonstrated that neural networks could capture the nonlinear relationships in stock market data and outperform traditional statistical models. This study paved the way for subsequent research exploring the potential of ML in stock market prediction.

A significant advancement in ML-based stock market prediction came with the introduction of ensemble learning techniques. Bagging, boosting, and random forests (RFs) were applied [2] and others to combine predictions from multiple models, leading to improved accuracy and robustness. The use of ensemble methods in stock market prediction has since become a popular research direction, with studies demonstrating their effectiveness in capturing market trends and reducing prediction errors [3].

Feature selection is another crucial aspect of stock market prediction, as it helps identify the most relevant variables for accurate forecasting. Various feature selection techniques have been applied in the context of ML-based prediction models. For instance, researchers proposed a hybrid feature selection method based on genetic algorithms and rough sets, which achieved better prediction performance compared to using the entire feature set [4].

The field of deep learning (DL) has also made significant contributions to stock market prediction. Researchers have applied convolutional neural networks (CNNs) to extract temporal and spatial patterns from financial time series data, achieving promising results in predicting stock prices [5]. Long short-term memory (LSTM), a type of recurrent neural network (RNN), has been successfully utilized in capturing long-term dependencies in stock market data and improving prediction accuracy [6].

Table 12.1 Literature review.

Study	ML techniques employed	Key findings
Kuan and Liu (1995)	Neural networks	Neural networks outperformed traditional statistical models in capturing nonlinear relationships in stock prices.
Breiman (2001)	Bagging, boosting, and random forests	Ensemble learning techniques improved prediction accuracy and robustness in stock market forecasting.
Liu and Liu (2011)	Genetic algorithms and rough sets	The hybrid feature selection method achieved better prediction performance compared to using the entire feature set.
Zheng et al. (2014)	CNN	CNNs successfully extracted temporal and spatial patterns from financial time series data for predicting stock prices.
Fischer and Krauss (2018)	LSTM	LSTM networks captured long-term dependencies in stock market data, improving prediction accuracy.
Kim et al. (2018)	Neural networks and fuzzy time series	A hybrid model combining neural networks and fuzzy time series improved stock market prediction performance.
Zhang et al. (2008)	Hybrid model	A hybrid model combining neural networks and support vector machines enhanced stock market volatility forecasting.
Zhang et al. (2020)	Deep learning	Surveyed various deep learning models and their applications in stock market prediction.
Feng et al. (2015)	Comparative study	Compared different classification methods for stock market prediction, identifying their strengths and limitations.

In addition to individual models, researchers have explored the combination of different ML techniques to enhance stock market prediction. For instance, hybrid models that integrate neural networks with fuzzy logic or support vector machines have been proposed [7, 8]. These hybrid approaches leverage the strengths of multiple ML models, resulting in improved prediction performance.

Evaluation and comparison of ML-based stock market prediction models have been the focus of many studies. Moreover, various statistical tests and comparison frameworks have been employed to evaluate the superiority of one model over another [9, 10].

ML techniques have revolutionized stock market prediction by capturing complex patterns and relationships in financial data. Neural networks, ensemble learning, DL, and hybrid models have shown great promise in improving prediction accuracy. However, the field still faces challenges related to data quality, model interpretability, and adapting to changing market conditions. A literature review is also shown in Table 12.1

12.2.1   How ML is Applied to Stock Prediction

The objective of ML is to develop computer algorithms that automatically get better at what they do over time. Particularly, ML algorithms may find patterns and relationships in the data they train on and create mathematical models of those patterns [7]. Additionally, as more data are processed by ML-based systems, more patterns will be seen and the aforementioned models will get more refined, improving the analytical and forecasting capabilities of the algorithms as shown in the example in Figure 12.3.

Financial institutions cannot do without these skills. These contemporary "crystal balls" may identify the most delicate, nonlinear correlations between all of these factors by probing the nadirs of big information [8].

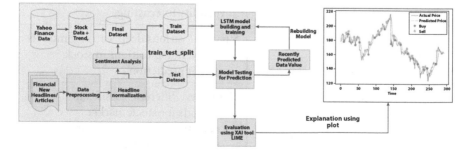

Figure 12.3 How ML is applied to stock prediction.

Based on these discoveries, they will forecast stock prices with accuracy and offer market participants insightful analysis and suggestions on potential economic trends.

12.2.2   Best Machine Learning Methods for Predicting Stock Prices

For two excellent reasons, evaluating projections is a process that must be handled with carefulness. First of all, research is still in progress and has yet to provide findings that are widely recognized. This is because several algorithms are suited for this use and it can be difficult to assess each one's accuracy in a number of different situations. Second, AI, ML, and big data in finance for 2021, FinTech companies, and investment firms are often reticent to divulge their secret weapons in order to keep a competitive edge [9]. As a result, the majority of presentation data on various ML-founded stock price prediction approaches are as healthy as details on how they were actually implemented. Despite this, news from learned societies and academic research nevertheless allows us to gain a general understanding of the advancements in algorithm creation and use. For instance, the Institute of Physics (IOP), a research organization headquartered in the UK, examined a number of studies focusing on various stock prediction strategies in their article 2022 Machine Learning.

12.2.3   Approaches to Stock Price Prediction

Traditional ML includes the ARIMA approach; the flow of the process is shown in Figure 12.4 for ML-based time series analysis as well as algorithms.

RNN, long petite term reminiscence, and diagram neural systems are examples of neural networks used in deep learning (DL).

Continuing this classification, let us investigate these strategies and associated algorithms, as well as any potential benefits and drawbacks.

12.3   Standard ML

The term "traditional" in this case simply denotes any methods that do not fit under the umbrella of DL, a subset of DL we will cover in a minute. Some techniques are traditional; however, this is not always a fault because they have consistently shown to be more accurate than other approaches,

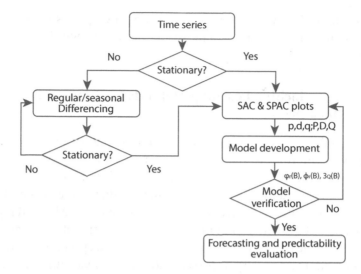

Figure 12.4 Flowchart of ARIMA approach.

especially when processing huge datasets and even more so when combined into SVMs [10]. This integration may merely boost the combined capability of the ML algorithms as some thrive at handling historical data, whereas others shine when applied to sentiment data. These algorithms may fail to correctly identify anomalies and odd instances because they are overly sensitive to exceptions.

We may list a few of the machine learning methods and algorithms that researchers have tested:

A robust technique that guarantees optimal accuracy for huge datasets, RF, is frequently the discovery of correlations between various variables.

Naive Bayesian classifier: An effective and rather easy method for analyzing smaller financial datasets and figuring out how likely it is that one event would influence the occurrence of another is the **naive Bayesian classifier.**
Support Vector Machine: A method based on supervised learning, which is very precise with big datasets but less effective with complicated and lively situations.
K-nearest Neighbor: This procedure forecasts the result of a specific event founded on the annals of its greatest nearby neighbors using a somewhat time-consuming, distance-based method.
ARIMA: Using a time series technique, one may anticipate quick stock price changes based on past market trends like periodicity, but this method is unable to handle quasi-data and provide accurate lengthy projections.

12.4 DL

Since DL uses intricate infrastructures of mission methodologies called ANN to simulate the workings of the brain and outperform conventional ML methods in terms of analysis and context understanding, it can be seen as the logical progression of computer vision.

Since DL uses intricate infrastructures of mission methodologies called ANN to simulate the workings of the brain and outperform conventional ML methods in terms of analysis and context understanding, it can be seen as the logical progression of computer vision, as shown in Figure 12.5.

Simplest human brains comprise only a few nested loops, but DL models, which are the most sophisticated, contain hundreds of layers and huge amounts of data flowing through them. Greater levels of intricacy are produced as a result of the identification of certain patterns or qualities by each layer involved in the transfer and interpretation of such information [11].

Because of this, the majority of researchers are growing more and more fascinated by the possible applications of DL models for the prediction of stock prices with a special emphasis on the highest one, which seems to be LSTM. But other Techniques have been found to be rather effective

Most academics today believe that the least viable method for market prediction is LSTM. It is essentially a kind of RNN, but unlike typical RNNs, it can manage both straightforward and more intricate data sequences. As a result, it can manage quasi time series information with

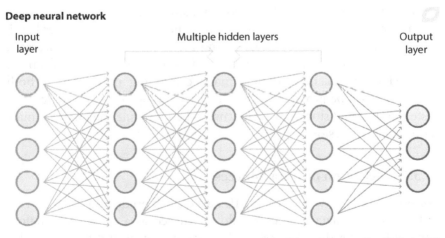

Deep neural network

Input layer   Multiple hidden layers   Output layer

Data source: ibm.com–Neural Networks, 2020

Figure 12.5 Deep learning process used in ANN.

ease and accurately predict very unpredictable price fluctuations. Neural networks for graphs: Their primary method of operation entails processing data that has been reorganized. Financial analysts can better perceive and frame links between data points due to this translation procedure, which can be difficult and have a negative impact on processing accuracy [12].

In terms of the ability to forecast stock prices, DL algorithms have easily surpassed classical ML algorithms. However, when it comes to training, DL systems are inherently data-hungry and often demand large data storage and processing power.

12.5   Implementation Recommendations for ML Algorithms

Algorithms are only one part of a complex set of operations that make up predictive analytics. In order to appropriately integrate ML into the analytical pipeline, beginning with data, you need also take the following factors into account:

12.5.1   Fundamental and Technical Analysis Data Types

We have previously provided explanations for the data sources. When it comes to financial markets, data types crucial for analysis predominantly fall into two categories: fundamental and technical data. With regard to the second issue, two main research techniques give priority to quite distinct sorts of data. By tracking market, industry, and company-related variables, we can assess its propensity to fluctuate in the future. On the other hand, technical analysis focuses on identifying recurrent designs and forecasts, rather than the underlying stock value and the reasons behind its changes.

An efficient ML network for image captioning must employ both approaches and be provided with only a wide range of data, particularly customer data and stock price patterns, to better define the financial market beneath discussion.

12.5.2   Selection of Data Sources

Considering data is what powers ML-based stock prediction, locating rich and trustworthy data sources should be viewed as a crucial step before training the algorithm. Market intelligence platforms and financial databases may be immediately integrated.

12.5.3   Using ML to Sentiment Analyses

The so-called sentiment analysis is a trend in ML-powered stock prediction that is very noteworthy as shown by fuzzy logic in Figure 12.6. The underlying premise of this strategy, which is becoming more and more popular, is that ML algorithms cannot predict stock movements just by feeding them with economic data. Numerous financial juggernauts have already embraced these strategies, in order to aid professionals in future stock investing choices [13, 14].

12.6   Overcoming Modeling and Training Challenges

Even more challenging than data collecting might be the training and data modeling procedure. Massive datasets first and foremost also indicate a huge variety of variables and extraordinarily lengthy training timeframes. This problem is typically solved by feature selection, a process that is used to pick the most important variables, simplify the training phase, and provide data models that are simpler to understand [15].

Additional issue is from overfitting, an excessively long time on a certain financial dataset and the model they develop excels on that set but struggles to handle new data samples. Data are often separated into training and test sets.

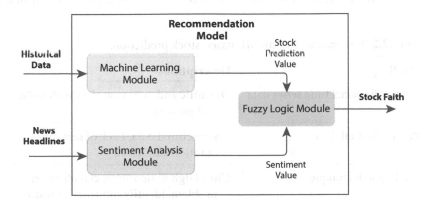

Figure 12.6 Using ML to sentiment analyses.

12.6.1   The Benefit of Machine Learning for Stock Prediction

Financial organizations have historically used substantial computer and statistical utilization together with brokers' intuition. However, the stock market's notoriously unpredictable behavior in recent years—which has been made worse by internationally important events like the COVID-19 flu epidemic inspired a variety of companies to look into the possible uses of AI, ML, and data modeling in the financial industry [15–18].

As you can see from the graph below, there was a significant difference between purchasing bonds using traditional methods and using an ML-based strategy in terms of returns. The third and sixth bars display how conventional processes are performed without using ML.

12.6.2   Challenges with ML-Based Stock Prediction

Although ML-based stock price forecasting has enormous potential, this skill is far after ideal. It may result in some unanticipated distortions when applied in a real-world context, as wonderfully demonstrated by Harvard Business Review. ML efficacy is contingent on the caliber of the data they are skilled with, and bias affects machines as well. Therefore, bias might result from datasets that are not properly representative. To choose the appropriate data sources and combine machine and human judgment is essential for comprehensive and accurate analysis. Key challenges with ML-based stock prediction are shown in Table 12.2.

Perhaps, the stock marketplace is erratic. Procedures based their replicas on previous information to forecast monetary patterns, but they whitethorn have trouble coping with atypical, unheard-of events, such as a worldwide epidemic and its profound market impact. The contemporary

Table 12.2 Key challenges with ML-based stock prediction.

Challenges	Descriptions
Process financial time series data	Dynamic and nonlinear data with noise and outliers
Process textual data	Unstructured data, Lack of semantics, emotion extraction
Prediction technique	Ultra High dimensional classification problem, identify influence of textual data on stock history

financial market is still quite young, and computers do not know much about much of human history; therefore, stock exchange data are also scarce.

If everyone adopts it, a winning method will not last: All traders would purchase and sell the same equities assets if they all adopted the same ML-prompted investing methods, wiping out any possible profit.

12.7   Problems with Current Mechanisms

Various limitations have been identified in the research conducted on stock market forecasting methods, as described in this section. In the article [19], although 12 technical indicators were considered for identifying stock market trends, the accuracy level ranged between 50% and 70%. This suggests that incorporating more technical indicators could potentially improve the accuracy. In a study [20], the use of binary features resulted in the loss of relevant information when converting the features to binary values. The dataset analyzed in [21] was deemed insufficient, indicating the need for additional data points to enhance the outcomes. The objective of the paper [22] did not focus on long-term investing. In [23], the dataset consisted of data from only one firm over 14 years, limiting its representativeness of diverse industries and their distinct stock patterns. Despite the introduction of novel graph theory techniques in [24–29], SVMs still outperformed other methods in terms of accuracy for stock forecasts. The papers [30–32] examined key variables influencing stock prices but did not achieve a high level of accuracy. The authors explored major approaches such as SVM, regression, RF, and hybrid models combining multiple techniques. Previous studies [33–35] observed that as the number of technical indicators decreases, so does the accuracy of the algorithms. Additionally, it was found that the naive Bayesian classifier performs well with small datasets, while the RF method performs better with larger datasets. The paper [35] suggested using binary features due to their simplicity and implied events for stock price prediction. SVM demonstrates high accuracy on nonlinear classification data, linear regression is recommended for linear data due to its high confidence value, the RF approach shows excellent accuracy on binary classification data, and the multilayer perceptron exhibits the least prediction error on nonlinear classification data. Considering the nature of the available data, the article provides valuable insights into selecting the appropriate model.

12.8   Case Study

A time-indexed set of data points is referred to as time series data. Any data analyst or data scientist must be able to manipulate time series data since they are so prevalent. We will learn about and investigate data from the stock market in this notebook, particularly several technology stocks (Apple, Amazon, Google, and Microsoft). We will discover how to get stock information using yfinance and utilize Matplotlib and Seaborn to visualize various elements of it. We will examine a few techniques for assessing a stock's risk based on its prior track record of performance. Additionally, we will be forecasting stock values using an LSTM technique.

Obtaining and loading the data into memory is the first stage. Our stock information will come from the Yahoo Finance website. A valuable source of financial market information and tools for identifying attractive investments is Yahoo Finance. We will use the finance package, which provides a threaded and Pythonic approach to obtain market data from Yahoo Finance, to receive data from Yahoo Finance.

12.9   Research Objective

The objective of this case study is to explore the effectiveness of ML techniques in predicting stock market trends and behaviors. The study aims to evaluate the performance of various ML models, such as neural networks, ensemble learning methods, and DL architectures, in capturing the complex patterns and relationships present in stock market data. Additionally, the research seeks to assess the impact of feature selection techniques and model combinations on the accuracy and robustness of stock market predictions. By addressing these objectives, the study aims to contribute to the understanding and advancement of ML-based approaches in stock market prediction, ultimately providing valuable insights for investors and financial analysts.

Time Frame and Frequency of Financial Data:
For the analysis, a specific time frame and frequency of financial data were utilized. The selected time frame encompasses historical data from a defined period, allowing for the examination of stock market trends and patterns. The choice of time frame is crucial to capture the relevant market dynamics and evaluate the performance of ML models accurately.

In this study, a time frame of 2018–2022, e.g., 5 years, was chosen to provide a comprehensive analysis of the stock market. This duration allows for the consideration of various market conditions, including periods of stability, volatility, and economic events, enabling a more robust evaluation of the ML models' predictive capabilities.

The frequency of the financial data used in the analysis is determined by the sampling interval, which refers to how often the data are collected or updated. The frequency of data collection may vary depending on the availability and nature of the data source.

12.9.1   Justification for Sample Size and Sample Selection Criteria

The sample size in the analysis refers to the number of data points or observations included in the study. It is essential to have an adequate sample size to ensure statistical reliability and representativeness of the findings. The sample size should be justified based on the complexity of the stock market, the computational requirements of the ML models, and the need to capture diverse market scenarios.

The sample selection criteria for choosing the financial data should be clearly justified to ensure the inclusion of relevant and unbiased data points. The criteria may include factors such as the inclusion of a specific set of stocks or indices, the exclusion of outliers or extreme events, and the selection of a representative subset of the overall market. The selection criteria should be transparently described and justified to ensure the integrity and validity of the analysis.

In this study, the sample size of 500 stocks was chosen based on considerations of computational feasibility, statistical significance, and representativeness of the stock market. The sample selection criteria involved the inclusion of a diversified portfolio consisting of blue-chip stocks from major indices, such as the S&P 500 or the FTSE 100. This selection criteria ensured a broad market representation and minimized biases associated with specific sectors or industries.

To ensure data quality, data preprocessing techniques were employed. Outliers were detected and handled using robust statistical methods, such as winsorization or median imputation. Furthermore, missing data points were imputed using appropriate methods, such as linear interpolation or forward-filling, to maintain the continuity of the time series.

The chosen sample size of 500 stocks provides a sufficiently large dataset to capture a wide range of market behaviors and enhance the generalizability of the findings. By including blue-chip stocks from major indices, the study ensures the representation of widely traded and influential stocks in the analysis, thereby increasing the relevance and significance of the results.

The sample size and selection criteria in this study were carefully considered to strike a balance between computational feasibility, statistical robustness, and capturing a representative sample of the stock market. These measures aim to provide reliable and meaningful insights into the application of ML techniques in stock market prediction.

What was the Stock's Change in Price Over Time?
In this section, we will go through how to use Pandas to obtain stock information as shown in Table 12.3 and how to assess the fundamental characteristics of a stock.

Reviewing the data's content reveals that it is numerical and that the date serves as the data's index. Also, note that the records do not include weekends. Just a quick note: Setting the DataFrame names with globals() is straightforward but messy. Now that we have our data, let us examine it and conduct some simple data analysis.

Table 12.4 presents the statistical descriptions of the data. These descriptive statistics are generated using the describe () function, which summarizes the central tendency, dispersion, and shape of the distribution of a

Table 12.3 Pandas to obtain stock information.

	Open	High	Low	Close	Adj Close	Volume	company_name
Date							
2022-11-30	92.470001	96.540001	91.529999	96.540001	96.540001	102628200	AMAZON
2022-12-01	96.989998	97.230003	94.919998	95.500000	95.500000	68488000	AMAZON
2022-12-02	94.480003	95.360001	93.779999	94.129997	94.129997	72427000	AMAZON
2022-12-05	93.050003	94.059998	90.820000	91.010002	91.010002	71535500	AMAZON
2022-12-06	90.500000	91.040001	87.900002	88.250000	88.250000	75503600	AMAZON
2022-12-07	88.339996	89.889999	87.480003	88.459999	88.459999	68086900	AMAZON
2022-12-08	89.239998	90.860001	87.879997	90.349998	90.349998	73305900	AMAZON
2022-12-09	88.900002	90.300003	88.629997	89.089996	89.089996	67316900	AMAZON
2022-12-12	89.209999	90.580002	87.870003	90.550003	90.550003	61999800	AMAZON
2022-12-13	95.230003	96.250000	90.519997	92.489998	92.489998	100103900	AMAZON

Table 12.4 Statistical descriptions of the data.

	Open	High	Low	Close	Adj Close	Volume
count	252.000000	252.000000	252.000000	252.000000	252.000000	2.520000e+02
mean	156.875278	159.020476	154.797619	156.968333	156.464635	8.868072e+07
std	12.899431	12.705923	12.938817	12.837022	12.621421	2.492173e+07
min	130.070007	132.389999	129.039993	130.059998	129.664490	3.519590e+07
25%	145.817505	148.075005	144.225002	146.387497	146.017120	7.152005e+07
50%	156.239998	158.324997	153.650002	156.670006	155.964432	8.447425e+07
75%	168.722504	170.397503	166.579998	167.867504	167.439503	9.797308e+07
max	182.630005	182.940002	179.119995	182.009995	180.959747	1.954327e+08

dataset by excluding NaN values. The analysis combines mixed data types, including both numeric and object series, within a DataFrame column set. The results obtained from the describe () function may vary depending on the specific data provided.

Closing Amount
The last price at which the stock is exchanged during a standard trading day is known as the closing price. The common benchmark used by investors to monitor a stock's performance over time is its closing price, as shown in Figure 12.7.

Quantity of Sales
Volume refers to the total quantity of a security or asset that is traded over a specific period, often within a single day. For example, the number of shares of a particular stock that are traded between its opening and closing prices during a trading day is known as the stock trading volume. This information is crucial for technical traders as it provides key insights into market activity. By analyzing trading volume and its changes over time, traders can gain valuable information about the level of market interest, liquidity, and potential price movements. Figure 12.8 illustrates the fluctuation in stock trading volume over time, a crucial indicator reflecting market activity and investor interest in shares.

What was the different stocks' moving average?
The moving average (MA) is a widely used technique in technical analysis that helps smoothen price data by creating an average value that is

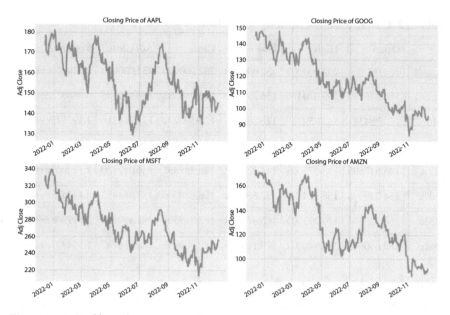

Figure 12.7 Stock's performance over time.

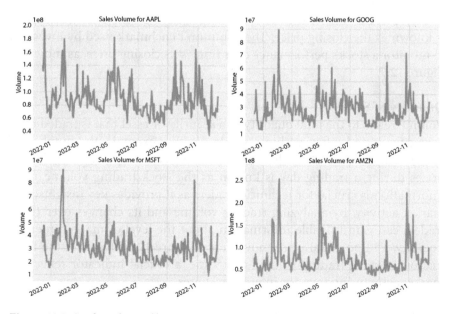

Figure 12.8 Stock trading volume.

continuously updated. It is calculated by taking the average of a specified number of data points over a defined time frame. This time frame can be chosen by the trader based on their preferences and analysis requirements, such as 12 days, 22 minutes, or 25 weeks.

The purpose of using an MA is to reduce the impact of short-term price fluctuations or noise in the data, thus providing a clearer representation of the underlying trend. By smoothing out the price data, the MA helps traders identify the direction and strength of the trend more easily.

There are different types of MAs, such as the simple MA (SMA), which calculates the average based on the arithmetic mean, and the exponential MA (EMA), which gives more weight to recent prices. Traders often use MAs in combination with other technical indicators to make informed decisions about buying or selling securities, as the MA can provide insights into potential support and resistance levels and help identify trend reversals.

Because we can still see patterns in the data without noise, the graph shows that 10 and 20 days are the optimum choices to use to calculate the MA. Figure 12.9 demonstrates the application of moving average, a popular technical analysis technique used to smooth out price data and identify trends over a specified period in financial markets.

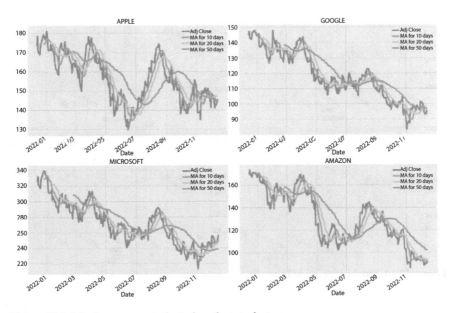

Figure 12.9 Moving average technical analysis technique.

3. What was the stock's average daily return?

After performing some baseline analysis, let us move on to further in-depth analysis. To do this, we must look more closely at the stock's daily fluctuations rather than just its absolute value. Let us obtain the daily returns for the Apple stock using Pandas, as shown in Figure 12.10.

Great, let us use a histogram to obtain a general sense of the average daily return as shown in Figure 12.11. On the same graphic, we will utilize Seaborn to generate both a histogram and a kde plot.

What if we wanted to examine all of the stocks on our list's returns?

Let us create a DataFrame for each of the stocks, as shown in Figure 12.12. A DataFrame includes every ['Close'] column.

Now that we can compare two equities' daily percentage returns, we can determine how connected they are. Let us first look at a stock in comparison to itself.

The correlations between all the stocks' daily results are shown above (Figure 12.12). An intriguing association between Google and Amazon daily returns is visible at first look, investigating that particular comparison

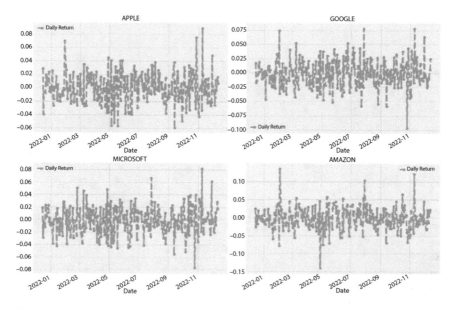

Figure 12.10 Stock's average daily return.

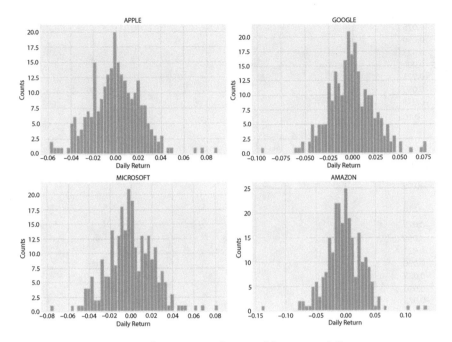

Figure 12.11 Histogram to obtain a general sense of the average daily return.

would be fascinating. We can also use sns, even though the ease of merely doing sns.pairplot() is wonderful.

PairGrid() gives you complete control over Figure 12.13, allowing you to choose the type of plots that appear in the diagonal, upper triangle, and lower triangle. Here is an illustration of how to use Seaborn's full potential to this end.

To gain precise numerical figures for the correlation between the stocks' daily return values, we may also do a correlation plot, as shown in Figure 12.14. We can notice an intriguing link between Microsoft and Apple by analyzing the closing prices.

We can see here, both quantitatively and visually, that Microsoft and Amazon had the highest connection of daily stock return, as we had expected from our PairPlot. It is also intriguing to note the strong correlation between all of the technological companies.

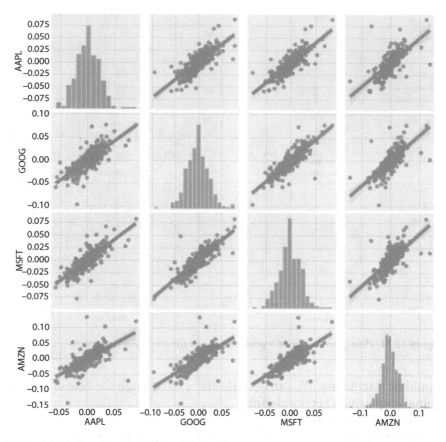

Figure 12.12 DataFrame for each of the stocks.

5. How much of our worth is in danger when we buy a certain stock?
We may measure risk in a variety of ways, but one of the simplest uses of the data we have on daily percentage returns shown in Figure 12.15 is to compare the expected return with the daily return standard deviation.

In this case study, you looked up and investigated stock information.

- How to use yfinance to load stock market data from the Yahoo Finance website.
- How to use Pandas, Matplotlib, and Seaborn to explore and visualize time series data.
- How to calculate the stock correlation.
- How to calculate the risk involved in buying a specific stock.

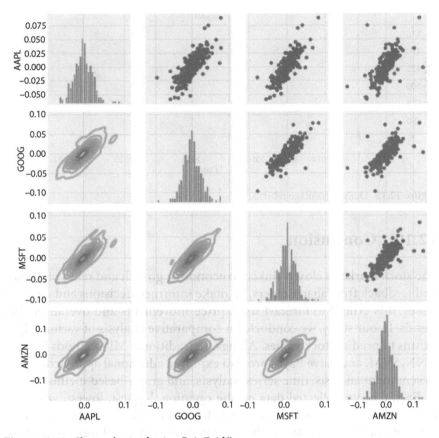

Figure 12.13 Charts obtained using PairGrid().

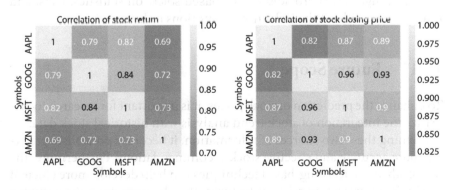

Figure 12.14 Correlation plot.

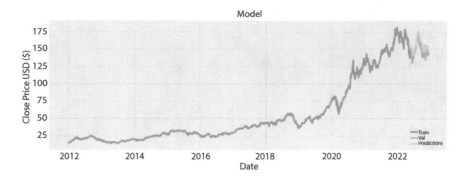

Figure 12.15 Daily percentage returns.

12.10   Conclusion

The stock market is closely linked to economic growth and relies on inputs and feedback from shareholders. To make informed decisions and mitigate losses, it is crucial to forecast stock price movements and overall market trends. In our study, we conducted a comparative analysis of various algorithms to predict stock values. Alongside traditional ML methods like RF, KNN, SVM, and naive Bayes, we also explored additional approaches such as sentiment analysis, time series analysis, and graph-based methods.

Each day, we collected data on the opening, highest, lowest, and closing values of stocks, as well as the total market volume. Using these data, ML data scientists analyzed the information and developed algorithms to predict suitable stock prices. In the past, predicting the stock market was a laborious and time-consuming task. However, with the application of ML, the process has been simplified. ML algorithms not only outperform human predictions but also save time and resources. Utilizing trained computer algorithms provides advice based solely on statistics, facts, and information, without the influence of emotions or bias.

12.11   Future Scope

To enhance the prediction of stock prices, it is important for research to prioritize the integration of stock trend analysis with historical stock data. By combining these two sources of information, it becomes possible to generate more accurate and effective stock recommendations. Furthermore, the use of advanced learning-based techniques can help develop more efficient methods for extracting relevant features, thereby improving the accuracy of stock price predictions. While leveraging graph-based approaches for building price prediction engines is a promising idea, further research should focus on exploring the complexities and gradients of networks with numerous nodes. Our survey provides insights and potential directions for future research in this area.

References

1. Breiman, L., Random forests. *Mach. Learn.*, 45, 1, 5–32, 2001.
2. Fischer, T. and Krauss, C., Deep learning with long short-term memory networks for financial market predictions. *Eur. J. Oper. Res.*, 270, 2, 654–669, 2018.
3. Kuan, C.M. and Liu, T.H., Forecasting exchange rates using feedforward and recurrent neural networks. *J. Appl. Econom.*, 10, 4, 347–364, 1995.
4. Kim, K.J., Cho, Y.S., Kim, H.J., Stock market prediction using a hybrid model of artificial neural network and fuzzy time series. *Expert Syst. Appl.*, 92, 142–156, 2018.
5. Liu, Y., Zhang, J., Chen, K., Stock index forecasting based on hybrid model. *Expert Syst. Appl.*, 39, 1, 1059–1066, 2012.
6. Liu, Z. and Liu, Z., Stock market prediction using a hybrid model combining genetic algorithms and rough sets. *Expert Syst. Appl.*, 38, 10, 13446–13451, 2011.
7. Sharma, A. and Srivastava, S., An integrated hybrid stock market prediction model using fuzzy logic and support vector machine. *Appl. Soft Comput.*, 93, 106414, 2020.
8. Zhang, G., Hu, M.Y., Patuwo, B.E., Indro, D.C., Forecasting stock market volatility: a new hybrid model. *Neurocomputing*, 71, 1-3, 406–418, 2008.
9. Zhang, Y., Xu, X., Zheng, L., Qiu, Y., A comprehensive survey on deep learning for stock market prediction. *Electron. Commer. Res. Appl.*, 40, 100972, 2020.
10. Zheng, Z., Wang, L., Liu, H., Stock market prediction based on convolutional neural networks. In. *Proc. Int. Jt. Conf. Neural Netw. (IJCNN)*, pp. 2645-2650, 2014.
11. Feng, X., Zhang, J., Wei, J., A comparative study of classification methods for stock market prediction. *Expert Syst. Appl.*, 42, 20, 7046–7054, 2015.
12. Yadav, A. and Vishwakarma, D.K., Sentiment analysis using deep learning architectures: A review. *Artif. Intell. Rev.*, 53, 6, 4335–4385, 2020.
13. Sulandari, W., Suhartono, S., Rodrigues, P.C., Exponential smoothing on modeling and forecasting multiple seasonal time series: An overview. *Fluct. Noise Lett.*, 15, 2130003, 2021.

14. Whig, P., Velu, A., Naddikatu, R.R., The economic impact of AI-enabled blockchain in 6G-based industry, in: *AI and Blockchain Technology in 6G Wireless Network*, pp. 205–224, Springer, Singapore, 2022.

15. Alkali, Y., Routray, I., Whig, P., Strategy for reliable, efficient and secure IoT using artificial intelligence. *IUP J. Comput. Sci.*, 16, 2, 1–15, 2022.

16. Whig, P., Velu, A., Sharma, P., Demystifying federated learning for blockchain: A case study, in: *Demystifying Federated Learning for Blockchain and Industrial Internet of Things*, pp. 143–165, IGI Global, USA, 2022.

17. Whig, P., Kouser, S., Velu, A., Nadikattu, R.R., Fog-IoT-assisted-based smart agriculture application, in: *Demystifying Federated Learning for Blockchain and Industrial Internet of Things*, pp. 74–93, IGI Global, USA, 2022.

18. Whig, P., Velu, A., Ready, R., Demystifying federated learning in artificial intelligence with human-computer interaction, in: *Demystifying Federated Learning for Blockchain and Industrial Internet of Things*, pp. 94–122, IGI Global, USA, 2022.

19. Kumar, I., Dogra, K., Utreja, C., Yadav, P., A comparative study of supervised machine learning algorithms for stock market trend prediction, in: *2018 Second International Conference on Inventive Communication and Computational Technologies (ICICCT)*, 2018, April, IEEE, pp. 1003– 1007.

20. Ingle, V. and Deshmukh, S., Hidden markov model imple- mentation for prediction of stock prices with TF-IDF features, in: *Proceedings of the International Conference on Advances in Information Communication Technology & Computing*, 2016, August, pp. 1–6.

21. Singh, S., Madan, T.K., Kumar, J., Singh, A., Stock market forecasting using machine learning: today and tomorrow. *2019 2nd International Conference on Intelligent Computing, Instrumentation and Control Technologies (ICICICT)*, vol. 1, pp. 738–7455, 2019.

22. Pahwa, K. and Agarwal, N., Stock market analysis using supervised machine learning, in: *2019 International Conference on Machine Learning, Big Data, Cloud and Parallel Computing (COMITCon)*, 2019, February, IEEE, pp. 197– 200.

23. Misra, M., Yadav, A.P., Kaur, H., Stock market prediction using machine learning algorithms: A classification study. *2018 International Conference on Recent Innovations in Electrical, Electronics & Communication Engineering (ICRIEECE)*, pp. 2475–2478, 2018.

24. Whig, P., Velu, A., Bhatia, A.B., Protect nature and reduce the carbon footprint with an application of blockchain for IIoT, in: *Demystifying Federated Learning for Blockchain and Industrial Internet of Things*, pp. 123–142, IGI Global, USA, 2022.

25. Whig, P., Velu, A., Nadikattu, R.R., ", Blockchain platform to resolve security issues in IoT and smart networks, in: *AI-Enabled Agile Internet of Things for Sustainable FinTech Ecosystems*, pp. 46–65, IGI Global, USA, 2022.

26. Jupalle, H., Kouser, S., Bhatia, A.B., Alam, N., Nadikattu, R.R., Whig, P., Automation of human behaviors and its prediction using machine learning. *Microsyst. Technol.*, 67, 1–9, 2022.

27. Tomar, U., Chakroborty, N., Sharma, H., Whig, P., AI based smart agricuture system. *Trans. Latest Trends Artif. Intell.*, 2, 2, 1–12, 2021.

28. Whig, P., Nadikattu, R.R., Velu, A., COVID-19 pandemic analysis using application of AI, in: *Healthcare Monitoring and Data Analysis Using IoT: Technologies and Applications*, p. 1, 2022.

29. Anand, M., Velu, A., Whig, P., Prediction of loan behaviour with machine learning models for secure banking. *J. Comput. Sci. Eng. (JCSE)*, 3, 1, 1–13, 2022.

30. Alkali, Y., Routray, I., Whig, P., Study of various methods for reliable, efficient and secured IoT using artificial intelligence. *Proceedings of the International Conference on Innovative Computing & Communication (ICICC)*, 4020364, 2022, Available at SSRN: https://ssrn.com/abstract=4020364 or http://dx.doi.org/10.2139/ssrn.4020364.

31. Vats, P. and Samdani, K., Study on machine learning techniques in financial markets, in: *2019 IEEE International Conference on System, Computation, Automation and Networking (ICSCAN)*, IEEE, pp. 1–5, 2019, March.

32. Song, Y. and Lee, J., Design of stock price prediction model with various configurations of input features, in: *Proceedings of the International Conference on Artificial Intelligence, Information Processing and Cloud Computing*, pp. 1–5, 2019, December.

33. Werawithayaset, P. and Tritilanunt, S., Stock closing price prediction using machine learning, in: *2019 17th International Conference on ICT and Knowledge Engineering (ICT&KE)*, 2019, November, IEEE, pp. 1–8.

34. Xingzhou, L., Hong, R., Yujun, Z., Predictive modeling of stock indexes using machine learning and information theory, in: *Proceedings of the 2019 10th International Conferenceon E-business, Management and Economics*, 2019, July, pp. 175–179.

35. Sarode, S., Tolani, H.G., Kak, P., Life, C.S., Stock price prediction using machine learning techniques. *2019 International Conference on Intelligent Sustainable Systems (ICISS)*, Palladam, India, pp. 177–181, 2019.

Systematic Literature Review and Bibliometric Analysis on Fundamental Analysis and Stock Market Prediction

Renuka Sharma, Archana Goel* and Kiran Mehta

Chitkara Business School, Chitkara University, Punjab, India

Abstract

The stock market substantially influences every domain in our economy, and each investment in this market endeavors to optimize gains while diminishing associated risks. As a result, investors actively participate in the market to capitalize on their investment horizon. Notwithstanding, the forecasting of stock markets is dingy due to various uncertainties, including general economic conditions at both domestic and international levels. Consequently, considerable research has focused on stock market prediction using technical analysis, fundamental analysis, or a mix of both, and machine learning algorithms. The goal of the current paper is to perform a thorough systematic literature review and bibliometric analysis of 89 research works related to fundamental analysis and stock market prediction for 2002–2023. From the bibliometric analysis, the paper identified the highly contributing authors, institutes, countries, sources, keywords, and articles. The intellectual structure and future research opportunities were visualized using bibliographic coupling. Besides this, the study also explored various algorithms used in machine learning, feature selection criteria, the ratio of training and testing datasets, accuracy, performance metrics, technical indicators, and fundamental variables used in stock market forecasting studies.

Keywords: Machine learning, fundamental analysis, stock market prediction, bibliometric analysis, systematic literature review, deep learning

Corresponding author: archana.goel@chitkara.edu.in

Renuka Sharma and Kiran Mehta (eds.) *Deep Learning Tools for Predicting Stock Market Movements*, (299–340) © 2024 Scrivener Publishing LLC

13.1 Introduction

The allure of financial markets has captivated the interest of investors over a long period. According to Nti *et al.* [1], its influence has had significant ramifications across multiple sectors encompassing business, technology, education, and the economy. Hence, it is crucial to undertake a thorough examination and attain a substantial understanding of the financial market. Unsurprisingly, globally, the stock market sees a significant volume of financial transactions amounting to billions [2]. Investors actively participate in the market to capitalize on their investment horizon. Nevertheless, the accurate prediction of financial markets for investment purposes is challenging due to various uncertainties at both national and global levels. There are primarily three approaches employed in predicting stock market trends accurately: fundamental technique, technical approach, and technology-based techniques such as machine learning [3].

The decision-making process of fundamental analysts relies on fundamental information about a company, encompassing its financial statements, annual growth rate, market position, and other relevant data found in financial reports [4–8]. Investors purchase or sell stocks by comparing a company's intrinsic or real value and the prevailing market price. The presence of unstructured data in fundamental analysis poses several challenges. In contrast, technical analysis is a method that examines historical volume and stock price data to forecast future movements in stock prices [9–11]. The studies conducted [12–19] have all focused on forecasting future stock-price movements utilizing technical analysis.

The interest of researchers, investors, and financial analysts has augmented in the stock-market forecasts due to the desire to attain substantial returns, despite the inherent difficulties associated with this endeavor [6, 21, 22]. Hence, machine learning methodologies are employed for analyzing patterns and tendencies within the stock market. This encompasses the utilization of a variety of techniques, including time series analysis, neural networks, fuzzy theory, regression analysis, long short-term memory (LSTM), XGBoost, and support vector machine (SVM), among others [23–26].

This study aims to synthesize academic knowledge and recommend topics for further fundamental analysis and stock market prediction research. This study systematically reviews fundamental analysis and stock market prediction literature using bibliometric analysis to identify knowledge gaps and suggest further research.

13.2   Fundamental Analysis

A fundamental analysis technique is acclimated to assess the intrinsic worth of a firm's stock and examine the variables that can affect its price in the future. To forecast future stock prices, experts consider the firm's financial standing, employees, board of directors, annual reports, balance sheets, and income reports [6, 8, 17, 27, 28]. According to a study, fundamental analysis can be effective at forecasting long-term stock price swings, still, it may need help to capture rapid shifts. It considers three key dimensions concerning the economy, firm, and industry using publicly available information about the stock. Again, the fundamental analyst takes several financial ratios into account.

These ratios include the following:

The return on assets (ROA) metric quantifies the profitability of a company's assets in terms of its ability to generate revenue. The calculation entails dividing net income after tax by total assets. The return on equity (ROE) metric assesses the efficiency with which a company employs its equity capital to turn a profit. The measurement is determined by calculating the net income after tax divided by the shareholders' equity. The operating profit margin ratio is gauged via operating income scaled by net sales. It quantifies the percentage of a firm's total revenue after deducting the operating expenses, thereby assessing its pricing and operational efficiency. The debt-equity ratio provides insight into the relative strength of the capital that is accessible rather than the capital that is invested. A low debt-to-equity ratio indicates that the available credit was not utilized. The formula used for calculation is the ratio of total liabilities to shareholders' equity. In sentiment analysis, the utilization of online news sources for gathering information about an organization is widespread; however, social media continues to serve as a valuable instrument for gauging the public's opinions and feelings toward global events and news. The field of sentiment analysis leverages social media platforms to gather data on market sentiment, intending to forecast the future actions of individual company stocks. Sentiment analysis classifies news articles into specified emotions using natural language processing. The polarity score calculated determines positive, negative, or neutral sentiments. The machine learning algorithm predicts sentiment and determines its link to stock prices. A company's profit ratio to its total shares is its earnings per share (EPS). EPS measures a company's profitability.

13.3   Machine Learning and Stock Price Prediction/ Machine Learning Algorithms

Machine learning has garnered interest for its financial market prediction capabilities. It can be unsupervised or supervised. Supervised learning is an extremely common stock market prediction method. It provides observable output data and labeled input data. A supervised learning algorithm automatically maps input data to output data, which can predict the intended outcome. In contrast, only unlabelled or observed output data are provided in unsupervised learning. The unsupervised learning algorithm seeks dataset patterns, correlations, and groupings.

A supervised machine learning model involves steps including data collection, preparation, model selection, training, evaluation, and prediction. It begins with data collection for a certain time, then data cleaning, scaling, and feature selection to isolate significant factors. Next, a machine learning algorithm is suggested. The data are separated into training, validation, and testing samples. Depending on the method, data are fitted into the model. The fitted model's correctness is then assessed. The model may need to be changed to improve accuracy or speed. Finally, the trained classification or regression model predicts.

Various algorithms forecast stock price direction. Random forest algorithm, logistic regression, and neural networks outperform discriminant analysis, single decision trees, and naive Bayes. Decision trees make decisions based on data features/attributes. Random forests use randomly generated decision trees. Each decision tree node calculates output using a random collection of characteristics. The random forest averages each decision tree's output and calculates the dataset's prediction accuracy. Multivariate analysis employing artificial neural network (ANN) and SVM has gained significant prominence in stock market analysis due to its remarkable efficacy in accurately predicting stock price forecasts. ANNs are computational models exhilarated by the human brain's layers of neurons. During training, the network modifies link strengths (weights) to learn from data flowing via these nodes. It allows it to discern patterns, forecast, and perform tasks in machine learning and artificial intelligence (AI). Deep learning has gained interest owing to stock market predicting advances. It can swiftly uncover latent nonlinear connections and extract relevant characteristics from noisy, complex data. LSTM and convolutional neural networks (CNNs) are often employed to anticipate stock market prices and returns.

13.4   Related Work

Much research has predicted stock markets. Still, we have yet to come across any comprehensive reviews and comparisons of the systems that are now in use based on the various methods, feature selection criteria, ratio of training and testing datasets, accuracy, performance metrics, technical indicators, and fundamental variables.

Polamuri *et al.* [22] examined 138 papers from 2000 to 2019, and 2173 distinct technical, macroeconomic, and fundamental indicators for markets, indexes, and stocks were identified. The authors selected ANN, SVM, fuzzy theory, and LSTM as popular stock market forecasting models.

After examining 122 works from 2007 to 2018, Nti *et al.* [1] found that SVMs along with ANN are the most popular stock market prediction methods. Shah *et al.* [3] classified stock market prediction strategies. They covered statistical analysis, pattern identification, machine learning, sentiment analysis, and hybrid algorithms for stock prediction. CNN, regression analysis, Pearson's correlation, Box-Jenkins model, random forest, CDPA, and NBA framework are typical stock market prediction techniques, according to Polamuri *et al.* [22]. Saini and Sharma [29] used multiple criteria to compare basic, technical, time series, and machine learning analyses. LSTM neural networks outperformed other machine learning methods. Rahul *et al.* [30] examined stock market prediction methodologies from previous research. Data mining, deep learning, and machine learning algorithms helped forecast stock values.

In recent years, stock market forecast review studies have gained popularity. Most review studies have focused on stock market prediction methods or taken a shorter time. Stock price prediction and bibliometric analysis need to explore the newest model-building factors. This paper conducts a structured review of stock market prediction methods, feature selection criteria, ratio of training and testing datasets, accuracy, performance metrics, technical indicators, and fundamental variables over a longer period to fill this gap.

13.5   Research Methodology

The identification of keywords was conducted with careful consideration of our research objective. The study focuses on the keywords "*Fundamental Analysis and stock market prediction*". The keyword was searched within the Scopus database, specifically within the abstract, title, and keywords fields.

Among the two prominent databases, namely, Web of Science and Scopus, it is worth noting that Scopus offers a more extensive range of journal coverage [31]. Therefore, this study limits itself to only those articles indexed in Scopus. The selected time frame spans from 2002 to 2023. The papers containing the specified keywords were exclusively downloaded if published in English within management and economics, econometrics, and finance. Initially, a total of 88 articles were obtained. Moreover, among the compilation of 89 articles, we could not get access to 18 articles. Consequently, a total of 71 research articles remained for subsequent evaluation. A comprehensive text review included the articles that successfully passed the screening process. The final selection of articles was determined based on adherence to the specified inclusion and exclusion criteria. The following inclusion criteria were employed: We included articles that elucidate the connections between fundamental analysis and stock market prediction in India. In conclusion, a total of 69 articles were obtained for this review.

VOS viewer and Excel have been used to conduct the systematic literature review based on bibliometric analysis. This study employed bibliometric analysis to present the performance of contributors, such as authors, institutes, countries, sources, keywords, and articles. The intellectual structure and future research opportunities were visualized using bibliographic coupling. Besides this, the study also addresses various methods, feature selection criteria, ratio of training and testing datasets, accuracy, performance metrics, technical indicators, and fundamental variables used in stock market prediction.

13.6 Analysis and Findings

13.6.1 Publication Activity of Fundamental Analysis and Stock Price Prediction

Figure 13.1 plots the number of papers published each year on fundamental analysis and stock market prediction research. It depicts that although research on fundamental analysis and stock market forecasting began in 2002, it took off in 2016. The years with the most articles published were 2019 (17), 2020 (10), 2021 (25), and 2022 (15). Additionally, in 2023, this upward tendency is anticipated to persist.

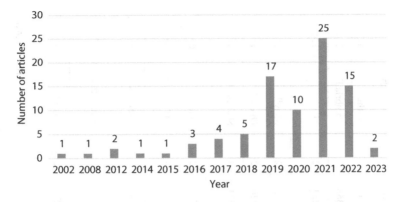

Figure 13.1 Publication activity of fundamental analysis and stock price prediction. Source: Authors compilation.

13.6.2   Top Authors, Countries, and Institutions of Fundamental Analysis and Stock Market Prediction

Table 13.1 lists the most prolific authors in fundamental analysis and stock market prediction research. From the list of 262 authors belonging to 89 papers, the top 15 authors that had written the maximum number of papers in our field were identified. The authors have been identified as the most significant and influential researchers in our research field based on the citations they have received. Each of these authors has garnered 124 citations, following closely behind with 98 and 60 citations, respectively. Studies are professors at Nanyang Technological University, Singapore. Simone Merello and Luca Oneto are professors at DIBRIS, University of Genova, Genova, Italy. They mainly focus on AI, machine learning, and neural networks. Anoop Sharma belongs to Singhania University, and Rajasthan and Jingjing Li belong to Beihang University, Beijing, China. Jingjing Li's research interests include forecasting, applied mathematics, marketing, and tourism. Anoop Sharma has demonstrated the highest level of productivity in the number of publications, having authored three publications.

The authors of each of the papers included in this study are from one of 38 different nations. The top 15 nations with the maximum number of papers on fundamental analysis and stock market prediction are listed in Table 13.1. The first author's country was acknowledged as the paper's origin. With 43 publications and the maximum number of citations (366), India has become a significant player in fundamental analysis and stock market prediction. Other leading nations in the subject of study with

Table 13.1 List of top authors, countries, and institutes of fundamental analysis and stock market prediction research.

TP	Organisation	TC	TP	Country	TC	TP	Author	TC
1	Clemson University, Clemson, United States	206	43	India	366	2	Cambria E.	124
1	Department of Management Information Systems, University of Central Florida, Orlando, United States	206	6	United States	234	2	Ma Y.	124
2	Dibris, University of Genova, Genova, Italy	124	3	Italy	167	2	Merello S.	124
1	School of Computing, Queen's University Kingston, Canada	124	2	Canada	126	2	Oneto I.	124
1	School of Computer Science and Engineering, Nanyang Technological University, Singapore	113	2	Singapore	124	3	Sharma A.	98
1	Govt. Women's Polytechnic, Indore, India	83	4	United Kingdom	77	2	Li J.	60
1	Electronics and Computer Science, University of Southampton, United Kingdom	68	3	China	60	2	Agrawal M.	35
1	Department of Computer Science and Informatics, University of Energy and Natural Resources, Sunyani, Ghana	65	3	Iran	43	2	Khan A.U.	35
1	Department of Computer Science, Sunyani Technical University, Sunyani, Ghana	65	2	Thailand	38	2	Shukla P.K.	35
1	Department of Computer Engineering and Information Technology, College of Engineering, Pune, India	53	2	Malaysia	27	2	Das S.R.	32

(Continued)

Table 13.1 List of top authors, countries, and institutes of fundamental analysis and stock market prediction research. (*Continued*)

TP	Organisation	TC	TP	Country	TC	TP	Author	TC
1	Department of Saeqm, University of Bergamo, Bergamo, Italy	43	4	Australia	25	2	Mishra D.	32
1	Faculty of Economics, všb Technical University of Ostrava, Ostrava, Czech Republic	43	2	Japan	8	2	Gite S.	21
1	Faculty of Industrial Engineering, al-Zahra University, Tehran, Iran	43	2	France	6	2	Khatavkar H.	21
1	School of Economics and Management, Beihang University, Beijing, China	39	3	Turkey	5	2	Maheshwari P.	21
1	School of Science, Beijing University of Chemical Technology, Beijing, China	39	2	Indonesia	0	2	Pandey N.	21

Source: Author's Compilation

more than 50 citations include the United States, Italy, Canada, the United Kingdom, Singapore, and China. Besides India, the field of study has received contributions from the United States, the United Kingdom, and Australia totaling more than three papers.

Moving toward the major institutions with the maximum number of published papers in our field, we found that the University of Central Florida and Clemson University are two of the most well-known universities, receiving 206 citations each, according to Table 13.1. The University of Genova, Queen's University, Nanyang Technological University, Government Women's Polytechnic, Indore, University of Southampton, University of Energy and Natural Resources, Sunyani Technical University, Ghana, and College of Engineering, Pune, are additional universities that have contributed papers with more than 50 citations.

13.6.3   Top Journals for Fundamental Analysis and Stock Market Prediction Research

All 89 papers included in this study are attributed to 73 sources. The top journals that publish fundamental analysis and stock market prediction articles are presented in Table 13.2. Regarding citations, Decision Support System, and Expert Systems with Applications, followed by the International Journal of Financial Studies, are the three leading journals, and their respective citation counts are 206, 134, and 124, respectively. In the realm of scholarly publications, it is noteworthy that "Expert Systems with Applications" has demonstrated exceptional productivity, boasting four publications. The top two journals belong to ScienceDirect publishers and MDPI which publishes the International Journal of Financial Studies.

13.6.4   Top Articles in Fundamental Analysis and Stock Market Prediction

Table 13.3 presents the most frequently cited publications about fundamental analysis and stock market prediction research. According to Scopus, the article of Leigh et al. [32] has garnered the most citations, indicating its significant impact and influence within the academic community, followed by the articles of Shah et al. [3] with 124 citations and Picasso et al. [33] with 113 citations. Leigh et al. [32] developed a decision support system by adopting a romantic approach facilitated by machine learning techniques such as neural networks along with genetic algorithms for predicting stock prices. Shah et al. [3] presented a succinct overview of stock markets and

Table 13.2 List of top journals for fundamental analysis and stock market prediction.

Source	Documents	Citations
Decision Support Systems	1	206
Expert Systems with Applications	4	134
International Journal of Financial Studies	1	124
Proceedings of the International Conference on Electronics, Communication and Aerospace Technology, Iceca 2017	1	83
Journal of Finance and Data Science	1	68
Artificial Intelligence Review	1	65
rteict 2017 – 2nd IEEE international conference on recent trends in electronics, information and communication technology, proceedings	1	53
Information Fusion	1	43
Applied Soft Computing Journal	1	39
International Journal of Recent Technology and Engineering	2	36
Proceedings of the International Conference on machine learning, big data, cloud and parallel computing: trends, perspectives and Prospects, Comitcon 2019	1	34
Expert systems with applications	1	31
Icssbe 2012 – proceedings, 2012 International conference on statistics in science, business and Engineering: "Empowering decision making with statistical sciences."	1	24
Proceedings of the 8th international conference on advanced computational intelligence, ICACI 2016	1	23
Neurocomputing	1	21

Table 13.3 List of top articles in fundamental analysis and stock market prediction research.

Articles	Title of the Document	Citations
Leigh W. (2002)	Forecasting the NYSE composite index with technical analysis, pattern recognizer, neural network, and genetic algorithm: A case study in romantic decision support	206
Shah D. (2019)	Stock market analysis: A review and taxonomy of prediction techniques	124
Picasso A. (2019)	Technical analysis and sentiment embeddings for market trend prediction	113
Sharma A. (2017)	Survey of stock market prediction using a machine learning approach	83
Atkins A. (2018)	Financial news predicts stock market volatility better than the close price	68
Nti I.K. (2020)	A systematic review of fundamental and technical analysis of stock market predictions	65
Khare K. (2017)	Short-term stock price prediction using deep learning	53
Barak S. (2017)	Fusion of multiple diverse predictors in the stock market	43
Yang F. (2019)	A novel hybrid stock selection method with stock prediction	39
Pahwa K. (2019)	Stock Market Analysis Using Supervised Machine Learning	34
Das S. R. (2019)	Stock market prediction using Firefly algorithm with evolutionary framework optimized feature reduction for OSELM method	31
Agrawal M. (2019a)	Stock price prediction using technical indicators: A predictive model using optimal deep learning	28
Siew H.I. (2012)	Regression techniques for the prediction of stock price trend	24
Boonpeng S. (2016)	Decision support system for investing in the stock market by using OAA-Neural Network	23
Gite S. (2021)	Stock Prices Prediction from Financial News Articles Using LSTM and XAI	21

a taxonomy for methods used in predicting stock market behavior. The paper centers on research accomplishments in stock analysis and forecasting. The text delved into the various methodologies employed in analyzing stocks, including technical, fundamental, short-term, and long-term approaches. Picasso A (2019) utilized data science and machine learning techniques to integrate technical with sentiment analysis to predict stock markets. This approach served as a foundation for the development of novel trading strategies. Atkins *et al.* (2018) observed that the level of predictability in volatility movements surpasses asset price fluctuations when employing financial news as input for machine learning algorithms. The research employed machine learning models, specifically latent Dirichl *et al.* location (LDA), to extract data from news feeds. Additionally, simple naive Bayes classifiers were used to predict the direction of stock indices within the US market. The study conducted by Nti *et al.* [1] aimed to conduct a comprehensive review of 122 relevant research studies spanning over 11 years (2007–2018) that focused on applying machine learning techniques in predicting stock market trends. The reports have identified several techniques categorized into three distinct groups: technical analysis, fundamental analysis, and combined analysis. The characteristics of a dataset, the number of data sources used, the scope of the data, algorithms, accuracy metrics, and the modeling software packages were used to categorize. Khare *et al.* [19] used feedforward and recurrent neural networks to forecast the short-term values of 10 New York Stock Exchange equities. The authors found that the feedforward multilayer perceptron predicted short-term stock values better than LSTM. Sharma *et al.* [34] utilized various regression methodologies, including polynomial regression, RBF regression, sigmoid regression, and linear regression, to forecast stock market prices with high efficiency. A closer look at other papers provides evidence that researchers have employed innovative algorithms to predict stock market trends [5, 35–37], utilized a variety of predictors to analyze the stock market [20], and applied regression techniques to predict stock prices [4, 34].

13.6.5 Keyword Occurrence Analysis in Stock Price Prediction Research

According to a study, the author's keywords best capture an article's important themes, hence this study prioritized them. Two author keywords appearing together in an article indicate a relationship between the two themes. Figure 13.2 shows the keywords network. The size of the node indicates the literature's keyword prevalence. A minimum threshold of

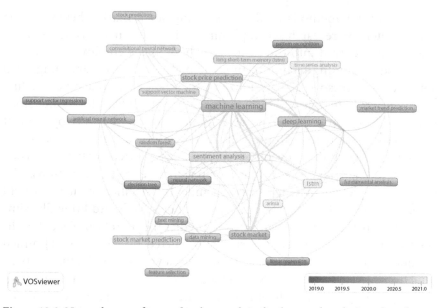

Figure 13.2 Network map of top author keywords in fundamental analysis and stock market prediction research. Source: Author's compilation.

three different occurrences is utilized. A total of 262 keywords have been used in stock price prediction research. The highly cited author keywords include machine learning, deep learning, stock market prediction, technical analysis, sentiment analysis, and the stock market, with the total number of occurrences as 31, 17, 17,14, 12, and 11, respectively, as shown in Table 13.4.

Furthermore, Figure 13.2 provides a term map illustrating the chronological development of our research field. The hue of each node's overlay represents the mean publication year of all papers in which the authors have specified the corresponding keyword. It can be observed that cold colors, such as blue, indicate keywords commonly found in older publications on average. Conversely, nodes with warmer colors, such as yellow, represent keywords with a more recent average publication year.

Until 2019, the predominant utilization of keywords encompassed pattern recognition, support vector regression, decision tree, neural network, and linear regression. Keywords such as fundamental analysis, market trend prediction, data mining, text mining, feature selection, and artificial neural networks gained prominence by the conclusion of 2019. In 2020, several new terms emerged in computer science and finance, including convolutional neural networks, machine learning, deep learning, random

Table 13.4 List of top author keywords in fundamental analysis and stock market prediction research.

Keywords	Occurrences	Total link strength
Machine Learning	31	69
Deep Learning	17	43
Stock Price Prediction	17	36
Technical Analysis	14	34
Sentiment Analysis	12	41
Stock Market	11	30
LSTM	9	30
Artificial Neural Network	8	20
Prediction	8	18
Stock Market Prediction	8	11
Data Mining	7	12
Fundamental Analysis	7	20
Neural Network	6	11

forest, support vector machine, stock market, and sentiment analysis. In 2021, notable keywords that have emerged include long short-term memory, time series analysis, and ARIMA. These keywords hold significance as they offer valuable insights and potential avenues for further investigation in the field of research.

13.6.6 Thematic Clusters of Stock Market Prediction Through Bibliographic Coupling

Bibliographic coupling identified six thematic clusters forming the foundation of fundamental analysis and stock market prediction research, as shown in Table 13.5.

Cluster 1 comprises scholarly papers about *Feature Learning and Stock Market Prediction*. The cluster's most prominent articles, with citation counts of 39, 31, and 11, respectively, are authored by Yang *et al.* [5], Das *et al.* [35], and Singh and Khushi [7]. Singh and Khushi [7] employed the

Table 13.5 Thematic clusters on fundamental analysis and stock market prediction research.

Theme	Authors	Title of the paper	Cluster	TC
Feature Learning and stock prediction	Singh and Khushi (2021)	Feature Learning for Stock Price Prediction Shows a Significant Role of Analyst Rating	1	11
	Das *et al.* (2019)	Stock market prediction using Firefly algorithm with evolutionary framework optimized feature reduction for OSELM method		31
	Yang *et al.* (2019)	A novel hybrid stock selection method with stock prediction		39
Technical Analysis and market trend prediction	Picasso *et al.* (2019)	Technical analysis and sentiment embeddings for market trend prediction	2	113
	Ratto *et al.* (2019)	Ensemble of Technical Analysis and Machine Learning for Market Trend Prediction		11

(Continued)

Table 13.5 Thematic clusters on fundamental analysis and stock market prediction research. (*Continued*)

Theme	Authors	Title of the paper	Cluster	TC
	Kanungsukkasem and Leelanupab (2019)	Financial Latent Dirichl *et al.* location (FinLDA): Feature Extraction in Text and Data Mining for Financial Time Series Prediction		15
Technical Indicators and Deep Learning Models	Agrawal *et al.* (2019a)	Stock Indices Price Prediction Based on Technical Indicators Using Deep Learning Model	3	28
	Agrawal *et al.* (2019b)	Stock Price Prediction Using Technical Indicators: A Predictive Model Using Optimal Deep Learning		7
	Mndawe *et al.* (2022)	Development of a Stock Price Prediction Framework for Intelligent Media and Technical Analysis		3

(*Continued*)

Table 13.5 Thematic clusters on fundamental analysis and stock market prediction research. (*Continued*)

Theme	Authors	Title of the paper	Cluster	TC
Neural Networks and Genetic Algorithms	He and Kita (2020)	Stock Price Prediction by Using Hybrid Sequential Generative Adversarial Networks	4	4
	Jiang *et al.* (2018)	Cross-domain Deep Learning Approach for Multiple Financial Market Prediction		8
	Leigh *et al.* (2002)	Forecasting the NYSE composite index with technical analysis, pattern recognizer, neural network, and genetic algorithm: a case study in romantic decision support		206
Stock Market Volatility and Machine Learning Algorithms	Verma *et al.* (2019)	Evaluation of Pattern-Based Customized Approach for Stock Market Trend Prediction with Big Data and Machine Learning Techniques	5	19

(*Continued*)

Table 13.5 Thematic clusters on fundamental analysis and stock market prediction research. (*Continued*)

Theme	Authors	Title of the paper	Cluster	TC
Neural Networks and Big data	Atkins *et al.* (2018)	Financial news predicts stock market volatility better than the close price.		68
	Barak *et al.* (2017)	Fusion of Multiple Diverse Predictors in Stock Market		43
	Boonpeng and Jeatrakul (2016)	Decision Support System for Investing in Stock Market by using OAA-Neural Network		23
	Ng *et al.* (2014)	LG-Trader: Stock trading decision support based on feature selection by a weighted localized generalization error model		21
	Attigeri *et al.* (2015)	Stock Market Prediction: A Big Data Approach		10

feature ranking technique to discern a reduced set of six indicators and revealed the significance of buy, hold, and sell analyst ratings. Subsequently, a conservative trading approach was employed to conduct a historical simulation on the stocks of FAANG (Facebook, Amazon, Apple, Netflix, and Google). In their study, Das *et al.* [35] investigated the efficacy of the Firefly algorithm for feature optimization, considering both the biochemical and social dimensions of the algorithm. The authors utilized four distinct datasets from the stock market: BSE Sensex, S&P 500, FTSE, and NSE Sensex. In their study, Yang *et al.* [5] proposed a novel hybrid model for selecting stocks that incorporates stock prediction techniques to anticipate future market trends. The authors demonstrated the effectiveness of this model in comparison to other similar approaches.

Cluster 2 encompasses articles that focus on *Technical Analysis and Market Trend Prediction*. The three most cited papers in this cluster are [13, 33], and [38], with citation counts of 113, 11, and 15, respectively. In their study, Picasso *et al.* [33] integrated technical and fundamental analyses using data science and machine learning methodologies to forecast market trends for the top 20 companies with the highest market capitalization listed in the NASDAQ 100 index. In their study, Ratto *et al.* [13] integrated technical analysis and machine learning methodologies to forecast the directional movement of the most heavily capitalized stocks in the NASDAQ instead of a singular stock. Kanungsukkasem and Leelanupab [38] developed a FinLDA model that extracts features from a composite of textual data, time series, and noteworthy news articles. The authors found that this approach enhances predictive accuracy and yields superior outcomes.

Cluster 3 comprises scholarly articles on *Technical Indicators and Deep Learning*. The cluster's most prominent articles are [24, 41, 42] with citation counts of 28, 7, and 4, respectively. The study conducted by centered on the Indian banking sector. It aimed to forecast the trajectory of stock prices by implementing optimal-LSTM deep learning and adaptive stock technical indicators (STIs) while also utilizing a correlation tensor constructed with suitable STIs. Agrawal *et al.* [24] proposed a comparative framework encompassing three indices: banks, automobiles, and metal. Mndawe *et al.* [39] introduced a framework that utilizes machine learning algorithms to forecast the stock prices of a telecommunications firm registered on the Johannesburg Stock Exchange. The employed methodology utilizes a text classifier model to conduct sentiment analysis within the framework. In conjunction with time series analysis and deep learning, technical indicators are employed to predict the stock price.

Cluster 4 comprises scholarly articles on neural networks and genetic algorithms. The three most prominent articles within this cluster are [16, 40] and [32] which have received citation counts of 206, 8, and 4, respectively. In their study, Leigh *et al.* [32] employed a decision support system that incorporated machine learning algorithms like neural networks and genetic algorithms, to forecast stock prices in a novel manner. In their study, Jiang *et al.* [40] presented an intriguing method known as the cross-domain deep learning approach (Cd-DLA) to predict multiple financial markets. The employed model analyzed correlations within the same domain and across different domains in financial forecasting by employing recurrent neural networks. Following this, all correlations were combined. In their study, He and Kita (2020) [16] utilized a hybrid sequential GANs model that integrated various RNN, LSTM, and GRU within the generator and discriminator components of GANs. The model was trained using data derived from the S&P 500. The experimental results exhibited superior performance in stock prediction compared to the prior research on single algorithm prediction.

Cluster 5 encompasses scholarly articles on *Stock Market Volatility and Machine Learning Algorithms*. The three primary articles within this cluster are [20, 23], and [12], with 206, 8, and 4 citations, respectively. According to Atkins *et al.* (2018) [23], utilizing news sources to extract information is more effective in predicting stock market volatility. The researchers employed LDA to represent data extracted from news feeds to develop machine learning models. Additionally, they utilized simple naive Bayes classifiers to forecast the stock movement direction. Verma *et al.* [12] introduced a tailored machine learning algorithm based on patterns to forecast the stock prices in the Indian stock market. The algorithm under consideration performs better than traditional machine learning methodologies, such as ANN and SVM. Polamuri *et al.* [20] introduced a fusion model that utilizes a combination of diverse base classifiers, such as Bagging, Boosting, and AdaBoost, to achieve accurate predictions of stock returns and risks for the companies registered in the Tehran Stock Exchange (TSE). The present model is subjected to a comparison analysis with the wrapper-GA algorithm regarding feature selection.

Cluster 6 consists of articles on *Neural Networks and Big Data*. The three most prominent articles within this cluster are [21, 36], and [10], with citation counts of 23, 21, and 10, respectively. Boonpeng and Jeatrakul [36] studied various multiclass classification techniques utilizing neural networks. The researchers empirically investigated the efficacy of one-against-one (OAO) and one-against-all (OAA) methodologies. The authors conducted a comparative analysis between multi-binary classification utilizing the OAA technique and traditional neural networks. The results indicated that the former outperformed the latter. Ng *et al.* [21] introduced the LG-Trader, which concurrently addresses the challenges of selecting classifier architecture and features. The approach employs a genetic algorithm that minimizes a novel weighted localized generalization error (wL-GEM). Attigeri *et al.* [10] presented a model based on big data that uses social media analysis and machine learning techniques to predict stock market trends.

13.6.7   List of Machine Learning Algorithms Used

Table 13.6 lists machine learning algorithms used with fundamental analysis in stock price prediction papers. Most studies, i.e., around 25%, have employed LSTM to forecast the stock prices, followed by SVM algorithm (22%) and regression techniques such as linear and logistic, i.e., around 16%.

Table 13.6 List of machine learning algorithm used.

Machine learning algorithms in stock price prediction		Number of documents
Long Short-Term Memory Networks (LSTM)	Jawahar *et al.* (2017); Chelladaraj *et al.* (2020); Agrawal *et al.* (2019a, b); Torralba (2019); Mndawe *et al.* (2022); Gite *et al.* (2021); Swain *et al.* (2021); Gite *et al.* (2021); Nadif *et al.* (2022); Mahadik *et al.* (2021); Shi *et al.* (2021); Puneeth *et al.* (2021); Sarkar *et al.* (2020); Heur *et al.* (2021); Raya *et al.* (2022); Kumar *et al.* (2020)	17
Support Vector Machine (SVM)	Verma, *et al.* (2019); Sharma *et al.* (2019); Ratto *et al.* (2018); Khairi *et al.* (2019); Barak *et al.* (2017); Singh and Khushi (2021); Allen *et al.* (2012); Kabran and Unlu (2020); Mndawe *et al.* (2022); Picasso *et al.* (2019); Azizi *et al.* (2021); Barak *et al.* (2016); Shrivastav and Kumar (2019); Kalaivani *et al.* (2022); Khekare *et al.* (2022)	15
Regression techniques such as Linear Regression, logistic regression, RBF regression, Sigmoid Regression, Polynomial regression	Sharma *et al.* (2017); Gaspareniene *et al.* (2021); Pawar (2019); Singh *et al.* (2022); Polamuri *et al.* (2019); Siew and Siew (2012); Attigeri *et al.* (2015); Azizi *et al.* (2021); Kristian *et al.* (2021); Kalaivani *et al.* (2022); Khekare *et al.* (2022)	11

(Continued)

Table 13.6 List of machine learning algorithm used. (*Continued*)

Machine learning algorithms in stock price prediction		Number of documents
Artificial Neural Network (ANN)	Verma *et al.* (2019); Hassan *et al.* (2021); Barak *et al.* (2017); Jiang *et al.* (2018); Barak *et al.* (2016); Puneeth *et al.* (2021); Choudhury and Sen (2017)	7
Random Forest	Gaspareniene *et al.* (2021); Singh and Khushi (2021); Polamuri *et al.* (2019); Mndawe *et al.* (2022); Picasso *et al.* (2019); Mandeep *et al.* (2022); Raya *et al.* (2022)	7
Decision Tree	Gaspareniene *et al.* (2021); Barak *et al.* (2017); Singh and Khushi (2021); Polamuri *et al.* (2019); Mndawe *et al.* (2022); Barak *et al.* (2016)	6
ARIMA	Mahadik *et al.* (2021); Shrivastav and Kumar (2019); Raya *et al.* (2022); Khekare *et al.* (2022)	4
K-Nearest Neighbour (KNN)	Singh and Khushi (2021); Azizi *et al.* (2021); Kristian *et al.* (2021); Khekare *et al.* (2022)	4
RNN	Shi *et al.* (2021); Sarkar *et al.* (2020); Heru *et al.* (2021)	3
Naïve Bayesian (NB)	Singh and Khushi (2021); Azizi *et al.* (2021); Atkins *et al.* (2018)	3
Extreme Learning Machine (ELM)	Yang *et al.* (2019); Zhang (2021); Das *et al.* (2019)	3
Recurrent Back Propagation Neural Network (RBPNN) and BPNN	Das *et al.* (2019); Kanungsukkasem and Leelanupab (2019); Choudhury, and Sen (2017)	3
XAI-LIME	Gite *et al.* (2021); Mandeep *et al.* (2022)	2

(*Continued*)

Table 13.6 List of machine learning algorithm used. (*Continued*)

Machine learning algorithms in stock price prediction		Number of documents
multiple classifier ensemble system (MCS)	Barak *et al.* (2017); Barak *et al.* (2016)	2
XG Boost	Raya *et al.* (2022); Wu(2021); Mandeep *et al.* (2022)	3
Fin LDA	Kanungsukkasem and Leelanupab (2019); Atkins *et al.* (2018)	2
Others	Ye *et al.* (2016); Boonpeng and Jeatrakul (2016); Picasso *et al.* (2019); Khare *et al.* (2017); Ratto *et al.* (2018); Ng *et al.* (2014); He and Kita (2020); Polamuri *et al.* (2019); Ratto *et al.* (2018); Ee *et al.* (2020); Gite *et al.* (2021)	11

Recently, studies have started using ANNs (11%), random forests (11%), decision trees (8%), ARIMA (6%), and K-nearest neighbor (6%). Only a few studies have used naive Bayesian, extreme learning machines, recurrent back propagation neural networks, XGBoost, XAI LIME, and FinLDA to predict stock prices. As shown in Table 13.6, other machine learning algorithms remain unexplored by researchers.

13.6.8   List of Training and Testing Dataset Criteria Used

We also identified various training and testing datasets used by the studies from the literature review, presented in Table 13.7. We observed that around 12 studies had used the 80-20 ratio to partition the datasets into training samples and testing samples, where 80 refers to the training dataset, and 20 refers to the testing dataset, followed by a 70-30 ratio used by ten studies. Very few studies have used 90-10 criteria (3), 75-25 (2), and 95-5 (2). Also, criteria such as 50-50 and 60-40 are hardly used, which can be used by the prior studies.

Table 13.7 List of training and testing dataset criteria used.

	Training and Testing data set	Number of documents
80-20	Yang *et al.* (2019); Ratto *et al.* (2018); Gaspareniene *et al.* (2021); Pawar (2019); Boonpeng and Jeatrakul(2016); Polamuri *et al.* (2019); Kabran and Unlu(2020); Torralba(2019); Mndawe *et al.* (2022); Ye *et al.* (2016); Gite *et al.* (2021); Jiang *et al.* (2018)	12
70-30	Verma *et al.* (2019); Hassan *et al.* (2021); Ee *et al.* (2020); Gaspareniene *et al.* (2021); Khare *et al.* (2017); Singh and Khushi (2021); Das *et al.* (2019); Mahadik *et al.* (2021); Kristian *et al.* (2021); Choudhury and Sen (2017)	10
90-10	Zhang (2021); Toochaei and Moeini (2023); Azizi *et al.* (2021)	3
75-25	Jawahar *et al.* (2020); Kanungsukkasem and Leelanupab (2019)	2
95-05	Shi *et al.* (2021); Nadif, *et al.* (2022)	2
50-50	Attigeri *et al.* (2015)	1
60-40	Suhail *et al.* (2022)	1

13.6.9   List of Evaluation Metrics Used

Table 13.8 displays the evaluation metrics used in fundamental analysis and stock price prediction research. Almost 13% of studies have focussed on the F1 score and RMSE, followed by R2 (10%), MSE (10%), accuracy (8%), precision (7%), recall (7%), MAE (6%), and MSE (6%). The evaluation indicators less used by the researchers include the Sharpe ratio, maximum drawdown, MAPE, and annualized return. As shown in Table 13.8, other evaluation parameters still need to be explored by the researchers.

13.6.10   List of Factors Used in Fundamental Analysis

Table 13.9 reveals various factors employed in the fundamental analysis and stock price prediction literature. Past studies have mainly employed

Table 13.8 List of evaluation metrics used.

	Evaluation metrics	Number of documents
F1 score	Ratto *et al.* (2018); He and Kita (2020); Singh and Khushi (2021); Jiang *et al.* (2018); Azizi *et al.* (2021); Toochaei and Moeini (2023); Sharma *et al.* (2019); Mndawe *et al.* (2022); Atkins *et al.* (2018)	9
RMSE	Swain *et al.* (2021); Nadif *et al.* (2022); Mahadik *et al.* (2021); Shrivastav and Kumar (2019); Shi *et al.* (2021); Puneeth, *et al.* (2021); Heru *et al.* (2021); Raya *et al.* (2022); Khekare *et al.* (2022)	9
R2	Verma *et al.* (2019); Kanungsukkasem and Leelanupab (2019); Gaspareniene *et al.* (2021); Pawar (2019); Singh *et al.* (2022); Atkins *et al.* (2018); Raya *et al.* (2022)	7
MSE	Verma *et al.* (2019); Kanungsukkasem and Leelanupab (2019); Gaspareniene *et al.* (2021); Agrawal *et al.* (2019); Mndawe *et al.* (2022); Kristian *et al.* 2021); Choudhury, and Sen (2017)	7
Accuracy	Agrawal *et al.* (2019); Azizi *et al.* (2021); Toochaei and Moeini (2023); Sharma *et al.* (2019); He and Kita (2020); Mndawe *et al.* (2022)	6
Precision	Toochaei and Moeini (2023); Sharma *et al.* (2019); He and Kita (2020); Mndawe *et al.* (2022); Atkins *et al.* (2018)	5
Recall	Toochaei and Moeini (2023); Sharma *et al.* (2019); He and Kita (2020); Mndawe *et al.* (2022); Atkins *et al.* (2018)	5

(Continued)

Table 13.8 List of evaluation metrics used. (*Continued*)

	Evaluation metrics	Number of documents
MAE	He and Kita 2020); Kanungsukkasem and Leelanupab (2019); Kristian *et al.* 2021); Raya *et al.* (2022)	4
Sharpe Ratio	Picasso *et al.* (2019); Chiu and Tsai (2021); Singh *et al.* (2022)	3
Maximum drawdown	Picasso *et al.* (2019); Chiu and Tsai (2021); Singh *et al.* (2022)	3
Annualised return	Picasso *et al.* (2019); Chiu and Tsai (2021)	2
Profit rate	Chiu and Tsai (2021); Singh *et al.* (2022)	2
MAPE	Khekare, *et al.* (2022)	1
Others (Random walk, g-mean, Directional accuracy rate (DAR), Adjusted R2, MAD, DSTAT	Atkins *et al.* (2018); Toochaei and Moeini (2023); Ye *et al.* (2016); Pawar (2019); Kanungsukkasem and Leelanupab (2019); Yang *et al.* (2019)	6

profitability ratios, growth ratios, liquidity ratios, efficiency ratios, macro-economic variables, leverage ratios, and sentiment analysis as fundamental factors. The most commonly used profitability ratios include ROA, ROE, OPM, NOM, and GPM. In contrast, return on working capital (RWC), pretax profit margin, and operating return on assets are the least employed profitability ratios. Similarly, the prior studies mainly used the debt-equity ratio among the leverage ratios. In contrast, debt ratio, debt coverage ratio, equity/fixed assets ratio, debt-to-equity ratio, equity ratio, and cash flow ratio were the least used by the authors. Most used liquidity ratios comprise current and quick ratios. In contrast, the less-used liquidity ratios encompass net working capital to total assets, operating cash flow ratio, current assets ratio, and cash flow coverage ratio. Among the efficiency ratios, fixed assets turnover, receivables turnover, total assets turnover, and current assets turnover ratios are used mainly by the prior studies. Most of

Table 13.9 List of factors used in fundamental analysis.

		Fundamental factors
Profitability ratios	Return on Assets (ROA)	Yang et al. (2019); Singh and Khushi (2021); Toochaei and Moeini (2023); Chiu and Tsai (2021); Ye and Schuller (2021); Siew and Nodin (2012)
	Return on Equity (ROE)	Yang et al. (2019); Toochaei and Moeini (2023); Chiu and Tsai (2021); Ye and Schuller (2021); Siew and Nodin (2012)
	Operating profit Margin (OPM)	Yang et al. (2019); Toochaei and Moeini (2023); Ye and Schuller (2021); Siew and Nodin (2012)
	Net profit Margin (NPM)	Yang et al. (2019); Khairi et al. (2019); Toochaei and Moeini (2023); Siew and Nodin (2012)
	Gross profit margin (GPM)	Toochaei and Moeini (2023); Ye and Schuller (2021); Siew and Nodin (2012)
	Return on Working Capital	Toochaei and Moeini (2023); Siew and Nodin (2012)
	Usefulness of Loan	Toochaei and Moeini (2023); Siew and Nodin (2012)
	Net Profit to Gross Profit ratio	Toochaei and Moeini (2023)
	Pretax profit margin	Toochaei and Moeini (2023)
	Operating Return on Assets	Toochaei and Moeini (2023)

(Continued)

Table 13.9 List of factors used in fundamental analysis. (*Continued*)

		Fundamental factors
Leverage	Debt equity ratio	Yang *et al.* (2019); Khairi *et al.* (2019); Siew and Nodin (2012); Toochaei and Moeini (2023); Chiu and Tsai (2021); Ye and Schuller (2021)
	Debt ratio	Toochaei and Moeini (2023); Siew and Nodin (2012)
	Debt coverage ratio	Toochaei and Moeini (2023); Siew and Nodin (2012)
	Long-term debt to-equity ratio	Toochaei and Moeini (2023); Siew and Nodin (2012)
	Current Debt to Equity ratio	Toochaei and Moeini (2023); Siew and Nodin (2012)
	Equity ratio	Toochaei and Moeini (2023); Siew and Nodin (2012)
	Equity to fixed assets ratio	Toochaei and Moeini (2023)
	Cash Flow Ratio	Yang *et al.* (2019)
	Quick Ratio	Yang *et al.* (2019); Siew and Nodin (2012); Toochaei and Moeini (2023); Ye and Schuller (2021); Barak *et al.* (2016)
	Current Ratio	Yang *et al.* (2019); Siew and Nodin (2012); Toochaei and Moeini (2023); Ye and Schuller (2021); Barak *et al.* 2016)
	Inventory turnover rate	Toochaei and Moeini (2023); Ye and Schuller (2021); Yang *et al.* (2019)
Liquidity	Net working capital to total assets ratio	Toochaei and Moeini (2023); Barak *et al.* 2016)
	Current assets ratio	Toochaei and Moeini (2023); Barak *et al.* (2016)

(*Continued*)

Table 13.9 List of factors used in fundamental analysis. (*Continued*)

		Fundamental factors
	Operating Cash Flow ratio	Toochaei and Moeini (2023)
	Cash Flow Coverage Ratio	Toochaei and Moeini (2023)
	Total asset turnover ratio	Toochaei and Moeini (2023); Barak *et al.* (2016); Siew and Nodin (2012)
	Receivables turnover rate	Toochaei and Moeini (2023); Yang *et al.* (2019)
	Fixed asset turnover ratio	Toochaei and Moeini (2023); Barak *et al.* (2016)
Efficiency	Current assets turnover ratio	Toochaei and Moeini (2023); Barak *et al.* (2016)
	Operating income growth rate	Yang *et al.* (2019); Toochaei and Moeini (2023)
	Days' sales in accounts receivable ratio	Toochaei and Moeini (2023)
	Working capital turnover ratio	Toochaei and Moeini (2023)
	Cash turnover ratio	Toochaei and Moeini (2023)
	Inventory to total assets ratio	Toochaei and Moeini (2023)
	Net Income growth rate	Yang *et al.* (2019); Toochaei and Moeini (2023); Chiu and Tsai (2021)

(Continued)

Table 13.9 List of factors used in fundamental analysis. (*Continued*)

		Fundamental factors
	Constant net assets growth ratio	Toochaei and Moeini (2023)
	Total income growth ratio	Toochaei and Moeini (2023)
Growth	Operating cash flow growth ratio	Toochaei and Moeini (2023)
	Net working capital growth ratio	Toochaei and Moeini (2023)
	Long-term debt growth ratio	Toochaei and Moeini (2023)
	Producer Price index	Toochaei and Moeini (2023)
	Bank Interest Rates	Kabran & Unlu (2020); Toochaei and Moeini (2023)
	Unemployment Rates	Kabran & Unlu (2020); Toochaei and Moeini (2023)
	Growth	Kabran & Unlu (2020); Toochaei and Moeini (2023)
	Inflation	Kabran and Unlu (2020)
	Exchange Rate	Toochaei and Moeini (2023)
Macroeconomic variables	Gross Domestic Product	Kabran and Unlu (2020)
	Balance of Payments	Kabran and Unlu (2020)
	Total assets of listed companies, IRR	Toochaei and Moeini (2023)

(*Continued*)

Table 13.9 List of factors used in fundamental analysis. (*Continued*)

		Fundamental factors
	Cash	Ye and Schuller (2021)
	DCF Analysis	Hassan *et al.* (2021)
	Sentimental Analysis	Verma *et al.* (2019); Sharma *et al.* (2019); Ratto *et al.* (2018); Hassan *et al.* (2021); Jawahar *et al.* (2020); Khairi *et al.* (2019); Kanungsukkasem and Leelanupab (2019); Attigeri *et al.* (2015); Suhail *et al.* (2022); Mndawe *et al.* (2022); Picasso *et al.* (2019); Gite *et al.* (2021); Atkins *et al.* (2018); Gite *et al.* (2021); Puneeth *et al.* (2021); Sarkar *et al.* (2020)
	EPS	Singh and Khushi (2021); Toochaei and Moeini (2023); Chiu and Tsai (2021); Ye and Schuller (2021); Siew and Nodin (2012)
	PB Ratio	Singh and Khushi (2021); Toochaei and Moeini (2023); Chiu and Tsai (2021); Ye and Schuller (2021)
	Price to Sales ratio	Toochaei and Moeini (2023); Chiu and Tsai (2021); Ye and Schuller (2021); Siew and Nodin (2012)
	PE Ratio	Khairi *et al.* (2019); Singh and Khushi (2021); Siew and Nodin (2012)
	Market Capitalisation	Toochaei and Moeini (2023); Chiu and Tsai (2021)
	Dividend per share	Khairi *et al.* (2019); Chiu and Tsai (2021)
	Capital expenditure	Singh and Khushi (2021)
Others	Altman z score	Siew and Nodin (2012)

(*Continued*)

Table 13.9 List of factors used in fundamental analysis. (*Continued*)

		Fundamental factors
	Net tangible asset	Siew and Nodin (2012)
	Price to cash flow	Toochaei and Moeini (2023)
	Book to market value	Toochaei and Moeini (2023)
	Earning Price Ratio	Toochaei and Moeini (2023)
	Shareholding Pattern	Khairi *et al.* (2019)
	consumer price index	Toochaei and Moeini (2023)
	Predicted returns	Yang *et al.* (2019)
	Cash from Operating Activities	Ye and Schuller (2021)
	Dividend Payout ratio	Ye and Schuller (2021)
	Dividend Yield	Ye and Schuller (2021)
	Free Cash Flow	Ye and Schuller (2021)
	Income from Continued Operations	Ye and Schuller (2021)
	Net Debt to EBIT	Ye and Schuller (2021)
	Net Income	Ye and Schuller (2021)
	Operating Expenses	Ye and Schuller (2021)
	Operating Income	Ye and Schuller (2021)

(Continued)

Table 13.9 List of factors used in fundamental analysis. (*Continued*)

		Fundamental factors
	Short Term Debt	Ye and Schuller (2021)
	Total Assets	Ye and Schuller (2021)
	Total Liabilities	Ye and Schuller (2021)
	Total Inventory	Ye and Schuller (2021)
	Fama and French model	Siew and Nodin (2012)
	Capital Asset Pricing model	Siew and Nodin (2012)
	Walter model	Siew and Nodin (2012)
	Gordon model	Siew and Nodin (2012)

the prior studies used the net income growth rate to estimate the growth rate of the companies. The authors have also studied macroeconomic variables to check the fundamentals of the companies by using bank interest rates, growth, and unemployment rates. To predict the stock price, many researchers have used sentiment analysis. As shown in Table 13.9, other ratios still need to be explored by the researchers.

13.6.11 List of Technical Indicators Used

Table 13.10 reveals the variety of technical indicators employed in the fundamental analysis and stock price prediction literature. The most commonly used technical indicator is open, high, low, and close, used by 28% of studies, followed by MACD (16%), relative strength index (16%), moving average (15%), and stochastic oscillator (15%). At the same time, only some studies have focussed on Bollinger Bands, Williams Overbought, momentum indicators, volume, CR indicator, trend, and ROC. The authors hardly explored other indicators such as volatility indicators, pseudo log return (PLR), max, min, average, VAR, rank correlation index (RCI), commodity channel index, average true range, ADX, support, and resistance lines.

Table 13.10 List of technical indicators used.

	Technical indicators	Number of documents
Open, high, low, close	Zhang (2021); Jawahar et al. (2020); He and Kita (2020); Pawar (2019); Attigeri et al. (2015); Ng et al. (2014); Suhail et al. (2022); Agrawal et al. (2019); Torralba (2019); Verma et al. (2019); Swain et al. (2021); Nadif et al. (2022); Mahadik et al. (2021); Shrivastav and Kumar (2019); Puri and Shrivastav (2019); Mandeep et al. (2022); Sarkar et al. (2020); Heru et al. (2021); Raya et al. (2022)	19
MACD	Ratto et al. (2016); Ma, and Cambria (2018); Khairi et al. (2019); Khare et al. (2017); Ng et al. (2014); Agrawal et al. (2019); Mndawe et al. (2022); Ye et al. (2016); Picasso et al. (2019); Chiu and Tsai (2021); Kalaivani et al. (2022)	11
Relative strength index	Ratto et al. (2018); Khairi et al. (2019); Khare et al. (2017); Boonpeng and Jeatrakul (2016); Ng et al. (2014); Agrawal et al. (2019); Das et al. (2019); Picasso et al. (2019); Chiu and Tsai (2021); Ye and Schuller(2021); Kalaivani et al. (2022)	11
Simple and exponential moving average	Ratto et al. (2018); Singh et al. (2022); Khare et al. (2017); Ng et al. (2014); Agrawal et al. (2019); Das et al. (2019); Mndawe et al. (2022); Picasso et al. (2019); Chiu and Tsai (2021); Ye and Schuller (2021)	10
Stochastic Oscillator	Ratto et al. (2018); Hassan et al. (2021); Khairi et al. (2019); Ng et al. (2014); Agrawal et al. (2019); Das et al. (2019); Ye et al. (2016); Picasso et al. (2019); Chiu and Tsai (2021); Kalaivani et al. (2022)	10

(Continued)

Table 13.10 List of technical indicators used. (*Continued*)

	Technical indicators	Number of documents
Bollinger Bands	Ratto *et al.* (2018); Khairi *et al.* (2019); Singh *et al.* (2022); Mndawe *et la.* (2022); Picasso *et al.* (2019)	5
Williams Overbought/ Oversold Indicator	Ratto *et al.* (2018); Ng *et al.* (2014); Agrawal *et al.* (2019); Das *et al.* (2019); Picasso *et al.* (2019)	5
Momentum indicators	Hassan *et al.* (2021); Khare *et al.* (2017); Das *et al.* (2019); Chiu and Tsai (2021)	4
Volume	Hassan *et al.* (2021); Boonpeng and Jeatrakul (2016); Ng *et al.* (2014); Verma *et al.* (2019)	4
CR indicator	Ratto *et al.* (2018); Picasso *et al.* (2019)	2
Trend	Hassan *et al.* (2021); Zhang (2021)	2
ROC	Das *et al.* (2019); Ye *et al.* (2016)	2
Others (volatility indicators, Pseudo Log Return (PLR), max, min, average, VAR, rank correlation index (RCI), Commodity chanel index, average true range, ADX, Support and resistance lines	Hassan *et al.* (2021); Zhang (2021); Singh *et al.* (2022); Khare *et al.* (2017); Das *et al.* (2019); Agrawal *et al.* (2019); Kalaivani *et al.* (2022)	7

13.6.12   List of Feature Selection Criteria

Table 13.11 lists feature selection criteria in fundamental analysis and stock price prediction literature. Looking into the fewer studies mentioning the feature selection criteria in their papers, it was found that authors have mainly used correlation, statistical analysis, Loughran and McDonald's

Table 13.11 List of feature selection criteria.

	Feature selection	Number of documents
Correlation	Attigeri *et al.* (2015); Agrawal *et al.* (2019); Toochaei and Moeini (2023); Kristian *et al.* (2021)	3
Bag of Words	Kanugsukkasem and Leelanupab (2019); Chiu and Tsai (2021); Sharma *et al.* (2019)	3
Statistical Analysis	Sharma *et al.* (2019); Das *et al.* (2019)	2
Loughran and McDonald's dictionary	Ratto *et al.* (2018); Picasso *et al.* (2019)	2
Affective Space	Ratto *et al.* (2018); Picasso *et al.* (2019)	2
Wrapper-GA scheme	Barak *et al.* (2017); Barak *et al.* (2016)	2
Filters and voting techniques	Toochae and Moeini (2023); Verma *et al.* (2019)	2
Twitter daily sentiment score	Sharma *et al.* (2019)	1
Heuristic-Hypernym method	Hassan *et al.* (2021)	1
SpaCy library	Jawahar *et al.* (2020)	1
Term-Frequency	Khairi *et al.* (2019)	1

(Continued)

Table 13.11 List of feature selection criteria. (*Continued*)

	Feature selection	Number of documents
Binary weighting scheme	Khairi *et al.* (2019)	1
Literature Review	Singh and Khushi (2021)	1
Chi Square	Atkins *et al.* (2018)	1
NSGA-II	Ng *et al.* (2014)	1
LG trader	Ng *et al.* (2014)	1
Machine Learning Methods- stacked restricted Boltzmann machines (RBMs)	Jiang *et al.* (2018)	1

dictionary, affective space, a bag of words, wrapper-GA scheme, filters, and voting techniques. Other less explored criteria include Twitter daily sentiment score, heuristic/hypernym method, spaCy library, term frequency, binary weighting scheme, chi-square, NSGA-II, and LG-Trader.

13.7   Discussion and Conclusion

The present study aims to review fundamental analysis and stock market prediction studies comprehensively and systematically. Eighty-nine papers from the Scopus database were reviewed for 2002–2023. From the bibliometric analysis, the paper identified the highly contributing authors, institutes, countries, sources, keywords, and articles. The intellectual structure and future research opportunities were visualized using bibliographic coupling. Besides this, the study also explored various methods, feature selection criteria, ratio of training and testing datasets, accuracy, performance metrics, technical indicators, and fundamental variables used in stock market prediction.

It was identified that the authors Erik Cambria, Simone Merello, Yukun Ma, Luca Oneto, Anoop Sharma, and Jingjing Li have been identified as the most significant and influential researchers in this field. India is the most considered country for fundamental analysis and stock market prediction research. The research on this topic was mostly conducted by the University of Central Florida and Clemson University. Decision Support System and

Expert Systems with Applications, followed by the International Journal of Financial Studies, are the three most influential journals publishing articles on this topic. The most significant articles in this field were published by Leigh *et al.* [32], Shah *et al.* [3], and Picasso *et al.* [33]. The highly cited author keywords include sentiment analysis, deep learning, stock markets, stock market forecasting, machine learning, and technical analysis. The more recent keywords in 2021 include LSTM, time series analysis, and ARIMA, which provide directions for future research. Six clusters based on bibliographic coupling were identified with the titles *Feature Learning and Stock Market Prediction, Technical Analysis and Market Trend Prediction, Technical Indicators and Deep Learning, Neural Networks and Genetic Algorithms, Stock Market Volatility and Machine Learning Algorithms,* and *Neural Networks and Big Data.* The machine learning algorithms such as LSTM, SVM, and regression techniques were most frequently found in the literature. The prior literature used 80-20 criteria to split the data into training and testing samples, whereas some studies used 70-30 criteria. The most common evaluation metrics are F1 score, RMSE, R2, MSE, accuracy, precision, recall, MAE, and MSE. While the most commonly used factors in the fundamental analysis are ROA, ROE, current ratio, assets turnover ratio, quick ratio, debt-equity ratio, macroeconomic variables, net income growth rate, and sentiment analysis, the commonly used technical indicators are relative strength index, open, high, low, and close, MACD, moving average, and stochastic oscillator. Looking into the fewer studies mentioning the feature selection criteria in their papers, it was found that authors have mainly used correlation, statistical analysis, Loughran and McDonald's dictionary, affective space, a bag of words, wrapper-GA scheme, filters, and voting techniques.

References

1. Nti, I.K., Adekoya, A.F., Weyori, B.A., A systematic review of fundamental and technical analysis of stock market predictions. *Artif. Intell. Rev., 53,* 4, 3007–3057, 2020.
2. Kumbure, M.M., Lohrmann, C., Luukka, P., Porras, J., Machine learning techniques and data for stock market forecasting: A literature review. *Expert Syst. Appl., 197,* 116659, 2022.
3. Shah, D., Isah, H., Zulkernine, F., Stock market analysis: A review and taxonomy of prediction techniques. *Int. J. Financ. Stud., 7,* 2, 26, 2019.

4. Siew, H.L. and Nordin, M.J., Regression techniques for the prediction of stock price trend, in: *2012 International Conference on Statistics in Science, Business and Engineering (ICSSBE)*, IEEE, pp. 1–5, 2012, September.

5. Yang, F., Chen, Z., Li, J., Tang, L., A novel hybrid stock selection method with stock prediction. *Appl. Soft Comput.*, *80*, 820–831, 2019.

6. Başoğlu Kabran, F. and Ünlü, K.D., A two-step machine learning approach to predict S&P 500 bubbles. *J. Appl. Stat.*, *48*, 13-15, 2776–2794, 2021.

7. Singh, J. and Khushi, M., Feature learning for stock price prediction shows a significant role of analyst rating. *Appl. Syst. Innov.*, *4*, 1, 17, 2021.

8. Toochaei, M.R. and Moeini, F., Evaluating the performance of ensemble classifiers in stock returns prediction using effective features. *Expert Syst. Appl.*, *213*, 119186, 2023.

9. Ameen Suhail, K.M., Sankar, S., Kumar, A.S., Nestor, T., Soliman, N.F., Algarni, A.D., El-Shafai, W., El-Samie, A., Fathi, E., Stockmarket trading based on market sentiments and reinforcement learning. *Comput. Mater. Contin.*, *70*, 1, 935–950, 2022.

10. Attigeri, G.V., MM, M.P., Pai, R.M., Nayak, A., Stock market prediction: A big data approach, in: *TENCON 2015-2015 IEEE Region 10 Conference*, IEEE, pp. 1–5, 2015 November.

11. Allen, D.E., Powell, R.J., Singh, A.K., Machine learning and short positions in stock trading strategies, in: *Handbook of Short Selling*, pp. 467–478, Academic Press, Cambridge, United States, 2012.

12. Verma, J.P., Tanwar, S., Garg, S., Gandhi, I., Bachani, N.H., Evaluation of pattern based customized approach for stock market trend prediction with big data and machine learning techniques. *Int. J. Bus. Anal.*, *6*, 3, 1–15, 2019.

13. Ratto, A.P., Merello, S., Oneto, L., Ma, Y., Malandri, L., Cambria, E., Ensemble of technical analysis and machine learning for market trend prediction, in: *2018 IEEE Symposium Series on Computational Intelligence (SSCI)*, IEEE, pp. 2090–2096, 2018 November.

14. Zhang, F., Extreme learning machine for stock price prediction. *Int. J. Electr. Eng. Educ.*, 0020720920984675, 60, 2021.

15. Jawahar, N., Chelladurai, J., Sakthivel, I., Bajracharya, B., Stock volume prediction based on polarity of tweets, news, and historical data using deep learning, in: *Proceedings of the 2020 2nd International Conference on Big-Data Service and Intelligent Computation*, pp. 49–53, 2020, December.

16. He, B. and Kita, E., Stock price prediction by using hybrid sequential generative adversarial networks, in: *2020 International Conference on Data Mining Workshops (ICDMW)*, pp. 341–347, 2020 November.

17. Khairi, T.W., Zaki, R.M., Mahmood, W.A., Stock price prediction using technical, fundamental and news-based approach, in: *2019 2nd Scientific Conference of Computer Sciences (SCCS)*, pp. 177–181, 2019.

18. Singh, B., Henge, S.K., Sharma, A., Menaka, C., Kumar, P., Mandal, S.K., Debtera, B., ML-based interconnected affecting factors with supporting

matrices for assessment of risk in stock market. *Wirel. Commun. Mob. Comput.*, 2022, 2022.

19. Khare, K., Darekar, O., Gupta, P., Attar, V.Z., Short term stock price prediction using deep learning, in: *2017 2nd IEEE International Conference on Recent Trends in Electronics, Information & Communication Technology (RTEICT)*, pp. 482–486, 2017.

20. Barak, S., Arjmand, A., Ortobelli, S., Fusion of multiple diverse predictors in stock market. *Inf. Fusion*, 36, 90–102, 2017.

21. Ng, W.W., Liang, X.L., Li, J., Yeung, D.S., Chan, P.P., LG-trader: Stock trading decision support based on feature selection by weighted localized generalization error model. *Neurocomputing*, 146, 104–112, 2014.

22. Polamuri, S.R., Srinivas, K., Mohan, A.K., Stock market prices prediction using random forest and extra tree regression. *Int. J. Recent Technol. Eng. (IJRTE)*, 8, 1, 1224–1228, 2019.

23. Atkins, A., Niranjan, M., Gerding, E., Financial news predicts stock market volatility better than close price. *J. Financ. Data Sci. (JFDS)*, 4, 2, 120–137, 2018.

24. Agrawal, M., Khan, A.U., Shukla, P.K., Stock indices price prediction based on technical indicators using deep learning model. *Int. J. Emerg. Technol. Learn.*, 10, 2, 186–194, 2019.

25. Torralba, E.M., Development of a deep learning-LSTM trend prediction model of stock prices, in: *Proceedings of the 2019 International Conference on Management Science and Industrial Engineering*, pp. 126–133, 2019, May.

26. Azizi, Z., Abdolvand, N., Asl, H.G., Harandi, S.R., The impact of persian news on stock returns through text mining techniques. *Iran. J. Manage. Stud.*, 14, 4, 799–816, 2021.

27. Chiu, C.H. and Tsai, Y.C., Predicting period stock spread ranking using revenue indicators and machine learning techniques. *IOP Conf. Ser. Earth Environ. Sci.*, 704, 1, 012014, 2021, March, IOP Publishing.

28. Kadu, P.P. and Bamnote, G.R., Comparative study of stock price prediction using machine learning, in: *2021 6th International Conference on Communication and Electronics Systems (ICCES)*, IEEE, pp. 1200–1204, 2021 July.

29. Saini, A. and Sharma, A., Predicting the unpredictable: An application of machine learning algorithms in Indian stock market. *Ann. Data Sci.*, 9, 4, 791–799, 2022.

30. Rauniyar, K., Khan, J.A., Monika, A., Review of different machine learning techniques for stock market prediction, in: *Inventive Systems and Control: Proceedings of ICISC 2021*, pp. 715–724, Springer, Singapore, 2021.

31. Kumar, N., Chauhan, R., Dubey, G., Applicability of financial system using deep learning techniques, in: *Ambient Communications and Computer Systems: RACCCS 2019*, pp. 135–146, Springer, Singapore, 2020.

32. Leigh, W., Purvis, R., Ragusa, J.M., Forecasting the NYSE composite index with technical analysis, pattern recognizer, neural network, and genetic

algorithm: A case study in romantic decision support. *Decis. Support Syst.*, *32*, 4, 361–377, 2002.

33. Picasso, A., Merello, S., Ma, Y., Oneto, L., Cambria, E., Technical analysis and sentiment embeddings for market trend prediction. *Expert Syst. Appl.*, *135*, 60–70, 2019.

34. Sharma, A., Bhuriya, D., Singh, U., Survey of stock market prediction using machine learning approach, in: *2017 International Conference of Electronics, Communication and Aerospace Technology (ICECA)*, vol. 2, pp. 506–509, 2017.

35. Das, S.R., Mishra, D., Rout, M., Stock market prediction using firefly algorithm with evolutionary framework optimized feature reduction for OSELM method. *Expert Syst. Appl.*, *X*, 4, 100016, 2019.

36. Boonpeng, S. and Jeatrakul, P., Decision support system for investing in stock market by using OAA-neural network, in: *2016 Eighth International Conference on Advanced Computational Intelligence (ICACI)*, IEEE, pp. 1–6, 2016.

37. Gite, S., Khatavkar, H., Srivastava, S., Maheshwari, P., Pandey, N., Stock prices prediction from financial news articles using LSTM and XAI, in: *Proceedings of Second International Conference on Computing, Communications, and Cyber-Security: IC4S 2020*, pp. 153–161, Springer, Singapore, 2021.

38. Kanungsukkasem, N. and Leelanupab, T., Financial latent dirichlet allocation (FinLDA): Feature extraction in text and data mining for financial time series prediction. *IEEE Access*, *7*, 71645–71664, 2019.

39. Mndawe, S.T., Paul, B.S., Doorsamy, W., Development of a stock price prediction framework for intelligent media and technical analysis. *Appl. Sci.*, *12*, 2, 719, 2022.

40. Jiang, X., Pan, S., Jiang, J., Long, G., Cross-domain deep learning approach for multiple financial market prediction, in: *2018 International Joint Conference on Neural Networks (IJCNN)*, IEEE, pp. 1–8, 2018, July.

41. Agrawal, M., Khan, A.U., Shukla, P.K., Stock price prediction using technical indicators: A predictive model using optimal deep learning. *Learning*, *62*, 7, 2019.

42. Tamura, R. and Hukushima, K., Bayesian optimization for computationally extensive probability distributions. *PloS One*, 13, 3, e0193785, 2018.

14

Impact of Emotional Intelligence on Investment Decision

Pooja Chaturvedi Sharma

Department of Accounting and Finance, Apeejay School of Management, Delhi, India

Abstract

This study is conducted to analyze the impact of emotional intelligence on the investment decision-making of Indian investors. Investors can improve their decision-making process regarding investments by recognizing and comprehending their emotions, which can reduce the conflicts that arise during the decision-making process. The survey method was used for collecting the primary data to test the research model. Data have been sourced from 239 Indian investors with market experience of at least 3 years in the four major metro cities, namely, Delhi, Mumbai, Kolkata, and Chennai. Respondent categories included postgraduate students, entrepreneurs, professional investors, public and private organizations employees, and individual investors. The Likert scale–based questionnaire was administered. The research employed statistical techniques such as exploratory factor analysis (EFA) and multiple regression analysis to reveal the fundamental pattern among a significant number of variables. Data analysis identified four factors affecting emotional intelligence and investment decisions, namely, attitude, emotions, perception, and low risk. The study's results validated a significant and straightforward link between investment choices and emotional intelligence, highlighting the considerable influence of emotional intelligence on investment decisions. Therefore, this study has wide-ranging implications for all sections of the population regarding developing basic EI as it also saves investors and noninvestors from potential financial frauds and will be helpful for the government in making stringent investor safety policies and spreading financial literacy that will lead to a change in the attitude of noninvestors and eventually pull more investors to Indian financial markets.

Email: poojamitsharmaa@gmail.com

Renuka Sharma and Kiran Mehta (eds.) *Deep Learning Tools for Predicting Stock Market Movements*, (341–362) © 2024 Scrivener Publishing LLC

Keywords: Emotional intelligence, investment decision, exploratory factor analysis, multiple regression, India

14.1   Introduction

Emotional intelligence (EI) is a vital skill that encompasses recognizing, understanding, and managing emotions in oneself and others. Whereas emotions were once seen as secondary to the decision-making process, recent research has highlighted their significance in various domains, including education and leadership [1]. In the realm of investment decision-making, EI plays a crucial role. Investors often encounter complex and uncertain situations where emotions can heavily influence their judgments and choices. Emotionally intelligent individuals are better equipped to recognize and regulate their emotions, leading to more informed and rational investment decisions. Goleman [1] suggested that EI accounts for 67% of the abilities required for excellent leadership performance, surpassing technical expertise and IQ. However, it is essential to consider additional factors that interact with EI and influence leadership and management outcomes. Studies have found that the impact of EI on these outcomes diminishes when ability and personality traits are taken into account. General intelligence, as measured by IQ, has also been found to be highly correlated with leadership effectiveness. Therefore, a comprehensive understanding of the relationship between EI and investment decisions necessitates considering multiple factors. The field of behavioral economics, pioneered by researchers such as Mullainathan and Thaler [2], explores the complex interplay between psychological, sociological, and economic factors that shape decision-making in the real economy. Economic agents, including investors, are subject to cognitive biases and limitations that hinder their ability to make purely rational decisions. Recent research has acknowledged EI as a crucial element in investment decisions and portfolio performance [3, 4].

To achieve the research objectives, the study aims to identify the factors influencing EI and investment decision-making. This objective involves investigating individual, situational, and environmental factors impacting EI and its influence on investment decisions. Personal traits, education, experience, and the sociocultural context will be explored to understand their role. The correlation between investment decisions and EI will be analyzed to assess how EI levels affect the quality of investment decisions, risk perception, portfolio diversification, and the ability to withstand market fluctuations. This analysis will shed light on the relationship between EI and investment outcomes. Furthermore, the study seeks to examine the causal impact of EI on investment decision-making. It aims to explore whether targeted interventions or training programs designed to improve EI can lead to better investment outcomes and financial well-being. By understanding the effect of EI on investment decisions, this research will provide valuable insights into improving financial behavior and decision-making processes.

Recent studies [4–7] have emphasized the importance of EI in investment decisions and portfolio performance. By recognizing and managing emotions effectively, investors can navigate the complexities of the financial markets more efficiently. Understanding the factors that influence EI and exploring its correlation with investment decisions will contribute to enhancing financial decision-making practices and optimizing investment strategies. The novel contribution of this study lies in exploring the interplay between EI and investment decisions in four major metro cities of India by identifying the factors that influence EI in the investment context and examining the causal impact of EI on investment outcomes. This research provides valuable insights for improving financial behavior and decision-making processes.

14.2 Literature Review

EI is a vital component of decision-making and behavior that has attracted significant attention in recent years. EI refers to the ability to recognize and regulate one's emotions, as well as those of others, and to use this information to guide thinking and behavior [8]. Investment decisions, on the other hand, are complex and often risky decisions that require careful consideration of various factors, including market trends, financial analysis, and emotional factors such as fear and greed. This literature review aims to explore the impact of EI on investment decision-making. A study conducted by Lopes *et al.* [9] investigated the impact of EI on investment decision-making among 100 participants. The results revealed that individuals with higher EI scores tend to make more rational investment decisions, whereas those with lower EI scores tend to make impulsive and emotional decisions. The study concluded that EI plays a crucial role in investment decision-making, and individuals with higher EI tend to be more successful in their investments. Another study by Goleman [1] investigated the relationship between EI and investment success among 80 investment managers. The results indicated that investment managers with higher EI scores tend to outperform those with lower EI scores. The study concluded that EI is an essential component of investment success and that investment managers should strive to improve their EI skills to improve their investment performance. Furthermore, a study by Arun and Ananthan [10] examined the impact of EI on investment decision-making among 200 retail investors. The study found a positive correlation between EI and investment performance, indicating that investors with higher EI tend to make more informed and successful investment decisions. The study concluded that EI is a vital factor in investment decision-making, and investors should focus on developing their EI skills to improve their investment performance.

Several studies have contributed to our understanding of investment decisions and the factors that influence them. For instance, Ahmed et al. [11] investigated the factors influencing investment decisions in financial investment companies listed on Iraqi stock exchanges, shedding light on the decision-making process and factors affecting investment choices. Another study by Bertagni et al. [12] presented an immersive setting for practicing EI, enabling participants to interact with various situations and enhance empathy, self-awareness, and self-regulation. In Vietnam's stock market, Luu et al. [13] explored the link between behavioral factors (mood, overconfidence, underreaction, overreaction, and herding behavior) and investment decisions among individual investors, considering the impact of investor demographics. Furthermore, Sashikalav and Chitramani [14] examined the factors influencing investors' long-term investment intentions, including risk tolerance, personality traits (extraversion and openness to experience), and behavioral biases (overconfidence bias). These studies collectively contribute to our understanding of investment decision-making and provide valuable insights for investors and financial professionals [12, 13, 15, 16].

Muttath and Menachery [17] conducted a study to investigate the impact of EI on investment decision-making among individual investors in India. The research revealed that individuals who possess higher EI tend to make better investment decisions, suggesting a positive correlation between EI and investment decision-making. Chen and Sheu [18] examined the relationship between EI and investment behavior among Taiwanese investors. The study found that EI was positively associated with investment behavior, suggesting that individuals with higher EI were more likely to engage in investment activities. Abbas et al. [15] researched to explore how EI affects investment decision-making among investors from Pakistan. Their findings revealed a positive correlation between EI and investment decision-making, suggesting that people with higher EI tend to make better investment decisions. Kim and Lee [19] investigated how EI relates to investment performance in Korean individual investors. On the other hand, Sabri *et al.* [20] conducted a study on Malaysian investors to explore the association between EI and investment decision-making. Their findings showed that EI had a positive impact on investment performance, indicating that those with higher EI tend to achieve better investment outcomes. The study found that EI was positively associated with investment decision-making, indicating that individuals with higher EI tended to make better investment decisions.

Ana *et al.* [21] investigated the impact of EI on investment behavior and performance among UK individual investors. Ana *et al.* [21] investigated the influence of EI on investment behavior and stock market participation in China. The research found that EI had a positive association with investment behavior and stock market participation. This suggests that individuals who had higher EI tended to participate more in investment activities. Yang and Zhao [22] conducted a study to investigate how EI relates to investment decision-making among Chinese investors. The findings showed that EI was linked to better investment decision-making, indicating that individuals with higher EI tend to make better investment decisions. Yen *et al.* [23] conducted a similar study with Taiwanese individual investors and also found a positive relationship between EI and investment decision-making. Bagul and Patil [24] investigated the relationship between EI and investment decision-making among Indian investors and found that higher EI was positively related to better investment decision-making.

According to Kunnanatt [25], people with high EI tend to produce positive outcomes in relationships, whereas those with low EI may create negative outcomes. Training programs focused on EI can improve attitudes, perceptions, and relationships in life. Avsec *et al.* [26] conducted research on the association between EI and personality traits among university students in Croatia and Slovenia. The study involved 257 students from Croatia and 171 from Slovenia, and the statistical analysis included regression, correlation, and two-way ANOVA. The results of the study revealed that extraversion and conscientiousness were significant factors of EI, and neuroticism was the most powerful predictor.

Ezadinea *et al.* [27] researched to examine the correlation between EI and the performance of investment portfolios. The study collected data from 122 Iranian investors and analyzed it using regression and t-tests. The results of the study indicated that EI had a beneficial effect on portfolio performance and that the experience of the investors also influenced portfolio performance and return.

EI has gained considerable attention in recent years as a crucial factor influencing decision-making and behavior. This literature review aims to explore the impact of EI on investment decision-making. The review examines various studies that investigate the relationship between EI and investment decisions, considering factors such as rationality, investment performance, risk tolerance, and behavioral biases.

Lopes *et al.* [9] conducted a study on the impact of EI on investment decision-making. Their findings indicated that individuals with higher EI scores tend to make more rational investment decisions compared to those with lower scores. Similarly, Abbas *et al.* [15] found that investment managers with higher EI outperform those with lower scores, highlighting the importance of EI in investment success.

The study by Luu *et al.* [13] explored the link between EI, behavioral factors, and investment decisions among individual investors in Vietnam. They discovered a positive correlation between EI and investment performance, taking into account the impact of investor demographics. These findings suggest that factors such as age, gender, and education may influence the relationship between EI and investment decision-making. Researchers [16] examined the factors influencing investors' long-term investment intentions, including EI, risk tolerance, personality traits, and behavioral biases. Their research revealed that EI, along with personality traits like extraversion and openness to experience, significantly influences long-term investment intentions. This suggests that EI plays a crucial role in shaping investors' preferences for long-term investment strategies. It also investigates the factors influencing investment decisions in financial investment companies listed on Iraqi stock exchanges, shedding light on the decision-making process and factors affecting investment choices [15]. Another study [12] presented an immersive setting for practicing EI, enabling participants to interact with various situations and enhance empathy, self-awareness, and self-regulation.

Several studies have investigated the relationship between EI and investment performance. Another recent study [15] has found a positive correlation between EI and investment decision-making among investors from Pakistan. Likewise, previous research [19] has observed that EI positively impacts investment performance in Korean individual investors. These findings suggest that individuals with higher EI tend to achieve better investment outcomes. Investor behavior is often influenced by behavioral biases, such as overconfidence and herding behavior. Chen and Sheu [18] found a positive association between EI and investment behavior among Taiwanese investors. This suggests that individuals with higher EI are more likely to engage in investment activities and may exhibit more rational decision-making.

14.3   Research Methodology

In this study, the research instrument utilized to assess EI and investment decision-making factors was a Likert scale questionnaire. The questionnaire was designed specifically for this research, taking into consideration the objectives and hypothesis of the study. The process of designing the research instrument involved several steps. Firstly, a thorough review of existing literature on EI and investment decision-making was conducted to identify relevant constructs and dimensions to be included in the questionnaire. Based on this literature review, a pool of potential items was generated. Next, a panel of experts consisting of researchers, practitioners, and subject matter experts in the field of EI and investment decision-making reviewed the pool of items. The experts provided feedback and suggestions regarding the relevance, clarity, and appropriateness of the items. This feedback was incorporated into the questionnaire refinement process. The refined questionnaire included items that assessed different aspects of EI, such as self-awareness, self-regulation, empathy, and social skills. It also included items related to investment decision-making factors, such as risk tolerance, information processing, and decision-making style. The Likert scale was chosen as the response format for the questionnaire. Participants were asked to rate their agreement or disagreement with each statement on a five-point scale ranging from "Strongly Disagree" to "Strongly Agree." This response format allowed for capturing the participants' perceptions and attitudes regarding EI and investment decision-making. To ensure the validity and reliability of the questionnaire, a pilot study was conducted with a small group of participants. The pilot study aimed to assess the clarity and understandability of the questionnaire items, as well as to examine the internal consistency of the scales. Based on the pilot study results, minor revisions were made to improve the wording and clarity of certain items. Once the final version of the questionnaire was established, data collection was carried out among the target population of Indian investors in major cities. Participants were approached through various channels, such as investment forums, professional networks, and online platforms. The questionnaire was administered online, ensuring anonymity and confidentiality of responses.

The researcher utilized the statistical software package SPSS to analyze the collected data and examine the relationship between EI and investment decisions. The sample selection was based on purposive sampling, ensuring that respondents represented a diverse range of backgrounds and experiences in the investment field. A total of 239 Indian investors with a minimum of 3 years of market experience participated in the study. The respondent categories included postgraduate students, entrepreneurs, professional investors, employees from public and private organizations, and individual investors. To achieve the research objectives, the study formulated a hypothesis that explored the relationship between EI and investment decisions. Data analysis was conducted using exploratory factor analysis (EFA) and multiple regression techniques. EFA was utilized to identify the underlying factors that influence investment decisions in the presence of EI. This analysis helps to determine the key dimensions or constructs that drive investors' decision-making processes. Multiple regression analysis was then employed to examine the relationship among these factors, specifically focusing on how EI impacts investment decisions. H1: There is a significant impact of EI on investor decisions.

14.4   Data Analysis

The researcher has adopted a self-designed questionnaire and the pilot testing was done. Therefore, the researcher has conducted Kaiser-Meyer-Olkin (KMO) and Bartlett's test to calculate the value of KMO to pursue the test measure of sampling adequacy of the questionnaire used. Pilot testing was done by taking responses from 100 respondents. Bartlett's test of sphericity and the KMO measure of sampling adequacy are statistical tests used to determine whether a factor analysis is appropriate for a given dataset. In this case, the results of Bartlett's test of sphericity were statistically significant with a p-value of less than 0.001, indicating that the data are suitable for factor analysis. Initially, this test is conducted to measure the sampling adequacy. The statistical analysis showed that the value of Bartlett's test of sphericity was significant with a chi-square value of 147.144, indicating that the matrix was factorable. Furthermore, the KMO measure was 0.575, which exceeded the threshold of 0.5, indicating that the sample was adequate for conducting factor analysis. As a result, the researchers determined that it was appropriate to proceed with factor analysis to investigate the relationship between EI and investment decision-making among investors in selected Indian metro cities. Further total variance explained was calculated at six stages for factors that affect investors' decisions. Extraction of the sum of square loadings generated five factors with a cumulative factor loading of 72.787%. The rotated component matrix is an important result of the principal components analysis (PCA) that displays the correlations between each variable and the identified components. It is also referred to as the loading matrix. After performing Varimax Rotation with Kaiser Normalization five factors were successfully constructed out.

To ensure the questionnaire's reliability, a reliability analysis was performed to calculate the value of Cronbach's alpha. Cronbach's alpha is a popular measure of reliability. According to Nunnally [28], a reliability score of 0.70 or higher is adequate for research in its early stages. The results of the reliability analysis showed that the Cronbach's alpha value for the nine items was 0.815, which is higher than the acceptable threshold of 0.70, indicating that the tool used in this study is reliable. This suggests that the items in the questionnaire are internally consistent and measure the same construct consistently. Therefore, the factor analysis performed in this study is considered appropriate and reliable.

Data cleaning refers to the process of identifying and rectifying errors and inconsistencies in a dataset or database, which may arise from incorrect data entry or data corruption. This involves detecting incomplete, inaccurate, or irrelevant data and either modifying or removing it. In this study, the researcher has performed data cleaning and screening by removing unengaged responses. As a result, the sample size was reduced to 239 from 325 after the removal of unengaged and missing responses.

Table 14.1 demonstrates that out of 239 respondents, the maximum number of respondents, i.e., 64%, lies in the age group of 18 to 25, and the least number of respondents, i.e., 3%, lies in the age group of 36 to 36 years. It shows that investors of the 18-to-25 age group are more interested in making investment decisions than working investors of all other age groups. The maximum percentage of respondents, i.e., 50%, lies in the category of female, whereas the minimum percentage of respondents lies in the category of prefer not to say, i.e., 1%. It shows that females are slightly more interested in making investment decisions than males in the selected group of respondents. The maximum percentage of respondents, i.e., 48%, is postgraduate. The lowest percentage of respondents, i.e., 9%, is indulged in others and the rest 43% are graduates.

EFA is a statistical approach that aims to identify the latent structure or underlying patterns within a large set of variables. EFA is utilized to reduce the complexity of data by summarizing the variables into a smaller set of underlying factors or components and to examine the theoretical framework that governs the relationships between the variables. It is used to find out the relationship between the variable and the respondent. PCA is a statistical method that is used to identify the underlying patterns and structure of a large set of variables by transforming them into a smaller set of summary variables while still retaining the essential information.

Table 14.1 Demographic profile of respondents.

Variables		Frequency	Percent (%)	Cumulative frequency
Age	18–25 years	153	64	64
	26–35 years	43	18	82
	36–46 years	7	3	85
	47 years and above	36	15	100
	Total	239	100	100
Gender	Male	118	49	49
	Female	119	50	99
	Prefer not to say	2	1	100
	Total	239	100	100
Education	Graduate	103	43	43
	Postgraduate	115	48	91
	Others	21	9	100
	Total	239	100	100

Source: Author's compilation

This method aims to reveal the underlying theoretical structure of the phenomenon by describing the variability among observed variables in terms of a smaller number of unobserved variables, known as factors. Table 14.2 shows the KMO and Bartlett's tests are also performed on the final dataset of 239 respondents. The significance level of Bartlett's test of sphericity is very high, with a chi-square value of 221.647 ($p < 0.001$, $p = 0.000$), and the KMO measure is 0.714, which is above the recommended threshold of 0.6. Therefore, it is suitable to continue with factor analysis.

In Table 14.3, the variance explained is presented. The "total" column displays the eigenvalue for EI and the amount of variance explained by each component for the original variables. The "% of variance" column shows the ratio of the variance explained by each component, expressed as a percentage of the total variance in all of the variables.

Table 14.2 KMO and Bartlett's tests.

KMO and Bartlett's tests		
Kaiser-Meyer-Olkin measure of sampling adequacy:		0.714
Bartlett's test sphericity	Approx. chi-square	221.467
	df	237
	Sig.	0.000

Table 14.3 Total variance explained.

Total variance explained						
	Initial emotional intelligence eigenvalues			Extraction sum of squares loading		
Component	Total	% of variance	Cumulative %	Total	% of variance	Cumulative %
1	2.984	21.318	21.318	2.984	21.318	21.318
2	1.509	10.777	32.095	1.509	10.777	32.095
3	1.362	9.726	41.820	1.362	9.726	41.820
4	1.205	8.604	50.424	1.205	8.604	50.424
5	1.160	8.289	58.713	1.160	8.289	58.713
6	0.954	6.816	65.529			
7	0.943	6.735	72.263			
8	0.824	5.887	78.150			
9	0.732	5.228	83.378			
10	0.634	4.532	87.910			
11	0.550	3.931	91.841			
12	0.416	2.974	94.815			
13	0.379	2.710	97.525			
14	0.347	2.475	100.000			

Five factors affecting EI were extracted. The eigenvalues were greater than one, which explains 58.713% of the variance. Eigenvalues are a measure of the amount of variance in a dataset that is accounted for by each principal component in a PCA. In general, the larger the eigenvalue, the more variance is explained by the corresponding principal component. Eigenvalues are greater than one, which means that each principal component explains more variance than would be expected by chance (i.e., if the data were randomly distributed). This is a common criterion for selecting the number of principal components to retain in a PCA. In this case, the eigenvalues add up to 58.713% of the total variance, which suggests that the first few principal components capture most of the important patterns in the data. Table 14.4 displays the rotated component matrix, also known as the loadings matrix, which is an essential outcome of PCA. It provides estimates of the correlation between each variable and the estimated components.

14.4.1   Reliability Analysis

The researcher used a self-designed questionnaire and conducted a pilot test. Subsequently, a reliability test was performed to determine the reliability of the questionnaire, and the result showed that Cronbach's alpha was 0.688 (as shown in Table 14.5), which is higher than 0.60. Since the value of Cronbach's alpha is above 0.60, it indicates that the scales in the questionnaire are internally consistent. Thus, the instrument used in this study has high reliability.

Table 14.5 depicts that Cronbach's alpha is 0.885 which is more than 0.70. Thus, it is depicted that there was inner consistency of scales.

14.4.2   Factors Naming

After conducting all the tests in EFA, the rotated component matrix resulted in the extraction of four factors. These factors were identified based on their factor loadings. Factor 1 consisted of three items with factor loadings ranging from 0.602 to 0.850. Factor 2 consisted of two items with factor loadings ranging from 0.678 to 0.797. Factor 3 consisted of two items with factor loadings ranging from 0.718 to 0.826. Factor 4 consisted of two items with factor loadings ranging from 0.686 to 0.716. The author

Table 14.4 Rotated component matrix.

Rotated component matrix				
Component	1	2	3	4
I usually consider public information (news) when trading stocks.	0.626			
I have a good understanding of my own emotions.		0.797		
I usually feel composed, confident, and content with my investment returns.			0.718	
I frequently find myself thinking about my previous and upcoming investments or trades.			0.826	
I frequently overestimate the market.				0.686
My happy mood influences my market activity.	0.602			
I am optimistic and that motivates me to invest in the market.				0.716
Despite any negative emotions that may affect me, I am actively engaged in market activities.	0.850			
My calm mindset influences my investment activity.		0.678		

a. Extraction method: principal components analysis.
b. Rotation method: Varimax Rotation with Kaiser Normalization.
c. Rotation converged in eight iterations.

Table 14.5 Reliability analysis.

Reliability statistics		
Cronbach's alpha	Cronbach's alpha based on standardized items	No. of items
.885	.888	9

Table 14.6 Factor naming table.

Attitude	Emotions	Perception	Low risk
I usually consider public information (news) when trading stocks.	I have a good understanding of my own emotions.	I usually feel composed, confident, and content with my investment returns.	I frequently overestimate the market.
My happy mood influences my market activity.	My calm mindset influences my investment activity.	I frequently find myself thinking about my previous and upcoming investments or trades.	I am optimistic and that motivates me to invest in the market.
Despite any negative emotions that may affect me, I am actively engaged in market activities.			

Source: Author's compilation

provided names for these factors based on their characteristics, which are presented in Table 14.6.

This table shows the four factors and their names as per the statements. Because these statements lead to a single factor. Therefore, four factors are extracted which are named attitude, emotion, perception, and low risk.

14.4.3   Multiple Regression Analysis

Multiple regression is a flexible statistical method used to examine relationships between a dependent variable and two or more independent variables. It allows researchers to make predictions of a particular variable based on known values of other variables and to test hypotheses regarding the extent to which independent variables explain variations in the dependent variable. This technique can also test associations between continuous and categorical variables and interactions among multiple independent variables and the dependent variable. In multiple regressions, models are created with one dependent variable and two or more independent variables, with the dependent variable being the one the researcher aims to predict. The impact of independent variables on the dependent variable can be analyzed using regression analysis, which can be conducted with the help of statistical software such as SPSS.

The multiple regression equation of Y on X_1, X_2, ..., X_k is given by:

$$Y = b_0 + b_1 X_1 + b_2 X_2 + ... + b_k X_K$$

Table 14.7 summarizes the results of the regression analysis, which provides information on the strength of the relationship between the independent variables and the dependent variable. The multiple correlation coefficient (R) measures the linear correlation between the observed values and the predicted values of the dependent variable by the model. A larger R-value suggests a stronger relationship between the independent and dependent variables. The analysis results show that the R-value is 0.548, indicating a moderate level of prediction. The R square value, also called the coefficient of determination, represents the proportion of variability in the dependent variable that can be explained by the independent variables. The R square value of 0.683 indicates that 68.3% of the variation in the dependent variable can be explained by the independent variables in the model, whereas the remaining 31.7% is due to other factors not considered in the model. The standard error of 3.44 in the analysis represents the standard deviation of the residuals, which reflects how far the predicted values are from the actual values. As the R square value increases, the standard error decreases, indicating that the estimates of performance become more accurate. Therefore, the standard error of 3.44 is considered negligible.

The results of the ANOVA test, as shown in Table 14.8, determine how well the regression model fits the data. The F-ratio is used to compare the variance explained by the regression model with the residual variance.

Table 14.7 Regression model summary.

Model summary				
Model	R	R square	Adjusted R square	Std. error of the estimate
1	0.548[a]	0.683	0.614	3.44541

[a] Predictors: (constant), emotional intelligence.

Table 14.8 ANOVA table.

ANOVA[a]						
Model		Sum of squares	Df	Mean square	F	Sig
1	Regression	385.380	1	385.380	32.465	0.000[b]
	Residual	1139.599	235	11.871		
	Total	1524.980	236			

[a]Dependent variable: ID
[b]Predictors: (constant), EI

In this study, the independent variables have a significant influence on predicting the dependent variable, as indicated by the F-value of 0.32 and a p-value of 0.000. This indicates that the model is a good fit for the data. A high F-value implies that the model is significant and can explain a substantial portion of the variance in the dependent variable.

Table 14.9 displays the coefficients that show the magnitude and direction of the association between the dependent variable, which is investment decisions, and the independent variable, which is EI. When the coefficient of an independent variable is positive, it suggests that an increase in those variables increases the dependent variable. Conversely, if the coefficient is negative, it implies that an increase in the independent variable leads to a decrease in the dependent variable. In this study, a linear analysis was conducted to test the hypothesis, and the findings demonstrate that EI has a considerable positive effect on investment decisions. The Sig. value of 0.000

Table 14.9 Coefficients table[a].

Coefficients						
Model		Unstandardized coefficients		Standardized coefficients	t	Sig
		B	Std. error	Beta		
1	(Constant)	14.084	2.311		6.094	0.00
	Emotional intelligence	0.640	0.112	0.503	5.698	0.00

[a]Dependent variable: ID

indicates that the relationship is strong and statistically significant, with a significance level below the threshold of 0.05.

14.5 Discussion, Implications, and Future Scope

The findings of this study reveal that several factors significantly influence the investment decisions of investors. These factors include the attitude of investors, their perception of investment options, their emotions, and their inclination toward low-risk investments. The study also establishes a positive and significant impact of EI on investment decision-making. This suggests that individuals with higher EI tend to make more informed and rational investment decisions. The findings of this research have important implications for various stakeholders [29–33]. The study highlights the importance of EI in investment decision-making. By recognizing the significance of EI, society can promote the development of EI skills among individuals, which can lead to better financial decision-making and improved financial well-being. The research findings provide valuable insights for investment practitioners, such as financial advisors and portfolio managers. Practitioners can incorporate EI training and strategies into their practices to enhance investor decision-making processes and outcomes. By understanding the emotional aspects that influence investment decisions, practitioners can better assist their clients in making more rational and informed investment choices. The findings of this study are particularly relevant for retail investors who make investment decisions on their own. By enhancing their EI, retail investors can improve their ability to manage emotions, mitigate biases, and make more rational investment decisions. This can contribute to better investment performance and financial outcomes for individual investors [34–39].

This study contributes to the existing literature by investigating the impact of EI on investment decision-making among Indian investors. It provides new insights into the factors that influence investment decisions and highlights the significance of EI in this context. Furthermore, the research expands the understanding of EI beyond traditional measures of risk tolerance and financial knowledge, emphasizing the role of emotional factors in shaping investment choices [40, 41].

Although this study has shed light on the relationship between EI and investment decision-making, there are several avenues for future research. Firstly, the current study focused on investors in four major Indian cities, limiting its generalizability. Future research could include a more diverse and representative sample of investors from different regions of the country to enhance the external validity of the findings. Additionally, the sample size of this study was relatively small [42–46]. Future research could employ a larger sample size to ensure more robust and reliable results. A larger sample would allow for a more comprehensive analysis of the impact of EI on investment decisions and facilitate more accurate generalizations to the wider investor population. Furthermore, future research could explore the effectiveness of interventions and training programs aimed at improving EI among investors. By examining the outcomes of such interventions, researchers can provide evidence-based recommendations for enhancing EI skills and improving investment decision-making [47–49].

14.6   Conclusion

In conclusion, this research work highlights the positive impact of EI on investment decision-making. The findings consistently demonstrate that individuals with higher EI tend to make better investment decisions, engage more actively in investment activities, and achieve better investment outcomes. These results emphasize the importance of developing EI skills for investors and investment managers. The implications of this research extend to various stakeholders, including investors, financial advisors, and investment managers. By recognizing the significance of EI, these individuals can enhance their decision-making processes and ultimately improve investment performance. Future research should explore the relationship between EI and investment decision-making in different cultural contexts to further enhance our understanding. Overall, incorporating EI into investment strategies and decision-making processes holds great potential for optimizing investment outcomes and benefiting both individual investors and financial professionals.

References

1. Goleman, D., What makes a leader? *Harv. Bus. Rev.*, 76, 6, 93–102, 1998.
2. Mullainathan, S. and Thaler, R.H., *Behavioral economics (NBER working paper series no. 7948)*, National Bureau of Economic Research, USA, 2000.
3. Durand, R.B., Newby, R., Sanghani, J., An intimate portrait of the individual investor. *J. Behav. Financ.*, 9, 193–208, 2008.
4. Smith, H. and Lee, T.M., Emotional intelligence and portfolio performance: The mediating role of risk perception. *J. Informetr.*, 32, 1, 24–39, 2023.

5. Goyal, S. and Singh, R., Emotional intelligence and investment decision making: An empirical study. *Int. J. Financ. Stud.*, 9, 3, 42, 2021.

6. Jones, D.A. and Hensher, D.A., Emotional intelligence and investor behavior. *J. Behav. Exp. Finance*, 33, 101971, 2022.

7. Kim, S. and Gannon, M.J., The role of emotional intelligence in stock investment decision-making: Evidence from individual investors. *J. Behav. Exp. Finance*, 39, 101798, 2023.

8. Salovey, P. and Mayer, J.D., Emotional intelligence. *Imagin. Cogn. Pers.*, 9, 3, 185–211, 1990.

9. Lopes, P.N., Salovey, P., Straus, R., Emotional intelligence, personality, and the perceived quality of social relationships. *Pers. Individ. Differ.*, 35, 3, 641–658, 2003.

10. Arun, T.G. and Ananthan, B., Impact of emotional intelligence on investment decision making: A study among retail investors in India. *Int. J. Account. Financial Manage. Res.*, 6, 1, 1–10, 2016.

11. Abdul-Kareem, A.A., Fayed, Z.T., Rady, S., El-Regaily, S.A., Nema, B.M., Factors influencing investment decisions in financial investment companies. *Systems*, 11, 3, 146, 2023.

12. Bertagni, B., Gardner, R., Minehart, R., Salvetti, F., An immersive and interactive setting to practice emotional intelligence. *Int. J. Adv. Corp. Learn.*, 16, 3, 21–26, 2023.

13. Quang, L.T., Linh, N.D., Nguyen, D.V., Khoa, D.D., Behavioral factors influencing individual investors' decision making in Vietnam market. *J. East. Eur. Cent. Asian Res.*, 10, (2), 2023.

14. Sashikala, V. and Chitramani, P., A review on emotional intelligence and investment behavior. *Indian J. Sci. Technol.*, 9, 10, 32–41, 2016.

15. Abbas, F., Ahmed, N., Ishaque, M., Jadoon, I., Impact of emotional intelligence on investment decision making: A study of individual investors in Pakistan. *J. Behav. Appl. Manage.*, 19, 2, 197–218, 2017.

16. Ferreira, S. and Dickason, Z., Analysing the factors affecting the long-term investment intention of investors. *Int. J. Econ. Financial Issues*, 13, 1, 112–120, 2023.

17. Muttath, B.T. and Menachery, A., Impact of emotional intelligence on investment decision. *Int. J. Res. Mark.*, 8, 3, 1–14, 2018.

18. Chen, Y.L. and Sheu, H.J., Emotional intelligence and investment behavior: Evidence from Taiwan. *J. Appl. Finance Bank.*, 6, 1, 1–18, 2016.

19. Kim, S.J. and Lee, S., Emotional intelligence and investment performance: Evidence from korean individual investors. *Asia-Pac. J. Financ. Stud.*, 46, 2, 193–215, 2017.

20. Sabri, M.F.M., Shah, A.H., Yusoff, M.Y.Z.M., Emotional intelligence and investment decision-making: A study among malaysian investors. *J. Financ. Rep. Account.*, 17, 2, 315–330, 2019.
21. Rosales-Pérez, A.M., Fernández-Gámez, M.A., Torroba-Díaz, M., Molina-Gómez, J., A study of the emotional intelligence and personality traits of university finance students. *Educ. Sci.*, 11, 1, 25, 2021.
22. Yang, X. and Zhao, L., The relationship between emotional intelligence and investment decision-making: Evidence from China. *J. Behav. Exp. Finance*, 28, 100418, 2020.
23. Yen, H.R., Chen, C.W., Huang, C.Y., The impact of emotional intelligence on investment decision-making: Evidence from taiwanese individual investors. *J. Appl. Finance Bank.*, 10, 2, 67–81, 2020.
24. Bagul, A. and Patil, S., Emotional intelligence and investment decision-making: Evidence from indian investors. *Int. J. Emerg. Mark.*, 17, 3, 669–686, 2022.
25. Kunnanatt, J.T., Emotional intelligence: The new science of interpersonal effectiveness. *Hum. Resour. Dev. Q.*, 15, 4, 489–495, 2004.
26. Avsec, A., Taksic, V., Mohoric, T., The relationship of trait emotional intelligence with the big five in croatian and slovene university student samples. *Psihol. Obz. /Hor. Psych.*, 3, 18, 99–110, 2009.
27. Ezadinea, N., Fathi, S., Salami, S., The effect of emotional intelligence on portfolio performance of stakeholders: Empirical evidence from Iran. *Interdiscip. J. Contemp. Res. Bus.*, 3, 5, 679–685, 2011.
28. Nunnally, J.C., *Psychometric theory. 2nd edition*, McGraw-Hill, New York, 1978.
29. Awais, M., Nawaz, M.A., Asghar, N., Impact of financial literacy and investment experience on risk tolerance and investment decisions: Empirical evidence from Pakistan. *J. Appl. Account. Res.*, 19, 1, 58–77, 2018.
30. Bhardwaj, M.K. and Kumar, M., The empirical impact of emotional intelligence on decision making styles among adolescents. *Int. J. Soc Sci.*, 7, 11, 33–43, 2017.
31. Mehta, K. and Sharma, R., Contrarian and momentum investment strategies: Evidence from indian stock market. *Int. J. Appl. Bus. Econ. Res.*, 15, 9, 107–118, 2017.
32. Mehta, K. and Sharma, R., Management of forex risk exposure: A study of SMEs and unlisted non-financial firms in India, *Int. J. Appl. Bus. Econ. Res.*, 15, 9, 43–54, 2017.
33. Mehta, K., Sharma, R., Vyas, V., Efficiency and ranking of sustainability index of India using DEA-TOPSIS. *J. Indian Bus. Res.*, 11, 2, 179–199, 2019, https://doi.org/10.1108/JIBR-02-2018-0057.

34. Dhiman, B. and Raheja, S., Do personality traits and emotional intelligence of investors determine their risk tolerance? *J. Commer. Account. Res.*, 7, 1, 1–12, 2018.

35. Haldi, M., Effect of emotional intelligence on investment decision making with a moderating role of financial literacy. *J. Bus. Econ. Dev.*, 2, 1, 20–28, 2017.

36. Johnsi, S. and Sunitha, K., Impact of personality and emotional intelligence on investor behaviour. *Int. J. Pure Appl. Math.*, 116, 24, 213–219, 2017.

37. Sharma, R., Mehta, K., Sharma, O., Exploring deep learning to determine the optimal environment for stock prediction analysis. *International Conference on Computational Performance Evaluation, ComPE*, pp. 148–152, 2021.

38. Sharma, R., Mehta, K., Vyas, V., Responsible investing: A study on non-economic goals and investors' characteristics. *Appl. Finance Lett.*, 9, SI, 63–78, 2020, https://doi.org/10.24135/afl.v9i2.245.

39. Vyas, V., Mehta, K., Sharma, R., The nexus between toxic-air pollution, health expenditure, and economic growth: An empirical study using ARDL. *Int. Rev. Econ. Finance*, 84, 154–166, 2023, https:// doi.org/10.1016/j.iref.2022.11.017.

40. Vyas, V., Mehta, K., Sharma, R., Investigating socially responsible investing behaviour of Indian investors using structural equation modelling. *J. Sustain. Finance Invest.*, 12, 1–23, 2020, DOI: 10.1080/20430795.2020.1790958.

41. Mitroi, A. and Opruți, A., Behavioral finance: New research trends, socionomics, and investor emotions. *Proc. Econ. Financ.*, 15, 1217–1224, 2014.

42. Ntim, C.G., Mensah, J.T., Mensah, P.N., Emotional intelligence, investment behavior and performance of UK individual investors. *J. Behav. Exp. Finance*, 31, 100539, 2021.

43. Sekscinska, K. and Markiewicz, L., Financial decision-making and individual dispositions, in: *J. Behav. Decis.Mak*, T. Zaleskiewicz and J. Traczyk (Eds.), pp. 99–120, Springer, 2020.

44. Mehta, K., Sharma, R., Vyas, V., A quantile regression approach to study the impact of aluminium prices on the manufacturing sector of India during the COVID era. *Mater. Today: Proc.*, 65, 8, 3506–3511, 2022, ISSN 2214-7853, https://doi.org/10.1016/j.matpr.2022.06.087.

45. Mehta, K., Sharma, R., Vyas, V., Kuckreja, J.S., Exit strategy decision by venture capital firms in India using fuzzy AHP. *J. Entrep. Emerg. Econ.*, 14, 4, 643–669, 2022, https://doi.org/10.1108/JEEE-05-2020-0146.

46. Sharma, R., Mehta, K., Goel, A., Non-linear relationship between board size and performance of Indian companies. *J. Manage. Gov.*, 27, 1277–1301, 2022, https://doi. org/10.1007/s10997-022-09651-8.

47. Tauni, M.Z., Fang, H.X., Iqbal, A., The role of financial advice and word-of-mouth communication on the association between investor personality and stock trading behavior: Evidence from chinese stock market. *Pers. Individ. Differ.*, 108, 55–65, 2017.

48. Yip, J.A. and Côté, S., The emotionally intelligent decision-maker: Emotion understanding ability reduces the effect of incidental anxiety on risk-taking. *Organ. Behav. Hum. Decis. Process.*, 132, 29–44, 2016.

49. Sharma, R., Mehta, K., Rana, R., Cryptocurrency adoption behavior of millennial investors in India, in: *Perspectives on Blockchain Technology and Responsible Investing*, pp. 135–157, IGI Global Publisher, USA, 2023.

15

Influence of Behavioral Biases on Investor Decision-Making in Delhi-NCR

Pooja Gahlot[1]*, Kanika Sachdeva[1], Shikha Agnihotri[2] and Jagat Narayan Giri[1]

[1]School of Business, Sushant University, Gurugram, India
[2]School of Business, IMS Ghaziabad, Uttar Pradesh, India

Abstract

The traditional view in finance is that investments must be made using rational processes. Before making decisions, investors evaluate both risks and returns to maximize their long-term profits. Behavioral finance presents a challenge to traditional finance because it introduces psychological factors that impact their choices. The fluctuations in the price of securities are caused by irrational activity on the part of investors and abnormalities in the market. As a direct result, analyses have been done to investigate the influence of various biases and factors on traders' decisions. The primary objective of this paper research is to study and analyze the consequences of three biases in IT, banking sectors, and academic industry. There are three cognitive biases: overconfidence, optimism, and the illusion of control. A total of 362 people filled out the structured questionnaire, which was utilized to gather data. Data analysis involved using SmartPLS software to apply the PLS algorithm and bootstrapping technique in partial least squares structural equation modeling. The research showed that there is a meaningful connection between having an excessive amount of confidence and making financial decisions. At the same time, optimism and the illusion of control did not significantly affect their decisions. Although this study provides valuable insights into investor biases in Delhi-NCR, it is essential to acknowledge its limited scope. Investors may benefit from this study by understanding the factors that influence the market through this research. It will ultimately lead to more rational investment decisions and increase market productivity.

Keywords: Behavioral finance, investor decision, behavioral biases, overconfidence, illusion of control, optimism, rationality, market anomalies

Corresponding author: Poojagahlot36@gmail.com

Renuka Sharma and Kiran Mehta (eds.) Deep Learning Tools for Predicting Stock Market Movements, (363–390) © 2024 Scrivener Publishing LLC

15.1   Introduction

Some options are easy, whereas others are more complex and need a more systematic approach. Individuals make many decisions throughout their lives, some of which are important and some of which are not. It is often held that people do not seek information that may help them make better decisions, preferring to rely on their own experience and instincts. It is commonly believed that people do not search for information that could help them make better decisions, instead relying on their experience and intuition. Financial theories have been developed based on the assumption that traders always act rationally in efficient markets. Important conventional theories in the field of finance, such as the efficient market hypothesis (1970) and the modern portfolio theory (1952), hold that individual investors are logical and risk-averse, opting for security above potential gain. According to studies conducted by Fernandez [1] and Sharpe [2], the pricing approach for capital assets accurately evaluates the economy's tendencies and the options available to investors. Conventional financial theory suggests that individuals are rational when identifying, utilizing, and executing optimal decisions [3]. The rational person does two things: first, they adjust their opinions in light of new evidence, and second, they invest in a way consistent with the explanations provided by standard financial theories [4]. It suggested that individual investors choose their investments to behave logically and sensibly. The studies reveal that investors often use financial models and theories to evaluate their investment choices' potential risks and returns [5–8]. It is widely acknowledged that people in the marketplace frequently make illogical decisions. It is evident in their tendency to engage in excessive trading, invest in stocks without fully understanding their true worth, make purchase decisions based on peer pressure, rely on past performance to guide current actions, and hold onto underperforming stocks while selling off successful ones. Investors frequently rely on all fallacies when making decisions. Unfortunately, these biases can lead to investments that do not increase utility [9].

After the energy crisis in 1970, a study produced results challenging the expected utility theory (EUT). In uncertain situations, it may be more beneficial to consider the theory developed by, and applying this theory might result in a deeper comprehension of the better choices [9]. Because of the integration of behavioral and psychological considerations into economic and financial choices, a new subject known as behavioral finance has emerged. The significant contribution of prospect theory facilitated this. Behavioral finance has emerged as a credible alternative to the EUT, acknowledging the limitations of this theory. This field emphasizes the significance of biases in comprehending irrational investment choices.

Behavioral finance investigates and discusses how investors' behavioral tendencies and emotions influence their investment decisions. Investors often need to deviate from the principles outlined in traditional finance theory. Well-documented studies on psychological features in behavioral finance have outweighed logical concepts. Most researchers have conducted extensive research and established that the origins of the current discipline of behavioral finance exist in cognitive psychology. Cognitive psychologists investigate how the thoughts and beliefs of individuals impact their fiscal decisions. Individuals make errors while investing because they need help solving the enhancement issues that classical theory's principles need. To deal with the increasing amount of data, people use rules of thumb, heuristics, or biases [10]. Investors in the field of finance are recognized as having distinct values and decision-making methods that are shaped by their beliefs and emotions. Consequently, their thoughts and actions play a critical role in making investment choices, significantly influencing the outcomes of their assets. The field of behavioral finance explores how mental and psychological biases affect the decisions made by investors and how these decisions can impact market prices and returns. The investors are influenced by cognitive and psychological biases leading to market prices that deviate from their actual value. It is essential to consider financial decisions, which account for emotions [11].

As per Shefrin [12], bias is a "predisposition toward error." In simpler terms, bias tends to make judgments influenced by preconceived notions. Investors may make better financial decisions if they know and can control every possible source of bias. This paper explores three human biases: overconfidence, the illusion of control, and optimism. It is essential to acknowledge these biases as they can significantly impact decision-making and overall outcomes. In addition to biases, people judge based on other psychological influences. It is standard for people to exhibit bias, which can result in irrational decisions. It can lead to distorted perceptions, inaccurate assessments, or flawed outcomes in certain situations. The "decision-making" process is the cognitive or mental process that ultimately chooses one action over another. Making investment decisions is a complex process that requires much more than money. Time, patience, and discipline are necessary for a successful investment [13]. Furthermore, the author classified finance biases into three categories: judgmental biases, preference mistakes, and biases related to dealing with the consequences of decisions. Overconfidence, optimism, and overreaction to random occurrences are all examples of judgmental biases. Investors also behave irrationally due to biases, and each bias results in a distinct pattern of decision [14].

Overly confident people can suffer against outcomes when making personal or business choices. These individuals tend to overvalue their abilities and disregard valuable input from others. They rely solely on their judgments, diminishing their willingness to seek guidance or advice during decision-making. Investors need to pay more attention to facts and models since they are confident that they are correct and overconfident. People only sometimes recognize when they are doing more harm than good because they disregard warning signs. Overconfidence increased as the investor's investing experience increased. Studies have shown that investors may become overly confident in their trading skills after a period of high market returns. It can result in excessive trading, which may not be justified. Investors must maintain a balanced approach and avoid making hasty decisions based on temporary market conditions [15].

The illusion of control is a common human tendency to believe that one has the power to impact outcomes that are outside of their control. Despite this, individuals often exhibit overconfidence in their abilities to control outcomes, which can lead to errors and mistakes. Recognizing this illusion and avoiding overestimating one's influence on uncontrollable events is essential. The concept of the "gamblers' fallacy" exposes a common misconception about control. According to this idea, individuals who gamble often apply more force to their dice rolls when hoping for a higher number but use less energy when aiming for a lower one. It has been demonstrated that this factor substantially reduced the profits of investors who were already susceptible due to inadequate analysis, risk management, and trading gains. Sometimes, investors experience an illusion of control where they become overly confident in their capacity to influence the outcomes of incidents. It can lead to a downfall; as the saying goes, "pride comes before a fall" [16].

Optimism bias is common in many domains where positive and negative outcomes are overestimated. This tendency involves overemphasizing the likelihood of achieving desired goals while minimizing the risk of failure. In addition, optimism impacts people and organizations regarding their financial decisions and how they live their daily lives. The critical takeaway from this bias is that investors are more likely to make impulsive investing decisions. Optimism bias causes investors unrealistically high expectations for their portfolio's success [17–19].

The investor does not invest in a single nation but in several other countries. Several biases influence the decision to invest. If the investor is aware of every possible bias, it will be easier to make rational decisions about their financial future [13]. Our research addresses three biases—overconfidence, the illusion of control, and optimism—and examines their impact on investors' decision-making in Delhi-NCR, India. Although numerous studies have been conducted on this subject worldwide, more research in India must be explicitly done. When investors are aware of the possible biases they face, it allows them to act more rationally. The following are some of the primary objectives that the research aims to accomplish:

1. To analyze how biases impact the investment decision-making procedure.
2. To identify the behavioral biases of investors in the Delhi-NCR region.

The following is an outline of the remaining parts of the paper. As the literature on cognitive biases of three behavioral biases was selected, the illusion of control, optimism, and overconfidence will be reviewed in Section 15.2. The hypothesis and suggested study framework will be reviewed in Section 15.3. The methodology used, an overview of the analysis, and the initial outcomes are all covered in Section 15.4 and Section 15.5 discusses the results and suggests further study.

15.2   Literature Review

Based on the conventional literature on finance, investors are commonly advised to use the EUT to make rational investment decisions and maximize their returns. However, behavioral finance sheds light on the influence that mental and psychological factors have on investors' irrational choices. The study revealed that investors can be categorized into two distinct groups: the logical and the illogical. Irrational investors base their investing choices on their emotions and intuition, unlike rational investors, who base their judgments on factual information and logic [20, 21].

Behavioral finance focuses on the psychological factors that affect investment decision-making. Numerous anomalies in investor behavior have been identified through research, which go against logical and rational decision-making and contradict traditional financial theory. These anomalies, also known as biases or cognitive errors, significantly impact investors.

The prospect theory clarifies how individuals make decisions in uncertain or risky situations. It proposes that people tend to avoid risk when there is a chance of making a profit but become more willing to take risks when confronted with potential losses [22].

15.2.1   Overconfidence Bias

Overconfidence makes investors overestimate their abilities, believing they have more excellent knowledge than they do. This financial bias is often found among investors. Many people tend to underestimate their strengths and overemphasize their weaknesses. Investors overestimate their abilities and engage in excessive stock market trading. The issue of overconfidence focuses on how accurately investors estimate their skills and identify their knowledge issues. Investors trade more aggressively when they are over-confident. The investor's confidence was positively influenced by the information provided, but unfortunately, it led to biased decision-making, as evidenced by the outcomes [23]. Overconfidence is characterized by an individual's excessive faith in their knowledge and analytical abilities, leading them to believe that they are superior to others and possess an inflated self-esteem [18]. Simply put, it is a condition where investors perceive themselves as more capable than they are. When many people in the market are too sure of themselves, the market does not act rationally. The more actively an investor trades, the less money they make. This study classified 66,465 families into five categories based on the amount of turnover in their joint stock holdings. The 20% of investors who traded the most frequently got a net yearly return of 7.2% lower than the 20% of those who sold the least [24]. Oskamp (1965) was the first psychologist to identify excessive confidence. Psychologists suggest that extreme confidence can lead individuals to overestimate their capacity to manage situations while simultaneously underestimating the time required to evaluate potential risks. It also includes overestimating one's capacity to execute specific jobs and displaying greater confidence in making decisions. When buying and selling stocks, the tendency to be overly confident can result in varied decisions among securities dealers. This bias can impact the overall outcome [25].

The too-confident investors tend to overreact to signals based on personal knowledge while disregarding readily available data. Sometimes, investors who are too confident may make trades even if the expected profits may not be enough to cover the costs of making the trade [26]. The data were taken from a prominent discount brokerage firm in the US between 1991 and 1996. The study found that numerous investors exhibit overconfidence and engage in excessive trading, resulting in lower household net returns, even though gross returns (excluding transaction costs) remain normal [27]. A study focused on how behavioral biases affect investment decisions made by securities firms in Ho Chi Minh City, Vietnam. After analyzing information from 188 individual investors, the researchers identified five behavior traits that impact investment choices [28]. Overconfidence may influence business investment decisions, and the manager's confidence increases the debt burden. The result demonstrates that increased debt levels in the capital structure result from management confidence [29].

According to behavioral theory, investors with overconfidence tend to exaggerate their level of knowledge and disregard uncertainties. As a result of their study, increased interest in high-risk investments, and pursuit of lower-risk premiums, asset prices rise and become inflated. This study investigates how Saudi Arabia's expanding stock market's company value is impacted by this overconfidence. According to the findings, overconfidence significantly and favorably affects a company's value [30–33]. Different research explores how investor overconfidence affects investment decisions and how it can impact a company's performance. The study proves that overconfidence can lead to mismanagement of resources that can harm a company [34]. The research shows that overconfident investors can make irrational decisions, but obtaining information can help prevent this. In particular, the study indicates that overconfidence can affect the rationality of individual investors' decisions. Investors frequently need help resulting from overconfidence bias, which can result in suboptimal investment decisions. This bias causes people to overestimate their understanding of financial markets or specific assets, causing them to ignore evidence and expert advice [35].

15.2.2 Illusion of Control Bias

As stated by Grou and Tabak [36], individuals tend to maintain the conviction that they can manipulate and impact circumstances that are out of their control, even if this belief is inaccurate. It is referred to as the "illusion of control." Illusions caused by overconfidence induce investors to overestimate their predictive capacity (which, according to EMH, they do not have) and to seek to "time" the market by purchasing or selling shares ahead of an expected share movement. Excessive trading increases spending and negatively impacts future choices. This bias affects the importance of skill, chance, and incentives in manipulating the financial market. As a result, investors tend to prioritize options they have already considered [37]. Additionally, individuals agree to spend proportionally in situations over which they have control and in situations over which they have no control. The individuals wanted to avoid investing in cases that they did not like, even when they influenced the problem. People's preferences emerged due to their beliefs and understanding of the conditions [38].

Many individuals may experience a sense of control over their circumstances, often due to the illusion of control and behavior bias. This bias can cause overestimating success levels that cannot be attributed to chance. Their control-illusion beliefs impact the efficiency of investors' transactions in financial instruments [39]. The illusion of control bias directly affects the performance of traders. In the research, a comparison was made between high and low levels of the illusion of control and the influence these levels have on various financial instruments. The concepts of the illusion of control, first introduced by Ising and Pompian [40], have since gained widespread acceptance and recognition in the relevant field. These ideas contribute to investors' overconfidence, negatively affecting the stock market. To succeed, traders need to improve their skills. Research has shown that self-control bias can lead to decreased savings and increased spending, risking earlier retirement and less money saved. Investors may try to recover lost time through various investment strategies, which can lead to potential difficulties.

The cognitive biases significantly impact business students' choice-making abilities. The authors in this study surveyed both graduate and undergraduate students enrolled at Jacksonville University, and the findings showed that biases influenced them and rationality is limited in their practices; however, they are less optimistic about investment ability and athletic ability [41]. Another research on the influence of biases on investors' choices. The study included a sample of 100 individuals, comprising both students and workers (55%). Information was collected through a questionnaire, and the study considered confirmation biases, the illusion of control, overconfidence, and loss aversion as independent variables, with male and female participants as dependent variables. Chi-square analysis was employed in this investigation. Results showed no substantial difference in overconfidence bias between male and female decision-makers [42].

The cognitive and emotional biases impact the investing choices of investors in Bangladesh. The information was gathered from a representative sample of 196 active investors on the exchange in Dhaka through a structured questionnaire. The findings indicate that investors are only somewhat unbiased and are impacted by different biases. These biases substantially influence the choices that investors in Bangladesh make about their investments [43]. This study focused on three cognitive biases that can cause overconfidence, affecting investment performance. The study found that these biases increase risk propensity, ultimately impacting investment performance. Furthermore, the research indicates that the "illusion of control" can be used to anticipate both the outcome of financial investments and risky behavior [44].

15.2.3   Optimism Bias

Optimism bias is often associated with overconfidence bias. A study stated that inaccurate beliefs about knowledge and control can lead to overconfidence and optimism [45]. The former is a state in which a person feels confident in their ability. It impacts their confidence in the likelihood of achievement. Optimism bias is the tendency to overestimate the chance of success (getting what you want) and underestimate the event of failure. Investors commonly exhibit an optimism bias, believing their investments will always generate positive returns. The vital point to take away from this bias is that investors are likelier to make rash investment decisions [46]. Investors with a higher optimism bias will likely view their investment portfolios with a more positive outlook. Although reality may vary from predictions, this optimistic outlook encourages them to increase trading frequency and volume [47].

Optimism can be described as expecting more positive outcomes than negative ones. This specific kind of bias may be seen in a wide range of different areas. The primary cause for present debt troubles in financing and debt-to-equity ratio is the excessive optimism that was expressed by corporate management in the past. It is essential to recognize that when new products are introduced to the market, it can lead to a bias in forecasting [48]. The predictions always need some degree of accuracy. It is hardly unexpected, given that many businesses may unknowingly participate in excessive optimism, mainly if their survival depends on optimistic estimates [49–51]. Excessive optimism influences the financial decisions and day-to-day actions of people and companies. The relationship between investor opinions and the value of shares was analyzed by Brown and Cliff [15]. It was determined that the pricing of capital can be influenced by sentiment. Excessive optimism is one of the behavioral factors influencing investing decisions. People tend to ignore the negative aspects of positive situations due to excessive optimism. In an attempt to gain profits, investors may sometimes make impulsive decisions without proper evaluation [52–54].

The influence of dispositional optimism on options trading in Netherlands by utilizing survey data and trade records as their primary sources of information. According to the life orientation test (LOT) results, options traders use more options when optimistic about the future. A study has shown that having an optimistic outlook can influence one's trading behavior. However, more research needs to be conducted on how optimism can impact decision-making when taking risks, even though it has significant potential importance [55]. Individuals with a positive outlook overestimate the potential benefits of high-risk investments and underestimate the risks and volatility involved. As a result, they introduce risk that is above average into portfolios [56]. It has been shown in this study that an individual's financial optimism significantly affects their portfolio selections. The study also found that optimistic individuals tend to make riskier portfolio selections while they are less likely to choose risk-free options. In business and finance, making accurate judgments about probabilities is essential [57]. People often overestimate the likelihood of positive outcomes when making financial decisions. They believe that the optimistic bias influencing corporate executives, entrepreneurs, and asset managers will similarly affect ordinary families. Since optimistic business and finance experts pursue hazardous investment possibilities, families with a positive outlook on their future financial condition may make less sensible, riskier portfolio decisions [16, 58].

Financial biases affect investors' choices in developing countries. It focuses on two cognitive biases, namely, anchoring and optimism biases, and how information asymmetry can moderate their effects. This study carefully investigates how risk perception affects the relationship between biases. Based on the results, it is clear that biases hold a considerable influence over an investor's choices. Furthermore, the perception of risk is crucial in regulating the connection between these two aspects [59, 60]. Investors with a positive outlook are more likely to invest because they are optimistic. When it comes to making choices, investors who feel they need additional incentives often focus entirely on the present status of the market. They are more likely to invest if they see that the market is performing well [17]. Optimistic investors also tend to diversify their holdings to increase their profits. Many investors make behavioral mistakes such as being pessimistic, optimistic, anxious, or sad regarding the stock market. These emotions often go against logical decision-making. Despite this, some investors benefit from irrational activity in the stock market. Some individuals rely on animal instincts to feel comfortable and follow the crowd [61].

15.3   Research Hypothesis

H1: There is a significant and positive relationship between the illusion of control bias and investment decisions.

H2: There is a significant and positive relationship between optimism bias and investment decisions.

H3: There is a significant and positive relationship between overconfidence bias and investment decisions.

The model developed from this research investigates how irrational behavioral tendencies like overconfidence, the illusion of control, and optimism affect investors. Following an exhaustive literature study, a model was built with the three biases serving as independent factors and investment decisions playing the role of dependent factors (Figure 15.1).

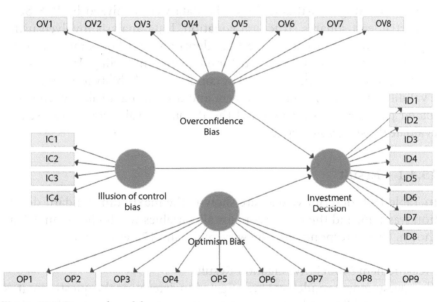

Figure 15.1 Proposed model.

15.4   Methodology

This research aimed to identify behavioral biases' impact and analysis on investors' choices. To attain this objective, we gathered a representative sample from a group of people who utilize financial tools through convenience sampling. The study focuses on individuals who belong to the investing class and can save and invest money in different financial markets. Furthermore, Delhi–National Capital Region (NCR) participants were chosen for the study due to the substantial growth of per capita income by 7.54% in the 2022–23 survey, which is 2.6 times higher than the national average [1]. The sample consists of people from the IT and banking industries. Few respondents were from the academic sector, including faculties and students. The data were collected using a rating system from 1 to 5, where 1 indicates strong disagreement, and 5 indicates strong agreement. The independent variable overconfidence bias scale has eight items, and the illusion of control bias has four items; both were adopted from. A few items of overconfidence bias were adopted from [61–64]. The independent variable optimism bias scale adopts nine items from [65, 66]. The independent variable optimism bias scale adopts nine items from [70]. The investment decision scale consists of eight items from [67, 68]. A set of 500 questionnaires were distributed, and 362 were used for data analysis after eliminating non-usable ones. The data were analyzed by PLS-SEM or partial least squares structural equation. Data analysis involved using SmartPLS software to apply the PLS algorithm and bootstrapping technique in partial least squares structural equation modeling. We evaluated the suggested measurement model by conducting reliability tests and doing a validity analysis utilizing convergent and discriminant validity. The estimated path coefficient values and the R square evaluation were used to evaluate the suggested framework.

15.4.1 Result

In Table 15.1, descriptive data are shown. The maximum standard deviation was 1.46, and the mean score for all variables was higher than 3.2, as shown. Of 362 respondents, 189 were male, and 173 were female.

Measurement Model Investigation Results
The measurement model was investigated to determine the questionnaire's indicator reliability and validity in determining its convergent and discriminant validity. Content validity was demonstrated through the opinion of six experts regarding the questionnaire. Due to the adaptable scales in this investigation, exploratory factor analysis was not performed, as stated in the previous work [69]. It was determined by confirmatory factor analysis that each statement does belong to the variable to which it is most closely related.

   All factor loadings for the statements in Table 15.2 exceeded the 0.7 thresholds set by the criterion [70]. According to Table 15.3, the scale

Table 15.1 Descriptive statistics.

Construct	Mean	SD
Overconfidence bias	3.902	1.337
Illusion of control bias	3.427	1.394
Optimism bias	3.20	1.460
Investment decision	3.832	1.268
Total number of respondents	362	
Male	189	
Female	173	

Source: Author's calculation

Table 15.2 Factor loadings.

Variable	Factor loadings
Illusion of control bias	
IC1	0.877
IC2	0.851
IC3	0.870
IC4	0.737
Investment decision	
ID1	0.871
ID2	0.795
ID3	0.880
ID4	0.807
ID5	0.710
ID6	0.780
ID7	0.776
ID8	0.877

(Continued)

Table 15.2 Factor loadings. (*Continued*)

Variable	Factor loadings
Optimism bias	
OB1	0.800
OB2	0.867
OB3	0.811
OB4	0.832
OB5	0.757
OB6	0.706
OB7	0.729
OB8	0.729
OB9	0.855
Overconfidence bias	
OV1	0.887
OV2	0.865
OV3	0.811
OV4	0.889
OV5	0.894
OV6	0.875
OV7	0.767
OV8	0.711

Source: Author's calculation

demonstrates consistency based on Cronbach's alpha and composite reliability measurements. It is essential to highlight that both values exceed the minimum requirement of 0.7 [71]. To verify convergent validity, the average variance extracted (AVE) was determined for each independent variable. Table 15.3 shows that the AVE values for all variables were higher than the minimum acceptable value of 0.5 [72], indicating the convergent validity of all.

Table 15.3 Internal consistency and convergent validity.

	Cronbach's alpha	Composite reliability	Average variance extracted
Illusion of control bias	0.859	0.902	0.698
Investment decision	0.866	0.892	0.517
Optimism bias	0.912	0.928	0.590
Overconfidence bias	0.905	0.923	0.607

Source: Author's calculation

Table 15.4 HTMT ratio-discriminant validity.

HTMT Ratio-discriminant validity				
	Illusion of control bias	Investment decision	Optimism bias	Overconfidence bias
Illusion of control bias				
Investment decision	0.573			
Optimism bias	0.487	0.510		
Overconfidence bias	0.768	0.640	0.511	

Source: Author's calculation

Heterotrait-monotrait (HTMT) ratio data were used to illustrate the discriminant validity of the instrument. The HTMT ratio of all the variables, as shown in Table 15.4, was less than the maximum limit of 0.85 [73], demonstrating that the instrument is valid in its ability to discriminate across groups of people.

Structural Model Investigation Results
After confirming the measurements, we analyzed the R square and model fit outcomes using the structural model. Furthermore, the bootstrapping method was used to assess path coefficient values. As depicted in Table 15.5, the model fitness was demonstrated with SRMR criteria, wherein the

Table 15.5 Model fit results.

Model fit	Saturated model	Estimated model
SRMR	0.096	0.096
d_ULS	4.016	4.016
d_G	1.887	1.887
Chi-square	883.501	883.501
NFI	.627	.627

Source: Author's calculation

Table 15.6 R Square results.

Dependent variable	R Square	R Square adjusted
Investment decision	0.444	0.426

Source: Author's calculation

SRMR value was found to be 0.096, below the set criteria of 0.80 [74], illustrating the proposed model to be of good fit.

Table 15.6 shows that the R square value for investment decisions is 0.444. It means that 44% of the variance in investment decisions is caused by a combination of biases, including the illusion of control, optimism, and overconfidence.

All the structural relationships were measured through the path coefficient results. Table 15.7 shows a strong and positive relationship between

Table 15.7 Hypothesis testing results.

Hypothesis	Proposed structural relationship	Beta	P values	Inference
H1	Illusion of control -> investment decision	0.226	0.157	Not supported
H2	Optimism bias -> investment decision	0.149	0.191	Not supported
H3	Overconfidence bias -> investment Decision	0.399	0.008	Supported

Source: Author's calculation

overconfidence bias and investment decisions ($\beta = 0.399$, $p < 0.05$), accepting H3. However, we discovered an insignificant but positive relationship between the illusion of control and investment decisions, leading us to reject H1. Likewise, we found that optimism bias had an insignificant positive relationship with investment decisions; thus, we reject H2. Therefore, the relationship between optimism bias and the illusion of control in investment decisions cannot be generalized to the whole population.

15.5 Discussion

In today's world, making investment decisions is a challenging task that requires the expertise of many financial specialists. Every investor faces the difficulty of operating in an increasingly unpredictable financial environment. In today's unpredictable environment, decision-making has become challenging [75]. The significance of investors in financial investments has grown over time, leading to a rise in the number of studies conducted in this field. The emergence of this field has captured the attention of numerous academics, drawn to its increasing relevance. The global importance of risk aversion only adds to its appeal. Extensive study has demonstrated that various behavioral biases impact investors' choices. These biases affect the investor's ability to make money. The current study also aims to assess the impact of three types of cognitive biases on the choices about financial investments that Indian investors make.

The research's first hypothesis states a significant positive relationship between investment choices and the illusion of control bias. The findings, however, show that there is no significant relationship between these two factors ($\beta = 0.226$, $p > 0.05$). According to Gino et al. [76], there was no substantial impact of the illusion of control on investment choices. This result aligns with recent studies; however, the findings seem to contradict those of Iqbal [79], Qureshi et al. [80], and Bashir et al. [81]. As per the article, it has been observed that the illusion of control bias affects stock market decision-making by investors. The study's second hypothesis also emphasizes optimism's significant influence on investing choices. Contrary to early predictions, the results show that there is no statistically significant link between the two variables ($\beta = 0.149$, $p > 0.05$); this conclusion aligns with those of Chhapra et al. [77] and supports the fact that these factors hold no significant value when it comes to investment decisions. However, empirical research like those by Rupinder Kaur Gill [78] and Iqbal [79] indicates that the overoptimism bias causes excessive trading by investors and leads them to believe they have a lesser chance of experiencing an adverse event than others. Therefore, based on the evidence gathered, it can be concluded that the influence of optimism and the illusion of control over investment decisions is irrelevant.

The third hypothesis has been analyzed that overconfidence influences investing decisions significantly. The results suggest that overconfidence favors investors' choices ($\beta = 0.399$, $p < 0.05$), consistent with other investigations' outcomes. It indicates that a large number of investors have an extensive amount of confidence in their decisions and believe they have made the right choices. The investors credit their investment skills for the profit growth they have experienced. Research conducted by Mufti *et al.* [85] and Isidore and Christie [86] consistently shows that investors' investment decision-making is positively impacted by their overconfidence. In terms of psychology, this indicates that investors cannot make better investment selections because of the overconfidence bias. Many studies have shown that being too confident in investments can have adverse financial consequences. This discovery contradicts previous research and emphasizes the significance of being cautious and knowledgeable in managing personal finances [87].

15.5.1   Conclusion and Implications

This study aims to assess investors' optimism, overconfidence, or control illusions when making investing decisions. The goal was accomplished using a systematic questionnaire to get accurate information from current investors knowledgeable about the market and their prior results, skills, and viewpoints on prospective investing strategies and stock markets. Five hundred people participated in the survey, and 362 responses were used after removing irrelevant ones. Male respondents comprised 52% of the sample, whereas female respondents comprised 47%. This study supports earlier studies that overconfidence affects investment decisions in a good way. However, the study did not discover a significant impact of the illusion of control and optimism bias on investing choices, in contrast to expectations. As a result, the statistics could not precisely reflect the respondents' genuine sentiments or opinions. All investors are advised to consider these biases as risk considerations to their investing decisions. To be regarded as informed investors, they must make a checklist of these variables before making investment decisions. The research also advises investors to construct a suitable investment portfolio, thoroughly identify and examine behavioral aspects that influence investing decisions, avoid mindlessly adopting the viewpoints of others, and think carefully and rationally while making investments.

This study has several implications for individuals and institutions, as it will help them learn about the effects of behavioral biases. Investors must clearly understand their preferences and results to make informed decisions in their best interests. This awareness can help prevent poor investment decisions. These findings may also be of great use to brokerage firms and other financial organizations when formulating policies about the operations of stock markets and their business sectors. Financial advisers can enhance clients' portfolios by considering their psychology, resulting in more effective financial planning. The result of this study can be tremendously valuable for policymakers in the stock market. By gaining crucial insights, policymakers can effectively promote the efficient functioning of the stock market and make informed decisions.

15.5.2   Limitations and Future Directions

The understanding has some limits that require special attention:

1. First, the study only focuses on three behavior biases: the illusion of control, optimism, and overconfidence. Other factors, such as risk acceptance, financial knowledge, and personality traits, can also impact investors' decisions. Future research should consider these other factors to understand better how biases influence investing choices.
2. Second, the research is based only on Delhi-NCR city. The findings need to be more generalizable to other parts of India or the world, and a futuristic approach is required in different regions to judge the consistency.
3. Third, the study focuses only on the salaried group working in IT and banking professions, faculties, and students. The findings may need to be more generalizable to other salaried groups of professionals, such as those in the healthcare or retail industries. Future research should focus on other salaried groups to see if the findings are consistent.

The study provides valuable insights into how behavior foundations affect investment outcomes. However, the limitations of the research should be considered when evaluating the results. Here are some specific examples of other factors that could be studied in future research:

- Risk appetite: What level of risk are investors ready to accept?
- Financial literacy: How knowledgeable are investors about financial markets and products?
- Personality traits: Do certain personality traits make investors more or less susceptible to biases?

15.5.3   Notes

[1] Source: The Hindu.com survey 2022-23. Available at:https://www.thehindu.com/news/cities/Delhi/delhis-per-capita-income-grew-by-754-in-2022-23-survey/article66643488.eceni

References

1. Fernandez, P., The capital asset pricing model, in: *Economic Ideas You Should Forget*, vol. 18, pp. 47–49, 2017, https://doi.org/10.1007/978-3-319-47458-8_19.
2. Sharpe, W.F., Capital assest prices: A theory of market equilibrium under conditions of risk. *J. Finance*, *XIX*, 3, 425–442, 1964, https://doi.org/10.1111/j.1540-6261.1964.tb02865.
3. Shah, S.Z.A., Ahmad, M., Mahmood, F., Heuristic biases in investment decision-making and perceived market efficiency. *Qual. Res. Financ. Mark.*, *10*, 1, 85–110, 2018, https://doi.org/10.1108/qrfm-04-2017-0033.
4. Mishra, K.C. and Metilda, M.J., A study on the impact of investment experience, gender, and level of education on overconfidence and self-attribution bias. *IIMB Manage. Rev.*, *27*, 4, 228–239, 2015, https://doi.org/10.1016/j.iimb.2015.09.001.
5. Kumar, V., Dudani, R., Latha, K., The big five personality traits and psychological biases: An exploratory study. *Curr. Psychol.*, *42*, 8, 6587–6597, 2023. https://doi.org/10.1007/s12144-021-01999-8.
6. Kumari, S. and Arora, M., Risk taking in financial decisions as a function of age, gender: Mediating role of loss aversion and regret. *Int. J. Appl. Psychol.*, *5*, 4, 83–89, 2015, https://doi.org/10.5923/j.ijap.20150504.01.
7. Mehta, K. and Sharma, R., Contrarian and momentum investment strategies: Evidence from indian stock market. *Int. J. Appl. Bus. Econ. Res.*, 15, 9, 107–118, 2017.
8. Sharma, M. and Firoz, M., Delineating investors' rationality and behavioural biases-evidence from the indian stock market. *Int. J. Manage. Pract.*, *15*, 1, 59–86, 2022, https://doi.org/10.1504/IJMP.2022.119925.

9. Kahneman, D. and Tversky, A., Prospect theory: An analysis of decision under risk. *Econometrica*, 47, 263–292, 1979, https://www.worldscientific.com/doi/abs/10.1142/9789814417358_0006.

10. Trehan, B. and Sinha, A.K., A study of existence of overconfidence biases among investors and its impact on investment decision, *ELK Asia Pacific Journals – Special Issue (2018)*, 3, 697–703, 2017.

11. Qadri, S.U. and Shabbir, M., An empirical study of overconfidence and illusion of control biases, impact on investor's decision making: An evidence from ISE. *Eur. J. Innov. Bus. Manage.*, 6, 14, 38–44, 2014, www.iiste.org.

12. Shefrin, H.M., Behavioral corporate finance. *SSRN Electron. J.*, 14, 3, 113–126, 2005, https://doi.org/http://dx.doi.org/10.2139/ssrn.288257.

13. Qasim, M., Hussain, R.Y., Mehboob, I., Arshad, M., Impact of herding behavior and overconfidence bias on investors' decision-making in Pakistan. *Accounting*, 5, 2, 81–90, 2019, https://doi.org/10.5267/j.ac.2018.7.001.

14. Kahneman, D. and Riepe, M.W., Portfolio construction forum kahneman aspects of investor psychology. *J. Portf. Manag*, 24, 4, 67–91, 1998.

15. Brown, G.W. and Cliff, M.T., Investor sentiment and asset valuation. *J. Bus.*, 78, 2, 405–440, 2005, https://doi.org/10.1086/427633.

16. Camerer, C. and Lovallo, D., Overconfidence and excess entry: An experimental approach. *Am. Econ. Rev.*, 89, 1, 306–318, 1999, https://doi.org/10.1257/aer.89.1.306.

17. Chen, C., Ishfaq, M., Ashraf, F., Sarfaraz, A., Wang, K., Mediating role of optimism bias and risk perception between emotional intelligence and decision-making: A serial mediation model. *Front. Psychol.*, 13, June, 1–9, 2022, https://doi. org/10.3389/fpsyg.2022.914649.

18. Sharma, R., Mehta, K., Goel, A., Non-linear relationship between board size and performance of Indian companies. *J. Manage. Gov.*, 27, 1277–1301, 2022, https://doi. org/10.1007/s10997-022-09651-8.

19. Sharma, R., Mehta, K., Sharma, O., Exploring deep learning to determine the optimal environment for stock prediction analysis. *Int. Conf. Comput. Perform. Evaluation (ComPE)*, 1, 148–152, 2021.

20. Kartini, K. and Nahda, K., Behavioral biases on investment decision: A case study in Indonesia. *J. Asian Finance Econ. Bus.*, 8, 3, 1231–1240, 2021, https://doi.org/10.13106/jafeb.2021.vol8.no3.1231.

21. Mehta, K., Sharma, R., Vyas, V., Kuckreja, J.S., Exit strategy decision by venture capital firms in India using fuzzy AHP. *J. Entrep. Emerg. Econ.*, 14, 4, 643–669, 2022, https://doi.org/10.1108/JEEE-05-2020-0146.

22. Goyal, N. and Kumar, S., Evidence on rationality and behavioural biases in investment decision making. *Qual. Res. Financial Market*, 8, 4, 270–287, 2015, https://doi.org/10.1108/QRFM-05-2016-0016.

23. Chira, I., Adams, M., Thornton, B., Behavioral bias within the decision making process. *J. Bus. Econ. Res. (JBER)*, 6, 8, 11–20, 2011, https://doi.org/10.19030/jber.v6i8.2456.

24. Barber, B.M. and Odean, T., Why do investors trade too much?, *Am. Econom. Rev.*, 89, 1279–1298, 2006, https://www.safalniveshak.com/wp-content/uploads/2012/07/Why-Do-Investors- Trade-Too-Much.pdf.

25. Ahmad, M., Zulfiqar, S., Shah, A., Overconfidence heuristic-driven bias in investment decision-making and performance: Mediating effects of risk perception and moderating effects of financial literacy. *J. Econ. Admin. Sci.*, 38 1, 60–90. 2020, https://doi.org/10.1108/ JEAS-07-2020-0116.

26. Barnes, J.H., Cognitive biases and their impact on strategic planning. *Strateg. Manage. J.*, 5, 2, 129–137, 1984, https://doi.org/10.1002/smj.4250050204.

27. Statman, M., Thorley, S., Vorkink, K., Investor overconfidence and trading volume. *SSRN Elec. J.*, 19, 1531–1565, 2003, https://www.jstor.org/ stable/4123481.

28. Ngoc, L.T.B., Behavior pattern of individual investors in stock market. *Int. J. Biol. Macromol.*, 9, 1, 1–16, 2014, https://doi.org/10.5539/ijbm.v9n1p1.

29. Malmendier, U. and Tate, G., Does overconfidence affect corporate investment? CEO overconfidence measures revisited. *Eur. Financ. Manage.*, 11, 5, 649–659, 2005, https://doi.org/10.1111/ j.1354-7798.2005.00302.x.

30. Aljifri, R., Investor psychology in the stock market: An empirical study of the impact of overconfidence on firm valuation. *Borsa Istanb. Rev.*, 23, 1, 93–112, 2023, https://doi.org/10.1016/j.bir.2022.09.010.

31. Sharma, R., Mehta, K., Vyas, V., Responsible investing: A study on non-economic goals and investors' characteristics. *Appl. Finance Lett.*, 9, SI, 63–78, 2020, https://doi.org/10.24135/afl.v9i2.245.

32. Vyas, V., Mehta, K., Sharma, R., The nexus between toxic-air pollution, health expenditure, and economic growth: An empirical study using ARDL. *Int. Rev. Econ. Finance*, 84, 154–166, 2023, https://doi.org/10.1016/j.iref.2022.11.017.

33. Mehta, K., Sharma, R., Vyas, V., Efficiency and ranking of sustainability index of India using DEA-TOPSIS. *J. Indian Bus. Res.*, 11, 2, 179–199, 2019, https://doi.org/10.1108/JIBR-02-2018-0057.

34. Metwally, A.H., The effect of overconfidence bias on investors decisions in the egyptian stock market: The role of information. *Alex. Univ. Adm. Sci.*, 60, 47–85, 2023.

35. Manani, K.N., Pednekar, D., Maurya, A.M., Impact of behavioural finance on investment decision-a study of investment behaviour in Mumbai region. *Korea Rev. Int. Stud.*, 16, 43, 42–53, 2023, https://doi.org/https://www.researchgate.net/publication/370229666.

36. Grou, B. and Tabak, B.M., Ambiguity aversion and illusion of control: Experimental evidence in an emerging market. *J. Behav. Finance*, 9, 1, 22–29, 2008, https://doi.org/10.1080/15427560801897162.

37. Prosad, J.M., Kapoor, S., Sengupta, J., Behavioral biases of indian investors: A survey of Delhi-NCR region, in: *Qualitative Research in Financial Markets*, vol. 7, 2015, https://doi.org/10.1108/QRFM-04-2014-0012.

38. Banerji, J., Kundu, K., Alam, P.A., Influence of behavioral biases on investment behavior. *SCMS J. Indian Manage.*, 17, 1, 81–98, 2020.

39. Syarkani, Y. and Alghifari, E.S., The influence of cognitive biases on investor decision-making: the moderating role of demographic factors. *J. Struct. Biol.*, 26, 2, 183–196, 2022, https://doi.org/10.20885/jsb.vol26.iss2.art5.

40. Ising, A. and Pompian, M., Behavioral finance and wealth management – How to build optimal portfolios that account for investor biases. *Financial Mark. Portf. Manage.*, 21, 4, 491–492, 20072006, https://doi. org/10.1007/s11408-007-0065-3.

41. Mahina, N.J., Muturi, W.M., Memba, F.S., Influence of over-optimism bias on investments at the Rwanda stock exchange. *Int. J. Manage. Commerce*, 5, 1, 169–181, 2017, http://www.ijssit.com.

42. Bashir, D.T., Rasheed, U., Raftar, S., Maqsood, M., Impact of behavioral biases on investors decision making: Male vs female. *IOSR J. Bus. Manage.*, 10, 3, 60–68, 2013, https://doi.org/10.9790/487x-1036068.

43. Yasmin, F. and Ferdaous, J., Behavioral biases affecting investment decisions of capital market investors in Bangladesh: A behavioral finance approach. *Invest. Manage. Financ. Innov.*, 20, 2, 149–159, 2023, https://doi.org/10.21511/imfi.20(2).2023.13.

44. Abdin, S.Z.U., Qureshi, F., Iqbal, J., Sultana, S., Overconfidence bias and investment performance: A mediating effect of risk propensity. *Borsa Istanb. Rev.*, 22, 4, 780–793, 2022, https://doi.org/10.1016/j.bir.2022.03.001.

45. Chen, G., Kim, K.A., Nofsinger, J.R., Rui, O.M., Trading performance, disposition effect, overconfidence, representativeness bias, and experience of emerging market investors. *J. Behav. Decis. Mak.*, 20, 4, 425–451, 2007, https://doi.org/10.1002/bdm.561.

46. Hoffmann, A.O., II, Post, T., Pennings, J.M.E., Individual investor perceptions and behavior during the financial crisis. *J. Bank. Financ.*, 37, 1, 60–74, 2013, https://doi.org/10.1016/j.jbankfin.2012.08.007.

47. Germain, L., Rousseau, F., Vanhems, A., Optimistic & pessimistic trading in financial markets. *SSRN Elec. J.*, 1, 1–33, 2005 *May 2014*, https://doi.org/https://www.researchgate.net/ publication/253509560.

48. Sukanya, R. and Thimmarayappa, R., Impact of behavioural biases in port-folio investment decision making process. *Int. J. Commer. Bus. Manage.*, 4, 4, 1278–1289, 2015.

49. Beuselinck, C., Heyman, D., Pronk, M., Individual investors and option trading: Attention grabbing versus long-term strategies. *SSRN Elec. J.*, 3. 1–57, 2012, https://doi.org/10.2139/ssrn.1745728.

50. Mehta, K., Sharma, R., Vyas, V., A quantile regression approach to study the impact of aluminium prices on the manufacturing sector of India during the COVID era. *Mat. Today: Proc.*, 65, 8, 3506–3511, 2022, ISSN 2214-7853, https://doi.org/10.1016/j.matpr.2022.06.087.

51. Sharma, R., Mehta, K., Rana, R., Cryptocurrency adoption behaviour of millennial investors in India, in: *Perspectives on Blockchain Technology and Responsible Investing*, pp. 135–157, IGI Global, 701 E. Chocolate Avenue Hershey, PA 17033, USA, 2023.

52. Felton, J., Gibson, B., Sanbonmatsu, D.M., Preference for risk in investing as a function of trait optimism and gender. *J. Behav. Finance*, 4, 1, 33–40, 2003, https://doi.org/10.1207/s15427579jpfm0401_05.

53. Chander, R., Sharma, R., Mehta, K., Dividend announcement and informational efficiency: An empirical study of indian stock market. *ICFAI J. Appl. Finance*, 13, 10, 29–42, 2007.

54. Chander, R., Sharma, R., Mehta, K., Impact of dividend announcement on stock prices. *NICE J. Bus.*, 2, 1, 15–29, January-June 2007, ISSN: 0973-449X.

55. Balasuriya, J., Muradoglu, Y.G., Ayton, P., Optimism and portfolio choice. *SSRN Electronic J.*, 1, 1–90, 2012, https://doi.org/10.2139/ssrn.1568908.

56. Vaid, A.J. and Chaudhary, R., Review paper on impact of behavioral biases in financial decision-making. *World J. Adv. Res. Rev.*, 16, 2, 989–997, 2022, https://doi.org/10.30574/wjarr.2022.16.2.1236.

57. Rashid, K., Tariq, Y., Rehman, M.U., Behavioural errors and stock market investment decisions: Recent evidence from Pakistan. *Asian J. Account. Res.*, 7, 2, 129–145, 2022, https://doi.org/10.1108/AJAR-07-2020-0065.

58. Mehta, K., Sharma, R., Vyas, V., Kuckreja, J.S., Exit strategy decision by venture capital firms in India using fuzzy AHP. *J. Entrep. Emerg. Econ.*, 14, 4, 643–669, 2022, https://doi.org/10.1108/JEEE-05-2020-0146.

59. Mouna, A. and Anis, J., A study on small investors' sentiment, financial literacy and stock returns: Evidence for emerging market. *Int. J. Account. Econ. Stud.*, 3, 1, 10, 2015, https://doi.org/10.14419/ijaes.v3i1.4098.

60. Mehta, K., Sharma, R., Chugh, A., Management of forex risk exposure: A study of SMEs and unlisted non-financial firms in India. *Int. J. Appl. Bus. Econ. Res.*, 15, 9, 43–54, 2017.

61. Barber, B.M. and Odean, T., Boys will be boys: Gender, overconfidence, and common stock investment. *Q. J. Econ.*, 116, 1, 261–292, 2001, https://doi.org/10.1162/003355301556400.

62. Dhamija, S. and Agrawal, A., Factors influencing investment decision making process – A select study, 2020, Published at: Shodhganga@INFLIBNET http://hdl.handle.net/10603/350882.

63. Singh, B. and Boora, A., Modelling of behavioural biases effect on investment decision making, 435, 2019, Published at: Shodhganga@INFLIBNET https://doi.org/10.4324/9780429328589-6.

64. Barber, B.M. and Odean, T., Trading is hazardous to your wealth: The common stock investment performance of individual investors. *J. Finance, LV2*, 2, 46–47, 2000.

65. Ullah, S., An empirical study of illusion of control and self-serving attribution bias, impact on investor's decision making: Moderating role of financial literacy. *Res. J. Finance Account.*, 6, 19, 109–118, 2015, www.iiste.org.

66. Hulland, J., Baumgartner, H., Smith, K.M., Marketing survey research best practices: Evidence and recommendations from a review of JAMS articles. *J. Academy Market. Sci.*, 46, 92–108, 2017, https://doi.org/10.1007/s11747-017-0532-y.

67. Sarstedt, M., Ringle, C.M., Hair, J.F., Treating unobserved heterogeneity in PLS-SEM: A multi-method approach. *J. Acad. Mark. Sci.*, 43, 1, 197–217, 2017, https://doi.org/10.1007/978-3-319-64069-3.

68. Hair, J.F., Risher, J.J., Sarstedt, M., Ringle, C.M., When to use and how to report the results of PLS-SEM. *Euro. Bus. Rev.*, 31, 1, 2–24, 2019, https://doi.org/10.1108/EBR-11-2018-0203.

69. Wong, K.K.-K., Mediation analysis, categorical moderation analysis, and higher-order constructs modeling in partial least squares structural equation modeling (PLS-SEM): A B2B example using smartPLS. *Mark. Bull.*, 1, 26, May, 1–22, 2016, https://doi.org/10.13140/RG.2.1.1643.0562.

70. Henseler, J., Ringle, C.M., Sarstedt, M., A new criterion for assessing discriminant validity in variance-based structural equation modeling. *J. Acad. Mark. Sci.*, 43, 1, 115–135, 2015, https://doi.org/10.1007/s11747-014-0403-8.

71. Henseler, J., Hubona, G., Ray, P.A., Using PLS path modeling in new technology research: Updated guidelines. *Ind. Manage. Data Syst.*, 116, 1, 2–20, 2016, https://doi.org/10.1108/IMDS-09-2015-0382.

72. Kannadhasan, M. and Nandagopal, R., Influence of decision makers' characteristics on risk analysis in strategic investment decisions. *J. Mod. Account. Audit.*, 6, 4, 38–44, 2010, https://www.researchgate.net/ publication/235951247.

73. Riaz, T. and Iqbal, H., Impact of overconfidence, illusion of control, self control and optimism bias on investors decision making; Evidence from developing markets. *Res. J. Finance Account.*, 6, 11, 2222–2847, 2015, www. iiste. org.

74. Miller, K.D. and Shapira, Z., An empirical test of heuristics and biases affecting real option valuation. *Strategic Manage. J.*, 29, 3, 269–284, 2004, https://doi.org/10.1002/smj.374.

75. Schwenk, C.R., Cognitive simplification processes in strategic decision-making. *Strateg. Manage. J.*, *17*, 1, 10792–10796, 2016, https://doi.org/ https://doi.org/10.1108/MD-07-2019-1006.

76. Gino, F., Sharek, Z., Moore, D.A., Keeping the illusion of control under control: Ceilings, floors, and imperfect calibration. *Organ. Behav. Hum. Decis.*, *114*, 2, 104–114, 2011, https://doi.org/10.1016/j. obhdp.2010.10.002.

77. Chhapra, I.U., Kashif, M., Rehan, R., Bai, A., An empirical investigation of investor's behavioral biases on financial decision making. *Asian J. Econ. Empir.*, *8*, 3, 99–109, 2018, https://doi.org/10.18488/ journal.1007/2018.7.3/1007.3.99.109.

78. Rupinder Kaur Gill, R.B., Study on behavioral finance, behavioral biases, and investment decisions. *Int. J. Account. Financial Manage. Res.*, *8*, 3, 1–14, 2018, https://doi.org/10.24247/ijafmraug20181.

79. Iqbal, N., Impact of optimism bias on investment decision: Evidence from Islamabad stock exchange, Pakistan. *Res. J. Finance Account.*, *6*, 19, 74–79, 2015.

80. Qureshi, S.A., Rehman, K., Hunjra, A., II, Factors affecting investment decision making of funds managers. *Wulfenia J.*, *19*, 10, 280–291, 2012.

81. Bashir, T., Azam, S.N., Butt, S.A.A., Javed, S.A., Tanvir, S.A., Are behavioral biases influenced by demographic characteristics & personality traits? Evidence from Pakistan. *Eur. Sci. J.*, *9*, 29, 277–293, 2013.

82. Nareswari, N., Balqista, A.S., Negoro, N.P., The impact of behavioral economics on investment decision. *Jurnal Manajemen Dan Keuangan*, *10*, 1, 15–27, 2021.

83. Kengatharan, L. and Kengatharan, N., The influence of behavioral factors in making investment decisions and performance: Study on investors of colombo stock exchange, Sri Lanka. *Asian J. FInance Account.*, *6*, 1, 1, 2014, https://doi.org/10.5296/ajfa.v6i1.4893.

84. Al-Dahan, N.S.H., Hasan, M.F., Jadah, H.M., Effect of cognitive and emotional biases on investor decisions: An analytical study of the Iraq stock exchange. *Int. J. Innov. Creat. Change.*, *9*, 10, 30–47, 2019, https://www. researchgate.net/publication/338955870.

85. Mufti, S.A. and Shah, D.Z.A., Impact of illusion of control on perceived efficiency in pakistani financial markets. *J. Soc Sci.*, *5*, 2, 100–110, 2011.

86. Isidore R, R. and Christie, P., The relationship between the income and behavioural biases. *J. Econ. Finance Adm. Sci.*, *24*, 47, 127–144, 2019, https://doi. org/10.1108/JEFAS-10-2018-0111.
87. Waweru, N.M., Munyoki, E., Uliana, E., The effects of behavioural factors in investment decision-making: A survey of institutional investors operating at the Nairobi stock exchange. *Int. J. Bus. Emerg. Mark.*, *1*, 1, 1399, 2008, https://doi.org/10.1504/IJBEM.2008.019243.

16

Alternative Data in Investment Management

Rangapriya Saivasan* and Madhavi Lokhande

*International School of Management Excellence, Research Centre,
Affiliated with the University of Mysore, Bangalore, Karnataka, India*

Abstract
Alternative data refers to nontraditional, unstructured information from various
sources, offering unique insights to enhance investment decision-making. This
study explores data quality and validation in alternative data analysis for investments, aiming to gain a competitive edge and make informed decisions. In this
study, qualitative research, utilizing secondary sources, thematic, and user analysis,
explores prominent themes and practices in alternative data adoption. The challenges of alternative data in investment management include data quality, privacy
concerns, and lack of standardization. Best practices like data governance, integrating multiple sources, and continuous monitoring enhance insights from alternative
data. Data quality and validation are crucial for leveraging alternative data effectively, aiming to gain an edge with robust validation and best practices for informed
investment decisions. High-quality data and validation processes are imperative for
harnessing the power of alternative data in investment analysis. Embracing alternative data and overcoming challenges opens doors to innovation and improved
investment outcomes in the evolving investment management landscape.

Keywords: Alternative data, investment management, data standardization,
data privacy

16.1 Introduction

Alternative data in investment management refers to data that is not
conventionally available or considered while analyzing a company or

Corresponding author: rangapriyas.isme20@gmail.com

Renuka Sharma and Kiran Mehta (eds.) *Deep Learning Tools for Predicting Stock Market Movements*,
(391–408) © 2024 Scrivener Publishing LLC

investment opportunity. By utilizing these sources of data, industry practitioners can gain insights into markets and investments that are not available to traditional players. Furthermore, this data can provide valuable information about a company or investment opportunity that would otherwise be overlooked [1]. Hedge funds have actively adopted alternative data into their conventional decision-making framework. The private equity ecosystem is close to follow, given the limited financial data and public information available for their investment opportunities [2–6]. These first adopters of data analytics stand to gain a competitive edge before alternative data becomes a widespread phenomenon and essential to the conventional decision-making framework. The alternative data market is projected to experience substantial growth, reaching a value of $135.7 billion by 2030, with a remarkable compound annual growth rate (CAGR) of 52.1% from 2022 to 2030. This growth is primarily fuelled by the escalating demand for nontraditional data sources from financial institutions and other organizations. Alternative data encompasses various types such as social media data, mobile phone data, and satellite imagery, offering insights into market trends and behavior beyond the scope of traditional data sources. The market is segmented based on data type (including social media data, mobile phone data, satellite imagery, and others), application (such as risk management, investment research, and marketing), and end-user (including financial institutions, insurance companies, and other organizations). Driving factors for this market include the increasing demand for nontraditional data sources, the rise of big data analytics, and the growing adoption of artificial intelligence (AI). The primary market for alternative data is projected to be the financial institutions' sector, with the insurance companies segment ranking second in terms of market size. These trends highlight the industry's shift toward leveraging alternative data and advanced analytics techniques to drive informed decision-making and gain a competitive edge. The market for alternative data is anticipated to experience the highest growth rate in the Asia-Pacific region, with North America and Europe following closely behind [7–10].

"Alternative data is untapped alpha"; however, the phenomenon is clouted with risks [11]. Some of the risks around alternative data in investment management include challenges with data quality, limited data availability, privacy concerns due to sensitive information, lack of regulatory framework, and the potential for model risk stemming from complex and less transparent modeling techniques. The alternative data also encounters several other issues, such as difficulty evaluating a dataset's/finding's value to investors and technical difficulties in effectively exploiting these datasets on a large scale. It is also being observed that the earliest alternative datasets are now less robust in supporting alpha generation. This subdued impact may be attributed to the proliferation which has led to a decrease in information advantage derived from the dataset. Alternative data, to sustain its success and find a permanent place in the conventional decision-making framework, should be able to generate deeper and more meaningful insights, firms that use these insights should continue to generate innovative investment ideas and alternative data sources at regular intervals [12–14].

It is evident that alternative data has the potential to tap into hidden alpha; however, there is a need to mitigate the challenges prudently to achieve optimal insights from alternative data to enable market outperformance. The objective of this study is to emphasize the significance of data quality and validation in alternative data analysis for investment purposes. It aims to highlight the importance of ensuring accurate and reliable alternative data when making investment decisions. The study discusses various validation techniques and best practices that can be employed to enhance the quality of alternative data and improve its usability in investment analysis. By exploring the subject of data quality and validation, the study aims to provide valuable insights and recommendations to investment professionals on effectively leveraging alternative data for informed decision-making. The rest of the chapter is organized; thus, Section 16.2 presents the literature review, Section 16.3 outlines the research methodology, Section 16.4 presents the results and discussions, Section 16.5 lays out the implications of this study, and finally Section 16.6 presents the concluding observations.

16.2   Literature Review

A study by Element22 (2019) [15] surveyed 20 asset management firms with a combined $14 trillion AUM (assets under management) and reaffirmed the notion that most leading fund houses were turning to advanced analytics and alternative data sources to enhance their performance, generate alpha consistently, improve operational efficiency, and grow their clientele. The study indicated that 85% of the fund houses were already employing advanced analytics and 55% were turning toward alternative data to capture the edge in finding deeper insights that were not yet exploited by competitors. There are efforts to combine alternative data with conventional data to build AI models to enable sustained outperformance and robust risk management [16]. Ekster and Kolm [3] explored alternative data in the institutional investment industry, highlighting its use to enhance portfolio returns. The work discusses the challenges in valuing alternative datasets and addresses technical obstacles such as entity mapping and ticker-tagging. They present methodologies, including the golden triangle event study and report cards, to assess the value of alternative data. Through a case study on healthcare data, they demonstrate a significant improvement in revenue prediction accuracy, reducing mean absolute error from 88% to 2.6%. Overall, the article provides valuable insights into the industry and methodologies for leveraging alternative data effectively. A study examines the use of alternative data, specifically social media commentary, satellite imagery, and GPS data, in trading and investment management. The research methodology employed involved conducting interviews with professionals from investment management, algorithmic trading firms, and alternative data providers. A comprehensive collection of interview data was gathered between 2014 and 2020, encompassing global financial hubs such as London, New York, Chicago, Amsterdam, and the Bay Area. From the extensive pool of 213 interviews, a subsample of 58 interviews was selected, comprising individuals involved in alternative data provision, sourcing, utilization for investment management and trading, and leveraging machine learning techniques. The findings highlight the growing importance of alternative data in these industries, particularly the use of social media sentiment analytics for predicting stock prices. The study emphasizes the open-ended nature of alternative data and the need for standardization efforts. It also explores the processes of prospecting and association related to utilizing alternative data. Additionally, the study uncovers the financialization of data and raises governance concerns arising from the widespread adoption of alternative data [17, 18]. There is an increase in the use of data that originates outside of the standard repertoire of data that is relevant to the market. The application of alternative data is slowly but steadily gaining ground, it is the next frontier in data-driven decision-making.

Monk *et al.* [1] proposed six dimensions to characterize alternative datasets in this study reliability, actionability, freshness, scarcity, comprehensiveness, and excludability. These dimensions contribute to the value of alt-data in defensive and defensible strategies. Reliability ensures trustworthiness, actionability enables informed decision-making, and freshness ensures the use of up-to-date information. Comprehensiveness provides a deeper understanding of risks and inefficiencies in defensive strategies, whereas scarcity affects excludability and the rate at which alt-data spreads, impacting defensive and defensible approaches differently. By re-evaluating the approach toward handling and using alternative data, experts will be able to choose alternative data that aligns best with their resources and objectives. Another study aims to enhance the reliability of information acquisition and the accuracy of data processing in the financial industry by exploring the utilization of AI technologies, specifically in analyzing alternative financial data. It addresses the absence of appropriate standards in integrating the financial industry with the Internet of Things (IoT). Through an examination of relevant research papers and standards, the study proposes a standardized evaluation framework. Performance verification of the framework demonstrates exceptional results, with comparative experiments showcasing a remarkable prediction accuracy of 95.44% and significantly reduced prediction errors compared to other model algorithms. The developed financial intelligence standard model exhibits effectiveness in precisely predicting alternative financial data while ensuring reliability and validity. Moreover, the study presents a comprehensive evaluation method for smart technology in alternative financial data, encompassing various steps such as identifying the evaluation object, assembling the evaluation team, selecting evaluation indicators, constructing the evaluation system, implementing the evaluation process, and determining comprehensive outcomes [19].

Considering the novelty of this phenomenon, the existing literature in this field remains relatively sparse and in its nascent stages. However, this study aims to bridge the gap by uncovering the multifaceted implications of alternative data. It explores the current landscape, identifying key stakeholders and their utilization of alternative data while also highlighting the inherent risks involved in its application. Furthermore, the work provides insights into the way forward for alternative data in investment management, outlining potential strategies and opportunities for maximizing its benefits. By offering a comprehensive analysis of this evolving field, this study contributes to the advancement and understanding of alternative data's role in shaping investment management practices.

16.3   Research Methodology

A qualitative research methodology was employed which involved a thorough examination of existing literature, industry reports, scholarly articles, and other relevant secondary sources. These sources provided valuable insights and data on the adoption and utilization of alternative data in investment management. By drawing on a wide range of secondary data, the study aimed to capture a holistic view of the subject matter. Thematic analysis was employed as a primary analytical technique. This method enables the identification of recurring themes and patterns in the data, allowing for a systematic exploration of the phenomenon [20]. This analysis provided a deeper understanding of the various applications, benefits, and challenges associated with alternative data. In addition to thematic analysis, user observation played a significant role in the research methodology. User observation involves directly observing or interacting with individuals to gain insights into the behaviors, experiences, and perspectives of any phenomenon [21]. The current best practices within the industry based on secondary data sources across prominent hedge fund houses, private equity firms, and other investment management institutions were analyzed. This user observation provided valuable insights into the practical aspects of using alternative data, including the challenges faced, the strategies employed, and the potential benefits realized. The combination of thematic analysis and user observation allowed for a comprehensive exploration of the novel phenomenon, it provided deep insights into the nuances of the opportunities and risks associated [22]. The insights drawn using the above methodology are important as they provide a comprehensive understanding of alternative data for informed decision-making and guided utilization.

16.4   Results and Discussion

16.4.1   Understanding the Current Landscape

A survey across 25 asset managers, fund managers, and chief investment officers provides the insight that 45% of the buy-side respondents have already induced alternative data as part of their portfolio construction process, 24% of the respondents plan to include alternative data as part of their conventional decision framework over the next 12 months. Around 44% of the respondents were using alternative data for over 4 years. A predominant portion of consumption of alternative data came from quantitative finance/systematic equity firms (44%), followed by fundamental/discretionary equity providers (32%), and the balance was by the firms that implemented the hybrid framework which is now known as the "quantamental" approach [23].

There is growing acknowledgment that such data is useful in the detection of risk exposures, prediction of market direction, and identifying new factors that have an impact on the stock's returns. The most popular alternative data that is making headway in the conventional decision-making framework is social media sentiment analytics. This phenomenon is at a very nascent stage, hence the term "alternative data" has become a placeholder for any data that has some potential to facilitate deeper insights. There is a need to standardize the definition and scope of "alternative data" by various stakeholders in the market, and this will enable advancements in this phenomenon in a meaningful and purposeful manner.

- User community and data type: At present, the main consumers of alternative data are hedge funds and private equity, in every likelihood it may soon become a part of the conventional decision-making framework in mutual fund houses, pension funds, insurance companies, portfolio management services, alternative investment fund houses, and other Banking, Financial Services, and Insurance (BFSI) entities. It is also expected the alternative data can be used to detect risk exposures, and hence, risk mitigation efforts could also be a key driver for the growth in the alternative data market. From the perspective of alternative data sources, credit card and debit card transaction data is expected to rise at the fastest CAGR due to the high levels of accuracy, this dataset is increasingly demanded by asset managers to gain insights on the consumer spending pattern which could potentially provide insight on the direction of the economy. At present, hedge fund managers are the most avid consumers of alternative data, they are under constant pressure to deliver alpha; hence, in their consistent endeavor to find cost-effective methods of generating alpha, there is increased demand for new and meaningful information from alternative datasets [24, 25].

  The data sources have increased over time, it is not limited to credit card and debit card transactions and email receipts but extend to social media activity, mobile activity, IoT-based devices, sensor-based tracking, satellites, and e-com portal activity. There is a constant endeavor to the identification of correlations and patterns within the datasets to deepen the insights which could help in the ideation of new investment opportunities [5, 26, 27].

- Usage by geography: North America was the early adopter of alternative data, as ~68% of the usage in 2021 was attributed to this region. This region is likely to lead the demand over the period between 2022 and 2030, and there are many emerging alternative data providers mushrooming within this region, which remains the driving factor for the dominance of this region. However, the Asia-Pacific (APAC) region is likely to emerge as the fastest-growing alternative data consumer over the forecasted period. Within the APAC region, economies like Singapore, India, Thailand, and China are likely to drive the demand [5].

- Data providers: Prominent companies such as Eagle Alpha, Quandl, Advan, YipitData, and M Science are providing various types of alternative data including credit and debit card transactions, geo-location traffic records, email receipts, satellite and weather data, social and sentiment data, web-scraped data, and mobile usage data. The acquisition of Quandl by NASDAQ in the year 2018 solidified the pertinence of alternative data. In the words of Quandl CEO Tammer Kamel, "Investors demand actionable intelligence from new and expensive data sources at an increasingly rapid pace." He further added that it is pertinent to work closely with industry practitioners and the decision-making community to evaluate the huge quantum of data which when streamlined as information can provide deep insights and investment ideas to deliver alpha consistently [28, 29].

The growing acceptance of alternative data is still clouted with certain risks. Mitigation of these risks is crucial as it could lead to enhanced decision-making, improved investment strategies, and unlocking the full potential of alternative data in driving financial success.

16.4.2   Challenges in the Adoption of Alternative Data

Incorporating alternative data into the mainstream decision framework presents unique challenges. This section explores the key obstacles and considerations associated with the adoption of alternative data in traditional decision-making processes.

Privacy and Data Protection: There are several privacy regulations related to consumer privacy and general data protection which are being curated to ensure that data snooping does not lead to personal privacy violations. Any dataset that is being analyzed should be free from personally identifiable information (PII), multiple datasets can conveniently mine personal information alongside data and, this could lead to a severe breach of personal privacy. Data providers' stringent compliance with privacy policies remains a critical factor for long-term sustenance [5]. This is an impediment that alternative data providers need to account for in the future, and this reiterates the need to define the scope and limitation of alternative data which could eventually lead to standardization. Such standardization can then provide the arena for the measurability of informational value drawn from alternative data in the decision-making framework, a key to large-scale adaptation of the phenomenon as part of the conventional decision-making framework.

Consistent Competitive Edge: There is increasing evidence that alternative data can provide the much-needed competitive edge, there are practically no hedge funds that shy away from using alternative data. Pipino *et al.* [31] announced that the data from Thasos, RS Metrics, Apptopia, TipRanks, Orbital Insight, PredictWallStreet, 280 First, Predata, OWL Analytics, and Symphony Pharma, all high-quality alternative data companies, will be available on their terminal for consumption by the investor community, this is a leading sign that indicates the adoption of the alternative dataset within the conventional decision framework across a large set of stakeholders. However, there is a growing need for new datasets as the edge derived from the earliest alternative data starts waning with its increased adoption across the community. The competitive edge remains only when there are a select few who are party to the information derived from the dataset, however, for the data provider scalability becomes inevitable to build a sustainable business practice. Alternative data is indeed a "mixed blessing" that has a few challenges to overcome before it finds its way into a legacy framework.

Quality and Accuracy: There have been concerns about the accuracy, quality, completeness, cost, and accessibility of alternative data. The improvement of quality is seemingly a "double-edged sword," there is a requirement for both the end user and the provider to know the nuances of the data available and the potential use of the data to help improve the quality. With the growing need to tap into new data sources to gain a competitive edge, it is only a matter of time before alternative data becomes a part of the conventional decision framework. There will, however, be a constant endeavor to source new data and identify patterns and trends to gain an informational edge. This essentially entails the endeavor to improve the data quality and accuracy for all emerging alternative datasets. It becomes important to identify data quality metrics for each category of alternative data, thus ensuring that accuracy and quality are of optimal level. The ability to gauge the informational value derived from each of the alternative datasets will not only translate to greater acceptance among the stakeholders but will also facilitate weeding out noise from the dataset, thus increasing the signal-to-noise ratio [30, 32, 33]. The study by Caserta [32] indicated that credit/debit card transactions and data scraped on the web are considered to be highly accurate and thus can provide deeper/meaningful insights. Data providers are required to scrub the PII from the dataset, the skeletal data received in many cases such as geolocation can be inaccurate and less impactful. Many critiques are of the view that a large part of the data generated in the name of alternative data is practically useless to identify the stock market direction, this can be attributed to the high noise in the dataset and the associated costs to clean/vet the data to separate the signals (if any) [34].

Privacy and Compliance: Financial consumer protection (FCP) principles refer to the legal and regulatory framework that applies to all alternative data service providers. There is a growing need to establish a standardized and comprehensive approach to consumer and data protection problems. There are specific points that need to be addressed concerning data sourcing:

- Lawful data collection aligned with a compatible and specific purpose.
- Role of consent for the usage of data collected beyond the original purpose.
- Defining and reinforcing the period of data retention
- In the era of APIs (application programming interfaces), will this information be akin to public information?

Alternative data providers must scrub the data of their last trace of PIIs and adhere to rigorous standards of security, reliability, and efficiency. Furthermore, it becomes vital to protect the data from any loss, corruption, damage, destruction, and misuse. The legal and regulatory framework around alternative data and big data, in general, is quite hazy. There is a need to standardize the dos and don'ts, with the cross-border data flows, it is extremely tough to hold regional security standards. There is a requirement for a decentralized regulatory framework that can be developed after an in-depth investigation of the implications of a potential data breach for financial consumers. This can help in developing an appropriate regulatory and industry-level response [35–37]. As a proactive step, SEC's (Securities Exchange Commission) Division of Examinations observes that alternative data needs to be examined on a priority basis, it is an area where the authorities expect the companies (service providers and end users) to have relevant, consistent, and established oversight on compliance. Section 204A within the Investment Advisers Act of 1940 states that investment professionals have to "establish, maintain, and enforce written policies and procedures reasonably designed, taking into consideration the nature of such investment adviser's business, to prevent the misuse of material, non-public information" [38].

Prohibitively High Costs: The cost of alpha generation has risen manifold with the market evolution. In the words of Tim Gaumer, Director of Research at Refinitiv, "Proving skill as an investment manager has never been harder. A lot of what was once considered alpha can now be explained by exposure to factors." Finding alpha just got harder, asset managers are always scouting for new datasets, patterns, and trends which can help them deliver value to investors. The best service providers are expected to lower the cost of finding alpha in data. It is apparent that due to the abysmally low alternative data quality, quant analysts spend anywhere between 40% and 80% of their time cleaning and normalizing the data for further use. Sourcing alternative data not only requires specialized tools but also requires trained hands to depersonalize, cleanse, and normalize them for further analysis. These factors have added to the cost of procuring alternative data by the decision-making community [39]. In a survey by Fama [40], where 69 US-based and European industry practitioners (fund managers, CIOs, and portfolio managers) were interviewed, around 38% of the respondents indicated that "prohibitively high fees" of acquiring alternative data was the primary reason for them not including alternative data into their mainstream decision framework. The management is also unsure of the informational value that alternative data brings to the model's ability to outperform the index, thus making them question the expense of such data where there is no proven legacy of value. It is also a concern that alternative datasets that are robust and accurate today, seem to diminish in value as they are adopted by a larger set of audience, they no longer provide the much-needed informational edge needed for alpha generation. The yearly subscription fee for alternative datasets can range between $25,000 and more than $500,000, and transactional data such as credit card/debit card spending and GPS tracking data is highly expensive. However, the correlation between the dataset and the stock returns has no sound empirical backing which makes it a questionable expense from the management's perspective. The cost can be lowered only by achieving economies of scale; however, if the data is available to all the decision-making community and investors alike, it is akin to public information which is already priced into the stock's value leaving no room for alpha generation [41, 42].

Integration with Traditional Data: Another impediment to the adoption of alternative data as cited by the decision-making community is the lack of human capital needed to integrate the new dataset within the existing model framework. Nearly 17% of the 69 respondents provided the aforesaid cause as the impediment to the implementation of alternative data into their mainstream systems. While there was no instance of alternative data integration within the OMS (order management system) by portfolio managers, about 40% of the hedge fund managers integrated alternative data within their EMS (execution management system) to generate signals through trading hours. This indicates that there is a possibility for both of these decision-making communities to integrate alternative data into their conventional framework provided that there is empirical evidence on the informational value that alternative data has a positive correlation with stock returns [43]. Integration with legacy framework becomes critical to enable industry practitioners to make timely decisions. Apart from the human talent to integrate the data appropriately, it is also important to have the infrastructure to shift between different types of alternative data, for example, image loading would require higher bandwidth than any textual data. It has been observed that alternative data with high quality can be easily integrated into the legacy decision framework [2, 44]. Recent research suggests that there can be two approaches to integrating alternative data into a mainstream framework, one is the accelerated approach where a single process is used as a case and vendors are shortlisted to identify the informational advantage they bring to the decision-making process [45]. This effort would enable coming up with the final few alternative datasets that add meaning to the entire process. Another method is the comprehensive approach where the firm re-evaluates its current tech process and assesses the key gaps that can be potentially filled in by means of advanced analytics and unstructured data. This would weed out the redundant processes, those that have minimal value addition, and bring in datasets that offer higher informational value.

Assessment of Informational Value: There is a challenge in the assessment of the informational value, given that it is not stationary. Efficient and rapid onboarding of data sources requires evaluation of existing infrastructure, assessment format of the data and quality thereof, examination of compliance and legality, data validation and cleaning for integration, and understanding of the scope and limitations [44]. Over the years, there have been efforts to tackle each of these obstacles methodically; however, the entire gamut of alternative data boils down to a vicious cycle of scalability, competitive edge, and informational value, the cross-correlation of these factors is severely negative making it tough to find an optimal solution to the issue at hand.

16.4.3   The Way Forward

The future of alternative data in investment management relies on addressing essential considerations. It is imperative to ensure the quality and reliability of the data through effective governance and validation techniques. Collaboration among data providers, financial institutions, and regulators plays a crucial role in establishing industry standards and facilitating integration. Advancements in data analysis technologies, such as machine learning and AI, unlock the untapped potential of alternative data. Regulatory frameworks need to evolve to provide clarity and address legal and ethical concerns. Ongoing education and upskilling initiatives for investment professionals are vital to enhancing their competence in utilizing alternative data. By embracing these strategies, the investment management industry can fully harness the power of alternative data, leading to innovation, informed decision-making, and superior investment outcomes.

16.5   Implications of This Study

The study has several implications that span various stakeholders in the realm of alternative data in investment management.

- Investment Management Firms: The study provides investment management firms with insights into the current landscape of alternative data, highlighting the benefits and risks associated with its usage. It offers guidance on incorporating alternative data into decision-making processes, enhancing investment strategies, and gaining a competitive edge.
- Data Providers: The study emphasizes the importance of data quality, reliability, and standardization. Data providers can use these insights to improve their data collection, validation, and delivery processes, ensuring that their alternative data offerings meet the needs and expectations of investment management firms.
- Regulatory Bodies: The findings of the study shed light on the regulatory challenges and considerations surrounding alternative data usage. Regulatory bodies can use this information to develop frameworks and guidelines that address privacy, data usage, and compliance issues, fostering a balanced and transparent environment for alternative data integration.
- Academic and Research Community: The study contributes to the existing body of knowledge on alternative data in investment management. It provides researchers with a

comprehensive understanding of the current landscape, risks, and the way forward. This knowledge can inspire further research and exploration of alternative data's impact on investment strategies.

16.6   Conclusion

Alternative data has gained significant attention in recent years, particularly among hedge fund and quant fund specialists, due to its potential to drive consistent alpha generation. However, the exclusivity and high cost of certain alternative data sources have posed challenges for experimental studies. Nevertheless, the increased usage of alternative data by asset managers and hedge fund managers aligns with the industry's data-driven and machine learning–oriented framework. Data can tell stories in ways in which it is shared, offered, and explained, hence a human expert who is capable of unearthing the most optimal relationship between data and processes to be able to extract the most valuable information becomes the need of the hour [45, 46]. Alternative data is gaining momentum alongside advanced analytics, driven by factors like computing power and cloud infrastructure. However, challenges such as data quality, privacy concerns, and high costs need to be addressed. Experimental studies are necessary for effective implementation within existing frameworks. Alternative data has the potential to transform the investment industry, offering unique insights, a competitive edge, and innovative product ideation. Early adopters can benefit from incorporating alternative data for consistent alpha generation and improved customer satisfaction. The industry is on the brink of a transformative shift in the utilization of alternative data and advanced analytics.

References

1. Monk, A., Prins, M., Rook, D., Rethinking alternative data in institutional investment. *J. Financ. Data Sci.*, 1, 1, 4–31, 2019, DOI 10.3905/jfds.2019.1.1.014.
2. In, S.Y., Rook, D., Monk, A., Integrating alternative data (also known as ESG data) in investment decision making. *Global Econ. Rev.*, 48, 3, 237–260, 2019, https://doi.org/10.1080/1226508X.2019.1643059.

3. Ekster, G. and Kolm, P.N., Alternative data in investment management: Usage, challenges, and valuation. *J. Financ. Data Sci.*, 3, 4, 10–32, 2021, DOI 10.3905/jfds.2021.1.073.

4. Dun & Bradstreet, *Alternative Data: The Hidden Source of Alpha*, Dun & Bradstreet, NJ, 2016.

5. Sharma, R., Mehta, K., Goel, A., Non-linear relationship between board size and performance of indian companies. *J. Manage. Gov.*, 27, 4, 1277–1301, 2022, https://doi. org/10.1007/s10997-022-09651-8.

6. Mehta, K., Sharma, R., Vyas, V., A quantile regression approach to study the impact of aluminium prices on the manufacturing sector of India during the COVID era. *Mat. Today: Proceed.*, 65, 8, 3506–3511, 2022. ISSN 2214- 7853, https://doi.org/10.1016/j.matpr.2022.06.087.

7. Grand View Research, *Alternative Data Market*, Grand View Research, San Francisco, 2022.

8. Precedence Research, *Global Industry Analysis, Size, Share, Growth, Trends. Regional Outlook, and Forecast 2022-2030*, Precedence Research, Canada, 2022.

9. The Business Research Company, *Alternative Data Global Market Report 2023*, The Business Research Company, London, 2023.

10. Sharma, R., Mehta, K., Sharma, O., Exploring deep learning to determine the optimal environment for stock prediction analysis. *International Conference on Computational Performance Evaluation, ComPE*, pp. 148–152, 2021.

11. Monk, A., Prins, M., Rook, D., Rethinking alternative data in institutional investment. *J. Financ. Data Sci.*, l, 1, 14–31, 2019, DOI: 10.3905/ jfds.2019.1.1.014.

12. Denev, A. and Amen, S., *The Book of Alternative Data: A Guide for Investors, Traders and Risk Managers*, John Wiley & Sons, NY, 2020.

13. Deloitte, *Alternative Data Adoption in Investing and Finance*, Deloitte, NY, 2018.

14. Mehta, K., Sharma, R., Vyas, V., Kuckreja, J.S., Exit strategy decision by venture capital firms in India using fuzzy AHP. *J. Entrep. Emerg. Econ.*, 14, 4, 643–669, 2022, https://doi.org/10.1108/JEEE-05-2020-0146.

15. Element 22, *Analytics Power*, Element 22, New York, 2019.

16. Bean, R., UBS asset management taps alternative data to increase alpha. *Forbes*, 18 November 2018, https://www.forbes.com/sites/ciocentral/2018/11/18/ubs-assetmanagement-taps-alternative-data-to-increase-alpha/?sh=7e17f3465d3a.

17. Hansen, K.B. and Borch, C., Alternative data and sentiment analysis: Prospecting non-standard data in machine learning-driven finance. *Big Data Soc*, 9, 1, 20539517211070701, 2022, https://doi.org/10.1177/20539517211070701.

18. Mehta, K., Sharma, R., Vyas, V., Efficiency and ranking of sustainability index of India using DEA-TOPSIS. *J. Indian Bus. Res.*, 11, 2, 179–199, 2019, https://doi.org/10.1108/JIBR-02-2018-0057.

19. Lv, Z., Wang, N., Ma, X., Sun, Y., Meng, Y., Tian, Y., Evaluation standards of intelligent technology based on financial alternative data. *J. Innov. Knowl.*, 7, 4, 100229, 2022, https://doi.org/10.1016/j.jik.2022.100229.

20. Braun, V. and Clarke, V., Using thematic analysis in psychology. *Qual. Res. Psychol.*, 3, 2, 77–101, 2006, doi/abs/10.1191/1478088706QP063OA, 2006.

21. Kuniavsky, M., *Observing the user experience*, Elsevier Science, Netherlands, 2003.

22. A.A., Iyanu, Combining user experience design & service design: Theory meets practice, Hochschule Rhein-Waal University of Applied Sciences, Germany, 2022.

23. Easthope, D., Alt data for investing: not so alternative anymore, Greenwich Research, London, 2021.

24. Distenfeld, L., NASDAQ acquires quandl, solidifies rise of alternative data, in: *Outside Insight*, 31 December 2018, https://outsideinsight.com/insights/why-nasdaqs- acquisition-of-quandl-solidifies-the-rise-of-alternative-data/.

25. Research and markets, *Alternative Data Market*, Research and markets, Dublin, 2022.

26. Sharma, R., Mehta, K., Vyas, V., Responsible investing: A study on non-economic goals and investors' characteristics. *Appl. Finance Lett.*, 9, SI, 63–78, 2020, https://doi.org/10.24135/afl.v9i2.245.

27. Vyas, V., Mehta, K., Sharma, R., The nexus between toxic-air pollution, health expenditure, and economic growth: An empirical study using ARDL. *Int. Rev. Econ. Finance*, 84, 154–166, 2023, https://doi.org/10.1016/j. iref.2022.11.017.

28. Jones, D., Nasdaq Acquires Quandl For Alternative Data, Seeking Alpha, New York, 10 December 2018, https://seekingalpha.com/article/4227483-nasdaq-acquires-quandl-for- alternative-data.

29. Bloomberg, *Bloomberg Enterprise Access Point Expands to Include Alternative Data*, Bloomberg, London, 21 February 2019, https://www.bloomberg.com/company/press/bloomberg-enterprise-access-point-expands-include-alternative-data/.

30. Olson, J.E., *Data quality: The accuracy dimension*, Elsevier, San Francisco, 2003.

31. Pipino, L.L., Lee, Y.W., Wang, R.Y., Data quality assessment. *Commun. ACM*, 45, 4, 211–218, 20022002, doi: doi/10.1145/505248.506010.

32. Caserta, Caserta, Caserta Concepts LLC. dba Caserta, New York, 14 March 2023, [Online], Available: https://caserta.com/alternative-data/. [Accessed 14 March 2023].

33. Dezember, R., Your smartphone's location data is worth big money to wall street. *Wall Str. J.*, 02 November 2018, https://www.wsj.com/articles/your-smart-phones-location-data-is-worth-big-money-to-wall-street-1541131260.

34. World Bank Group, *Financial Consumer Protection and New Forms of Data Processing Beyond Credit Reporting*, World Bank Group, Washington DC, 2018.

35. Nasdaq Data Link, *The Future of Data Privacy in Alternative Data*, Nasdaq, NY, 2020.
36. Weilbacher, D., Curran, S., Jarcho, J., Wagner, A., Helgans, G., Alternative data compliance considerations for investment advisers, Promontory, NY, 2021.
37. Sharma, R., Mehta, K., Rana, R., Cryptocurrency adoption behaviour of millennial investors in India, in: *Perspectives on Blockchain Technology and Responsible Investing*, pp. 135–157, IGI Global, Pennsylvania, 2023.
38. Ribando, J. M. & Bonne, G., 2010. A new quality factor: Finding alpha with asset4 ESG data, New York: Thomson Reuters.
39. Malkiel, B.G., Efficient market hypothesis, in: *Finance*, pp. 127–134, The New Palgrave. Palgrave Macmillan, London, 1989.
40. Fama, E.F., Efficient capital markets: A review of theory and empirical work. *J. Finance*, 25, 2, 383–417, 1970, https://doi.org/10.2307/2325486.
41. McPartland, K., Alternative data for alpha, Greenwich Associates, London, 2017.
42. Rodda, S., Five Considerations for Bringing Alternative Data into Your Workflow. *Dow Jones Newswires*, 07 May 2020, https://www.dowjones.com/professional/resources/blog/five-considerations-for-bringing-alternative-data-into- your-workflow.
43. Valentine, J., The risk-reducing stages of alternative data implementation, GARP, NJ, 2022.
44. Dourish, P. and Edgar, G.C., Datafication and data fiction: Narrating data and narrating with data. *Big Data Soc*, 5, 2, 1–10, 2018, https://doi.org/10.1177/2053951718784083.
45. Hansen, K. and Borch, C., The absorption and multiplication of uncertainty in machine-learning-driven finance. *Br. J. Soc*, 72, 4, 1015–1029, 2021, https://doi.org/10.1111/1468-4446.12880.
46. Denev, A. and Amen, S., The value of alternative data, in: *The Book of Alternative Data: A Guide for Investors, Traders and Risk Managers*, pp. 27–46, Wiley, New Jersey, 2020.

17

Beyond Rationality: Uncovering the Impact of Investor Behavior on Financial Markets

Anu Krishnamurthy

Department of Management Studies, Mount Carmel College, Autonomous, Bangalore, Karnataka, India

Abstract

Traditional finance theories rely on rational behavior in investors, who seek to optimize returns through fundamental analysis, technical analysis, and personal judgment. However, recent research has identified inconsistencies in these theories when applied in practical scenarios. Retail investors in the equity market are prone to various influences, biases, and emotional factors that can impact their decision-making process. Market irregularities arise due to suboptimal responses from investors, who exhibit irrational behavior by deviating from the consistent mathematical framework. Behavioral finance, an interdisciplinary field that integrates behavioral and cognitive psychology with traditional economics and finance, aims to elucidate irrational financial decision-making by employing psychological principles and other theories about human behavior. It examines the influence of investors' emotions and psychology on their investment decision-making processes, focusing on the convergence of intellectual acumen and emotional restraint for rational conduct. Warren Buffet emphasized the importance of understanding how emotions contribute to irrational behavior, and the examination of investor psychology becomes increasingly intriguing. Despite progress in various scientific disciplines, the field of psychology remains relatively nascent. Therefore, it is crucial to examine the dynamics of group behavior within markets and the specific behavioral characteristics exhibited by individual investors to achieve success in investment endeavors.

Keywords: Investor behavior, behavioral finance, behavioral biases

Email: anu.krishnamurthy@mccblr.edu.in

Renuka Sharma and Kiran Mehta (eds.) Deep Learning Tools for Predicting Stock Market Movements, (409–428) © 2024 Scrivener Publishing LLC

17.1   Introduction

The traditional finance model has dominated the field of finance since the mid-1950s, primarily developed by economists from the University of Chicago. The underlying premise of the conventional finance model posits that individuals exhibit rational behavior. Nevertheless, psychologists argue that individuals frequently experience grief influenced by cognitive and emotional biases, leading them to behave irrationally. The finance industry exhibited reluctance in embracing the perspective put forth by psychologists advocating for the behavioral finance model. The field of behavioral finance has experienced increased recognition due to the mounting evidence supporting the significant impact of psychology and emotions on decision-making processes. There exists a divergence of opinions regarding the timing, manner, and rationale behind the impact of psychology on investment decisions. However, the conferral of the 2002 Nobel Prize in Economics upon psychologist Daniel Kahnemann and experimental economist Vernon Smith is widely regarded as a validation of the discipline of behavioral finance.

17.1.1   Traditional Finance

The dominant theories within the realm of academic finance are widely recognized as standard or traditional finance. The theoretical foundations of traditional finance are intricately connected to the principles of modern portfolio theory (MPT) and the efficient market hypothesis (EMH). The development of MPT can be attributed to Harry Markowitz, who formulated this framework in 1952 while pursuing his doctoral studies at the University of Chicago. MPT involves the assessment of the expected return, standard deviation, and correlation of a specific stock or portfolio about other stocks or mutual funds held within that portfolio. By integrating these three principles, it is feasible to formulate an optimal portfolio for a specific collection of stocks or bonds. An efficient portfolio can be defined as a compilation of stocks that provides the greatest expected return about the level of risk assumed or, alternatively, demonstrates the minimum attainable risk for a given anticipated return. The EMH is a prominent theme within the field of finance. The underlying assumption suggests that the market value or price of security encompasses all accessible information, thereby indicating that the present trading price of a stock or bond signifies its equitable value. According to proponents, the concept of stocks being valued at their fair market value suggests that active traders or portfolio managers face challenges in consistently achieving superior returns that surpass the performance of the overall market. As a result, advocates contend that investors ought to embrace a strategy of owning the entire market rather than endeavoring to surpass its performance.

The allocation of funds toward equity shares occupies a prominent position in the realm of capital markets owing to its capacity to yield superior rates of return when compared to other investment options. Investors have the option to make investment decisions based on subjective risk criteria or objective risk criteria. The foundational assumption of rational investor behavior underlies traditional finance theories, including MPT [1] and the capital asset pricing model (CAPM) [2]. Investors acquainted themselves with the plethora of information disseminated within the market. As a result, a process of logical decision-making followed, leading to the manifestation of efficient market behavior through the dissemination of comprehensive information to investors [3–5].

The CAPM was originally introduced by Jack Treynor in 1962 and later expanded upon by William Sharpe in 1964 [6]. This theory was formulated based on the groundwork laid by Markowitz's prior research. The Nobel Prize in Economics was bestowed upon Sharpe, Markowitz, and Merton Miller in 1990 as a testament to their noteworthy contributions to the discipline of financial economics. The year 1973 marked the introduction of an alternative version of the CAPM by Black and Scholes [7], which is commonly referred to as the Black CAPM or Zero-Beta CAPM. This particular variation deviates from the underlying assumption of an asset devoid of risk.

The CAPM is a commonly employed theoretical framework within the field of finance that is utilized to ascertain the suitable valuation of a specific security or a collection of securities. This specific model employs the security market line (SML) as a mechanism for investors to assess the risk-reward trade-off of any security in the market. The CAPM was subsequently revised to incorporate the integration of size premium and specific risk. In order to provide further clarification, it should be noted that the traditional market risk premium has been replaced with the result of multiplying beta by the market risk premium.

In contrast, the EMH posits that stocks are consistently traded at their intrinsic value, rendering it unfeasible for investors to acquire undervalued stocks or dispose of overpriced stocks. The theory further posited that it is not feasible for an investor to surpass the market's performance, and the sole avenue for achieving greater returns is by investing in securities with higher levels of risk. The categorization of such investments as falling within the realm of behavioral science is becoming more prevalent due to their reliance on trends and collective behavior [8, 9].

Traditional finance theories were subject to certain limitations. In their study conducted in 2004, Fama and French [10] put forth the argument that the CAPM did not pass empirical tests, suggesting that the model's application lacks validity. The process of decision-making is intricate and cannot be solely predicated upon imperfect information obtained from unreliable sources. The act of decision-making involves the selection of one option from a set of alternatives. The achievement of wealth maximization is therefore only possible through the selection of an optimal investment decision.

According to financial theory, it is posited that investors exhibit rational behavior and that the presence of both individual and collective rationality contributes to the efficiency of the market. Nevertheless, it is important to acknowledge that in practical scenarios, individual investors do not consistently exhibit rational behavior, and it is evident that markets do not consistently operate with perfect efficiency. Investors exhibit heterogeneity as a result of diverse factors such as socioeconomic background, educational attainment, age, gender, and other relevant variables. Recent studies have revealed that specific behavioral biases are responsible for the aforementioned situation. These discoveries have led to the emergence of behavioral finance, an academic discipline that examines the impact of psychology on the actions of financial professionals and the resulting consequences on the market [11, 12].

17.1.2   Behavioral Factors Affecting Investment Decisions

The theory of limited arbitrage posits that the presence of irrational investors can lead to anomalies in the fundamental value, whereas rational investors may exhibit vulnerability in their behavior. Behavior models have been formulated as a consequence of experimental investigations carried out by financial economists in conjunction with cognitive psychologists, stemming from this irrationality. These models propose that investors develop certain beliefs or expectations that subsequently influence their investment decisions.

The diagram below illustrates the diverse behavioral factors that influence investors' investment decisions.

17.1.3   Investor Behavior

The cost associated with participating in the stock market has experienced a significant decline, resulting in an increasing number of individuals engaging in equity investments. Furthermore, there has been an increased awareness among individuals regarding the importance of saving for their postretirement period. As a result, individuals are now inclined toward making defined contributions to retirement schemes as a means to ensure their future financial security. The available evidence indicates that investors exhibit a preference for portfolio diversification as a means of mitigating risks. They exhibit a preference for investing in familiar avenues rather than unfamiliar ones. Nevertheless, investors tend to diversify their portfolios simplistically. According to rational investing models, the expectation is that minimal trading activity should be observed in order to mitigate potential risks. Overconfidence stands out as the primary factor contributing to excessive trading. This finding presents a more suitable behavioral rationale for investors who engage in higher levels of trading, operating under the belief that they possess ample and dependable market information.

The investment decisions made by individuals are contingent upon their objectives of achieving either short-term or long-term gains. The demographic of individuals engaged in investment activities, driven by a desire for immediate financial gains, has experienced notable growth in recent years. The market has been disrupted as a result of the lack of foresight and erratic actions exhibited by these investors. Therefore, it is imperative to effectively handle investors' perceptions and mitigate stock price volatility by comprehending investor behavior.

17.1.4   Emergence of Behavioral Finance

Although the study of behavioral finance places significant emphasis on traditional finance, it is the underlying psychological and sociological factors that serve as the primary drivers in this area of research. Consequently, individuals pursuing the field of behavioral finance must possess a foundational comprehension of the principles encompassing psychology, sociology, and finance in order to familiarize themselves with the overarching tenets of behavioral finance. Behavioral finance endeavors to elucidate and enhance comprehension of the cognitive patterns exhibited by investors, encompassing the emotional mechanisms at play and the extent to which they impact the decision-making process. Behavioral finance seeks to provide an understanding of the fundamental aspects of finance and investment through the lens of human behavior, encompassing the what, why, and how of these phenomena. There has been extensive discourse surrounding the precise definition and legitimacy of behavioral finance, given its ongoing evolution and continuous refinement as a scholarly discipline. The ongoing occurrence of this evolutionary process can be attributed to the extensive and varied academic and professional expertise possessed by numerous scholars. Behavioral finance is an academic discipline that examines the impact of psychological and sociological factors on the financial decision-making process of individuals, groups, and entities. Rational decision-making is inherently grounded in the cause-and-effect relationship; however, in practice, comprehending this relationship can prove to be exceedingly challenging. Therefore, scholars and researchers who have conducted studies to comprehend the process of financial decision-making assert that investment is a cognitive choice influenced by psychological factors. In the 1990s, the emergence of a novel conceptual framework known as "Behavioral Finance" became increasingly prevalent in numerous scholarly publications. Nevertheless, the origins of behavioral finance can be traced back to a period spanning 150 years. During the 19th and early 20th centuries, there was a notable reference to this concept in specific primary literature. In his 1841 publication titled "Extraordinary Popular Delusions and the Madness of Crowds," Scottish journalist Charles Mackay [13] analyzed crowd psychology. In 1895, Gustave Le Bon [14] authored "The Crowd: A Study of the Popular Mind," a seminal work that also delved into the realm of crowd psychology and explored the phenomenon of herd behavior. In 1912, Charles Selden [15] authored the book "Psychology of the Stock Market," which marked the initial application of psychological principles to the domain of stock market analysis.

In 1969, Howard and Sheth [16] introduced a behavioral equation model that pertains to the process of decision-making. The individual proposed that the process of decision-making can be conceptualized as a mathematical equation, wherein the resultant outcome is determined by various factors including the level of need, cues, returns, and satisfaction. According to the individual's perspective, the factors of perception, motivation, incentive potential, and intensity of cues play a significant role in shaping purchase intention, ultimately leading to the final purchase decision. The consequences of these decisions have the potential to yield either favorable or unfavorable outcomes for investors. The researchers made modifications to this model about investment decisions within the mutual fund industry. Lintner [17] conducted a study examining how individuals utilize information to formulate investment decisions. According to Shefrin, Hersh, and Meir Statman [18], the field of behavioral finance pertains to the examination of how psychological factors influence the decision-making behavior of investors. The author delineated the four fundamental themes that underpin behavioral finance as heuristics, framing, emotions, and market impact.

In their seminal work, Kahnemann and Smith [19] examined the interplay between financial economics and psychological decision-making, thereby introducing the concept of behavioral finance. In their seminal work, Barberis and Thaler [20] conducted a comprehensive investigation into the impact of emotional judgments on financial markets, revealing the existence of a dichotomy between rational and irrational investors within these markets. The decision-making process of irrational investors is influenced by emotional factors, leading to disruptions in market equilibrium. Conversely, rational investors, driven by logic and reason, act as a counterbalance to prevent these irrational investors from rectifying price deviations from the fundamental value [21, 22]. In the year 2017, Richard H. Thaler [23] was awarded the Nobel Prize in recognition of his significant contributions to the field of behavioral economics. The foundation of his research was the examination of how human characteristics influence the economic choices made by individuals and the subsequent impact these choices have on the overall functioning of markets.

Behavioral finance is an amalgamation of different schools of thought, resulting in a distinctive approach. The methodology employed in this study involves the integration of financial theories and principles with psychological perspectives, thereby adopting an interdisciplinary approach. This theory presents a contradiction to the conventional CAPM and EMH. The field of behavioral finance encompasses the examination of human behavior in financial decision-making, which can be analyzed at both the micro and macro levels. Micro behavioral finance is a branch of study that examines the behavioral patterns and decision-making processes of individual investors. In contrast, macro behavioral finance is concerned with analyzing the behavioral dynamics and tendencies exhibited by the overall financial markets. Furthermore, it aids in the examination of the behavioral characteristics exhibited by equity investors and the recurring trends observed in their investment choices.

A crucial factor in achieving success in investment lies in comprehending one's intended course of action. This implies that stocks should be regarded as commodities of enterprises and acquired solely when their valuation is deemed appropriate. Consumers make purchasing decisions based on the perceived value of a business, which must surpass the price of the product or service being offered. Nevertheless, the likelihood of such a scenario is contingent upon a significant degree of apprehension and negativity. Proficient investors engage in the practice of purchasing assets at a reduced price and subsequently divesting them at a higher valuation. However, investors often find themselves in a state of uncertainty regarding the consensus on their decisions, as such scenarios appear to be nonexistent. Consequently, investors engage in purchasing assets at elevated prices with the expectation of subsequently selling them at even higher prices. Regrettably, their endeavors often culminate in the sale of said assets at lower prices than initially anticipated.

In the immediate term, intelligence and brilliance can be advantageous; however, it is ultimately wisdom that proves to be effective over an extended period. A discerning and judicious investor employs diverse methodologies to assess a business and diligently endeavors to anticipate future outcomes. Regrettably, as a result of time constraints, investors often make impulsive decisions. Despite the diligent efforts invested, the mathematical equations employed to assess the risk and return associated with investments prove inadequate in informing investment decisions. In order to address these irregularities, investors employ diverse investment strategies, among which is the practice of "value investing."

17.1.5   Traditional Finance vs. Behavioral Finance

Traditional finance operates under the assumption that individuals possess the ability to effectively and accurately process data. On the other hand, behavioral finance acknowledges that individuals tend to utilize imperfect cognitive shortcuts, known as heuristics when processing information. These heuristics can lead to biases in their beliefs and predispose them to make errors.

Traditional finance assumes that individuals evaluate all decisions based on the transparent and objective factors of risk and return. Put differently, the choice of the framework employed to delineate a problem holds no significance. On the other hand, behavioral finance asserts that the way decision problems are presented has a substantial impact on individuals' perceptions of risk and return. Behavioral finance operates under the assumption of frame independence.

Traditional finance operates under the assumption that individuals are driven by rationality, logic, and autonomous decision-making. In contrast, behavioral finance acknowledges the significant impact of emotions and herd behavior on decision-making processes.

According to the traditional finance perspective, it is posited that markets operate efficiently, thereby suggesting that the price of every security reflects an impartial estimation of its inherent value. On the other hand, behavioral finance presents a counterargument to the influence of heuristic-driven biases and errors. It emphasizes the importance of frame independence, as well as the impact of emotions and social influence, which frequently result in a disparity between market price and fundamental value.

Behavioral finance is increasingly recognized as a significant field of study in the context of the current volatile economic climate. The presence of uncertainty engenders fear and impedes the investor's capacity to make logical and reasoned choices. Several decades ago, research advanced without taking into account the influence of human factors on decision-making. The aforementioned ideologies were centered on the conventional CAPM and EMH, which posited that investors were expected to exhibit rational behavior and that markets were expected to operate efficiently. Empirical evidence demonstrates that in practical contexts, traditional theories encounter significant contradictions, thereby highlighting the presence of diverse anomalies that investors must navigate. Different investment vehicles such as mutual funds and life insurance are designed to cater to individual investors who may lack the expertise required to navigate the complexities of the stock market. The investor encounters difficulties in the realm of decision-making due to the abundance of profitable financial products present in the market.

The comprehension of behavioral finance enhances investors' ability to make more informed investment decisions. This platform offers investors the chance to gain insight into their own biases and errors in judgment. The implementation of a structured trading strategy can assist investors in making logical and informed decisions. Therefore, the present study aims to investigate the primary tool of behavioral finance, known as value investing [24–27].

17.2   Statement of the Problem

The practice of value investing necessitates a heightened level of discipline in the realm of financial modeling. This resource offers a set of principles to inform investment decision-making and assists individuals in achieving higher investment yields. Recent research has indicated a disparity between conventional finance theories and practical scenarios, as empirical evidence suggests that average investors tend to base their decision-making on emotional factors rather than logical considerations. Investors may experience confusion when confronted with uncertainties surrounding investment decisions. Consequently, individuals are susceptible to making irrational decisions. Markets often deviate from anticipated behavior, leading investors to make decisions that diverge from expected norms.

The value investing process is widely regarded as a prudent long-term strategy, wherein value investors engage in independent research to analyze financial statements and evaluate key metrics such as profit margins, price-to-earnings ratios, and book value. These assessments serve as the basis for their investment selection. In the context of the burgeoning interest in the Indian stock market, it has been observed that investors tend to refrain from employing fundamental analysis when making investment decisions. Therefore, it was deemed imperative to gain a comprehensive understanding of the behavioral factors that influence these investment decisions.

17.3   Need for the Study

Despite excelling in their respective professional domains, the average amateur investor may lack expertise in identifying suitable stocks for investment. Therefore, he engages in speculative activities rather than simply investing. This distinction sets apart an investor who possesses a comprehensive understanding of the concept of "value investing" and utilizes it when making investment choices. Therefore, it was considered necessary to comprehend the primary factors in value investing that are taken into account by individual investors when making equity investments. This knowledge would assist ordinary investors in comprehending the behavioral elements that influence their investment choices.

Additionally, formulating an optimal investment strategy aids investors in making rational decisions to maximize their returns.

17.4   Significance of the Study

The primary objective of an equity investor is to generate wealth. In essence, the process of generating wealth can be understood as a cognitive endeavor rather than a mere quantitative pursuit. Value investing not only facilitates the optimization of individual investors' wealth at a micro level through the selection of favorable stocks but also fosters business expansion and guides the economy toward its intended trajectory. In light of this correlation, it can be argued that value investing holds social significance and merits scholarly investigation

There are three ways of investing—intellectually difficult, physically difficult, and emotionally difficult ways.

The intellectually difficult path is adopted by investors who have a sound knowledge of the market and who are ready to take risks while investing. It is a kind of cash flow approach wherein investors understand the different concepts of investing. Investors are expected to understand the different kinds of businesses, the economic policy of the country, and the various market forces that affect investing. Hard work is the key to success in this path and patience is the game changer. Such investors have a strong conviction in their decisions and aim at achieving long-term goals. Such investors are emotionally strong and are least affected by the behavioral factors that influence investment decisions. A living example of such investing is Warren Buffet who has beaten the market with his intellect.

The physically difficult path is adopted by investors who would like to overload themselves with market information. Such investors continuously monitor the stock market movements through various channels like newspapers, magazines, and television. They also update their knowledge about companies and their key performance indicators. These investors strongly believe that the knowledge so obtained would help them pick winning stocks. This indicates that even those investors who are not intellectually competent can work hard physically throughout the day to update themselves with market information and remain successful investors.

The emotionally difficult path is adopted by the investors who adopt neither the intellectual way nor the physical way. These investors are guided by emotional discipline and are not carried away by market sentiments. They follow the thumb rule that investors need to be fearful when others are greedy and they have to be greedy when others are fearful. This path emphasizes patience while investing as the sole aim of investors is to reap higher returns in the long run. The principle of compounding over a long period plays a very important role in such investment decisions. This requires a proper understanding of the various behavioral factors that affect investment decisions. Value investing provides an optimal solution for an emotionally independent investor.

17.4.1   Types of Investors

There are four types of investors, namely, risk-averse, risk seeker, greedy, and hopeful.

17.4.1.1   Risk-Averse

These investors adopt certain strategies that are risk-free or of low risk such that they expect higher returns than what they are earning at present on their investments. Such investors invest in high-dividend stocks that resemble coupons on safe bonds and expect an appreciation of their investments. Hence, stocks with a low price-earnings ratio are considered safe stocks for risk-averse investors as they continue to make earnings over a long period. These stocks are traded in the market at less than book value. In short, risk-averse investors are value investors who believe that stocks that are traded at less than book value are underpriced and fetch higher returns over a long period.

17.4.1.2   Risk Seeker

These investors prefer stocks with an upside risk rather than stocks that resemble bonds. The stock of a company is considered good if the key financial indicators are good. Such companies have an excellent track record of accounting rate of return in the past along with social benefits for their stakeholders. The stocks with high earnings and usually risky without offering many dividends are preferred by such investors. Sometimes, these investors prefer investing in loser stocks too as they believe that the prices of such stocks would not fall much more and expect the prices to increase over a period. The risk seekers reap hidden bargains by investing in stocks that are least tracked by analysts.

17.4.1.3   Greedy

It is the greed of investors that makes them go behind stocks that offer at least something for nothing. Some companies accelerate the growth of other companies by acquiring them and these investors invest in such growth companies. The newly acquired company attracts the market and takes advantage of being in the race. Greedy investors use "arbitrage" to the fullest by identifying such stocks that are priced differently in two different markets and are expected to converge at some point in time. Such investors believe that there is a significant momentum in stock prices and invest huge amounts as stocks traded on high volume are always better than stocks traded on low volume.

17.4.1.4   Hopeful

These investors religiously believe that success comes only with patience as stocks always win in the long term. They rely on the expertise of financial analysts whose advice helps them reap higher returns. Investors do not get carried away by the information overload or negativity surrounding the stocks. In fact, it is the conventional wisdom that helps such investors to make rational decisions. The simple rule followed by hopeful investors is investing during good years and staying away from the market during bad years.

Value investing necessitates a heightened level of discipline in the realm of financial modeling. This resource offers a set of principles to inform investment decision-making and assist individuals in achieving higher investment yields. Recent studies have revealed a disparity between conventional financial theories and practical scenarios, as evidenced by the tendency of average investors to make decisions driven by emotions rather than rationality. Investors may experience confusion when faced with uncertainties surrounding investment decisions. Consequently, individuals are susceptible to making irrational decisions. Markets often deviate from anticipated patterns of behavior, leading investors to make decisions that diverge from conventional expectations [28, 29].

Despite excelling in their respective career fields, the average amateur investor may lack expertise in identifying suitable stocks for investment. Therefore, his actions can be characterized as speculative rather than purely investment-oriented. This distinction separates an investor who possesses a comprehensive understanding of the concept of "value investing" and applies it in their investment decision-making process from another investor. Therefore, it was deemed necessary to conduct this research in order to gain insight into the primary factors in value investing that individual investors take into account when making equity investments.

The value investing process is widely regarded as a prudent long-term strategy, wherein investors engage in independent research to assess financial statements and key metrics, including profit margins, price-to-earnings ratios, and book value, in order to make informed investment decisions. Within the framework of the burgeoning interest surrounding the Indian stock market, it has been ascertained that investors exhibit a dearth of engagement in fundamental analysis when formulating their investment choices. Therefore, it was deemed imperative to undertake a comprehensive investigation in order to comprehend the behavioral factors that influence said investment choices [30, 31].

The comprehensive examination of existing literature suggests that there exists a deficiency in the conceptual comprehension of individual equity investors when it comes to distinguishing a value investor from a typical investor. Research on value investing strategies from the Indian perspective is currently in its early stages. There exists a scarcity of scholarly literature pertaining to the evaluation of the performance of value and growth stocks, as well as the presence of a value premium. Value investing not only contributes to the financial prosperity of investors but also facilitates the expansion of businesses, thereby enhancing the overall economic value at a macroeconomic scale. Additionally, it aids the comprehension of the significance of fundamental analysis in stock selection for the average investor and promotes value investing as an optimal investment strategy.

17.5 Discussions

Investment can be undertaken through two distinct approaches, namely, concentration or diversification. Concentration refers to the strategic management of the patient and enduring capital over an extended duration. On the other hand, diversification means passive investing which an average investor follows. However, if investing is done scientifically with special emphasis on the right companies at the right prices, an investor can reap the joy of compounding as mentioned in the note by Warren Buffet. The right way of choosing stocks starts with an initial screening process using fundamental analysis and eliminating stocks that do not fall under the criteria [32, 33].

A potential investor must look for three aspects, namely, price, longevity of growth, and superior rate of returns. It is better to understand that value does not mean cheap when a value investor buys underpriced stocks. Most of the value investors have proved that risk and return are negatively correlated. There has been a misconception that an investor should take high risks to get optimum returns. An investor should be process-oriented and develop a checklist to filter only good stocks out of the stocks available in the market.

As mentioned by Shri Kuntal Shah, a founding partner of Sage One Investment Advisors, in one of his interviews, the essence of compound interest can be applied to value investing as follows:

Wealth creation = longevity of growth + high rate of returns + reasonable price.

When compared to a traditional investor, a value investor always focuses on a growth-driven investment strategy. This is supported by the argument that the magnitude of the future growth of a business determines the present value of the business today. Hence, a value investor calculates the difference between the firm's true value and the market-designated value to understand the intrinsic value of the business [34, 35].

Following are the points which have emerged out of the discussions:

- An investor should invest in companies that have strong growth strategies in terms of earnings, earnings growth drivers, and capital allocation decisions.
- In the words of Warren Buffet, "Be greedy when others are fearful and fearful when others are greedy." This has to be applied by any prudent investor in order to reap benefits in the long run.
- It is always advisable to read the history of business houses whereby harder lessons can be learned more easily than going through one's own hard experience.
- Even though time is equivalent to money, investors should have the patience to reap greater benefits.

Hence, it is understood that a good forecast of future earnings growth and future price-earnings ratios and the use of the concept of "margin of safety" would lead to rational investment decisions and investors can reap higher returns [36–38].

17.6   Implications

The investment decisions of individual equity investors are influenced by various behavioral factors. The variation in investment factors can be attributed to a range of socioeconomic characteristics, including but not limited to age, gender, and educational attainment. Middle-class salaried employees who are investors tend to prioritize the preservation of their investments over engaging in speculative activities that may result in losses. The investors demonstrate prudence and prioritize long-term gains, aligning with the principles of value investing as articulated by Warren Buffet.

The primary objective of any investment is to enhance the financial stability and overall welfare of the investor. The responsibility for addressing minor errors at the outset, rather than enduring long-term consequences, lies with the investor. A prudent investor consistently integrates their financial acumen with a well-balanced psychological approach. Value investing is a strategy that introduces a higher level of discipline when making investment decisions. The strategy in question is widely regarded as conservative in nature while also being oriented toward long-term objectives. In the context of the expanding Indian stock market, value investing emerges as a favorable investment strategy for investors seeking to attain elevated long-term returns.

17.7   Scope for Further Research

The present study is aimed at individual investors who invest in equity. The same can be tested for other alternative avenues for investment. There are also institutional investors in Bangalore City and the impact of the same behavioral factors may be studied in the future. For this study, only the five most important behavioral factors have been considered as suggested by individual investors. However, there are other behavioral factors too which influence investment decisions. The scope of the study may be extended to other cities to bring in a more statistical database of investors. Also, the conceptual understanding of value investing has still been an open-ended question that provides a platform for further research in this field. The findings of the study may be validated by conducting a longitudinal study after a fixed interval of time. The time lag may cause a change in the investment decisions as experience has a significant impact on decision-making.

References

1. Markowitz, H., Portfolio selection. *J. Finance*, 7, 1, 77–91, 1952.
2. Treynor, J., Towards a theory of market value of risky assets, in: *Asset Pricing and Portfolio Performance*, pp. 15–22, Risk Books, London, 1962.
3. Chander, R., Sharma, R., Mehta, K., Dividend announcement and informational efficiency: An empirical study of indian stock market. *ICFAI J. Appl. Finance*, 13, 10, 29–42, 2007.
4. Chander, R., Sharma, R., Mehta, K., Impact of dividend announcement on stock prices. *NICE J. Bus.*, 2, 1, 15–29, 2007.
5. Sharma, R., Mehta, K., Rana, R., Cryptocurrency adoption behaviour of millennial investors in India, in: *Perspectives on Blockchain Technology and Responsible Investing*, pp. 135–157, 2023.
6. Sharpe, W., Capital asset prices: A theory of market equilibrium under conditions of risk. *J. Finance*, 19, 3, 425–442, 1964.
7. Fischer, B. and Scholes., M., The pricing of options and corporate liabilities. *J. Polit. Econ.*, 81, 3, 637–659, 1973.
8. Sharma, R., Mehta, K., Sharma, O., Exploring deep learning to determine the optimal environment for stock prediction analysis. *International Conference on Computational Performance Evaluation, ComPE*, pp. 148–152, 2021.
9. Sharma, R., Mehta, K., Vyas, V., Responsible investing: A study on non-economic goals and investors' characteristics. *Appl. Finance Lett.*, 9, SI, 63–78, 2020, https://doi.org/10.24135/afl.v9i2.245.
10. Fama, F., The capital asset pricing model: Theory and evidence. *J. Econ. Perspect.*, 18, 3, 25–46, 2004.
11. Mehta, K., Sharma, R., Vyas, V., Efficiency and ranking of sustainability index of India using DEA-TOPSIS. *J. Indian Bus. Res.*, 11, 2, 179–199, 2019, https://doi.org/10.1108/JIBR-02-2018-0057.
12. Mehta, K., Sharma, R., Vyas, V., A quantile regression approach to study the impact of aluminium prices on the manufacturing sector of India during the COVID era. *Mat. Today: Proc.*, 65, 8, 3506–3511, 2022, ISSN 2214- 7853, https://doi.org/10.1016/j.matpr.2022.06.087.
13. Mackay, C., *Extraordinary popular delusions and the madness of crowds*, Richard Bentley, London, 1841.

14. Le Bon, G., *The crowd: A study of the popular mind*, Sparkling Books Edition, Sparkling Books, London, 1895.

15. Selden, C., *Psychology of the stock market*, Fraser Publishing Company, New York, 1912.

16. Howard, J.A. and Sheth, J.N., The theory of buyer behavior. *J. Am. Stat. Assoc.*, III, 467–487, 1969.

17. Lintner, G., Behavioral finance: Why investors make bad decisions? *Planner*, 13, 1, 7–8, 1998.

18. Shefrin, H. and Statman, M., Behavioral portfolio theory. *J. Financial Quant. Anal.*, 35, 1, 27–52, 2000.

19. Kahnemann, S., *Advanced information on the Prize in Economic Sciences 2002*, The Royal Swedish Academy of Sciences, Stockholm, Sweden, 17 December 2002, 1–25, 2002, http://www.nobelprize.org/prizes/economicsciences/2002/press-.

20. Barberis, T., A survey of Behavioral Finance, National Bureau of Economic Research, Cambridge, 2003.

21. Mehta, K. and Sharma, R., Contrarian and momentum investment strategies: Evidence from indian stock market. *Int. J. Appl. Bus. Econ. Res.*, 15, 9, 107–118, 2017.

22. Sharma, R., Mehta, K., Goel, A., Non-linear relationship between board size and performance of Indian companies. *J. Manage. Gov.*, 27, 1277–1301, 2022, https://doi. org/10.1007/s10997-022-09651-8.

23. Thaler, R.H., The Prize in Economic Sciences 2017, *The Royal Swedish Academy of Sciences*, pp. 1(6) to 6(6), Stockholm, Sweden, 9th October, 2017. http://www.nobelprize.org/prizes/economicsciences/2017/thaler/facts-.

24. Browne, C.H., *The little book of value investing*, John Wiley and Sons Inc., New Jersey, 2007.

25. Lynch, P., *One upon a wall street*, Simon & Schuster Paperbacks, New York, 1989.

26. Graham, B., *The intelligent investor*, Harper, New York, 1973.

27. Graham, B., *Security analysis*, McGraw–Hill, New York, 1934.

28. Buffet, M. and David, C., *Buffetology*, A Fireside Book, New York, 1999.

29. Munger, C., *The complete investor*, Columbia University Press, New York, 2015.

30. Fisher, P., Investment advice from mutual fund companies. *J. Portf. Manage.*, 24, 09–26, 1997.

31. Templeton, J., *Templeton's way with money*, John Wiley and Sons Inc., USA, 2012.

32. Lynch, P., *One upon a wall street*, Simon & Schuster Paperbacks, New York, 1989.

33. Jhunjhunwala, R., *The Indian dream*, Create Space Independent Publishing Platform, California, 2016.

34. Parikh, P., *Value investing and behavioral finance*, Tata McGraw - Hill Publishing Company Limited, New Delhi, 2012.

35. Agarwal, R., *The art of wealth creation*, Motilal Oswal, Mumbai, 2018.
36. Bhattacharya, S., Investors often play the odds to feel good, Forbes, India, Mumbai, 2014.
37. Vyas, V., Mehta, K., Sharma, R., The nexus between toxic-air pollution, health expenditure, and economic growth: An empirical study using ARDL. *Int. Rev. Econ. Finance*, 84, 154–166, 2023, https://doi.org/10.1016/j.iref.2022.11.017.
38. Shah, B., *Of long–term value and wealth creation from equity investing*, Mumbai, Novel Investor, 2013.

18

Volatility Transmission Role of Indian Equity and Commodity Markets

Harpreet Kaur* and Amita Chaudhary

University School of Business, Chandigarh University, Mohali, India

Abstract

The rate at which a security's price swings, i.e., increases or decreases for a specific set of returns, is how volatility is expressed. When one financial market's volatility disruption has a significant negative effect on another financial market's volatility (i.e., conditional variance), this is known as volatility spillover. In the modern day where financial markets are highly interconnected, it is essential to comprehend such transmission to capitalize on the benefits of portfolio diversification. The present paper investigates the volatility transmission role of two major Indian financial markets, mainly the commodity and equity futures markets. Specifically, we examine the unconditional volatility spillover among equity future index and commodity composite (Comdex) as well as sectoral (energy, metal, and agricultural) future indices. We have applied two stationarity tests along with the Diebold-Yilmaz (DY) volatility spillover model on daily realized volatility series of selected indices. Since the volatility series of sampled indices are not directly available, it is calculated for each index using the range method. Therefore, the official websites of MCX and NSE have been used to extract information regarding the high and low daily futures prices of equity and commodity indices respectively, for the period from 2007 to 2022. Initially, the descriptive analysis revealed that the energy index has the highest average volatility as well as unconditional volatility followed by equity, metal, comdex, and agri indices, respectively. Furthermore, all the sampled series are asymmetrically distributed as these are positively skewed and leptokurtic. Both stationarity tests confirmed that none of the volatility series have a unit root. Therefore, we proceed further by applying a DY volatility spillover model with lag order 5, forecast horizon of 10 and 200 days of rolling window to examine connectedness among indices through static analysis. The study found that, on average, 29.20% of the forecast error variances have been explained by the

---

Corresponding author: harpreetresearcher@gmail.com

Renuka Sharma and Kiran Mehta (eds.) Deep Learning Tools for Predicting Stock Market Movements, (429–444) © 2024 Scrivener Publishing LLC

spillover effect. Furthermore, Comdex acts as the highest net volatility transmitter followed by Equity. In contrast, the energy index acts as the highest net volatility receiver followed by the metal index and the agri index. Nonagricultural indices are more sensitive to other indices volatility than agricultural indices. All these insights into the volatility transmission role of the stock as well as commodity markets will certainly assist practitioners, individual as well as institutional investors along with policymakers.

Keywords: Volatility, commodity, stock, Diebold, futures market

18.1   Introduction

Financial liberalization and globalization have increased the volatility among international financial markets over the past two decades [1]. Volatility means oscillation in asset prices of a particular financial market. It is a barometer used by analysts and investors to understand fluctuation and inefficiency in the financial markets [2]. Whether the flow of information from one financial market encompasses the volatility-generating process of one more similar or different market depends upon the rate at which the information flows [3]. The ultimate goal of investors is to contract the risk and expand the returns. One of the most effective strategies to achieve investors' objectives is through proper portfolio diversification. However, due to the presence of integration among financial markets, investors cannot exploit the potential diversification fruits. Because of this increased stock market integration, the gigantic and enduring effect of the East Asian crisis (1997) along with the subprime crisis-GFC (2007) has been witnessed by developed and emerging economies concurrently [4]. The shocks or volatility transmission takes place not only among financial markets across economies but also among financial markets of a particular country. Such transmission of financial shocks across counties and within the financial markets of a country is known as volatility transmission [5].

Commodities can be used as a supplement to traditional asset classes due to various reasons such as it helpful in enhancing the risk-return trade-off as it is believed to have a low correlation with conventional financial assets in the long run [6, 7]. It can be further used as a hedging tool especially during times of inflation [7–9] and during financial stress [10]. Due to these reasons, investors are now considering commodities not only as a hedging tool but also wholly as investments just like other financial assets [11]. However, investors cannot reap the benefits of commodities as asset class along with other traditional asset classes if markets are integrated and there is a presence of volatility spillover among commodity derivative markets and other financial markets of a country or commodity markets of various countries [12].

The core objective of the study is to find the volatility interrelationship between the Indian commodity and equity market to capture active net volatility transmitters and receivers. The findings of the study will be helpful to the global as well as domestic investors for asset allocation or portfolio decisions. If there is the transmission of volatility from one asset class to another, especially in a volatile period, then the investors cannot reap the benefits of diversification to reduce their risk.

The rest of the document is structured as follows. The second part reviews some basic literature. The methods and data used are displayed in the third part. The empirical findings are discussed in the fourth part, with the conclusion covered in the final paragraph.

18.2   Literature Review

A review of past literature reveals that many studies have analyzed volatility spillover either across the financial markets of countries or across the financial assets of a country. Most of these studies are related to the intercountry financial market's volatility spillover [13–23]. However, examining the volatility spillover among various financial markets within a nation has only been the subject of a very limited number of research studies. Even in the context of commodities, most studies usually focus on the interaction of crude oil prices with other securities such as equity and other commodities [24–30], foreign exchange rates [31–34], and other energy markets [35–37].

The finance literature comes up with countless studies that investigated the volatility transmission between different financial markets. A majority of these research studies have been carried out to capture the volatility spillover effect between developed nations' financial markets. The existing studies related to developed financial markets include the application of the Dynamic Conditional Correlation (DCC) model to test whether 25 commodities and 13 traditional asset classes of the US and other major economies were different from each other or not over the period from 1980 to 2006 [38]. Their result suggested that in more than half cross sections, the conditional correlation between commodity futures with equity returns and with Treasury bills fell, especially during market turbulence. The researchers found the presence of considerable spillover of volatility between oil prices and returns of the European stock market [39]. A recent study employed the MSIAH to test the relationship between returns of US commodities, real estate assets, and financial assets from 1987 to 2008. They confirmed the existence of a "tranquil" regime which was characterized by positive equity returns with low volatility and a "crisis" regime which had the opposite characteristics to those of the earlier one. Furthermore, there was evidence of contagion between stock, real estate, and oil too [40]. Furthermore, researchers [41] applied VAR(-1)-GARCH(1,1) systems to find out correlation along with the transmission of volatility across the US equity (S&P500) and five commodity indices from 2001 to 2011. They found that the equity index has the highest conditional correlation with the gold index followed by the oil, wheat, and beverage indices, respectively. Furthermore, they analyzed optimal weights and hedge ratios and concluded that commodities should be added to stock-diversified portfolios with a motive to enhance returns. It is also concluded that the correlation between most of the selected assets has changed especially in the post-crisis period [42]. Another research carried out a study over 16 years and confirmed the presence of volatility spillover mostly from commodities to the Russian stock index (RTS) in all three subsample periods; however, it was high, especially in World Financial Crises. There was the presence of the strongest volatility transmission from three commodities such as gasoline, Brent oil, and palladium to the selected RTS index [43]. Akkoc and Civcir employed SVAR-DCC-GARCH and provided evidence for the presence of dynamic volatility spillover from crude oil and gold to the equity market of Turkey, with a stronger impact of later commodity rather than the former one on the sampled stock market [44]. Research based on G20 markets concluded that during turbulent times, developed markets among G20 stock markets have more sway than emerging markets, and underdeveloped stock markets are always more excessively vulnerable to shocks than the counter markets [45]. A dynamic nonsymmetric return spillover is tested among oil, gold, and 22 equity indices of distinct sectors in Europe, concluding that the majority of equities sectors are the net transmitters, whereas oil markets and gold act as the net recipients of return spillovers [30]. The researchers have employed one of the frequency connectedness approaches to examine the dynamic volatility spillover among financial markets and energy commodities from January 2018 to April 2022. They concluded that the COVID-19 outbreak caused a notable but transient rise in the volatility spillover [46].

We will now turn tear viewing a few of the significant studies related to developing markets except India. Zhong *et al.* (2004) [47] examined spillovers in the volatility of the emerging Mexican stock markets by applying the bivariate EGARCH model. They concluded that the sampled index futures market was the main source of provoking instability in its underlying spot market. The researchers Sadorsky (2014) [48] have also examined the conditional correlation and volatility spillover across prices of various commodities (oil, copper, and wheat) and stock markets of emerging nations. They used VARMA-AGARCH and DCC-AGARCH models and concluded that negative residuals were more responsible for increasing the variance as compared to positive residuals. Furthermore, after the global financial crises, correlation among sampled assets has increased significantly and approaching precrisis figures. It is concluded that oil prices and BRICS stock market prices are obliquely affected by the volatilities of other prices [49].

Studies related to Indian financial markets are Adrangi *et al.* (2014) [50] who ensure the existence of an extremely fragile linkage between the Indian stock and commodity market when they examined co-movements among three financial markets, namely, equity, exchange rate, and commodity. Bouri *et al.* [51] have used linear (ARDL) as well as nonlinear asymmetric causality tests on implied volatility indices over a period ranging from 2009 to 2016. They highlighted the sturdy association among implied volatilities of gold, oil, and the Indian stock market. Furthermore, they reported causality in one direction from the volatilities of both commodities to the volatilities of the Indian stock market only [51]. Researchers also used the DCC and Diebold-Yilmaz (DY) model to find financial contagion along with volatility spillover among five asset markets of India, namely, stock, bond, commodity, currency, and gold market for the period 2006 to 2016. They concluded that the commodity market has the largest financial contagion with the equity market, however, slightest with the gold [10]. Indian stock and commodity market were playing the role of net volatility transmitters and only the stock market was a source of transmitting volatility to the Indian commodity market. Likewise, Maitra (2019) [52] have confirmed the presence of slightly more return as well as volatility spillover between Indian stock and commodity during the postcrisis period in contrast to the precrisis period. The another author used DY spillover index to investigate the dynamic volatility and return connectedness among the financial markets of India over a period from 2006 to 2017. Their study confirmed the presence of a time-varying correlation among all selected markets. Moreover, the stock market works as the largest transmitter of return and volatility pursued by the Forex and commodity markets [53].

It is evident from the previous works of literature that there was hardly any study that analyzed the transmission of volatility among equity and individual commodities in the context of India. Therefore, to bridge this research gap, the present research is carried out to help investors while carrying out investment-related decisions.

18.3   Data and Methodology

The dataset retrieved to analyze the volatility spillover in Indian future markets consists of daily near-month low and high prices of stock future index and composite as well as sectoral future indices of commodity market from official websites of the National Stock Exchange of India (NSE) and Multi Commodity Exchange of India Ltd (MCX), respectively, over the period January 1, 2007 until March 31, 2022. A total number of 3456 observations were obtained; however, 450 observations have been deleted from all commodity indices to deal with the problem of nonsynchronous trading days between the selected markets.

18.3.1   Conversion of Price Series into Volatility Series

The range-based estimator is used for quantifying volatility using the following equations including information about intraday low and high prices instead of daily closing prices of each index. Literature has proven the advantage of using a range-based volatility estimator as compared to the traditional method of estimating volatility [54–57].

For index i on day t, we have

$$\text{Daily variance } (\tilde{\sigma}_{it}^2) = 0.361[\ln (P_{it}^{high}) - \ln(P_{it}^{low})]^2$$

where $\ln (P_{it}^{high})$ and $\ln(P_{it}^{low})$ are the natural logs of high price and low price in market i on day t, respectively. After calculating the daily variance, we calculate daily volatility or the annualized daily percent standard deviation with the help of the following formula:

$$\text{Daily volatility } (\hat{\sigma}_{it}^2) = 100 \sqrt[2]{365 * \tilde{\sigma}_{it}^2}$$

18.3.2   Test of Stationary

Stationarity of series is an essential perquisite before applying time series models. Therefore, to check whether all the sampled indices' log volatilities are stationary at level or not, the augmented Dickey-Fuller (ADF) test [58] along with the Phillips-Perron (PP) test [59] is used. These tests have been applied with trend and intercept having the null hypothesis of the unit root.

18.3.3   Diebold-Yilmaz Index—A Vector Autoregressions-Based Approach

To capture the static volatility transmission across selected Indian stock indices and commodity futures through the construction of a total volatility spillover index, the methodology of Diebold and Yilmaz (2012) has been employed in the study. This total volatility index, a nondirectional spillover index, is a distillation of several directional volatility spillovers into a single index and typically appears in the extreme lower right-hand corner of the variance decomposition matrix [5]. It calculates the percentage of the total forecast error variance (FEV) that volatility shock spillovers across the eleven stocks and commodity futures indices under consideration have contributed to. The volatility contributions produced by the Diebold-Yilmaz research paper (KPPS) variance decomposition were used to construct the index, represented by VSg (H) Koop, Pesaran and and Potter (1996) [60]and Pesaran and Shin (1998) [61].

$$VS^g(H) = \frac{\sum_{\substack{i,j=1 \\ i \neq j}}^{N} \tilde{\theta}_{ij}^g(H)}{\sum_{i,j=1}^{N} \tilde{\theta}_{ij}^g(H)} \times 100 = \frac{\sum_{\substack{i,j=1 \\ i \neq j}}^{N} \tilde{\theta}_{ij}^g(H)}{N} \times 100 \qquad (18.1)$$

18.4   Results and Discussions

18.4.1   Descriptive Analysis

Table 18.1 presents the descriptive statistics of daily volatilities of five selected future indices, namely, stock future index (FUTIDX), commodity composite (COMDEX), and sectoral (METALS, ENERGY, and AGRI) future indices. It is evident from the following table that the energy index has the highest average volatility (represented by mean) as well as unconditional volatility (represented by standard deviation) followed by futidx, metal, comdex, and agri indices, respectively. We also observe that all sampled series are asymmetrically distributed because all are positively skewed and leptokurtic (Kurtosis, >3). Furthermore, to check the robustness of the above results, the Jarque-Bera (J-B) test has been applied which confirms the normal distribution of converted volatility series at a very high level of significance. It might be due to the presence of extreme values in all the sample series.

Table 18.1 Descriptive statistics of volatility series.

	NIFTY	COMDEX	METAL	ENERGY	AGRI
Mean	18.4593	14.63844	15.467	26.35892	11.0542
Median	14.3336	12.48656	13.0827	23.00017	9.89317
Maximum	168.04	82.27191	104.246	112.6267	48.3558
Minimum	2.55154	2.44555	1.92547	2.653779	1.83471
Std. Dev.	14.2401	8.388521	9.10917	14.65279	5.72987
Skewness	3.35573	2.100677	2.44617	1.64917	1.69363
Kurtosis	23.0355	9.949638	14.0255	6.760935	7.72618
Jarque-Bera	55398.7*	8183.152*	18053.8*	3105.021*	4195.3*

Note: * denotes significant at a 1% level of significance.

18.4.2   Stationary Test

Before applying any regression model to the time series, we checked the stationary feature of the selected indices to avoid spurious results. Therefore, parametric and nonparametric unit root tests, namely, ADF test and PP test, have been applied, respectively. Table 18.2 depicts that the volatility series of Nifty, Comdex, Metal, Energy, and Agriculture do not only have a significant trend but are stationary at a level as a p-value of t-statistics is statistically significant at 1%. Thus, both tests reject the null hypothesis of unit root ($\rho = 1$) in each index. In other words, the volatility series of all selected individual commodities and indices are stationary.

Table 18.2 Unit Roots tests on volatility series.

Unit root tests	NIFTY	COMDEX	METAL	ENERGY	AGRI
ADF	-9.4350*	-6.6563*	-9.7840*	-5.3032*	-9.14331*
PP	-51.8190*	-56.8704*	-55.0452*	-55.8036*	-53.7171*

Note: * denotes significant at a 1% level of significance.

18.4.3   Volatility Transmission

After ensuring about stationarity of all volatility series, we have applied the VAR-based Diebold- Yilmaz model to check volatility spillover among selected commodity and stock indices. Table 18.3 shows the gross and net volatility transmissions among stock and various commodity indices. We have calculated volatility connectedness measures based on the VAR of order 5 (as per Schwarz information criterion), rolling window of 200, and generalized variance decomposition of 10 days ahead forecast errors. In Table 18.3, the contribution "FROM" others (off-diagonal row sums) and contribution "TO" others (off-diagonal column sums) are the total volatility spillover from all selected indices to the ith index and the total volatility spillover from the ith index to all selected indices, respectively. Net volatility spillover is calculated by subtracting "contribution FROM others" from "contribution TO others". The index is considered to be a net transmitter of volatility if it has a positive value of net volatility spillover; however, in the vice versa situation, it is named a net volatility receiver. The total volatility index is approximately the fraction of "grand off-diagonal column sum"

Table 18.3 Volatility transmission.

	NIFTY	COMDEX	METAL	ENERGY	AGRI	From others (gross)
NIFTY	92.4	6.5	0.5	0.2	0.4	7.6
COMDEX	5.3	94.1	0	0.3	0.2	5.9
METAL	5.9	55.2	38	0.3	0.6	62
ENERGY	1.9	53.9	10.9	33.1	0.1	66.9
AGRI	0.2	2.5	0.3	0.7	96.3	3.7
Contribution to others (gross)	13.4	118.1	11.8	1.5	1.4	146.1
Contribution including own	105.8	212.2	49.7	34.6	97.6	Total volatility index= 29.20%
Net volatility spillover	5.8	112.2	-50.2	-65.4	-2.3	

(or "grand off-diagonal row sum") to "grand column sum (or "grand row sum"), expressed as a percentage. It is a single index that comprises the distillation of the numerous directional volatility spillover.

It is evident from Table 18.3 that COMDEX grossly transmits a high degree of volatility (118.1); however, ENERGY grossly receives a high degree of volatility (66.9) from other indices. Furthermore, on the basis of net volatility spillover, COMDEX is the largest net transmitter of volatility followed by NIFTY, whereas ENERGY, METAL, and AGRI are net receivers of volatility. Thus, we conclude that whether it is gross or net volatility spillover, the commodity market composite index is the largest volatility transmitter; on the other hand, its sectoral index, ENERGY, is the utmost volatility receiver. As per the total volatility index, across the entire sample, on average, 29.20% of the volatility FEV in all selected indices is due to all these transmissions.

18.5   Conclusion

Volatility is a barometer used by analysts and investors to understand fluctuation and inefficiency in the financial markets. Using the methodology of Diebold and Yilmaz (2012), this study investigates the static volatility transmission between Indian equity and commodity market, using intraday high and low prices over the period ranging from April 1, 2007 to March 31, 2022 [5]. Initially, all selected indices and individual commodity price series are converted into volatility series using the range method, and then two unit root tests are applied. The ADF and PP test results confirmed the stationarity of all the volatility series. The study found that, on average, 29.20% of the FEVs have been explained by the spillover effect. Moreover, the static net volatility spillover results depict that Comdex acts as the highest net volatility transmitter followed by equity. On the other hand, the energy index acts as the highest net volatility receiver followed by the metal indices and agri index. Nonagricultural indices (such as metal and energy indices) are more sensitive to other indices' volatility than agricultural indices as the former indices show a huge negative volatility spillover of 65.4 (energy) and 50.2 (metal) as compared to the latter one. Since the agricultural index is the nominal transmitter/recipient of volatility spillovers to/from the equity index as well as the nonagricultural commodity market during the sample period, it suggests that portfolio managers and investors can diversify the risk of the Indian equity sector and nonagricultural commodities by including agricultural commodities in their portfolios. Thus, the findings of the study will be helpful to global and domestic investors for asset allocation or portfolio decisions.

References

1. McGough, T. and Berry, J., Real estate risk, yield modelling and market sentiment: the impact on pricing in european office markets. *J. Eur. Real Estate Res.*, *15*, 2, 179–191, 2022.

2. Yaşar, B., The impact of COVID-19 on volatility of tourism stocks: Evidence from BIST tourism index, in: *Handbook of Research on the Impacts and Implications of COVID-19 on the Tourism Industry*, pp. 23–44, IGI Global, 2021. https://www.igi-global.com/dictionary/the-impact-of-covid-19-on-volatility-of-tourism-stocks/100407

3. Ross, S.A., Information and volatility: The no-arbitrage martingale approach to timing and resolution irrelevancy. *J. Finance*, *44*, 1, 1–17, 1989.

4. Srivastava, A., Bhatia, S., Gupta, P., Financial crisis and stock market integration: An analysis of select economies. *Glob. Bus. Rev.*, *16*, 6, 1127–1142, 2015.

5. Diebold, F.X. and Yilmaz, K., Better to give than to receive: Predictive directional measurement of volatility spillovers. *Int. J. Forecast*, *28*, 1, 57–66, 2012.

6. Lee, C.F., Leuthold, R.M., Cordier, J.E., The stock market and the commodity futures market: Diversification and arbitrage potential. *Financial Anal. J.*, *41*, 4, 53–60, 1985.

7. Jensen, G.R., Johnson, R.R., Mercer, J.M., Efficient use of commodity futures in diversified portfolios. *J. Futures Mark.: Futures, Options, Other Derivative Products*, *20*, 5, 489–506, 2000.

8. Bodie, Z., Commodity futures as a hedge against inflation. *J. Portf. Manage.*, *9*, 3, 12–17, 1983.

9. Edwards, F. and Park, J., Do managed futures make good investments? *J. Futures Mark.*, 16, 475–517, 1996.

10. Roy, R.P. and Roy, S.S., Financial contagion and volatility spillover: An exploration into indian commodity derivative market. *Econ. Model.*, *67*, 368–380, 2017.

11. Vivian, A. and Wohar, M.E., Commodity volatility breaks. *J. Int. Financial Mark. Inst. Money*, *22*, 2, 395–422, 2012.

12. Kannadas, S. and Viswanathan, T., Volatility spillover effects among gold, oil and stock markets: Empirical evidence from the G7 countries. *Econom. Stud.*, *31*, 4, 18–32, 2022.

13. Yilmaz, K., Return and volatility spillovers among the east asian equity markets. *J. Asian Econ.*, *21*, 3, 304–313, 2010.

14. Li, Y. and Giles, D.E., Modelling volatility spillover effects between developed stock markets and asian emerging stock markets. *Int. J. Finance Econ.*, 20, 155e177, 2015.

15. Jebran, K. and Iqbal, A., Examining volatility spiilover between asian countries' stock markets. *China Finance Econ. Rev.*, *4*, 1, 6, 2016.

16. Bala, D.A. and Takimoto, T., Stock markets volatility spillovers during financial crises: A DCC-MGARCH with skewed-t density approach. *Borsa Istanbul Rev.*, *17*, 1, 25–48, 2017.

17. Vardar, G., Coşkun, Y., Yelkenci, T., Shock transmission and volatility spillover in stock and commodity markets: Evidence from advanced and emerging markets. *Eurasian Econ. Rev.*, *8*, 2, 231–288, 2018.

18. Hung, N.T., Financial connectedness of GCC emerging stock markets. *Eurasian Econ. Rev.*, *11*, 4, 753–773, 2021.

19. Vuong, G.T.H., Nguyen, M.H., Huynh, A.N.Q., Volatility spillovers from the Chinese stock market to the US stock market: The role of the COVID-19 pandemic. *J. Econ. Asymmetries*, *26*, e00276, 2022.

20. Saâdaoui, F. and Ghadhab, I., Investigating volatility transmission across international equity markets using multivariate fractional models. *Int. Trans. Oper. Res.*, *30*, 5, 2139–2157, 2023.

21. Yahya, F., Abbas, G., Lee, C.C., Asymmetric effects and volatility transmission from metals markets to solar energy stocks: Evidence from DCC, ADCC, and quantile regression approach. *Resour. Policy*, *82*, 103501, 2023.

22. Mehta, K., Sharma, R., Vyas, V., Efficiency and ranking of sustainability index of India using DEA-TOPSIS. *J. Indian Bus. Res.*, 11, 2, 179–199, 2019, https://doi.org/10.1108/JIBR-02-2018-0057.

23. Mehta, K., Sharma, R., Vyas, V., A quantile regression approach to study the impact of aluminium prices on the manufacturing sector of India during the COVID era. *Mater. Today: Proc.*, 65, 8, 3506–3511, 2022, ISSN 2214- 7853, https://doi.org/10.1016/j.matpr.2022.06.087.

24. Zhang, Y.J. and Wei, Y.M., The crude oil market and the gold market: evidence for cointegration, causality and price discovery. *Resour. Policy*, 35, 168–177, 2010.

25. Filis, G., Degiannakis, S., Floros, C., Dynamic correlation between stock market and oil prices: The case of oil-importing and oil-exporting countries. *Int. Rev. Financial Anal.*, *20*, 3, 152–164, 2011.

26. Lee, Y.H., Huang, Y.L., Yang, H.J., The asymmetric long-run relationship between crude oil and gold futures. *Global J. Bus. Res. (GJBR)*, *6*, 1, 9–15, 2012.

27. Anand, B., Paul, S., Ramachandran, M., Volatility spillover between oil and stock market returns. *Indian Econ. Rev.*, 49, 1, 37–56, 2014.

28. Ewing, B.T. and Malik, F., Volatility spillovers between oil prices and the stock market under structural breaks. *Glob. Finance J.*, *29*, 12–23, 2016.

29. Kumar, S., Singh, G., Kumar, A., Volatility spillover among prices of crude oil, natural gas, exchange rate, gold, and stock market: Fresh evidence from exponential generalized autoregressive conditional heteroscedastic model analysis. *J. Public Aff.*, *22*, 4, e2594, 2022.

30. Mensi, W., Yousaf, I., Vo, X.V., Kang, S.H., Asymmetric spillover and network connectedness between gold, BRENT oil and EU subsector markets. *J. Int. Financ. Mark. Inst. Money.*, 76, 101487, 2022.

31. Zhang, Y.J., Fan, Y., Tsai, H.T., Wei, Y.M., Spillover effect of US dollar exchange rate on oil prices. *J. Policy Model.*, 30, 6, 973–991, 2008.

32. Salisu, A.A. and Mobolaji, H., Modeling returns and volatility transmission between oil price and US–Nigeria exchange rate. *Energy Econ.*, 39, 169–176, 2013.

33. Mehta, K., Sharma, R., Chugh, A., Management of forex risk exposure: A study of SMEs and unlisted non-financial firms in India. *Int. J. Appl. Bus. Econ. Res.*, 15, 9, 43–54, 2017.

34. Sayadi, M., Rafei, M., Sheykha, Y., Asymmetric volatility spillovers of oil price and exchange rate on chemical stocks: Fresh results from a VAR-TBEKK-in-mean model for Iran. *Iran. Econ. Rev.*, 26, 4, 885–904, 2022.

35. Serletis, A., *Quantitative and empirical analysis of energy markets*, vol. 1, World Scientific, 2007. https://www.worldscientific.com/worldscibooks/10.1142/8624#t=aboutBook

36. Charfeddine, L., True or spurious long memory in volatility: Further evidence on the energy futures markets. *Energy Policy*, 71, 76–93, 2014.

37. Li, J., Umar, M., Huo, J., The spillover effect between Chinese crude oil futures market and Chinese green energy stock market. *Energy Econ.*, 119, 106568, 2023.

38. Chong, J. and Miffre, J., Conditional return correlations between commodity futures and traditional assets, Working Paper, EDHEC, April 2008. https://climateimpact.edhec.edu/sites/ercii/files/EDHEC_Working_Paper_Conditional_Return_Correlations_between_Commodity_Futures_and_Traditional_Assets.pdf

39. Arouri, M., Jouini, J., Nguyen, D., On the impacts of oil price fluctuations on european equity markets: Volatility spillover and hedging effectiveness. *Energy Econ.*, 34, 611–617, 2012.

40. Chan, K.F., Treepongkaruna, S., Brooks, R., Gray, S., Asset market linkages: Evidence from financial, commodity and real estate assets. *J. Bank. Financ.*, 35, 6, 1415–1426, 2011.

41. Mensi, W., Beljid, M., Boubaker, A., Managi, S., Correlations and volatility spillovers across commodity and stock markets: Linking energies, food, and gold. *Econ. Model.*, 32, 15–22, 2013.

42. Mollick, A.V. and Assefa, T.A., U.S. stock returns and oil prices: The tale from daily data and the 2008–2009 financial crisis. *Energy Econ.*, 36, 1–18, 2013.

43. Živkov, D., Njegić, J., Momčilović, M., Bidirectional spillover effect between russian stock index and the selected commodities. *Zb. Rad. Ekon. Fak. Rij.: Časopis Za Ekonomsku Teoriju I Praksu*, 36, 1, 27–51, 2018.

44. Akkoc, U. and Civcir, I., Dynamic linkages between strategic commodities and stock market in Turkey: Evidence from SVAR-DCC-GARCH model. *Res. Policy*, 62, 231–239, 2019.

45. Zhang, W., Zhuang, X., Lu, Y., Wang, J., Spatial linkage of volatility spillovers and its explanation across G20 stock markets: A network framework. *Int. Rev. Financial Anal.*, 71, 101454, 2020.

46. Huang, J., Chen, B., Xu, Y., Xia, X., Time-frequency volatility transmission among energy commodities and financial markets during the COVID-19 pandemic: A novel TVP-VAR frequency connectedness approach. *Finance Res. Lett.*, 53, 103634, 2023.

47. Zhong, M., Darrat, A.F., Otero, R., Price discovery and volatility spillovers in index futures markets: Some evidence from Mexico. *J. Bank. Financ.*, 28, 12, 3037–3054, 2004.

48. Sadorsky, P., Modeling volatility and correlations between emerging market stock prices and the prices of copper, oil and wheat. *Energy Econ.*, 43, 72–81, 2014.

49. Boubaker, H. and Raza, S.A., A wavelet analysis of mean and volatility spillovers between oil and BRICS stock markets. *Energy Econ.*, 64, 105–117, 2017.

50. Adrangi, B., Chatrath, A., David-Christie, R., Maitra, D., Market comovements, regulation, and financial crisis: Evidence from indian markets. *Rev. Futures Mark.*, 22, 2, 21–47, 2014.

51. Bouri, E., Jain, A., Biswal, P.C., Roubaud, D., Cointegration and nonlinear causality amongst gold, oil, and the indian stock market: Evidence from implied volatility indices. *Resour. Policy*, 52, 201–206, 2017.

52. Maitra, D. and Dawar, V., Return and volatility spillover among commodity futures, stock market and exchange rate: Evidence from India. *Glob. Bus. Rev.*, 20, 1, 214–237, 2019.

53. Sobti, N., Domestic intermarket linkages: measuring dynamic return and volatility connectedness among indian financial markets. *DECISION: Off. J. Indian Inst. Manage. Calcutta*, 45, 4, 325–344, 2018.

54. Garman, M.B. and Klass, M.J., On the estimation of security price volatilities from historical data. *J. Bus.*, 53, 1, 67–78, 1980.

55. Parkinson, M., The extreme value method for estimating the variance of the rate of return. *J. Bus.*, 53, 1, 61–65, 1980.

56. Yang, D. and Zhang, Q., Drift-independent volatility estimation based on high, low, open, and close prices. *J. Bus.*, 73, 3, 477–492, 2000.

57. Petneházi, G. and Gáll, J., Exploring the predictability of range-based volatility estimators using recurrent neural networks. *Intell. Syst. Account. Finance Manage.*, 26, 3, 109–116, 2019.

58. Dickey, D.A. and Fuller, W.A., Distribution of the estimators for autoregressive time series with a unit root. *J. Am. Stat. Assoc.*, 47, 427–431, 1979.

59. Phillips, P.C. and Perron, P., Testing for a unit root in time series regression. *Biometrika*, 75, 2, 335–346, 1988.
60. Koop, G., Pesaran, M.H., Potter, S.M., Impulse response analysis in non- linear multivariate models, 0,000 results (0.33 seconds). *J. Econ.*, 74, 119–147, 1996.
61. Pesaran, M.H. and Shin, Y., Generalized impulse response analysis in linear multivariate models. *Econ. Lett.*, 58, 17–29, 1998.

Glossary

AI (Artificial Intelligence): Artificial Intelligence is the simulation of human intelligence processes by machines, including learning, reasoning, and problem-solving. In finance, AI is employed to analyze data, develop trading strategies, and automate tasks.

AI in option trading: Artificial Intelligence (AI) augments option trading by applying deep learning to assess market conditions and identify profitable opportunities. It assists traders in executing well-informed option trading strategies.

Alternative data: Alternative data refers to non-traditional, unconventional data sources used for analysis. In finance, it can include social media activity, satellite imagery, and web scraping data for predicting market movements.

ARCH and GARCH family: Autoregressive Conditional Heteroskedasticity (ARCH) and Generalized ARCH (GARCH) models are used to model volatility clustering in financial time series data. They provide insights into market volatility patterns.

ARIMA (AutoRegressive Integrated Moving Average): ARIMA is a time-series forecasting method that models a variable as a combination of its past values and forecast errors. It's commonly used in financial analysis for predicting stock prices and market trends. They capture temporal trends, seasonality, and autocorrelations in stock market data.

Artificial intelligence in stock market prediction: Artificial intelligence leverages deep learning and other techniques to analyze massive amounts of data for stock market predictions. It enhances decision-making by identifying intricate patterns and trends that impact stock prices.

Artificial neural network: An artificial neural network (ANN) is a computational model inspired by the human brain's structure. It consists of interconnected nodes and is used in various tasks, including pattern recognition and prediction. Prediction Models: Prediction models use historical data and mathematical algorithms to forecast future outcomes. In finance, prediction models are employed to estimate stock prices, market trends, and economic indicators.

Asset management companies (AMCs): AMCs manage investment portfolios on behalf of clients, aiming to optimize returns while managing risks. Deep learning can aid AMCs by offering data-driven insights for more informed decision-making.

Bearishness: Bearishness represents a negative outlook on the market or an asset. Those with a bearish view expect prices to decline. This sentiment might arise from negative news, weak fundamentals, or technical indicators suggesting downward movement.

Behavioral biases: Behavioral biases are systematic patterns of deviation from rational decision-making due to cognitive and emotional factors. They include biases like loss aversion, herding behavior, and overconfidence, which can impact investment choices.

Behavioral finance: Behavioral finance studies how psychological factors impact financial decisions and market behavior. It explores why individuals often deviate from rational decision-making, resulting in behavioral biases and market anomalies.

Bibliometric analysis: A quantitative assessment of patterns within scholarly literature, used to reveal prominent authors, significant topics, and citation interconnections.

Blind quantum computing: Blind quantum computing allows a user to delegate a computational task to a quantum server without revealing the specifics of the computation. This preserves privacy and security, making it useful for confidential calculations.

Bullishness: Bullishness refers to a positive outlook on the market or a specific asset. A person with a bullish view anticipates that prices will rise. This sentiment is often fueled by positive news, strong fundamentals, or technical indicators pointing towards upward movement.

Business: A business refers to an entity engaged in economic activities, producing goods or services for profit. In finance, understanding a business's financial health and performance is crucial for investment decisions.

Call and put option: Call and Put options are financial derivatives that provide the right but not the obligation to buy (Call) or sell (Put) an underlying asset at a predetermined price within a specified timeframe. Deep learning can assist in understanding option pricing and predicting their value changes.

Co-integration test: Co integration tests are statistical tools used to determine whether multiple non-stationary time series have a long-term equilibrium relationship. In finance, they help identify variables that move together over time, indicating a lasting connection.

Commodity: A commodity is a basic raw material or primary agricultural product that is interchangeable with other goods of the same type. Examples include crude oil, gold, wheat, and coffee. Commodity markets play a pivotal role in global trade and economics as they provide a standardized platform for buying and selling these goods.

Cumulative open interest: Cumulative open interest is the summation of open interest values across multiple trading periods. Analyzing cumulative open interest helps identify trends in market sentiment and potential shifts in market dynamics over time.

Data privacy: Data privacy pertains to the protection of sensitive information. In financial analysis, data privacy is crucial to ensure the confidentiality and security of investor data and sensitive financial information.

Data standardization: Data standardization involves transforming data into a consistent format or structure. In finance, standardizing data is essential for accurate analysis and comparison across different sources.

Deep learning and derivative markets: Derivative markets involve instruments whose value is derived from an underlying asset, like options and futures. Deep learning improves derivative market predictions by capturing complex relationships between these instruments and market variables.

Deep learning models: Deep learning models are intricate neural networks with multiple layers that autonomously learn from data. These models have shown promise in capturing intricate patterns in stock market data, improving prediction accuracy.

Deep learning: Deep learning is a specialized area of machine learning that involves artificial neural networks with multiple layers. It's particularly effective for tasks like image and speech recognition.

Deep learning: Deep learning is a subset of machine learning that involves artificial neural networks with multiple layers. It's designed to automatically learn patterns from large amounts of data and has gained prominence for its ability to analyze complex relationships in various fields, including stock market predictions.

Diebold: Diebold Nixdorf is a global company specializing in providing technology solutions and services to various industries, including banking and retail. They offer a range of products such as ATMs, point-of-sale systems, security solutions, and software to enhance operational efficiency and customer experiences.

DNN and stock market data: Deep Neural Networks (DNNs) analyze vast amounts of stock market data to identify intricate patterns. Their hierarchical architecture enables them to capture complex relationships within the data.

Econometric models: Econometric models are statistical frameworks that combine economic theory with data to analyze and quantify relationships between variables. These models help economists and analysts understand how changes in one variable can impact others within complex economic systems.

Efficient market hypothesis (EMH): EMH posits that stock prices reflect all available information, making it impossible to consistently outperform the market. Deep learning challenges aspects of EMH by identifying patterns that might be missed by traditional methods.

Emotional intelligence: Emotional intelligence is the ability to recognize, understand, manage, and effectively use one's own emotions and those of others. In the context of finance, emotional intelligence can impact investment decisions by helping individuals manage their emotions and make rational choices.

Event study: An event study analyzes the impact of specific events, such as earnings releases or economic announcements, on asset prices. It helps researchers understand how markets react to new information.

Exploratory factor analysis: Exploratory Factor Analysis (EFA) is a statistical technique used to identify underlying patterns and relationships among a set of observed variables. It helps researchers understand complex data structures and reduce them to a smaller number of factors.

Exponential moving averages (EMA): EMA is a technical indicator that emphasizes recent price data more than older data points. Deep learning can assist in optimizing EMA parameters for improved trend analysis.

Financial service sector and deep learning: The financial services sector leverages deep learning to enhance customer experiences, automate processes, detect fraud, and predict market trends, fostering more efficient and accurate decision-making.

Fundamental analysis: Fundamental analysis evaluates a company's financial health by examining its financial statements and market position. Deep learning can enhance this analysis by processing vast amounts of data for more informed investment decisions.

Future & options: Futures contracts and options are derivatives that derive their value from an underlying asset. Futures obligate the buyer to buy or sell the asset on a future date, while options provide the buyer with the choice to buy or sell the asset. Both instruments are used for speculation and risk management.

Future: In finance, a future is a standardized contract obligating the buyer to purchase or the seller to sell a specified asset at a predetermined price on a future date. Futures contracts are used for hedging and speculation.

Futures market: The futures market is a platform where participants trade standardized contracts known as futures contracts. These contracts obligate traders to buy or sell an asset at a predetermined price on a specified future date. The futures market enables hedging against price fluctuations and allows speculators to profit from price movements.

Granger causality test: The Granger causality test assesses whether the past values of one variable can predict the future values of another. It's a valuable tool for identifying potential causal relationships between economic or financial variables.

Graphics processing units (GPUs): GPUs accelerate deep learning computations due to their parallel processing capabilities. They significantly speed up tasks like training complex neural networks, crucial for timely stock market analysis.

Illusion of control: The illusion of control bias occurs when individuals believe they have more influence over outcomes than they actually do. In finance, it can lead to misguided trading strategies based on a false sense of control.

Image classification: Image classification assigns labels to images based on their content. Applied to stock market data, it can categorize visual information, aiding in identifying trends, sentiments, and potential signals.

Information efficiency in stock market: Information Efficiency theory classifies markets based on how quickly and accurately prices adjust to new information. Deep learning's rapid data processing can contribute to more efficient markets by facilitating quicker price adjustments.

Investment banks (IBs): Investment banks offer various financial services, including trading, mergers and acquisitions, and underwriting. Deep learning can enhance their analytical capabilities for better market predictions and risk assessment.

Investment decision: An investment decision is the process of choosing where to allocate funds with the intention of achieving financial returns. It involves assessing various factors such as risk tolerance, investment goals, market trends, and asset analysis.

Investment management: Investment management involves overseeing and making decisions about an investment portfolio on behalf of individuals or institutions. It includes asset allocation, risk assessment, and performance evaluation.

Investment: Investment refers to the allocation of funds with the expectation of generating future returns. In finance, investment decisions are based on factors like risk, expected returns, and market analysis.

Investor behavior: Investor behavior explores how psychological biases and emotional factors influence investment decisions. Integrating deep learning with behavioral finance can offer insights into understanding and predicting market reactions driven by human behavior. It's a central focus of behavioral finance, which studies deviations from rational behavior.

Investor decision: Investor decisions encompass the choices individuals make when allocating their funds for investment purposes. These decisions are influenced by various factors, including risk tolerance, financial goals, market information, and personal biases.

LSTM (Long Short-Term Memory): LSTM is a type of artificial neural network architecture designed for sequences and time-series data. It's used in various tasks, including stock market prediction, due to its ability to capture long-term dependencies.

Machine learning and stock market predictions: Machine learning techniques, including deep learning, analyze historical market data to identify patterns and trends that inform predictions. These models adapt and improve based on new data, enhancing their predictive accuracy over time.

Machine learning: Machine learning involves the development of algorithms that enable computers to learn from and make predictions or decisions based on data. It's used extensively in stock market prediction and risk assessment.

Market anomalies: Market anomalies are patterns or events that contradict traditional financial theories. Examples include the January effect, where stock prices tend to rise in January, and the momentum effect, where past winners continue to outperform.

Marketplace: A marketplace is where buyers and sellers interact to exchange goods or services. In finance, stock markets and commodity exchanges are examples of marketplaces where financial instruments are traded.

Mathematical tools: Mathematical tools, such as statistical methods and quantitative models, are used in financial analysis to quantify relationships, make predictions, and assess risks.

Monetary policy: Monetary policy refers to the actions taken by a central bank to manage a country's money supply, interest rates, and credit availability, with the aim of achieving economic stability and growth.

Multiple regression: Multiple regression is a statistical method used to analyze the relationship between a dependent variable and multiple independent variables. It helps quantify the impact of various factors on the dependent variable and aids in making predictions.

Mutual funds and use of deep learning: Mutual funds pool money from multiple investors to invest in diverse assets. Deep learning aids mutual funds by providing advanced tools for portfolio optimization and predicting market trends.

Neural network family: The Neural Network family encompasses various architectures inspired by the human brain's neural structure. This includes Convolutional Neural Networks (CNNs) for image analysis, Recurrent Neural Networks (RNNs) for sequence data, and more, each tailored for specific tasks, including stock market analysis.

NLP (Natural Language Processing): NLP is a branch of AI that focuses on enabling computers to understand, interpret, and generate human language. It's used in sentiment analysis and news processing for predicting market movements.

Object recognition: Object recognition involves identifying specific objects or patterns within images or visual data. In the stock market context, object recognition can aid in identifying relevant market signals from visual data sources.

Open interest: Open interest is the total number of outstanding futures or options contracts that have not been closed by offsetting trades or exercised by physical delivery. It provides insight into the level of market activity and can influence price movements.

Optimism: Optimism bias is the inclination to view outcomes as more favorable than they are statistically likely to be. It can lead investors to underestimate risks and make overly aggressive investment decisions.

Option chain: An option chain is a comprehensive list of all available options contracts for a specific underlying security. It includes different strike prices and expiration dates for both call and put options. Option chains provide traders with essential information for crafting options-based strategies.

Option trading strategies: Option trading strategies involve combinations of buying and selling options to capitalize on various market conditions. Deep learning models can help optimize these strategies by analyzing historical data and identifying optimal entry and exit points.

Overconfidence: Overconfidence bias leads individuals to overestimate their abilities, knowledge, and predictive accuracy. In investing, it can result in excessive trading, unwarranted risk-taking, and poor portfolio performance.

Panel data: Panel data refers to observations collected over time on multiple individuals, entities, or units. It's used in various economic and financial analyses to account for individual and time-specific effects.

Portfolio management: Portfolio management involves selecting and managing a mix of investments to achieve specific financial goals. Deep learning enhances this process by analyzing diverse data sources, optimizing asset allocation, and improving risk management.

Predict stock market: Predicting the stock market involves using various techniques, including fundamental and technical analysis, as well as advanced data-driven approaches like machine learning and artificial intelligence, to forecast future price movements of stocks and indices.

Predicting the stock prices: Predicting stock prices involves using historical data, market trends, and advanced techniques like deep learning to forecast future stock values. It aids investors in making informed decisions.

Prediction: Prediction involves estimating future outcomes based on historical data and other relevant information. In finance, prediction models are used to forecast stock prices, market trends, and economic indicators.

Price and volume study in stock market: Price and volume study involves analyzing the relationship between a stock's price movement and the trading volume. Deep learning techniques can uncover complex correlations between these variables for predictive insights.

Psychological traits and stock market trading: Psychological traits like fear and greed significantly influence trading decisions. Deep learning models can incorporate sentiment analysis and psychological factors to better predict market movements driven by these emotions.

Put-call ratio: The put-call ratio is a market sentiment indicator derived from the ratio of traded put options to call options. A high put-call ratio can suggest increased bearish sentiment, while a low ratio might indicate heightened bullishness among traders.

Quantitative finance: Quantitative finance is a field that uses mathematical models, statistical analysis, and computer programming to understand and predict financial markets' behavior. It blends financial theory with technology to make informed investment and risk management decisions.

Quantum computing and stock markets: Quantum computing's immense computational power has the potential to revolutionize stock market predictions by quickly analyzing vast amounts of data. Though in its early stages, its impact on financial modeling could be significant.

Quantum computing: Quantum computing is an emerging field that harnesses the principles of quantum mechanics to perform complex calculations. It has the potential to revolutionize fields such as cryptography, optimization, and material science by solving problems that are currently intractable for classical computers.

Quantum neural networks: Quantum neural networks combine quantum computing elements with neural network structures to enhance machine learning capabilities. They leverage quantum properties to potentially speed up certain computations.

Random walk and EMH: The random walk theory suggest stock prices move randomly, challenging the predictability of markets. Deep learning's ability to uncover hidden patterns can challenge this theory by offering insights into seemingly random movements.

Rationality: Rationality involves making decisions based on logical analysis, information, and sound reasoning, without being influenced by emotions or cognitive biases. Rational investors carefully weigh pros and cons before making choices.

Recent development in stock market prediction models: Recent developments incorporate advancements in deep learning architectures, optimization algorithms, and the integration of alternative data sources. These models offer higher prediction accuracy and adaptability to changing market dynamics.

Recent techniques of stock market analysis: Recent stock market analysis techniques encompass machine learning, deep learning, natural language processing, sentiment analysis, and more. These advanced techniques provide more comprehensive insights into market behavior and enhance predictive capabilities.

Regression analysis in stock prices: Regression analysis models relationships between variables, aiding in predicting stock prices based on historical data and other relevant factors. Deep learning improves regression accuracy by accounting for complex nonlinear interactions.

Returns in the stock market: Returns quantify the profitability of an investment over a specified period. Deep learning models help analyze historical returns to uncover trends and relationships with other market variables.

Risk analysis in security analysis: Risk analysis assesses potential financial losses associated with investments. In security analysis, deep learning models enhance risk assessment by analyzing vast amounts of data to identify potential risks and inform mitigation strategies.

RNN (Recurrent Neural Network): RNN is a type of artificial neural network architecture suitable for sequential data. It's often used in financial time-series analysis to capture dependencies in data across time steps.

Security markets: Security markets are platforms where various financial instruments like stocks, bonds, and derivatives are bought and sold.

Deep learning plays a crucial role in analyzing market data and predicting price movements within these markets.

Sentiment analysis: Sentiment analysis involves using NLP and AI techniques to analyze text data, such as social media posts or news articles, to determine the sentiment or emotional tone. It's used to gauge market sentiment and predict price movements.

Short-term and long-term predictions in stock market: Short-term predictions focus on immediate price movements, usually within days or weeks, while long-term predictions extend over months to years. Both employ deep learning techniques to uncover patterns for different investment strategies.

Soft computing and stock markets: Soft computing involves flexible, adaptive techniques like neural networks and fuzzy logic. Applied to stock markets, it helps capture uncertain and complex market dynamics for improved predictions.

Stock market prediction models: These specialized models use historical data, indicators, and machine learning techniques to predict future movements and trends in the stock market, aiding investors in decision-making.

Stock market prediction: Stock market prediction involves using data analysis, machine learning, and deep learning to forecast future stock price movements. It aims to assist investors and traders in making informed decisions about buying, selling, or holding securities.

Stock market: The stock market is a dynamic marketplace where financial instruments, such as stocks and bonds, are bought and sold. It's a crucial component of the global financial system, facilitating capital allocation and price discovery.

Stock price movements: Stock price movements refer to the fluctuations in the prices of individual stocks over time. Deep learning tools aim to decipher and predict these movements based on historical data and other relevant factors.

Stock price prediction: Stock price prediction involves using historical price data, market indicators, and advanced modeling techniques to forecast future price movements of stocks. Methods range from traditional time series analysis to sophisticated machine learning algorithms.

Stock returns: Stock returns represent the change in a stock's price over a specified period, often expressed as a percentage. They provide insights into the performance of investments.

Stock: A stock represents ownership in a company and represents a claim on a portion of the company's assets and earnings. When you own stocks, you're essentially a shareholder in the company. Stocks are traded on stock exchanges, and their prices fluctuate based on supply and demand, company performance, and market sentiment.

Support vector machine and stock price analysis: Support Vector Machines (SVMs) are machine learning algorithms used in stock price analysis to classify and predict market trends. They create decision boundaries based on historical data, aiding traders and investors in decision-making.

Systematic literature review: A meticulous approach that identifies, assesses, and summarizes existing research on a defined subject, offering a comprehensive snapshot of the present status within a particular field.

Technical analysis: Technical analysis studies historical trading data and patterns to predict future price movements. Combining deep learning with technical analysis can offer more sophisticated insights into market trends.

Technical indicators and deep learning: Technical indicators, such as moving averages and Relative Strength Index (RSI), help traders make decisions. Deep learning models can integrate these indicators with other data for enhanced predictions.

Text mining and stock market predictions: Text mining analyzes textual data from news articles, social media, and other sources to gauge market sentiment and extract relevant information. Deep learning techniques enhance sentiment analysis and text-based predictions.

Theoretical framework: A theoretical framework provides a structured approach for conducting research or analysis. It defines key concepts, variables, and relationships, guiding the formulation of hypotheses and research questions.

Time series analysis: Time series analysis involves studying data points collected at sequential time intervals. Deep learning models excel in recognizing complex patterns within time series data, making them valuable for stock market predictions.

Time series prediction: Time series prediction employs historical data to forecast future values. Deep learning models excel in capturing intricate temporal patterns, enabling accurate time series predictions for stock market movements.

Trading in stock market: Trading involves buying and selling financial instruments, such as stocks, to capitalize on price fluctuations. Deep learning and other techniques provide insights that traders use to execute well-informed strategies.

Traditional deep learning techniques: These encompass well-established methods in deep learning, such as feedforward neural networks, backpropagation, and gradient descent. While effective, they have evolved with newer techniques to tackle more complex challenges in stock market predictions.

Volatility of stock market: Volatility measures the rate at which stock prices fluctuate. Deep learning models can analyze historical volatility patterns and other data to predict future market volatility, assisting investors in managing risk.

Volatility test: A volatility test examines the level of price fluctuations in financial data. By quantifying the degree of uncertainty and risk, it assists investors and analysts in making informed decisions.

Volatility: Volatility measures the degree of price variability of a financial instrument over a specific period. It's a critical indicator for assessing risk and is often used by traders to make informed decisions. High volatility implies greater price fluctuations, while low volatility suggests more stable prices.

Index

Printed in the USA/Agawam, MA
May 21, 2024

866493.014